Arduino Applied

Comprehensive Projects for Everyday Electronics

Neil Cameron

Apress®

Arduino Applied: Comprehensive Projects for Everyday Electronics

Neil Cameron
Edinburgh, UK

ISBN-13 (pbk): 978-1-4842-3959-9   ISBN-13 (electronic): 978-1-4842-3960-5
https://doi.org/10.1007/978-1-4842-3960-5

Library of Congress Control Number: 2018965611

Managing Director, Apress Media LLC: Welmoed Spahr
Acquisitions Editor: Natalie Pao
Development Editor: James Markham
Coordinating Editor: Jessica Vakili

Cover image designed by Freepik (www.freepik.com)

Distributed to the book trade worldwide by Springer Science+Business Media New York, 233 Spring Street, 6th Floor, New York, NY 10013. Phone 1-800-SPRINGER, fax (201) 348-4505, e-mail orders-ny@springer-sbm.com, or visit www.springeronline.com. Apress Media, LLC is a California LLC and the sole member (owner) is Springer Science + Business Media Finance Inc (SSBM Finance Inc). SSBM Finance Inc is a **Delaware** corporation.

For information on translations, please e-mail rights@apress.com, or visit http://www.apress.com/rights-permissions.

Apress titles may be purchased in bulk for academic, corporate, or promotional use. eBook versions and licenses are also available for most titles. For more information, reference our Print and eBook Bulk Sales web page at http://www.apress.com/bulk-sales.

Any source code or other supplementary material referenced by the author in this book is available to readers on GitHub via the book's product page, located at www.apress.com/978-1-4842-3959-9. For more detailed information, please visit http://www.apress.com/source-code.

Printed on acid-free paper

Table of Contents

About the Author

Neil Cameron was a research scientist in quantitative genetics at Roslin Institute (of "Dolly the sheep" fame) with expertise in data analysis and computer programming. Neil has taught at the University of Edinburgh and Cornell University. He has a deep interest in electronics and "how things work," with a focus on programming the Arduino and its application on a range of comprehensive projects for everyday electronics, which inspired him to write this book.

About the Technical Reviewer

Fabio Claudio Ferracchiati is a senior consultant and a senior analyst/ developer using Microsoft technologies. He works at BluArancio S.p.A (www.bluarancio.com) as senior analyst/developer and Microsoft Dynamics CRM Specialist. He is a Microsoft Certified Solution Developer for .NET, a Microsoft Certified Application Developer for .NET, a Microsoft Certified Professional, and a prolific author and technical reviewer. Over the past ten years, he's written articles for Italian and international magazines, and co-authored more than ten books on a variety of computer topics.

Preface

Microcontrollers are incorporated in car control systems, domestic appliances, office machines, mobile phones, medical implants, remote controls, and the list goes on. The Arduino Uno is a microcontroller board that can be easily programmed and used to build projects. The objective of this book is to provide information to use the Arduino Uno in a range of applications, from blinking an LED to a motion sensor alarm, to route mapping with a mobile GPS system, to uploading information to the Internet. Prior knowledge of electronics is not required, as each topic is described and illustrated with examples using the Arduino Uno.

The book covers a comprehensive range of topics. In Chapters 1-3, the Arduino Uno and the Arduino programming environment are set up, and several sensors are described with practical examples to provide the basis for subsequent projects. Information display with the Arduino Uno using liquid crystal, LED, and dot matrix displays are described in Chapters 4-7. Several projects are developed with servo and stepper motors, infrared control, RFID, and SD card data logging in Chapters 8-12. Sensing and displaying color is outlined in Chapters 13-14, and recording images in Chapter 15. Bluetooth, wireless, and Wi-Fi communication systems are described in Chapters 16, 17 and 25, with practical examples of message scrolling, servo motor control, and web-based information display projects, respectively. The Arduino Uno is deconstructed to the microcontroller for use in a mobile GPS system, with timed events and power-saving methods in Chapters 18-21. Electronic sound projects are outlined in Chapter 22. An obstacle-avoiding robot car and a balancing robot are described in Chapters 23 and 24, with the robot car controlled by systems described in earlier chapters.

Projects covered in the book include and extend those in Arduino Uno starter kits to increase knowledge of microcontrollers in electronic applications. Many of the projects are practically orientated, such as information displays, GPS tracking, RFID entry systems, motion detector alarms, and robots. Building projects helps you understand how many electronic applications function in everyday life. Examples include flashing numbers on a screen, a scrolling message in the train station, electronic tags on items in a shop or books in the library, a desktop weather station, Bluetooth communication with a mobile phone, digital sound systems, and an obstacle-avoiding robot vacuum cleaner.

Each example in the book is accompanied by code and a description of that code, which helps you learn how to program a microcontroller and a computer, which is a highly valuable skill. The Arduino programming language is C, which is widely used. Learning to program an Arduino provides the framework for other computer programming languages. Throughout the book, schematic diagrams were produced with Fritzing software (`www.fritzing.org`), with an emphasis on maximizing the clarity of component layout and minimizing overlapping connections. The authors of the libraries used in the book are identified in each chapter, with library details covered in the appendix. There are several approaches to structuring sketches, and the approach taken in the book is to declare variables at the start of the sketch, rather than throughout the sketch.

All the code used in the book is available to download from `github.com/Apress/arduino-applied`. The Arduino programming environment and libraries are constantly being updated, so information on the consequences of those updates on the content of the book is also available at `github.com/Apress/arduino-applied`.

Many chapters of the book are stand-alone, so that you can delve into a section of the book rather than having to start from the beginning, while several chapters utilize information from earlier chapters to build a project. You learn how to break down a complex project into smaller projects, just as each chapter addresses a different topic, to then be able to build and enhance the initial project.

If you bought, or are thinking about buying, an Arduino Uno starter kit that contains a few LEDs, a variety of sensors, with some switches and resistors, then this book is for you. If you want to build electronics projects with a microcontroller, then the comprehensive range of topics covered in the book provides the detailed instructions to get started.

CHAPTER 1

Introduction

The Arduino Uno provides the framework to learn about electronics, and to understand and build electronic devices. The Arduino Uno can monitor an environment with sensors, drive LED message boards, generate sound and light patterns, take and display digital photos, communicate by Bluetooth or wirelessly with other electronic devices, communicate by Wi-Fi to the Internet, and record data on the route, speed, and altitude of a trip with GPS.

Arduino Uno

The Arduino Uno R3 (see Figure 1-1) contains the ATmega328P microcontroller to carry out programmed instructions and memory to store data. The Arduino is powered through a DC input or a USB connection, which is also used to upload instructions and communicate with a computer or laptop. An ATmega16U2 chip manages USB (Universal Serial Bus) to serial communication.

The power pins allow 5V (5 volts) or 3.3V and ground (GND) to connect other devices. Pins 0 and 1 are for transmitting and receiving serial data from other devices. Pins 2 to 13 are digital input and output, which input or output 5V for a digital one or 0V for a digital zero. Several output pins vary the time that a pin state is 5V to emulate voltages between 0V and 5V. The analog pins, A0 to A5, measure voltages between 0V and 5V and convert analog signals to digital values (ADC). Pins A4 and A5

© Neil Cameron 2019
N. Cameron, *Arduino Applied*, https://doi.org/10.1007/978-1-4842-3960-5_1

can also communicate with other devices, as can pins 10 to 13, but using different communication systems, I2C and SPI respectively, than the USB connection. Three LEDs (light-emitting diode) indicate power (ON), transmitting (TX), and receiving (RX), with a fourth LED connected to pin 13. The Reset button is used to restart the microcontroller.

The functionality of the Arduino Uno enables a comprehensive range of projects to be developed, which are described throughout the book. Several of the terms—such as ADC, I2C, and SPI—may mean little to you just now, but they are explained in the relevant chapters.

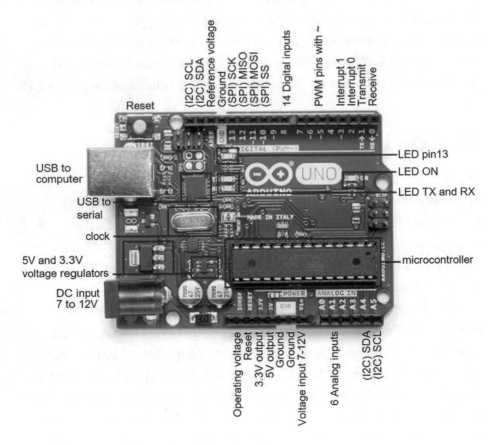

Figure 1-1. *Arduino Uno*

Breadboards

The solderless breadboard contains columns of connected sockets for positioning electronic components to create a circuit and for connecting to the Arduino (see Figure 1-2). The two rows along the length (left to right) of the breadboard are used to connect to power (red) or ground (blue) lines in a circuit. Holes in each short column (green) of the breadboard are connected together, but the columns are not connected, so that two components each with one "leg" in the same green column are connected together. The middle area in the breadboard separates the breadboard into two unconnected halves. Breadboards come in a variety of sizes.

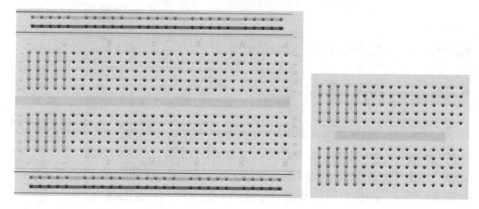

Figure 1-2. Breadboard

The term *breadboard* originates from radio amateurs attaching fixing points to a wooden breadboard and then connecting electronic components to the fixing points.

For example, Figure 1-3 shows a circuit with an LED, a 100Ω resistor, and a 3V battery. The positive or red terminal of the 3V battery is connected to the long leg of the LED, as the relevant component legs are in the same short column. Likewise, the short leg of the LED is connected to the "top" end of the 100Ω resistor, but not to the "bottom" end of the resistor due to the separating middle area of the breadboard. To complete the circuit, a black wire connects the negative or black terminal of the 3V battery to the "bottom" end of the resistor.

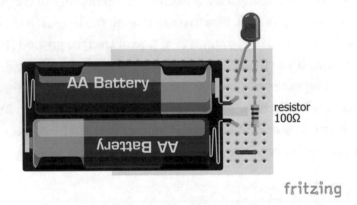

Figure 1-3. *LED and resistor circuit*

Arduino IDE Software

The Arduino IDE (interactive development environment) software is downloaded from www.arduino.cc/en/Main/Software, with the downloaded *arduino-version number-windows.exe* file saved to the desktop. The *.exe* file is double-clicked to start the installation.

The Arduino IDE program files are stored in *C:* ➤ *Program Files (x86)* ➤ *Arduino*, which includes example sketches located in *C:* ➤ *Program Files (x86)* ➤ *Arduino* ➤ *examples*. Each example sketch is accompanied by a text file outlining the objective of the sketch, the breadboard layout of the components, and a circuit diagram.

The Arduino IDE is used to write, compile, and upload files to the microcontroller. A file containing Arduino code is called a *sketch*. Within the Arduino IDE, clicking one of the five IDE symbols provides quick access to compile a sketch, to compile and upload a sketch, to open a blank sketch, to open an existing sketch from a list of all sketches,

and to save the current sketch. The *Open an existing sketch* option ⬆
does not scroll the complete list of sketches, so use *File* ➤ *Sketchbook*
instead. Some useful options from the drop-down menu are given in
Table 1-1.

Table 1-1. *Drop-down Menu Options of the Arduino IDE*

Options	Description
File ➤ *Open Recent*	A list of recently accessed sketches
File ➤ *Examples*	Arduino IDE built-in sketches
Edit ➤ *Find*	Find and replace text in a sketch
Sketch ➤ *Include Library*	Arduino and contributed libraries
Tools ➤ *Serial Monitor*	Displays serial data to serial monitor
Tools ➤ *Serial Plotter*	Graphic display of serial data
Tools ➤ *Board*	Description of the microcontroller for example Arduino/Genuino Uno
Tools ➤ *Port*	Detail of serial port, for example COM3 Arduino/Genuino Uno
File ➤ *Open Recent*	List of recently accessed sketches

Arduino IDE Sketch

An Arduino IDE sketch consists of three parts: variable definition, the
void setup(), and the void loop() functions. The first part includes
defining which Arduino pins are connected to sensors, LEDs, or devices,
and declaring the values of variables. For example, the int LEDpin = 9
instruction defines a variable, named *LEDpin*, with the integer value of 9.
The void setup() function implements definitions in the first part of the

sketch and only runs once. For example, the `pinMode(LEDpin, OUTPUT)` instruction defines the Arduino pin 9 as an output pin, rather than an input pin by default, since *LEDpin* has the value 9.

The `void loop()` function runs continuously and implements the sketch instructions. For example, a sketch may turn on and off an LED at given times.

Declaring variables in the first part of the sketch makes it easier to update the variable once at the start of the sketch, rather than having to check through the sketch and update variables throughout the sketch.

Comments are prefaced by //, such as // Set LED to pin 9, and are not implemented by the microcontroller. With a couple of exceptions, all instruction lines end with a semicolon.

Run the Blink Sketch

Follow these steps to run the blink sketch.

1. Connect the Arduino to a computer or laptop with the USB-to-serial cable.

2. In Arduino IDE, select *File ➤ Examples ➤ 01. Basics ➤ Blink.*

3. Click the *Compile and Upload,* ⊙ , button.

The built-in LED on the Arduino will now flash every second. Welcome to Arduino !

The `Problem uploading to board.` error message indicates that the serial port should be updated. Select *Tools ➤ Port* and choose the appropriate port (for example, *COM3* or *COM4*) for the Arduino. Go to step 3.

The error message `An error occurred while uploading the sketch` indicates that the description of the microcontroller should be updated. Select *Tools ➤ Board* and choose the relevant board (for example, *Arduino/ Genuino Uno*). Go to step 3.

Electricity Explained

An understanding of electricity is helpful before progressing further.

All materials are made of atoms, which consist of protons, neutrons, and electrons. Electrons have a negative charge and can move from one atom to another. Electricity is the movement of electrons between atoms, or rather the flow of an electrical charge.

A simple example of an electrical charge is rubbing a cloth over an inflated balloon. Electrons are rubbed off the cloth and onto the balloon, making the balloon negatively charged. If the balloon is now placed near an object, then the balloon "sticks" to the object. The negative charge of the balloon repels the negatively charged electrons of the object, leaving an excess of positive charge next to the balloon. Since positive and negative charges attract, then the balloon is attracted to the object.

The effect of moving an electric charge from one object to another has been known for centuries. More than two-and-a-half-thousand years ago, the Greeks knew that rubbed amber, which is fossilized tree resin, could attract light objects, such as hair. The word *electric* derives from the Greek word for amber, *elektron*.

A discharging battery is a source of electrons, and the electrons move from the negative terminal, the *anode*, to the positive terminal, the *cathode*. The words anode and cathode are derived from the Greek words *anodos* and *kathodos*, so cathode is abbreviated as *K*. Although electrons flow from anode to cathode, the *conventional current* flows from cathode to anode, or from positive to negative.

Describing electricity uses the terms *charge, voltage, current*, and *resistance*. The analogy of water flowing from a reservoir through a pipe can be used to envisage some of the electrical terms (see Table 1-2).

Table 1-2. *Electrical Parameter and Water Analogy*

Electrical Parameter	Water Analogy
Electrical charge (coulombs, C)	Amount of water in the reservoir
Voltage (volts, V)	Water pressure at the reservoir end of the pipe
Current (amperes or amps, A)	Rate of water flow
Resistance (ohms, Ω)	Inverse of pipe width (narrow pipe ⇒ high resistance)

The relationship between voltage (V), current (I), and resistance (R) is $V = I \times R$, which is Ohm's law.

Charge is measured in amp-hours (Ah), which is the charge transferred by a current of one amp for one hour. The length of time that a battery, such as a nickel metal hydride (NiMH) AA battery with a charge of 2400mAh, can supply a given current depends on the size of the current. For example, with discharge rates of 2400, 4800, or 7200mAh, the battery would last 60, 30, or 20 minutes.

Electrical power, measured in watts (W), is the rate that energy is transferred in unit time, equal to the product of voltage and current.

Revise the Blink Sketch

ANODE

CATHODE

The blink sketch can be changed to make a separate LED blink rather than the LED on the Arduino. The Arduino supplies a regulated 5V output from the pin marked 5V, but a resistor is required to ensure that the current does not exceed the LED's maximum permitted current of 20mA. Without the resistor, the high current would damage the LED.

Using Ohm's law, which states voltage equals the product of current and resistance, or $V = I \times R$, the value of the resistor (R) can be determined, given the known voltage (V) and current (I). The forward voltage drop across the LED is 2V, which is the minimum voltage required to turn on the LED. With a 5V output from the Arduino, there is 3V = 5V – 2V across the resistor (see Figure 1-4). If the current through the resistor and the LED is to be at most 20mA, then from Ohm's law, the resistor value (R = V/I) = 3/0.02 = 150Ω, which is equal to the voltage across the resistor divided by the current through the resistor. A resistor of at least 150Ω would protect the LED from an excessively high current and the widely available 220Ω resistor can be used. Resistors are color-coded (see Appendix) to identify the resistance, but checking the resistance with a multimeter is straightforward. Resistors are connected either way around in a circuit.

The power through the resistor should be checked to ensure that it is not greater than the maximum value for the resistor. In the example, the maximum power rating of the resistor is 250mW. With 3V across the resistor and 20mA maximum current, then power = V × I = 60mW, which is well below the maximum value.

An LED is a diode, which allows current to pass in one direction only. The long leg of the LED is the anode and the flat side of the LED is on the cathode side. LEDs contain semiconductor material, which determines the wavelength of light emitted: red, green, blue, or yellow. The forward voltage drop of red, yellow, and green LEDs is lower than for blue and white LEDs: 2.0V and 2.9V, respectively.

If an LED and resistor were connected as in the left-hand side of Figure 1-4, then the LED would stay on continuously. If the LED was connected to an Arduino pin, then changing the pin status from 5V (*HIGH*) to 0V (*LOW*) to *HIGH* repeatedly would turn on and off the LED. The revised circuit in the right-hand side of Figure 1-4 has the LED anode connected to pin 11 of the Arduino. Switching the LED on and off is a digital or binary operation, 0 or 1, requiring a `digitalWrite` instruction to pin 11 to enable or disable a power supply to the LED. Connections for the two examples in Figure 1-4 are given in Table 1-3.

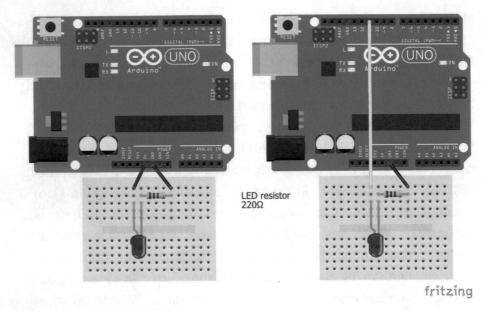

Figure 1-4. *Blink an LED*

Table 1-3. *Connections for LED*

Component	Figure 1-4 left-hand side		Figure 1-4 right-hand side	
	Connect to	and to	Connect to	and to
LED long leg	Arduino 5V		Arduino pin 11	
LED short leg	220Ω resistor	Arduino GND	220Ω resistor	Arduino GND

The revised blink sketch is shown in Listing 1-1. The LED is connected to Arduino pin 11. In the void setup() function, the Arduino pin defined by the *LEDpin* variable is defined as an OUTPUT pin, rather than an INPUT pin that would be used for input, such as measuring a voltage. In the void loop() function, the state of Arduino pin 11 is repeatedly changed from *HIGH* to *LOW* and *LOW* to *HIGH* at one-second intervals, which corresponds to changing the output voltage on the pin from 5V to 0V, and so the LED turns on and off.

Listing 1-1. Sketch to Blink an LED

```
int LEDpin = 11;                    // define LEDpin with integer value 11

void setup()                        // setup function runs once
{
  pinMode(LEDpin, OUTPUT);          // define LEDpin as output
}

void loop()                         // loop function runs continuously
{
  digitalWrite(LEDpin, HIGH);       // set pin state HIGH to turn LED on
  delay(1000);                      // wait for a second = 1000ms
  digitalWrite(LEDpin, LOW);        // set pin state LOW to turn LED off
  delay(1000);
}
```

Instructions within the void setup() and void loop() functions are included in curly brackets, indicating the start and end of the function, with the instructions indented to make the sketch easier to interpret. Sketches must include both the void setup() and void loop() functions, even if a function contains no instructions.

Comments are useful to interpret a sketch. A comment is text after the // characters. Several lines of comments can be included when bracketed by /* and */, such as

/* this is the first line of comment
this is the second line of comment
this is the last line of comment */

The schematic format has red and black wires for VCC (positive voltage) and GND (ground), with yellow, blue, or green wires connecting electronic components to Arduino pins. In general, green is used for an input signal and yellow for an Arduino output signal.

Pulse Width Modulation

Several Arduino pins, those marked with ~ support Pulse Width Modulation (PWM), which replaces a constant *HIGH* signal with a square wave, pulsing *HIGH* and *LOW*, and the pulse width can be modified (see Figure 1-5). The impact of PWM on an LED is to change the perceived continuous brightness of an LED, even though the LED is being turned on and off repeatedly.

PWM is also used to control the speed of motors and to generate sound. The PWM frequency on Arduino pins 5 and 6 is 976 cycles per second (Hertz or Hz), so the interval between pulses, indicated by the green dotted lines in Figure 1-5, is 1.024ms. Most people cannot detect flicker between images displayed above 400Hz, so an LED turned on and off at 976Hz appears to be constantly on.

The square wave is generated by the analogWrite(pin, value) instruction with a duty cycle of (*value*/255), so a 0% or 100% duty cycle corresponds to a *value* of 0 or 255. For example, in Figure 1-5, with a 5V supply, the PWM duty cycles of 0%, 25%, 50%, 75%, and 100% can be broadly thought of as supplying average voltages of 0V, 1.25V, 2.5V, 3.75V, and 5V, respectively. PWM is one mechanism for supplying "analog" signals from a "digital" 0V or 5V signal, and it is used in many projects throughout the book.

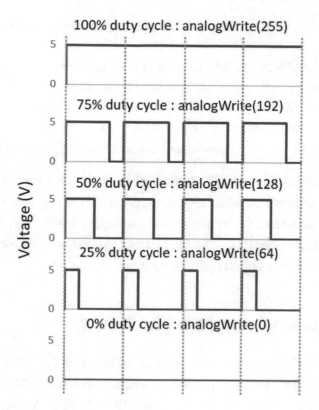

Figure 1-5. *Pulse width modulation*

The sketch (see Listing 1-2) uses PWM to change the brightness of an LED with the rate of change controlled by the *increm* and *time* variables.

Listing 1-2. LED Brightness and PWM

```
int LEDpin = 11;                 // define LED pin
int bright = 0;                  // initial value for LED brightness
int increm = 5;                  // incremental change in PWM frequency
int time = 25;                   // define time period between changes

void setup()                     // setup function runs once
{
  pinMode(LEDpin, OUTPUT);   // LED pin as output
}
```

```
void loop()                        // loop function runs continuously
{
  analogWrite(LEDpin, bright);   // set LED brightness with PWM
  delay(time);                   // wait for the time period
  bright = bright + increm;      // increment LED brightness
  if(bright <=0 || bright >= 255) increm = - increm;
}                        // reverse increment when brightness = 0 or 255
```

The symbols || denote *OR*, so the if(bright <= 0 || bright >= 255) increm = -increm instruction is equivalent to "if the *bright* variable is less than or equal to zero, or greater than or equal to 255, then change the sign of the *increm* variable." The *OR* instruction reverses the increasing brightness to decreasing brightness, and vice versa.

Opening and Saving Sketches

To open a saved sketch, within the Arduino IDE, select *File* ➤ *Open*. Choose the folder name containing the sketch, click *Open*, select the sketch, and click *Open*. Alternatively, select *File* ➤ *Open Recent*. A list of recently opened sketches is displayed, then click the required sketch.

The default location for saving sketches is determined by selecting *File* ➤ *Preferences* in the Arduino IDE. To save a sketch, select *File* ➤ *Save As*, which opens the default sketches folder, then choose a file name for the sketch and click *Save*. The file name must not contain spaces, so use an underscore instead, such as in *file_name*. When a sketch is saved, a folder is automatically generated to contain the sketch.

When a sketch has been edited in the Arduino IDE, a § symbol follows the sketch name to indicate that changes have been made since the sketch was last saved. To save an existing sketch, select *File* ➤ *Save*. If changes have been made to a sketch, then after saving the sketch, the § symbol disappears.

Summary

The Arduino Uno and the Arduino IDE programming environment were described. An introduction to programming the Arduino enabled a sketch to control an LED turning on and off. The blink sketch was changed to vary the brightness of the LED using Pulse Width Modulation. A summary of electricity, including Ohm's Law, helped you understand how an LED functions and that an LED requires a resistor to reduce the current.

Components List

- Arduino Uno and breadboard
- LED
- Resistor: 220Ω

CHAPTER 2

Switches

Switches are used to turn devices on or off, such as a room light or an electrical appliance, and when sending a signal, such as pressing a particular key on a keyboard. Switches can also be used to control devices; a device is on when the switch is initially pressed or while the switch is pressed. The metal contacts of switches can bounce when the switch is pressed, which could repeatedly turn a device on and off again. Switch bouncing can be controlled using software or by hardware, which is called debouncing a switch.

Tactile Switch

A switch can be connected to an Arduino pin to turn an LED on or off. When the switch is closed, the digital pin is connected to 5V and the pin state is *HIGH*. When the switch is open, the 10kΩ pull-down resistor permits a small current to flow between the digital pin and GND, so the pin state is pulled down to *LOW* (see Figure 2-1).

© Neil Cameron 2019
N. Cameron, *Arduino Applied*, https://doi.org/10.1007/978-1-4842-3960-5_2

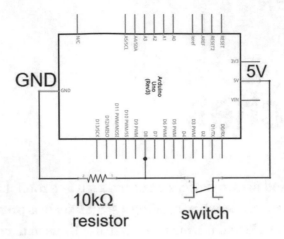

Figure 2-1. *Pull-down resistor*

If the switch and resistor are reversed, relative to the digital pin, then when the switch is open, the digital pin is connected to 5V, through the 10kΩ pull-up resistor, and the pin state is *HIGH*. Use of a pull-down or a pull-up resistor depends on whether the pin state is to be *LOW* or *HIGH* when the switch is open. If a pull-down or pull-up resistor was not included, then when the switch is open the digital pin would not be connected to GND or to 5V, so the pin state would be undefined. Incorporation of a switch with the pull-down resistor is shown in Figure 2-2.

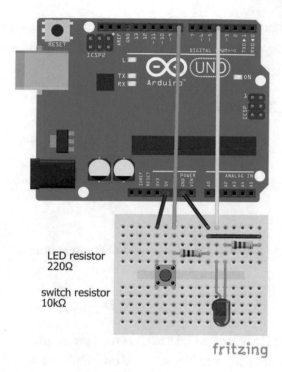

Figure 2-2. *LED switch with pull-down resistor*

The switch module consists of two pairs of connected pins, with the switch pins close together on the underside of the switch. Connections for Figure 2-2 are given in Table 2-1.

Table 2-1. *Connections for LED Switch with Pull-Down Resistor*

Component	Connect to	and to
Switch left	Arduino 5V	
Switch right	Arduino pin 8	
Switch right	10kΩ resistor	Arduino GND
LED long leg	Arduino pin 4	
LED short leg	220Ω resistor	Arduino GND

19

Listing 2-1 turns an LED on while the switch is pressed and off while the switch is not pressed. The `digitalRead(pin number)` instruction reads the state of the pin, *HIGH* or *LOW*.

Listing 2-1. LED Switch

```
int switchPin = 8;                    // define switch pin
int LEDpin = 4;                       // define LED pin
int reading;                          // define reading as integer

void setup()
{
  pinMode(LEDpin, OUTPUT);            // LED pin as output
}

void loop()
{
  reading = digitalRead(switchPin);  // read switch pin
  digitalWrite(LEDpin, reading);     // turn LED on if switch is HIGH
}                                     // turn LED off if switch is LOW
```

It would be more useful to turn the LED on or off only when the switch is pressed (see Listing 2-2). The states of the switch and LED are stored as variables, *switchState* and *LEDState*, respectively. When the switch is initially pressed, the switch state changes from *LOW* to *HIGH* and the state of the LED is updated from either *LOW* (off) to *HIGH* (on) or from *HIGH* to *LOW*. The *switchState* variable is also updated when the switch is initially pressed, but if the switch is continuously pressed, then the switch state does not change. Releasing the switch changes the switch state from *HIGH* to *LOW* and the *switchState* variable is updated, but there is no change in the LED state. The `void loop()` function continues to read the switch pin.

Listing 2-2. LED Switch Only When Pressed

```
int switchPin = 8;              // define switch pin
int LEDpin = 4;                 // define LED pin
int reading;                    // define reading as an integer
int switchState = LOW;          // set switch state to LOW
int LEDState = LOW;             // set LED state to LOW

void setup()
{
  pinMode(LEDpin, OUTPUT);      // LED pin as output
}

void loop()
{
  reading = digitalRead(switchPin); // read switch pin
  if(reading != switchState)        // if switch state has changed
  {                                  // if switch pressed, change LED state
    if(reading == HIGH && switchState == LOW) LEDState = !LEDState;
    digitalWrite(LEDpin, LEDState); // turn LED on or off
    switchState = reading;          // update switch state
  }
}
```

Comparison Operators

A logical *AND* is indicated with the && symbol, such as if(X>Y && A==HIGH), which indicates that if X is greater than Y and A is equal to *HIGH*, then the outcome is true.

A logical *OR* is indicated with the || symbol, such as if(X>Y || A==HIGH), which indicates that if X is greater than Y or A is equal to *HIGH*, then the outcome is true.

The double equals sign (==) denotes "is equal to" in a comparison, as in if(reading == HIGH), which means "if reading is equal to HIGH".

!= denotes "is not equal to" in a comparison as in if(reading != switchState), which means "if reading is not equal to *switchState*".

The exclamation mark ! denotes "the opposite value", as in LEDState = !LEDState, which means "change *LEDstate* to its opposite value", which is from *HIGH* to *LOW* or *LOW* to *HIGH*.

The equivalent of X = X + 1 is X++ and similarly, X-- is equivalent to X = X - 1.

The calculation y%x is y modulus x, or the remainder when integer y is divided by integer x.

Debouncing a Switch

When a switch is pressed, the springy nature of the metal used in the contact points can cause the contact points to touch several times; in other words, to bounce, before making a permanent contact. The Arduino clock speed of 16MHz equates to 16 million operations per second, so a bouncing switch contact appears to the microcontroller as having closed and opened several times when the switch is pressed. For example, when an LED is controlled by a switch, sometimes the LED does not turn on or off when the switch is pressed. The switch can be debounced by two software methods or by a hardware solution.

One software method initiates a delay, following a change in the switch state, and then rereads the switch state after the delay, defined by the delay(milliseconds) instruction. If the delay is too short, then the switch may still be bouncing at the end of the delay. The void loop() function in Listing 2-3 includes the debounce delay, rereads the switch pin and compares the new switch state with the switch state read before the delay. In Listing 2-3, the new instructions compared to Listing 2-2 are highlighted in bold.

Listing 2-3. LED Switch with Debounce Time

```
void loop()
{
  reading = digitalRead(switchPin);   // read switch pin
  if(reading != switchState)          // if state of switch has changed
  {
    delay(50);                        // debounce time of 50ms
    reading = digitalRead(switchPin); // read switch pin again
    if(reading != switchState)        // compare switch state again
    {
      if (reading == HIGH && switchState == LOW) LEDState =!LEDState;
      digitalWrite(LEDpin, LEDState);
      switchState = reading;
    }
  }
}
```

A second software method is to continue delaying until there is no longer a change in the switch state at the end of the delay or debounce time. The debounce time is essentially the time that the switch must be held in a constant state before the LED is turned on or off. The state of the switch has to be stored at three times: before the switch was pressed (*oldSwitch*), when the switch was pressed during the debounce time (*switchState*) and when the switch was last pressed (*reading*). The millis() function counts the number of milliseconds that the sketch has been running and is used to store the time when the switch was pressed. The state of the switch is continuously read, until the switch state is the same for longer than the debounce time, at which time the LED can be turned on or off. The number of milliseconds may be greater than the upper limit of an integer number $(2^{15}-1)$ms or 33 seconds, so the time variable is defined as an unsigned long with maximum value of $(2^{32}-1)$ms or 50 days.

In Listing 2-4, *lastSwitch* refers to the time the switch was last pressed during the debounce time and the changes relative to the non-debounced sketch, Listing 2-2, are highlighted in bold.

Listing 2-4. Debounced LED Switch with Continued Delay

```
int switchPin = 8;              // define switch pin
int LEDpin = 4;                 // define LED pin
int reading;                    // define reading as an integer
int switchState = LOW;          // set switch state to LOW
int LEDState = LOW;             // set LED state to LOW
unsigned long switchTime;       // define time as unsigned long
int lastSwitch = LOW;           // set last switch press in debounce time
int debounceTime = 50;          // define debounce time in ms

void setup()
{
  pinMode(LEDpin, OUTPUT);      // LED pin as output
}

void loop()
{
  reading = digitalRead(switchPin);   // read switch pin
  if(reading != lastSwitch)     // if reading different from last reading
  {
    switchTime = millis();      // time switch state change in debounce time
    lastSwitch  = reading;      // update last switch state
  }                             // is switch state the same for required time
  if((millis() - switchTime) > debounceTime)
  {
```

```
if(reading !=switchState)
{
  if (reading == HIGH && switchState == LOW) LEDState =!LEDState;
  digitalWrite(LEDpin, LEDState);
  switchState = reading;
}
}
}
```

When the outcome of an if() instruction cannot be included on the same line as the if() instruction, then the outcome of the if() instruction is contained in curly brackets, just as with the void loop() function. Indenting of instructions within an if() instruction makes the sketch easier to interpret.

Hardware Switch Debounce

 The hardware solution is to include a capacitor across the switch (see Figure 2-3). The capacitor charges while the switch is not pressed. When the switch is pressed, the capacitor discharges and the switch signal to the Arduino is *HIGH*. While the switch bounces, the capacitor maintains the switch signal at *HIGH*. With the hardware solution, there is no need for the software debouncing sketch. One resistor-capacitor combination is a 10kΩ pull-down resistor and 10µF capacitor.

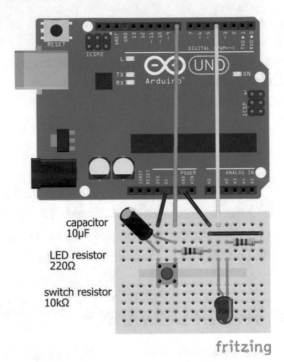

capacitor
10µF

LED resistor
220Ω

switch resistor
10kΩ

fritzing

Figure 2-3. *LED switch and capacitor*

The rate, RC, at which a capacitor charges or discharges depends on
the resistance (R) of the resistor and the capacitance (C) of the capacitor.
The voltage across the capacitor after t seconds of charging is $V(1 - e^{-t/RC})$,
where V is the supply voltage, and after t seconds of discharging the
voltage across the capacitor is $V(e^{-t/RC})$. The higher the RC value, the
longer the debounce delay. After the initial switch press and the capacitor
discharge, the capacitor has recharged to 50% of capacity and the switch
signal is again *HIGH* after a debounce delay of RC × ln(2) seconds. The
debounce delay time can be expressed as 0.693 × RC or RC/1.44 seconds.

With the resistor-capacitor combination of a 10kΩ resistor and a 10µF
capacitor, the debounce delay is 69ms. There are many resistor-capacitor
combinations that achieve a given debounce delay lasting RC × ln(2)
seconds, but a large resistor should be used to minimize the current through
the resistor.

Electrolytic capacitors are polarized and the anode must be at a higher voltage than the cathode. The cathode has a "–" marking and a colored strip on the side of the capacitor. The long leg of an electrolytic capacitor is the anode or positive leg (see Table 2-2).

Table 2-2. *Connections for Figure 2-3*

Component	Connect to	and to
Switch left	Arduino 5V	
Switch right	Arduino pin 8	
Switch right	10kΩ resistor	Arduino GND
Capacitor negative	Switch right	
Capacitor positive	Switch left	
LED long leg	Arduino pin 4	
LED short leg	220Ω resistor	Arduino GND

Ball Switch

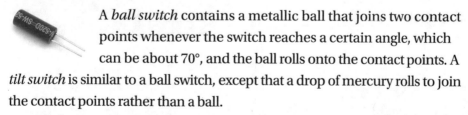

A *ball switch* contains a metallic ball that joins two contact points whenever the switch reaches a certain angle, which can be about 70°, and the ball rolls onto the contact points. A *tilt switch* is similar to a ball switch, except that a drop of mercury rolls to join the contact points rather than a ball.

The layout of the ball switch circuit (see Figure 2-4) is identical to the tactile switch circuit (see Figure 2-2), but the sketch (see Listing 2-5) contains an if else instruction to turn the LED on or off. The if else instruction is more efficient than two if() instructions and is used when there is more than one condition, each with a different outcome. In the ball switch sketch, if the reading is *LOW*, then the LED is turned on; otherwise, the LED is turned off.

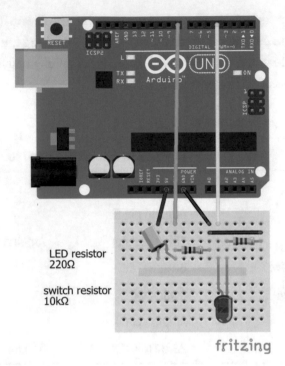

Figure 2-4. *LED and ball switch*

Listing 2-5. LED and Ball Switch

```
int switchPin = 8;                      // define switch pin
int LEDpin = 4;                         // define LED pin
int reading;

void setup()
{
  pinMode(LEDpin, OUTPUT);              // LED pin as output
}

void loop()
{
  reading = digitalRead(switchPin);    // read switch pin
```

```
if(reading == LOW) digitalWrite (LEDpin, HIGH); // ball switch tips
                                                // over, led on
    else digitalWrite(LEDpin, LOW); // ball switch not tipped over, led off
}
```

Summary

The chapter described how to program the Arduino so that a switch could control an LED. The bounce effect of a switch was described and the switch was debounced using two software solutions and a hardware solution with a resistor and a capacitor. The range of programming instructions was extended to enable the programming of more complex sketches.

Components List

- Arduino Uno and breadboard

- LED

- Resistors: 220Ω and 10kΩ

- Capacitor: 10µF

- Switches: tactile and ball

CHAPTER 3

Sensors

Sensors can be connected to the Arduino to measure aspects of the environment with sensor information displayed on the serial monitor or on the serial plotter. The Arduino can perform an instruction depending on the sensor signal being above or below a given threshold, such as turning on a light when a room is dark. This chapter describes several sensors with accompanying sketches to demonstrate uses of the sensors. In subsequent chapters, projects include one or more sensors, so it is useful to have all the sensors described in one chapter.

Temperature Sensor

The LM35DZ is a precision temperature sensor with an operating temperature range of 0°C to 100°C that outputs 10mV for every degree Celsius increase in temperature. The maximum output voltage of the LM35DZ sensor is 100 × 10mV, or one volt. The Arduino analog-to-digital conversion (ADC) converts a voltage to a digital value between 0 and 1023. When the default ADC maximum voltage of 5V is equated to a value of 1023, the range of output voltages from the LM35DZ sensor has an analog equivalent of 0 to 205 (= 1023/5). If the ADC maximum voltage is set to 1.1V rather than 5V, then the output voltages from the LM35DZ sensor map to an analog range of 0 to 930 (= 1023/1.1),

N. Cameron, *Arduino Applied*, https://doi.org/10.1007/978-1-4842-3960-5_3

providing greater resolution for the temperature sensor. For example, a temperature increase of 1°C corresponds to an increased analog reading of 9 rather than only 2, with ADC maximum voltages of 1.1V and 5V, respectively. The ADC voltage can be reduced from 5V to 1.1V with the analogReference(INTERNAL) instruction.

The Arduino has three analog reference values:

- analogReference(DEFAULT)   equates 5V to $1023 = 2^{10}-1$

- analogReference(INTERNAL)   equates 1.1V to 1023

- analogReference(EXTERNAL)   equates 3.3V to 1023 when the 3.3V pin is connected to the AREF pin

After setting the ADC reference voltage to 1.1V, the temperature in degrees Celsius is the temperature sensor's reading multiplied by 110.0/1023. The reading is divided by 1023 and multiplied by 1100 to convert the reading to mV, and then divided by 10 to convert mV to °C. The LM35DZ temperature sensor must be connected correctly, as in Figure 3-1, with the right-hand side of the flat side connected to 5V; otherwise, the LM35DZ temperature sensor rapidly overheats. The temperature sensor's output pin is connected to one of the Arduino's six analog input pins, marked A0 to A5 (see Table 3-1).

Figure 3-1. *Temperature sensor*

Table 3-1. *Connections for Temperature Sensor*

Component	Connect to
LM35DZ GND	Arduino GND
LM35DZ OUT	Arduino pin A0
LM35DZ VCC	Arduino 5V

The LM35DZ temperature reading can be displayed graphically using the Arduino IDE serial plotter by selecting *Tools* ➤ *Serial Plotter*. The communication speed between the Arduino and the serial plotter can be set to 9600 baud (see Figure 3-2). The serial plotter constantly updates the minimum and maximum values of Y axis. To prevent the updating, the minimum and maximum values are defined and then combined with the sensor reading into a string, with the three variables—minimum, sensor value, and maximum—plotted simultaneously (see Listing 3-1).

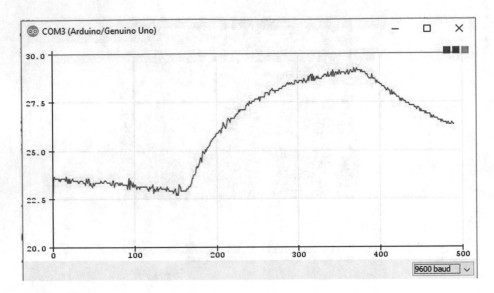

Figure 3-2. *Serial plotter with temperature*

Listing 3-1. Temperature Sensor

```
int tempPin = A0;              // define LM35DZ signal on analog pin A0
int min =20;                   // define minimum plot value
int max = 30;                  // define maximum plot value
int reading;                   // define reading as an integer
float temp;                    // define temp as a real number

void setup()
{
  Serial.begin(9600);          // define Serial output baud rate
  analogReference(INTERNAL);   // set ADC voltage to 1.1V rather than 5V
}

void loop()
{
  reading = analogRead(tempPin);    // read temperature sensor pin
  temp = (reading * 110.0)/1023;    // convert reading to temperature
              // convert minimum, temperature and maximum to a string
```

```
String axis = String(min) +" "+ String(temp) +" "+ String(max);
Serial.println(axis);          // update plot
delay(10);                     // delay 10ms between readings
}
```

The `temp = (reading * 110.0)/1023` instruction returns a real number for *temp* when there is a real number in the calculation. If all numbers in the calculation are integers, then an integer value is returned, even though *temp* is defined as a real number. For example, a reading of 500 produces *temp* values of 53.76 and 53 given the instructions `temp = (reading * 110.0)/1023` and `temp = (reading * 110)/1023`, respectively.

Variables

Variables are defined as integer, real, or text. Integers are stored as powers of 2. For example, $13 = (1 \times 2^3) + (1 \times 2^2) + (0 \times 2^1) + (1 \times 2^0)$, as $2^0 = 1$, so the 4-bit binary representation of 13 is B1101.

A Boolean variable, `bool`, takes the value 0 or 1, true or false, *HIGH* or *LOW*, and only requires one bit of memory (see Table 3-2).

A `byte` stores an integer between 0 and 255. A character, `char`, is stored as an integer, with values from –128 to 127, with each character allocated an ASCII (American Standard Code for Information Interchange) value, such as the letter A with value 65.

An integer, `int`, has maximum value $2^{15}-1$ and a long integer, `long`, has maximum value $2^{31}-1$, but requires 4 bytes of memory.

Table 3-2. *Variable Types and Their Properties*

name	Power of 2	Storage	Upper Value	Centered On Zero	Lower Limit	Upper Limit
bool	1	bit	1		0	1
byte	8	1 byte	255	char	−128	127
unsigned int	16	2 bytes	65535	int	−32768	32767
unsigned long	32	4 bytes	4,294,967,295	long	−2,147,483,648	2,147,483,647

Real numbers, float, require 4 bytes of storage, which is the same as for a long integer, but the maximum stored value of a real number is 3.403×10^{38}, as real numbers are converted into a fraction part multiplied by a power of two. Real numbers have only 6 to 7 decimal digits of precision, which is the total number of digits, not the number of digits to the right of the decimal point. Multiplying a real number by an integer value results in an integer, but if a value with a decimal point is included, then the result is a real number. For example, if X is a real number, then 2*X is an integer, but 2.0*X is a real number.

Variables can be defined using the C program language and the *uint* format (see Table 3-3).

Table 3-3. *Variable Types and Definition*

Name		bits	upper value
unsigned char	uint8_t	8	255
unsigned int	uint16_t	16	65535
unsigned long	uint32_t	32	4,294,967,295

An integer or real number that has a constant value throughout a sketch can be defined as a `const`, which reduces memory requirements. For example, the `const int tempPin = A0` instruction requires less memory storage than if *tempPin* is defined as an integer with `int tempPin = A0`.

Humidity Sensor

 The DHT11 humidity and temperature sensor measures temperatures between 0°C and 50°C and relative humidity between 20% and 90%. Measurements are taken every second, with an accuracy of ±2°C for temperature and ±5% for relative humidity. At a relative humidity of 0%, the air is completely dry, and at 100% condensation occurs.

The DHT11 sensor is supplied as a unit or mounted on a printed circuit board (PCB) that includes a 10kΩ pull-up resistor between the signal and 5V connections. The function of pull-up and pull-down resistors was described in Chapter 2. Connection pins for the DHT11 unit or PCB-mounted DHT11 are different, as shown in Figure 3-3. A 10kΩ pull-up resistor should be connected between the signal and 5V pins of the DHT11 unit. For illustration, connections for both the DHT11 unit and the PCB-mounted DHT11 are shown in Figure 3-3 and Table 3-4.

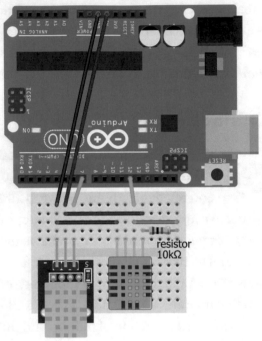

Figure 3-3. *DHT11 sensors*

Table 3-4. *Connections for DHT11 Sensors*

Component	Connect to	and to
PCB DHT11 GND	Arduino GND	
PCB DHT11 VCC	Arduino 5V	
PCB DHT11 OUT	Arduino pin 7	
DHT11 GND	Arduino GND	
DHT11 OUT	Arduino pin 12	10kΩ resistor
DHT11 VCC	Arduino 5V	10kΩ resistor

Library Installation

A library of instructions is required to use the DHT11 sensor. While the Arduino IDE includes several libraries for managing hardware, such as writing to an SD card or controlling a motor, a library for the DHT11 sensor must be downloaded and installed into the Arduino IDE. There are three methods for installing a library into the Arduino IDE.

Library Installation Method 1

1. Download the library in a *.zip* file and store on the computer/laptop.

2. Open the Arduino IDE and select *Sketch* ➤ *Include Library* ➤ *Add .zip Library*.

3. Select the location where the *.zip* file was saved when downloaded.

4. Select the *.zip* file containing the library and click *Open*. The library is installed in the default *Documents* ➤ *Arduino* ➤ *libraries* folder.

5. To confirm the location of the default folder, select *File* ➤ *Preferences* in the Arduino IDE.

Library Installation Method 2

1. Download the library in a *.zip* file and extract the *.zip* file to the default *Documents* ➤ *Arduino* ➤ *libraries* folder.

2. To confirm the location of the default library folder for the Arduino IDE, select *File* ➤ *Preferences*.

3. The Arduino IDE must be restarted before the installed library is listed in the Arduino IDE using *Sketch* ➤ *Include Library*.

Library Installation Method 3

1. Several libraries are directly accessible by the Arduino IDE and do not have to be downloaded as *.zip* files. Before downloading a library *.zip* file, first check if the library is not already available within the Arduino IDE framework.

2. Open the Arduino IDE and select *Sketch* ➤ *Include Library* ➤ *Manage libraries*.

3. In the *Library Manage* window, use the *Filter your search* option to locate the required library.

4. Click *More info*, select the library version number, and click *Install*.

For each library listing, within the Arduino IDE, select *More info* to access GitHub for library documentation and updates.

There are example sketches within each library, which are accessed within the Arduino IDE by selecting *File* ➤ *Example* ➤ *library name*.

There are several libraries for the DHT11 sensor. The *dht* library (*DHTlib*) by Rob Tilllaart is recommended. The *dht* library is contained within a *.zip* file available at `https://github.com/RobTillaart/Arduino`. Use installation method 1 or method 2 to install the *dht* library.

A library is included in a sketch with the `#include <libraryname.h>` instruction, which references the *libraryname.h* file located in the *Documents* ➤ *Arduino* ➤ *libraries* ➤ *libraryname* folder. Note there is no semicolon at the end of the library `#include` instruction. When a library is included in a sketch, a variable must be associated with the library, which is called "creating an instance of the class," where *class* is the library. The variable has the properties of the library, in a similar way that a variable defined as an integer has the properties of an integer. Instructions specific to a library are prefixed with the variable name.

For example, the *dht* library is included in the sketch with the #include <dht.h> instruction. The *DHT* variable is associated with the *dht* library with the dht DHT instruction. The *dht* library-specific temperature instruction is prefixed with *DHT* in the sketch DHT.temperature instruction.

Listing 3-2 displays (on the serial monitor) the temperature and humidity measurements from a DHT11 unit and a PCB-mounted DHT11 sensor, but only for consistency with Figure 3-3. Comment out instructions for the DHT11 unit or the PCB-mounted DHT11 sensor, as required.

Text is displayed on the serial monitor before the temperature or humidity reading is displayed. Text is included in quotation marks (" "), as is the tab character, which is \t. The sensors are read at one-second intervals, using the delay(1000) instruction to wait 1000ms. The humidity component of the DHT11 sensor is more responsive to change than the temperature component.

Listing 3-2. DHT11 Sensors

```
#include <dht.h>            // include dht library
dht DHT;                    // associate DHT with dht library
int DHTpin = 12;            // DHT11 unit on pin 12
int PCBpin = 7;             // PCB mounted DHT11 on pin 7
int check;

void setup()
{
  Serial.begin(9600);      // define Serial output baud rate
}
```

```
void loop()
{
  check = DHT.read11(DHTpin);          // read DHT11 sensor on DHTpin
  Serial.print("DHT11 Unit temp: ");   // print text followed by a space
  Serial.print(DHT.temperature,0);     // temperature reading, integer only
  Serial.print("\thumidity: ");        // print tab then text
  Serial.println(DHT.humidity,0);      // humidity reading, integer only
  check = DHT.read11(PCBpin);          // repeat for the DHT11 on PCB
  Serial.print("DHT11 PCB temp: ");
  Serial.print(DHT.temperature,0);
  Serial.print("\thumidity: ");
  Serial.println(DHT.humidity,0);
  delay(1000);                         // delay one second
}
```

Light Dependent Resistor

A light dependent resistor (LDR), or photoresistor, is used to quantify incident light, as the resistance of the LDR decreases with increasing incident light. The LDR is combined with a 4.7kΩ resistor to form a voltage divider (see Figure 3-4), which is outlined in more detail later in the chapter. The voltage divider's output voltage, reflecting the LDR resistance, is converted by the Arduino's analog to digital converter (ADC) to a digital value. The LDR's resistance is between 3kΩ and 5kΩ in average daylight, so a 4.7kΩ resistor provides a balanced resistance for the voltage divider. Like any resistor, an LDR can be connected either way around in a circuit.

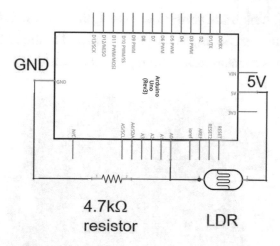

Figure 3-4. *LDR and voltage divider*

A voltage divider's output voltage, V_{out}, is $V_{in}\left(\dfrac{R_{resistor}}{R_{LDR} + R_{resistor}}\right)$, where R_{LDR} and $R_{resistor}$ are the LDR and known resistor resistances, respectively, and V_{in} is the input voltage of 5V from the Arduino. As the incident light increases, the LDR's resistance decreases and the output voltage of the voltage divider increases. The Arduino ADC converts the voltage divider's output voltage to a digital reading equal to $\dfrac{V_{out} \times 1023}{V_{in}}$. The LDR's resistance is $\left(\dfrac{1023}{reading} - 1\right) R_{resistor}$, which ranges from 700Ω in light conditions to 50kΩ in the dark, corresponding to light intensity readings of 890 and 90, respectively.

The LDR can be used to change the brightness of an LED, depending on the incident light, such as a night light (see Figure 3-5). The connections and sketch are shown in Table 3-5 and Listing 3-3. The LED is turned on only when the light intensity is low, with a threshold of 500 for the voltage divider reading. A high LED brightness is required in low light conditions, so the voltage divider reading is inversely mapped to the LED brightness, with low readings corresponding to high LED brightness.

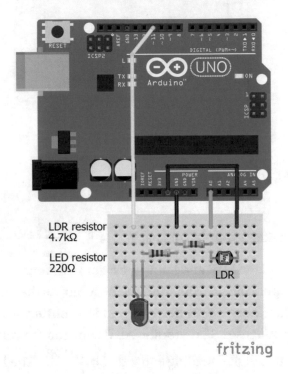

Figure 3-5. *Light dependent resistor and LED*

Table 3-5. *Connections for Light Dependent Resistor and LED*

Component	Connect to	and to
LDR right leg	Arduino 5V	
LDR left leg	Arduino A0	
LDR left leg	4.7kΩ resistor	Arduino GND
LED long leg	Arduino pin 11	
LED short leg	220Ω resistor	Arduino GND

Listing 3-3. Light Dependent Resistor and LED

```
int Vdivid = A0;                    // voltage divider analog pin
int LEDpin = 11;                    // LED on PWM pin
int thresh = 500;                   // threshold light intensity
int reading, bright;

void setup()
{
  pinMode(LEDpin, OUTPUT);          // LED pin as output
}
void loop()
{
  reading = analogRead(Vdivid);     // voltage divider reading
  bright = 0;                       // set LED brightness to zero
                                    // map reading to LED brightness
  if(reading<thresh) bright = map(reading, 0, thresh, 255, 0);
  analogWrite(LEDpin, bright);      // change LED brightness
  delay(1000);                      // delay 1000ms
}
```

The analogRead(Vdivid) instruction reads the value on the analog pin, *Vdivid*, with values between 0 and 1023. The bright = map(reading, 0, thresh, 255, 0) instruction maps a reading value between 0 and *thresh* (= 500) to a LED *bright* value of 255 to 0. Note that the low LDR readings are mapped to high LED brightness values. A mapping of analog inputs to analog outputs is often required, as the analog inputs are on a scale of 0 to 1023, while analog outputs are on a scale of 0 to 255.

Light Dependent Resistor and Several LEDs

A light dependent resistor can be used to turn on a number of LEDs, depending on the ambient light, with a brighter light turning on more LEDs (see Figure 3-6, Table 3-6, and Listing 3-4). The LEDs do not have to be connected to Arduino PWM pins, as the LEDs are only turned on or off. The map() function converts the output from the voltage divider to the number of LEDs to be turned on, equal to the *level* variable. In the sketch, *level* LEDs are turned on and (*nLEDs* – *level*) LEDs are turned off, where *nLEDs* is the total number of LEDs. The maximum value of *level* is the number of LEDs plus one, so that no LEDs are turned on in very low ambient light.

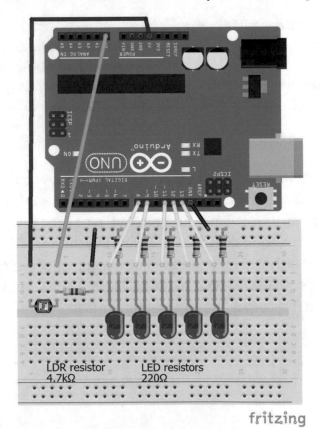

Figure 3-6. *LDR and several LEDs*

Table 3-6. *Connections for LDR and Several LEDs*

Component	Connect to	and to
LDR left leg	Arduino 5V	
LDR right leg	Arduino A0	
LDR right leg	4.7kΩ resistor	Arduino GND
LED long legs	Arduino pins 8,	9, 11, 12, 13
LED short legs	220Ω resistors	Arduino GND

Listing 3-4. LDR and Several LEDs

```
int Vdivid = A0;                     // voltage divider analog pin
int nLEDs = 5;                       // number of LEDs
int LEDpin[] = {8, 9, 11 ,12, 13};   // LED pins
int reading, level;

void setup()
{                                    // define LED pins as outputs
  for (int i=0; i<5; i++) pinMode(LEDpin[i], OUTPUT);
}

void loop()
{
  reading = analogRead(Vdivid);      // voltage divider reading
  level = 0;                         // set number of LEDs to zero
  level = map(reading, 0, 1023, 0, nLEDs+1);  // map reading to level
  for (int i = 0; i < nLEDs; i++)
  {                                              // turn on LED
    if (i < level) digitalWrite(LEDpin[i], HIGH);  // less than level
    else digitalWrite(LEDpin[i],LOW);   // otherwise turn off LED
  }
  delay(1000);                        // delay 1000ms
}
```

The int LEDpin[] = {8, 9, 11, 12, 13} instruction defines an array of integer values, with the values of the array referenced as *LEDpin[0]* to *LEDpin[4]* and not as *LEDpin[1]* to *LEDpin[5]*. The size of the array does not have to be explicitly defined, as it is implicitly defined by the number of values between the curly brackets. The size of an array can also be defined with the int LEDpin[5] instruction.

The for (int i = start; i < finish; i++) instruction repeats the series of instructions contained in the curly brackets (*finish – start*) times by incrementing the counter *i* from *start* to *finish*. For example, to repeat an instruction four times, the instruction is for (int i = 0; i < 4; i++) with the counter *i* taking the values 0, 1, 2 and 3. If the counter is to run from 10 to 6, for example, then the instruction is for (int i = 10; i >5; i--) with counter *i* taking the values 10, 9, 8, 7, and 6.

In Listing 3-4, a for() instruction is used to define the LED pins as *OUTPUT*, rather than having to repeat the pinMode(pin, OUTPUT) instruction several times. The second for() instruction repeats *nLEDs* times with the counter *i* incrementing from 0 to *nLEDs-1*, and an LED is turned on if *i* is less than *level*; otherwise, the LED is turned off.

Voltage Divider

A voltage divider (see Figure 3-7) can change an output voltage with a combination of resistors, as in the two examples with a light dependent resistor. A potentiometer is another example of a voltage divider when used for tuning to a radio station or controlling the movement of a motor. A second use of voltage dividers is as a logic level converter to reduce the voltage of a transmitted signal. For example, a logic level converter is required by a receiving Bluetooth module operating at 3.3V when connected to an Arduino transmitting a 5V signal.

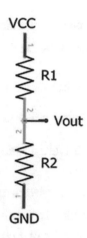

Figure 3-7. *Voltage divider*

A voltage divider consists of an input voltage, V_{in}, two resistors, $R1$ and $R2$, in series, and an output voltage, V_{out}, at the junction of the two resistors. From Ohm's law, as discussed in Chapter 1, the output voltage $V_{out} = I \times R2$, where I is the current through the circuit, equal to $\dfrac{V_{in}}{R1+R2}$, so

$V_{out} = V_{in}\left(\dfrac{R2}{R1+R2}\right)$. If the two resistors are equal, then the output voltage

is half the input voltage.

A signal voltage of 5V can be reduced to 3.3V by using the combination of 1kΩ and 2kΩ resistors or by using the combination of 5kΩ and 10kΩ resistors. The difference between using the two sets of resistors is in the power to reduce the signal voltage and the change in energy produces

heat. In Chapter 1, power was defined as V × I, which is $\dfrac{V_{in}^2}{R1+R2}$ for a

voltage divider. For the two combinations of resistors, the power is 8.33mW and 1.67mW, respectively, so the 5kΩ and 10kΩ resistor combination produces less heat as the current, and so the power, is lower than with the 1kΩ and 2kΩ resistors.

A voltage divider should never be used to reduce the voltage to supply a device or load. The Thevenin resistance of a voltage divider is $\dfrac{R1 \times R2}{R1 + R2}\ \Omega$ and the combination of a voltage divider and a load is essentially like another voltage divider with an output voltage to the load of $V_{in}\left(\dfrac{Rload}{RVD + Rload}\right)$, where *Rload* and *RVD* are the Thevenin resistance of the load and voltage divider, respectively.

If a 5kΩ and a 10kΩ resistor combination formed a voltage divider to reduce 5V to 3.3V for a device with a resistance of 66Ω, then the actual voltage supply to the device would be only 0.1V. Conversely, if a 50Ω and a 100Ω resistor combination formed the voltage divider, then the output voltage would be the required 3.3V, but the power output would be 250mW, which may be sufficient to burn out the resistors.

Ultrasonic Distance Sensor

 The HC-SR04 ultrasonic distance sensor estimates distance by transmitting (sensor T) an ultrasonic sound wave and measuring the time taken to receive (sensor R) the echo. The frequency of the sound wave is 40kHz, which is above the upper limit of human hearing of 20kHz. The distance, in centimeters, between the sensor and the target point is half the echo time, measured in microseconds, multiplied by 0.0343, assuming a speed of sound of 343m/s.

The minimum and maximum measureable distances are 2cm and 4m, respectively. For reliable distance measurements, the ultrasonic distance sensor should be perpendicular to the scanned surface, both horizontally and vertically, and the scanned surface should be flat. The time for the signal to return over a 5m distance is 29ms, so a delay between subsequent distance measurements of at least 40ms avoids interference between signals from different measurements.

To initiate the ultrasonic distance sensor, the trigger pin is held *HIGH* for at least 10µs. The sensor then sends out an eight-cycle signal at 40kHz with the pulseIn() function, automatically setting the echo pin to *HIGH*, and waits for the signal to return, when the echo pin is set to *LOW*. The time interval between the echo pin changing from *HIGH* to *LOW* is the echo time. If the echo pin is *HIGH* when the pulseIn() function is called, the pulseIn() function waits until the echo pin is set to *LOW* and then to *HIGH* before timing the signal.

An ultrasonic distance sensor to measure distance is given in Figure 3-8, with connections in Table 3-7 and a sketch in Listing 3-5.

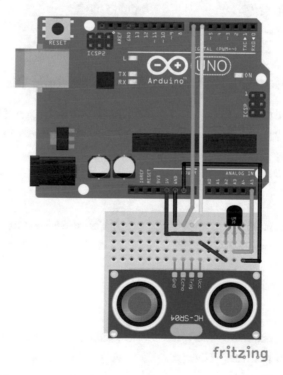

Figure 3-8. *Ultrasonic distance and temperature sensors*

Table 3-7. *Connections for Ultrasonic Distance and Temperature Sensor*

Component	Connect to
HC-SR04 VCC	Arduino 5V
HC-SR04 Trig	Arduino pin 6
HC-SR04 Echo	Arduino pin 7
HC-SR04 GND	Arduino GND
LM35DZ GND	Arduino GND
LM35DZ OUT	Arduino pin A5
LM35DZ VCC	Arduino 5V

Listing 3-5. Measure Distance with the Ultrasonic Distance Sensor

```
int trigPin = 6;                          // HC-SR04 trigger pin
int echoPin = 7;                          // HC-SR04 echo pin
float duration, distance;

void setup()
{
  Serial.begin(9600);                     // define Serial output baud rate
  pinMode(trigPin, OUTPUT);               // define trigger pin as output
}

void loop()
{
  digitalWrite(echoPin, LOW);             // set the echo pin LOW
  digitalWrite(trigPin, LOW);             // set the trigger pin LOW
  delayMicroseconds(2);
  digitalWrite(trigPin, HIGH);            // set the trigger pin HIGH for 10µs
  delayMicroseconds(10);
  digitalWrite(trigPin, LOW);
  duration = pulseIn(echoPin, HIGH);      // measure the echo time (µs)
```

```
distance = (duration/2.0)*0.0343;   // convert echo time to distance (cm)
if(distance>400 || distance<2) Serial.println("Out of range");
else
{
  Serial.print("Distance : ");
  Serial.print(distance, 1); Serial.println(" cm");
}
}
```

Ultrasonic distance sensor information can be displayed on the Arduino IDE serial monitor by selecting *Tools ➤ Serial Monitor* (see Figure 3-9). The communication speed of 9600 baud (Bd) between the Arduino and the serial monitor is defined in the void setup() function with the Serial.begin(9600) instruction.

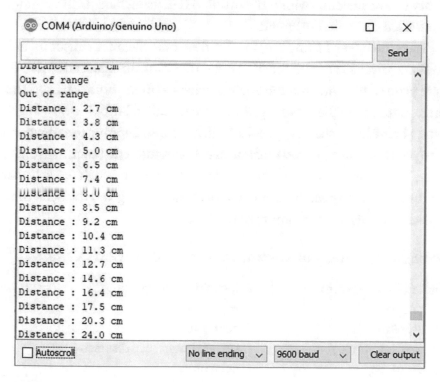

Figure 3-9. Serial monitor

There are several options for displaying information on the serial monitor.

- `Serial.print(X, d)`   print the real number X with d decimal places

- `Serial.print("abc")`   print *abc*

- `Serial.print("abc\tdef")`   insert a tab (\t) after *abc* and before *def*

- `Serial.println("abc")`   insert a carriage return (\r) and new line (\n) after *abc*

There are several libraries for the HC-SR04 ultrasonic distance sensor and the *NewPing* library by Tim Eckel is recommended. The *NewPing* library can be installed within the Arduino IDE using installation method 3, as outlined earlier in the chapter.

The sketch (see Listing 3-6) for the ultrasonic distance sensor includes the library, *NewPing*, with the `#include <NewPing.h>` instruction. Note there is no semicolon after the angle brackets with the library name. The sonar functions in the *NewPing* library are initialized with the `NewPing sonar(trigPin, echoPin, maxdist)` instruction, defining the trigger and echo pins and the expected maximum measurement distance to avoid noise. The distance between the start and target point is half the echo time multiplied by the speed of sound and divided by 10^4, given the echo time in μs and the distance in centimeters (cm).

Listing 3-6. Ultrasonic Distance Sensor and NewPing Library

```
#include <NewPing.h>          // include NewPing library
int trigPin = 6;              // trigger pin
int echoPin = 7;              // echo pin
int maxdist = 100;            // set maximum scan distance (cm)
int echoTime;                 // echo time
float distance;               // distance (cm)
```

```
NewPing sonar(trigPin, echoPin, maxdist); // associate sonar with
                                           // NewPing library
void setup()
{
  Serial.begin(9600);                      // set baud rate for Serial Monitor
}

void loop()
{
  echoTime = sonar.ping();                 // echo time (μs)
  distance = (echoTime/2.0)*0.0343;        // distance between sensor and target
  Serial.print("echo time: ");             // print text "echo time: "
  Serial.print(echoTime);                  // print echo time
  Serial.print(" microsecs\t");            // print text " microsecs" and tab
  Serial.print("distance: ");              // print text "distance: "
  Serial.print(distance,2);                // print distance with 2 DP
  Serial.println(" cm");                   // " cm" followed by a new line
  delay(500);
}
```

The following are other sonar functions in the NewPing library.

- `sonar.ping_cm()`: Returns the distance between the sensor and the target point, but there are no digits after the decimal point.

- `sonar.convert_cm(echotime)`: Returns the distance given the echo time, but outlier values can be observed. It is more robust to calculate the distance between the sensor and target point directly from the echo time.

- `sonar.ping_median(number of observations)`: Returns median echo time for the number of observations, with a minimum of five observations, after excluding out-of-range values.

Speed of Sound

The speed of sound depends on the air temperature and can be estimated as 331.3 + 0.606 *temp* m/s, where *temp* is the temperature in degrees Celsius. If an temperature sensor is connected to Arduino analog pin A5, then the speed of sound can be estimated based on the echo time over a known distance (see Figure 3-8 and Table 3-7). The known distance is defined at the start of the sketch (see Listing 3-7).

Listing 3-7. Speed of Sound

```
#include <NewPing.h>            // include NewPing library
int pinTrig = 6;                // trigger pin
int pinEcho = 7;                // echo pin
int maxdist = 100;              // max scan distance (cm)
int echoTime;
float distance = 15;            // known distance to scan (cm)
NewPing sonar(pinTrig, pinEcho, maxdist);  // associate sonar with
                                           // NewPing library
int tempPin = A5;               // temperature sensor on analog pin A5
float speed, temp, predict;

void setup()
{
  Serial.begin(9600);          // define Serial output baud rate
  analogReference(INTERNAL);   // set ADC voltage to 1.1V rather than 5V
}

void loop()
{
  echoTime = sonar.ping_median(5);          // median echo time (µs)
  speed = distance*2.0*pow(10,4)/echoTime;  // speed of sound (m/s)
  Serial.print(echoTime);Serial.print(" microsecs\t");  // print echo time
```

```
Serial.print("speed ");                        // print text "speed"
Serial.print(speed,1); Serial.print("\t");     // print speed to 1DP and tab
temp = (analogRead(tempPin)*110.0)/1023;       // read temperature
predict = 331.3 + 0.606 * temp;                // calculate speed of sound
Serial.print("predict ");
Serial.print(predict,1);Serial.println(" m/s");  // print prediction to 1DP
delay(500);
}
```

The pow(x,y) instruction raises the x variable to the power y, so pow(10,4) is 10^4.

Hall Effect Sensor

 Hall effect sensors are activated by a magnet field and are used to measure rotational speed of a car crankshaft or a bicycle wheel or for detecting the presence of a magnetic field, as in a door or window alarm system.

When the Hall effect sensor is in a magnetic field, the field exerts a force on the semiconductor material of the sensor and deflects the material's electrons away from the magnetic field. The movement of electrons creates a potential difference between the two sides of the semiconductor material, which indicates that the sensor is in a magnetic field. The Hall effect sensor is sensitive to the magnetic field's polarity, with the sensor activated when the South pole of the magnet is close to the label side of the sensor or when the North pole of the magnet is close to the flat side of the sensor (see Figure 3-10). The orientation of a magnet is determined with a compass.

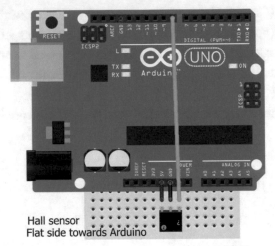

Hall sensor
Flat side towards Arduino

fritzing

Figure 3-10. *Hall effect sensor*

The 3144 Hall effect sensor (see Figure 3-10 and Table 3-8) requires a pull-up resistor (see Figure 3-11). The internal pull-up resistors of the Arduino input pins can be used, rather than connecting a resistor between the output and VCC pins of the sensor,. The Arduino's internal pull-up resistor is activated with the digitalWrite(pin, INPUT_PULLUP) instruction.

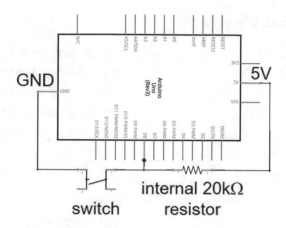

Figure 3-11. *Pull-up resistor*

Table 3-8. *Connections for Hall Effect Sensor*

Component	Connect to
Hall VCC (flat side left)	Arduino VCC
Hall GND	Arduino GND
Hall out (flat side right)	Arduino pin 8

The structure of the sketch for the Hall effect sensor (see Listing 3-8) is based on the switch sketch of Listing 2-2. The sketch determines the rpm, time per revolution and speed of a bicycle with 700×32 tyres, which have a circumference of 2.16m. The results are displayed on the serial monitor in this chapter, as display screens are outlined in Chapters 4 and 13.

Listing 3-8. Hall Effect Sensor

```
int switchPin = 8;                          // Hall effect sensor pin
int switchState = LOW;                      // set switch to LOW
int revolution = 0;                         // number of revolutions
float circum = 2.16;                        // tyre circumference
unsigned long time = 0;                     // time (ms) per revolution
float speed, rpm;
int reading;

void setup()
{                                           // pull-up resistor on hall
  pinMode(switchPin, INPUT_PULLUP);         // effect sensor pin
  Serial.begin(9600);                       // set baud rate for Serial Monitor
}

void loop()
{
  reading = digitalRead(switchPin);         // read Hall switch
  if(reading != switchState)                // switch state changed
  {
    if (reading == HIGH && switchState == LOW)
    {                                       // start of new revolution
      revolution = revolution +1;           // increment number of revolutions
      time = millis() - time;               // time (ms) since last revolution
      speed = 3600.0*circum/time;           // speed calculationin km/h
      rpm = 60000.0/time;                   // revolutions per minute
      Serial.print(revolution);             // print number of revolutions
      Serial.print("\t");                   // and a tab
      Serial.print(speed,1);                // print speed to 1DP
      Serial.print("km/h\t");               // with " km/h" and tab
```

```
      Serial.print(rpm,0);Serial.println("rpm"); // print rpm, "rpm"
      time = millis();                    //update revolution time
   }
   switchState = reading;            // update hall switch state
  }
}
```

Sound Sensor

 The LM393 sound sensor (see Figure 3-12 with connections in Table 3-9) detects sound above a threshold, which is controlled by adjusting the sensor's potentiometer. In the sketch (see Listing 3-9), an LED is turned on while the sound level is above a threshold level and the serial monitor displays that a new sound has been detected or that the previous sound has finished. A minimum time lag between sounds has to occur before two sounds are considered discrete rather than continuous. Reducing the time lag, increases the "sensitivity" to new sounds. When the detected sound is above the threshold, the output is set to *LOW* rather than to *HIGH*.

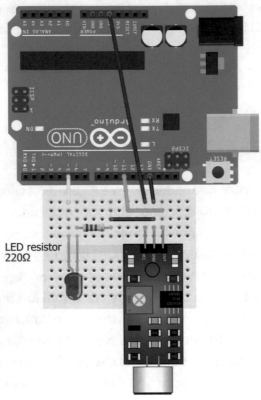

Figure 3-12. *Sound sensor*

Table 3-9. *Sound Sensor*

Component	Connect to	and to
Sound sensor VCC	Arduino 5V	
Sound sensor GND	Arduino GND	
Sound sensor OUT	Arduino pin 11	
LED long leg	Arduino pin 5	
LED short leg	220Ω resistor	Arduino GND

Listing 3-9. Sound Sensor

```
int soundPin = 11;            // sound sensor pin
int LEDpin = 5;               // LED pin
int detected = LOW;           // sound detect state to LOW
unsigned long detectTime;     // time sound detected
int lag = 1000;               // time between sounds (ms)
int sound;

void setup ()
{
  Serial.begin(9600);         // set baud rate for Serial Monitor
  pinMode(LEDpin, OUTPUT);    // LED pin as output
}

void loop ()
{
  sound = digitalRead(soundPin);    // read sound pin
  if (sound == LOW)                 // sound detected with LOW, not HIGH
  {
    detectTime = millis();   // start time of new sound
    if (detected == LOW)     // if currently no sound
    {                                // print "new SOUND" and tab
      Serial.print("new SOUND");Serial.print("\t");
      detected = HIGH;               // update sound detect state to HIGH
      digitalWrite(LEDpin, detected); // turn LED on
    }
  }
  else if (sound == HIGH)   // no sound detected
  {                                // continuous sound no longer detected
    if(detected == HIGH && (millis()-detectTime) > lag)
    {
      Serial.println("now quiet");   // print "now quiet" with a new line
```

```
    detected = LOW;                          // update sound detect state to LOW
    digitalWrite(LEDpin, detected);  // turn LED off
  }
 }
}
```

Infrared Sensor

Infrared (IR) remote controls are used to operate devices, such as television or machinery, by transmitting a signal consisting of pulses of infrared light. The VS1838B infrared sensor receives an IR signal, which is decoded to implement the appropriate action. For example, the IR signal in Figure 3-13 has binary and HEX representations of B011101 and 0x1D, respectively. Infrared light is not visible to the human eye, as the wavelength of IR light, 700 nm to 1000nm, is longer the wavelength of visible light, 400 nm to 700nm. However, the IR light from an IR transmitter is visible though the camera of a mobile phone or tablet, as generally the cameras do not have an IR filter.

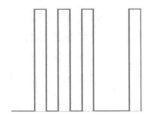

Figure 3-13. *Infrared signal*

The *IRremote* library by Ken Shirriff is recommended for sketches with an IR sensor. The *IRremote* library is available within the Arduino IDE and is installed using installation method 3, as outlined earlier in the chapter.

When the IR sensor detects a signal, the sketch (see Listing 3-10) displays the device type, HEX representation and bit count of an IR signal and turns the LED on for one second (see Figure 3-14 with connections in Table 3-10).

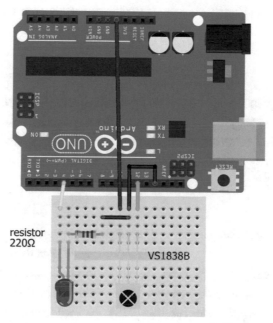

Figure 3-14. *Infrared sensor*

Table 3-10. *Infrared Sensor*

Component	Connect to	and to
IR sensor OUT	Arduino pin 12	
IR sensor GND	Arduino GND	
IR sensor VCC	Arduino 5V	
LED long leg	Arduino pin 4	
LED short leg	220Ω resistor	Arduino GND

Listing 3-10. Infrared Sensor

```
#include <IRremote.h>              // include IRremote library
int IRpin = 12;                    // IR sensor pin
IRrecv irrecv(IRpin);              // associate irrecv with IRremote library
decode_results reading;            // IRremote variable reading
int LEDpin = 4;                    // LED pin

void setup()
{
  Serial.begin(9600);             // set baud rate for Serial Monitor
  irrecv.enableIRIn();            // start the infrared receiver
  pinMode(LEDpin, OUTPUT);        // LED pin as output
}

void loop()
{
  if(irrecv.decode(&reading))     // read pulsed signal
  {                               // NEC, Sony, RC5 or RC6 signals
        if(reading.decode_type == NEC)  Serial.print("NEC: ");
    else if(reading.decode_type == SONY) Serial.print("Sony: ");
    else if(reading.decode_type == RC5)  Serial.print("RC5: ");
    else if(reading.decode_type == RC6)  Serial.print("RC6: ");
    else Serial.print("Other: ");
    Serial.print(reading.value, HEX); // display device type and
    Serial.print("\tBits: ");         // HEX code on Serial Monitor
    Serial.println(reading.bits);     // display number of IR signal bits
    digitalWrite(LEDpin, HIGH);       // turn LED on
    delay(100);                       // delay before next IR signal
    digitalWrite(LEDpin, LOW);        // turn LED off
    irrecv.resume();                  // receive the next infrared signal
  }
}
```

Infrared Distance Module

 Infrared can also be used to determine the distance from an object based on the time taken for the infrared signal to bounce off a target object and be received by the infrared sensor. The TCRT500 infrared distance module includes an infrared emitter and receiver on one side of the module, with a potentiometer on the other side. The analog value on the Arduino A0 pin is determined by both the distance to the target object and the color of the target object. For example, a black surface reflects less light than a white surface, so the distance to a black target object appears greater than the distance to a white target object in the same position. If the received signal is less than the threshold, set by the potentiometer, then the TCRT500 D0 pin state changes from *HIGH* to *LOW* and the built-in LED turns on. The TCRT500 infrared distance module is connected to 5V (see Figure 3-15 and Table 3-11).

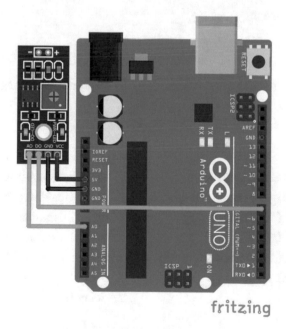

Figure 3-15. *Infrared distance sensor*

Table 3-11. *Connections for Infrared Distance Sensor*

Component	Connect to
TCRT500 VCC	Arduino 5V
TCRT500 GND	Arduino GND
TCRT500 D0	Arduino pin 7
TCRT500 A0	Arduino pin A0

The sketch (see Listing 3-11) displays the analog value on pin A0 and the state of the built-in LED.

Listing 3-11. Infrared Distance Sensor

```
int IRpin = A0;                        // IR sensor pin
int threshPin = 7;                     // threshold pin
int reading, thresh;

void setup()
{
  Serial.begin(9600);                  // set Serial Monitor baud rate
}

void loop()
{
  reading = analogRead(IRpin);         // read IR sensor pin
  thresh = 1-digitalRead(threshPin);   // read threshold pin
  Serial.print("Distance: ");          // print "Distance: " to Serial Monitor
  Serial.print(reading);               // print IR sensor value
  Serial.print("\tThreshold : ");      // print a tab and "Threshold"
  Serial.println(thresh);              // print threshold value
  delay(1000);                         // delay 1s
}
```

Passive Infrared Sensor

 All objects with a temperature above absolute zero emit heat energy in the form of infrared radiation. The HR-SC501 passive infrared (PIR) sensor converts the infrared radiation into an output voltage. The PIR sensor has two halves to detect a change in infrared radiation, caused by an object moving in front of the PIR sensor, as movement is indicated by a change in infrared radiation not the level of infrared radiation. The Fresnel lenses above the PIR sensor increase the field of view of the PIR sensor to about 110° with a range of six meters. PIR sensors are used in motion detector alarms.

The PIR sensor requires up to 60s to stabilize after switching on and the output stays *HIGH* for a minimum of 2.5s after movement is detected. The time delay (Tx) and the sensor sensitivity (Sx) are increased by turning clockwise the appropriate potentiometer on the side of the module. Smaller movements are detected with high sensitivity with a distance range between 3m and 7m. The time delay ranges from 2.5s to 5min, so initially the most counterclockwise position is useful.

The structure of the PIR sensor sketch (see Listing 3-12, Figure 3-16, and connections in Table 3-12) is the same as the structure of the sound sensor sketch (see Listing 3-9). In both sketches, the void loop() function consists of two halves, with the first half detecting the occurrence of a new event and the second half determining if the event has ended.

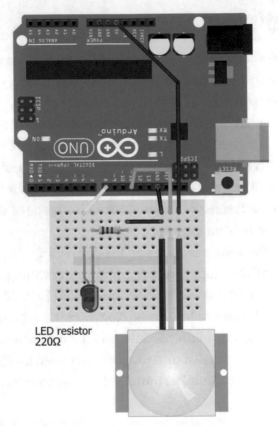

Figure 3-16. *PIR sensor*

Table 3-12. *PIR Sensor Connections*

Component	Connect to	and to
PIR sensor VCC	Arduino 5V	
PIR sensor OUT	Arduino pin 11	
PIR sensor GND	Arduino GND	
LED long leg	Arduino pin 8	
LED short leg	220Ω resistor	Arduino GND

Listing 3-12. PIR Sensor

```
int PIRpin = 11;                    // PIR sensor pin
int LEDpin = 8;                     // LED pin
int PIRstate = LOW;                 // set PIR state to LOW
int reading;
unsigned long detectTime;           // time lag on PIR sensor
float moveTime;

void setup()
{
  Serial.begin(9600);               // set Serial Monitor baud rate
  pinMode(LEDpin, OUTPUT);          // LED pin as output
}

void loop()
{
  reading = digitalRead(PIRpin);              // read PIR pin
  if (reading == HIGH && PIRstate == LOW)     // PIR detected new
  {                                           // movement
    Serial.print("New movement detected");    // print to Serial Monitor
    detectTime = millis();                    // time of movement
    PIRstate = HIGH;                          // update PIR state to HIGH
    digitalWrite(LEDpin, PIRstate);           // turn LED on
  }                                           // movement no longer detected
  else if (reading == LOW && PIRstate == HIGH)
  {
    moveTime = millis() - detectTime;   // duration of movement
    moveTime = moveTime/1000.0;
    Serial.print(" and lasted for ");   // print to Serial Monitor
    Serial.print(moveTime,1);           // print detect time (s) with 1DP
    Serial.println(" seconds");         // print text with a new line
```

```
    PIRstate = LOW;                          // update PIR state to LOW
    digitalWrite(LEDpin, PIRstate);   // turn LED off
  }
}
```

Accelerometer and Gyroscope

 An accelerometer measures an object's acceleration, but not relative to an observer. For example, an object at rest on the Earth's surface has an acceleration due to Earth's gravity of 9.81ms^{-2}. For example, an accelerometer detects the orientation of a laptop to ensure that an image is displayed upright. A gyroscope measures angular velocity and when combined with an accelerometer forms an inertial navigation system.

The GY-521 module includes an MPU-6050 accelerometer and gyroscope sensor, which can be powered by 3.3V or 5V, but 3.3V is preferable. The GY-521 module communicates with I2C (see Chapter 4) with an I2C address of *0x68*. The I2C address can be changed to *0x69* by setting the *AD0* pin to *HIGH* rather than the default *LOW*, to include a second GY-521 module. Only the VCC, GND and two I2C communication pins, SDA and SCL, are connected to the Arduino, with the latter two connected to pins A4 and A5, respectively.

The values for the three accelerometer and gyroscopic axes (X: left–right, Y: forward–back, and Z: up–down) are stored in six pairs of registers (see Table 3-13), with values in a pair of registers then combined. For example, if the values in the pair of registers for the accelerometer X axis are *AxHigh* and *AxLow*, then the combined value is $2^8 \times AxHigh + AxLow$ equivalent to the AxHigh<<8 | AxLow instruction, which shifts the value in the high register by eight positions and then adds the value in the low register.

Table 3-13. *Data Registers for Accelerometer and Gyroscope Sensor*

Variable	High address	Low address
Accel X-axis	0x3B	0x3C
Accel Y-axis	0x3D	0x3E
Accel Z-axis	0x3F	0x40
Temperature	0x41	0x42
Gyro X-axis	0x43	0x44
Gyro Y-axis	0x45	0x46
Gyro Z-axis	0x47	0x48

Using the YPR (yaw, pitch, roll) representation (see Appendix), the accelerometer measurements are converted to a roll angle $= arctan(y/z)180/\pi$ and a pitch angle $= - arcsin(x)180/\pi$, where, x, y, and z are the adjusted accelerometer measurements. Defining $|A| = \sqrt{a_x^2 + a_y^2 + a_z^2}$, where a_X, a_Y, and a_Z are the accelerometer measurements, each divided by 2^{14}, with the adjusted accelerometer measurement $x = a_X/|A|$ and similarly for a_Y and a_Z. The arctan(numerator/denominator) instruction in the Arduino IDE is *atan2(numerator, denominator)*, which is equivalent to *atan2 (denominator, numerator)* in Excel.

To illustrate using the GY-521 module for determining orientation, LEDs are positioned on four sides of the GY-521 module (see Figure 3-17) and when the module is tilted, the corresponding LEDs are turned on, based on the accelerometer measurements. In the void setup() function of the sketch, the I2C address of the MPU-6050 sensor is defined, the power management register is set to zero to "wake up" the sensor. Within the void loop() function of the sketch, the accelerometer measurements are adjusted to the x, y, and z values, to then calculate the roll and pitch angles.

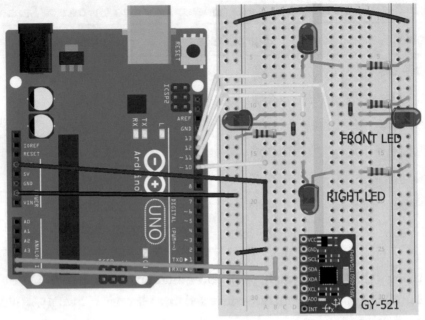

Figure 3-17. *GY-521 with LEDs*

Using an aircraft analogy, a positive roll angle is a turn with the right wing down and a positive pitch angle is the nose lifting up. If the roll angle is greater than 10° or less than –10°, then the right or left LED is turned on, with the front or back LED turned on when the pitch angle is greater than 10° or less than –10°, respectively.

The sketch (see Listing 3-13) uses the *Wire* library for I2C communication between the Arduino and the GY-521 module. The *Wire* library is included in the Arduino IDE, so only the I2C address of the GY-521 module is required. Connections for the GY-521 module are given in Table 3-14).

Table 3-14. *GY-51 Module Connections*

Component	Connect to	and to
GY-521 VCC	Arduino 3.3V	
GY-521 GND	Arduino GND	
GY-521 SCL	Arduino A5	
GY-521 SDA	Arduino A4	
LED long legs	Arduino pins 10,	11, 12, 13
LED short legs	220Ω resistors	Arduino GND

Listing 3-13. GY-521 Module

```
#include<Wire.h>                 // include Wire library
int I2Caddress = 0x68;          // I2C address of the MPU-6050
int frontLED = 13;
int backLED = 11;               // define LED pins
int rightLED = 12;
int leftLED = 10;
float accelX,accelY,accelZ;     // accelerometer measurements
float roll, pitch, sumsquare;

void setup()
{
  Serial.begin(9600);          // define Serial output baud rate
  pinMode(frontLED, OUTPUT);
  pinMode(backLED, OUTPUT);     // define LED pins as OUTPUT
  pinMode(rightLED, OUTPUT);
  pinMode(leftLED, OUTPUT);
  Wire.begin();                          // initiate I2C bus
  Wire.beginTransmission(I2Caddress);  // transmit to device at I2Caddress
```

```
  Wire.write(0x6B);                          // PWR_MGMT_1 register
  Wire.write(0);                             // set to zero wakes up MPU-6050
  Wire.endTransmission(1);                   // end of transmission
}

void loop()
{                                            // transmit to device at
  Wire.beginTransmission(I2Caddress);        // I2Caddress
  Wire.write(0x3B);                          // start reading from register 0x3B
  Wire.endTransmission(0);                   // transmission not finished
  Wire.requestFrom(I2Caddress,6,true);       // request data from 6 registers
  accelX=Wire.read()<<8|Wire.read();         // combine AxHigh and AxLow
  accelY=Wire.read()<<8|Wire.read();         // combine AyHigh and AyLow
  accelZ=Wire.read()<<8|Wire.read();         // combine AzHigh and AzLow
  accelX = accelX/pow(2,14);
  accelY = accelY/pow(2,14);                 // scale X, Y and Z measurements
  accelZ = accelZ/pow(2,14);
  sumsquare = sqrt(accelX*accelX+accelY*accelY+accelZ*accelZ);
  accelX = accelX/sumsquare;
  accelY = accelY/sumsquare;                 // adjusted accelerometer measurements
  accelZ = accelZ/sumsquare;
  roll = atan2(accelY, accelZ)*180/PI;       // roll angle
  pitch = -asin(accelX)*180/PI;              // pitch angle
  LEDs();                                    // call function to control LEDS
}
void LEDs()                                  // function to control LEDs
{
  int front = LOW;
  int back = LOW;                            // turn off all LEDs
  int right = LOW;
  int left = LOW;
  if(roll>10) right = HIGH;                  // right or left LEDS with roll angle
  else if(roll< -10) left = HIGH;
  if(pitch>10) front = HIGH;                 // front or back LEDs with pitch angle
  else if(pitch< -10) back = HIGH;
```

```
    digitalWrite(frontLED, front);        // if value = HIGH, LED on
    digitalWrite(backLED, back);          // if value = LOW, LED off
    digitalWrite(rightLED, right);
    digitalWrite(leftLED, left);
    delay(500);
}
```

The GY-521 module includes a temperature sensor, with the temperature measurement stored in the register after the accelerometer Z measurements. The temperature, in degrees Celsius, is equal to $temp/340.0 + 36.53$, where $temp$ is the combined value from the temperature pair of registers. Information on registers and temperature calculation is available from *InvenSense* register data pages. The instructions in Listing 3-14 can be included in Listing 3-13, between the `Wire.endTransmission(0)` and `accelX = accelX/pow(2,14)` instructions.

Listing 3-14. Temperature Reading from GY-521 Module

```
    Wire.requestFrom(I2Caddress,8,true);    // request data from 8 registers
    accelX=Wire.read()<<8|Wire.read();      // combine AxHigh and AxLow
    accelY=Wire.read()<<8|Wire.read();      // combine AyHigh and AyLow
    accelZ=Wire.read()<<8|Wire.read();      // combine AzHigh and AzLow
    temp=Wire.read()<<8|Wire.read();
    tempC = temp/340.0 + 36.53;             // temperature reading
```

Summary

A selection of sensors were described with a demonstration sketch for each sensor, because the sensors are used in subsequent projects. Sensors were used to measure temperature, humidity, light, distance, sound, and the speed of sound. The Hall effect sensor measured wheel revolutions with a magnet. The infrared sensor detected signals, such as from a television remote control, and measured distance with movement detected by the passive infrared sensor. The accelerometer and gyroscope module detected when it was tilted. The voltage divider was combined with several sensors. Installing libraries to the Arduino IDE was described. More programming instructions were introduced to develop sketches to control the sensors.

Components List

- Arduino Uno and breadboard

- LED

- Resistors: 220Ω, 4.7kΩ, and 10kΩ

- Light dependent resistor (or photoresistor)

- Temperature sensors: LM35DZ and DHT11

- Ultrasonic distance sensor: HC-SR04

- Hall effect sensor: 3144

- Magnet

- Sound sensor: LM393

- Infrared sensor: VM1838B

- Passive infrared (or PIR) sensor: TCRT500

- Accelerometer and gyroscope module: GY-521

CHAPTER 4

Liquid Crystal Display

The liquid crystal display (LCD) screen displays output from the Arduino, so that the Arduino does not need to be connected to a computer screen or laptop. A 16×4 LCD with a HD44780 controller is used in the chapter, which can display four rows of 16 characters per row, with each character defined by an 8×5–pixel array. LCDs have different sizes such as 16×2, 16×4, 20×2, and 20×4.

The LCD has 16 pins numbered from left to right, when looking down on the screen. Some LCDs have no backlight function, so pins 15 and 16 are unconnected. The LCD screen contrast is controlled with a 10kΩ potentiometer. Details of the LCD pin functions are given in Table 4-1. Register selection provides information on the type of signal received by the LCD, such as an instruction to move the cursor to a given position or the data on a character to be displayed.

Table 4-1. *LCD Pin Description*

Pin		Description	Arduino Pin
1	VSS	Ground	GND
2	VDD	5V power supply for logic	5V
3	V0	LCD contrast adjustment	Potentiometer signal pin
4	RS	Register Selection: data or instruction register for LCD controller	Pin 2

(continued)

© Neil Cameron 2019

N. Cameron, *Arduino Applied*, https://doi.org/10.1007/978-1-4842-3960-5_4

Table 4-1. (*continued*)

Pin		Description	Arduino Pin
5	RW	Read or Write mode	GND for Write to LCD
6	E	Enable data ready for transmission	Pin 3
7-10	D0–D3		Unconnected
11-14	D4–D7	Unconnected	Pin 4–Pin 7
15	A or LED+	LED backlight (anode)	5V for backlight
16	K or LED-	LED backlight (Cathode)	GND for backlight

The *LiquidCrystal* library by Adafruit is built into the Arduino IDE, so it does not need to be uploaded. The LCD control and data lines are mapped to the Arduino pins with the LiquidCrystal lcd(RS, E, D4, D5, D6, D7) instruction, where *RS, E,* and *D4* to *D7* are the Arduino pins connected to the LCD pins. For example, if Arduino pins 2, 3, 4, 5, 6, and 7 are connected to the LCD *RS, E* and *D4* to *D7* pins, then the pin definition instruction would be either

```
LiquidCrystal lcd(2, 3, 4, 5, 6, 7)
```

or

```
int RS = 2;
int E  = 3;
int D4 = 4;
int D5 = 5;
int D6 = 6;
int D7 = 7;
LiquidCrystal lcd(RS, E, D4, D5, D6, D7);
```

In Listing 4-1, the number of seconds that the sketch has been running and the temperature from an LM35DZ temperature sensor, described in

Chapter 3, are displayed on the LCD (see Figure 4-1). The void setup() function specifies the dimensions of the LCD screen and the text to be constantly displayed, so that during the void loop() function only the updated time and temperature are written to the LCD. The reference point of the LCD to position a character is the top left-hand corner with position (0,0). For example, the fifth column and second row position is (4,1). Connections, other than the LCD, for Figures 4–1 and 4–2 are given in Table 4-2.

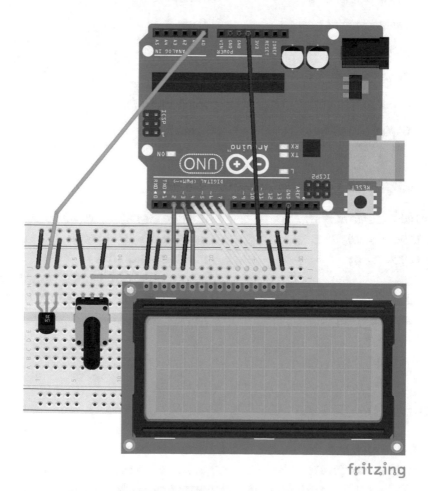

Figure 4-1. *LCD and temperature sensor*

Table 4-2. *Connections for LCD and Temperature Sensor*

Component	Connect to
LM35DZ GND	Arduino GND
LM35DZ OUT	Arduino pin A0
LM35DZ VCC	Arduino 5V
Potentiometer GND	Arduino GND
Potentiometer signal	LCD pin 3
Potentiometer VCC	Arduino 5V
Capacitor negative	Arduino GND
Capacitor positive	Arduino pin 9
Capacitor positive	LCD pin 3

Listing 4-1. LCD and Temperature Sensor

```
#include <LiquidCrystal.h>          // include the LiquidCrystal library
int LCDcol = 16;                    // number of LCD columns
int LCDrow = 4;                     // number of LCD rows
                                    // associate lcd with LiquidCrystal library
LiquidCrystal lcd (2,3,4,5,6,7);    // define LCD pins RS, E and D4 to D7
int tempPin = A0;                   // LM35DZ temperature sensor pin
int time = 0;
int reading;
float temp;

void setup()
{
  lcd.begin(LCDcol, LCDrow);        // define LCD dimensions
  lcd.setCursor(0,0);               // move cursor to start of first row
  lcd.print("LCD to display");      // print first row "LCD to display"
  lcd.setCursor(0,1);               // move cursor to start of second row
```

```
  lcd.print("time and temp");       // print second row "time and temp"
  lcd.setCursor(3,2);               // move cursor to insert "secs" on third row
  lcd.print(" secs");
  lcd.setCursor(5,3);               // move cursor to insert "C" in fourth row
  lcd.print(" C");
  analogReference(INTERNAL);        // set ADC voltage to 1.1V rather than 5V
}

void loop()
{
  lcd.setCursor(0,2);               // move cursor to start of third row
  if(time < 100) lcd.print(" ");    // spacing for 10s < time <100s
  if(time < 10) lcd.print(" ");     // spacing for time < 10s
  lcd.print(time);                  // print time (s)
  time++;                           // increment time
  reading = analogRead(tempPin);    // read temperature from sensor
  temp = (reading * 110.0)/1023;    // convert to Celsius given 1.1V range
  lcd.setCursor(0,3);               // move cursor to start of fourth row
  lcd.print(temp);                  // print temperature
  if(time>999) time = 0;            // reset time to zero
  delay (1000);                     // delay 1000ms
}
```

Contrast Adjustment with PWM

The LCD contrast can be adjusted with pulse width modulation (PWM),
as described in Chapter 1, smoothed with a 100µF (or 0.1mF) capacitor
(see Figure 4-2). The LCD contrast increases with decreasing PWM. Note
that electrolytic capacitors are polarized and the anode must be at a higher
voltage than the cathode. The cathode has a "–" marking and a colored
strip on the side of the capacitor.

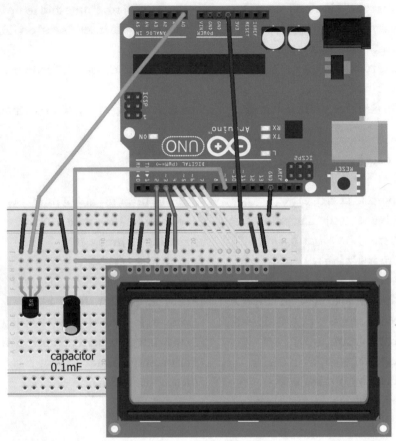

Figure 4-2. *LCD contrast and PWM*

The LCD contrast adjustment pin, *V0*, is connected to an Arduino PWM pin with the capacitor connected across the PWM output and ground. The following three instructions are added to the end of the void setup() function.

```
int contrast = 9;              // PWM pin for contrast
pinMode(contrast, OUTPUT);     // define contrast pin as OUTPUT
analogWrite(9, 80);            // PWM value of 80 (maximum is 255)
```

Decreasing the PWM value decreases the LCD contrast.

The LCD backlight can be turned on or off with the instructions `lcd.backlight()` and `lcd.noBacklight()`, respectively.

Scrolling Text

Rather than the displayed text being in a fixed position on the LCD, the text can be scrolled across the LCD screen. Substrings of up to 16 characters are printed, moving the start column from the right of the LCD screen to the left. When the first 16-character substring has been displayed across the LCD screen, the first character is dropped and a new last character is added to the substring. The process is repeated, dropping one character and adding another. The example text string is split over two lines of instructions with the continuation character (\) (see Listing 4-2).

Listing 4-2. Scrolling Text on LCD

```
#include <LiquidCrystal.h>          // include the LiquidCrystal library
int LCDcol = 16;                     // number of LCD columns
int LCDrow = 4;                      // number of LCD rows
LiquidCrystal lcd(2,3,4,5,6,7);      // define LCD pins RS, E and D4 to D7
int first;                  // position of first letter in 16 character substring
int last = 0;               // position of last letter in 16 character substring
int row = 1;                // row of LCD to display text
int col;
String text = "The quick brown fox jumps over the lazy dog \
contains every letter of the alphabet.";    // line continuation with \
                                             // character
void setup()
{
  lcd.begin(LCDcol, LCDrow);     // define LCD dimensions
  text = text + " ";             // add space at end of text as a buffer
}
```

```
void loop()
{
  if(last>text.length()+15) last=1;   // set first column of substring
  if(last<17) first = 0;  // substring<17 characters, start character =0
    else first = last-16;  // substring>=17 chars, start char = last-16
  if(last>16) col = 0;      // substring>16 characters, start column = 0
    else col = 16-last;     // substring<=16 chars, start col = last-16
  lcd.setCursor(col,row); // set cursor position
  lcd.print(text.substring(first, last));   // print substring
  last = last +1;                           // increment last
  delay(250);                               // delay 250ms
}
```

The if else instruction is more efficient than two if() instructions and is used when there is more than one condition, each with a different outcome. For example, if there are four mutually exclusive conditions, each with separate outcomes, then the following "instructions"

```
if (condition A is true) outcome A
else if (condition B is true) outcome B
else if (condition C is true) outcome C
else outcome D          // if conditions A, B and C are not true, then outcome D
```

are more efficient than the four "instructions":

```
if (condition A is true) outcome A
if (condition B is true) outcome B
if (condition C is true) outcome C
if (condition D is true) outcome D
```

When an else if condition is true, the sketch moves to the next instruction, rather than checking all the remaining else instructions, which is more efficient than checking each if() instruction in a series of if() instructions. For example, if condition B were true, then condition C would not need to be checked.

The text.length() function determines the length of the string *text*. The text.substring(first, last) function creates a substring consisting of characters *first* to *last* of the string *text*.

LCD with I2C Bus

 The Inter-Integrated Circuit (I2C) bus is used for communication between a microcontroller and other devices, such as an LCD. The I2C Two Wire Interface (TWI) bus uses two signal lines: serial data (SDA) and serial clock (SCL), irrespective of the number of devices. The microcontroller communicates with all devices and the message includes the address of the device to be communicated with, so that only the relevant device responds to the microcontroller. One pair of Arduino I2C pins are A4 for SDA and A5 for SCL. An I2C bus reduces the number of Arduino input pins to communicate with an LCD from six to two. The LCD screen contrast is controlled using an I2C bus potentiometer. The jumper at the end of the I2C bus can be disconnected to turn off the LCD backlight. Chapter 11 includes more information on I2C communication.

The microcontroller requires the hexadecimal address of the I2C bus to communicate with the I2C bus. I2C addresses for sensors and modules are available at https://learn.adafruit.com/i2c-addresses/ the-list. Listing 4-3 displays the address of all I2C devices connected to the Arduino. On transmitting to an I2C device, the device returns "0" to indicate a successful transmission, while, for example, a return of "4" indicates an error. The I2C addresses 0x00 to 0x07 and 0x78 to 0x7F are reserved, so are not scanned to detect an I2C device.

Listing 4-3. I2C Addresses

```
#include <Wire.h>                      // include Wire library
int device = 0;                        // set device counter to 0

void setup()
{
  Serial.begin (9600);                 // set Serial output baud rate
  Wire.begin();                        // start I2C bus
  for (int i=8; i<120; i++)            // scan through channels 8 to 119
  {
    Wire.beginTransmission (i);        // transmit to device at address i
    if (Wire.endTransmission () == 0)  // device response to transmission
    {
      Serial.print("Address 0x");      // print to screen "Address 0x"
      Serial.println(i, HEX);          // print to screen I2C address in HEX
      device++;                        // increment device count
      delay(10);                       // delay 10ms
    }
  }
  Serial.print(device);                // print to screen device count
  Serial.println(" device found");     // print to screen " device found"
}

void loop()
{}                                     // nothing in void loop() function
```

I2C with Temperature and Pressure Sensor

 To illustrate connecting more than one I2C device to the
Arduino, temperature and pressure are displayed on the LCD,
with readings from a BMP280 sensor, which can communicate
with the Arduino with either I2C or SPI (see Chapter 11 for
details). The BMP280 sensor measures temperature between

-40°C and 85°C with an accuracy of ±0.01°C and pressure with an accuracy of ±0.12hPa, equivalent to ±1m in altitude. There are several libraries available for the BMP280 sensor. The sketch uses the *Adafruit BMP280* and *Adafruit Unified Senso*r libraries, which are included in the Arduino IDE and installed using installation method 3, as outlined in Chapter 3.

The BMP280 sensor operates at 3.3V, so a logic level converter (LLC) is required to reduce the voltage of the transmitted signal from the Arduino, which operates at 5V. On the low voltage side, the logic level converter *TX* and *RX* pins are connected to the BMP280 SDI and SCK pins, respectively (see Figure 4-3). On the high voltage side, the logic level converter *TX* and *RX* pins are connected to the Arduino I2C pins A4 (SDA) and A5 (SCK), respectively. The BMP280 SD0 pin should be connected to GND. The I2C address of the BMP280 sensor is 0x76, as the SD0 pin is pulled to GND, but otherwise, the default I2C address is 0x77.

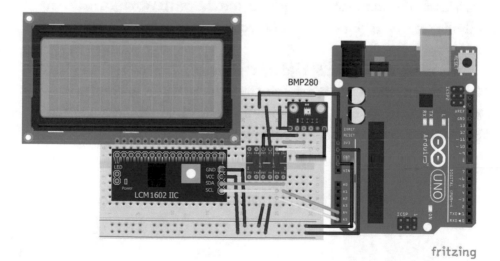

Figure 4-3. LCD with I2C bus and BMP280 sensor

The *LiquidCrystal_I2C* library by Frank de Brabander is included in the Arduino IDE and is installed using installation method 3, as outlined in Chapter 3. In the Arduino IDE, select *Sketch* ➤ *Include Library* ➤ *Manage Libraries*. Enter *LiquidCrystal_I2C*. Click *More Info*. Select the latest version and click *Install*.

After connecting the I2C bus and BMP280 sensor (see Table 4-3), the sketch (see Listing 4-4) includes the *Wire* and *LiquidCrystal_I2C* libraries, the I2C bus address, which is 0x3F, and initializes the LCD. The sketch displays the current time, temperature, and pressure, with the initial hour and minutes entered through the serial monitor buffer. The while (Serial.available() > 0) instruction ensures that the entire serial buffer is read. The Serial.parseInt()instruction extracts integers from the serial buffer by waiting until a non-numeric value enters the serial buffer and then converts the previous numeric values into an integer. In the sketch, the comma following hour and the carriage return following minutes are the required non-numeric values of the Serial.parseInt() function.

A similar instruction, Serial.parseFloat(), extracts real numbers from the serial buffer. In the sketch, the void setup() function prints constant text to the LCD, while updating of the time, temperature, and pressure occurs in the void loop() function.

Table 4-3. *Connections for LCD with I2C Bus and BMP280 Sensor*

Component	Connect to	and to
I2C bus GND	LLC high voltage GND	Arduino GND
I2C bus VCC	LLC high voltage 5V	Arduino 5V
I2C bus SDA	LLC high voltage TX	Arduino A4
I2C bus SCL	LLC high voltage RX	Arduino A5
BMP280 VCC	LLC low voltage 3.3V	Arduino 3.3V
BMP280 GND	LLC low voltage GND	
BMP280 SDI	LLC low voltage TX	
BMP280 SCK	LLC low voltage RX	
BMP280 SDO	LLC low voltage GND	

Listing 4-4. LCD with I2C Bus and BMP280 Sensor

```
#include <Wire.h>                    // include Wire library
#include <LiquidCrystal_I2C.h>       // include LiquidCrystal_I2C library
int I2Caddress = 0x3F;               // I2C address of I2C bus
int LCDcol = 16;                     // number of LCD columns
int LCDrow = 4;                      // number of LCD rows
LiquidCrystal_I2C lcd(I2Caddress,LCDcol,LCDrow); // I2C address
                                                 // and LCD size
#include <Adafruit_Sensor.h>         // include Unified Sensor library
#include <Adafruit_BMP280.h>         // include BMP280 library
Adafruit_BMP280 bmp;                 // associate bmp with Adafruit_BMP280 library
int BMPaddress = 0x76;               // I2C address of BMP280
int sec = 0;
int min, hour;
float temp, pressure;
```

```
void setup()
{
  lcd.init();                     // initialise LCD
  bmp.begin(BMPaddress);          // initialise BMP280 sensor
  Serial.begin(9600);             // define Serial output baud rate
  Serial.print("Enter time as hh,mm");  // print text to screen
  lcd.setCursor(0,0);             // move cursor to column 1 row 1
  lcd.print("Current");           // print "Current" to LCD
  lcd.setCursor(0,1);             // move cursor to column 1 row 2
  lcd.print("time");              // print "time" to LCD
  lcd.setCursor(0-4,2);           // move cursor to column 1 row 3
  lcd.print("temp");              // and reduce col by 4 for 3rd and 4th rows
  lcd.setCursor(0-4,3);           // move cursor to column 1 row 4
  lcd.print("pres");
}

void loop()
{
  while (Serial.available()>0)    // read data in Serial buffer
  {
    hour = Serial.parseInt();     // first integer in Serial buffer is hours
    min = Serial.parseInt();      // second integer in buffer is minutes
  }
  sec++;                          // short for sec = sec + 1
  if(sec>59)                      // increase minutes when seconds = 60
  {
    sec = 0;                      // reset seconds to 0
    min++;                        // increase minutes by 1
  }
  if(min>59)                      // increase hours when minutes = 60
  {
    min = 0;                      // reset minutes to 0
    hour++;                       // increase hours by 1
  }
```

```
if(hour>23) hour = 0;                       // set hours to 0 when hours = 24
lcd.setCursor(6, 1);                        // move cursor to column 6 row 2
if(hour < 10) lcd.print(" ");               // spacing for hours < 10
lcd.print(hour);                            // print hour to LCD
lcd.print(":");                             // print ":" to LCD
if(min<10) lcd.print("0");                  // leading zero for minutes < 10
lcd.print(min);                             // print minutes to LCD
lcd.print(":");
if(sec<10) lcd.print("0");                  // leading zero for seconds < 10
lcd.print(sec);                             // print seconds to LCD
temp = bmp.readTemperature();               // read temperature from sensor
pressure = bmp.readPressure()/100.0;        // read pressure from sensor
lcd.setCursor(6-4,2);                       // move cursor to column 6 row 3
lcd.print(temp, 1);                         // print temperature to LCD to 1DP
lcd.print(char(178));                       // print degree character to LCD
lcd.print("C");
lcd.setCursor(6-4,3);                       // move cursor to column 6 row 4
lcd.print(pressure, 1);                     // print pressure to LCD to 1DP
lcd.print(" hPa");
delay (1000);                               // delay 1000ms
}
```

16×4 LCD Cursor Positioning

The 16×4 LCDs have different starting addresses for the third and fourth rows than 20×4 LCDs for which the LCD library was written. To position the cursor at column N in the third row requires the lcd.setCursor(N-4, 2) instruction instead of lcd.setCursor(N ,2) and similarly for the fourth row. The effect is demonstrated for a 16×4 LCD (see Listing 4-5).

Listing 4-5. Cursor Position on 16×4 LCD

```
#include <Wire.h>                          // include Wire library
#include <LiquidCrystal_I2C.h>             // include LiquidCrystal_I2C
int I2Caddress = 0x3F;                     // address of I2C bus
int LCDcol = 16;                           // number of LCD columns
int LCDrow = 4;                            // number of LCD rows
LiquidCrystal_I2C lcd(I2Caddress,LCDcol,LCDrow);

void setup()
{
  lcd.init();                              // initialize the lcd
}

void loop()
{
  for (int col=0; col<16; col++)
  {
    lcd.clear();                           // clear the LCD
    lcd.setCursor(col,0);                  // first row
    lcd.print("A");
    lcd.setCursor(col,1);                  // second row
    lcd.print("B");
    lcd.setCursor(col-4,2);                // reduce col by 4 in the third row
    lcd.print("C");
    lcd.setCursor(col-4,3);                // reduce col by 4 in the fourth row
    lcd.print("D");
    delay(500);
  }
}
```

Further, when a string longer than 16 characters is written to the first and second rows of the 16×4 LCD, characters 17 onward are displayed on the third and fourth rows. For a long string, printing a substring of at most 16 characters on a 16×4 LCD is recommended.

Display Entered Values on LCD

Data entry from the keyboard, through the serial monitor, can be displayed on the LCD. The lcd.write() instruction is used to display alphanumeric characters on the LCD rather than lcd.print(). When a character in the serial monitor buffer is read by Serial.read(), the lcd.print(Serial.read())instruction displays the ASCII (American Standard Code for Information Interchange) code of the character, while lcd.write(Serial.read()) converts the ASCII code to display the alphanumeric character, provided that the *No line ending* option is selected on the serial monitor. The sketch (see Listing 4-6) displays on the LCD the characters entered on the keyboard through the serial monitor buffer.

Listing 4-6. Display on LCD Characters Entered on Keyboard

```
#include <Wire.h>                   // include Wire library
#include <LiquidCrystal_I2C.h>      // include LiquidCrystal_I2C library
int I2Caddress = 0x3F;              // address of I2C bus
int LCDcol = 16;                    // number of LCD columns
int LCDrow = 4;                     // number of LCD rows
LiquidCrystal_I2C lcd(I2Caddress,LCDcol,LCDrow);   // I2C address
                                                   // and LCD size
void setup()
{
  lcd.init();                       // initialize LCD
  Serial.begin(9600);               // define Serial output baud rate
}
```

```
void loop()
{
  if (Serial.available()>0)        // if data in Serial input buffer
  {
    lcd.clear();                   // clear the LCD
    while (Serial.available()>0) lcd.write(Serial.read());
  }                                // read and display input buffer
}
```

The if (Serial.available()) instruction determines if there are characters in the serial input buffer and the while (Serial. available() > 0) instruction ensures that all the buffer is read, as Serial.read() reduces the serial buffer by one character at a time. The lcd.clear()instruction clears the LCD screen and moves the cursor to position (0, 0).

LCD Character Set

Listing 4-7 displays the 256 possible characters on the 16×4 LCD in blocks of 64 characters, as the character set of an LCD can differ from the standard character set associated with an HD44780 controller. The screen number to display 64 characters is entered on the serial monitor, with screen number 1 corresponding to character values 0 to 63.

Listing 4-7. Display LCD Character Set

```
#include <Wire.h>                      // include Wire library
#include <LiquidCrystal_I2C.h>         // include LCD with I2C library
int I2Caddress = 0x3F;                 // I2C address of I2C bus
LiquidCrystal_I2C lcd(I2Caddress,16,4); // I2C address and LCD size
int screen = 1;
int j,start;
```

```
void setup()
{
  lcd.init();                 // initialise LCD
  Serial.begin(9600);         // define Serial output baud rate
  Serial.print("Enter screen number 1 to 4");
}                             // print message to Serial Monitor

void loop()
{                             // read screen from Serial buffer
  while (Serial.available()>0) screen = Serial.parseInt();
  for (j=(screen-1)*4; j<screen*4; j++)   // 4 rows of characters per screen
  {
    lcd.setCursor(0,(j%4));       // position cursor at start of row
    if((j%4)>1) lcd.setCursor(0-4,(j%4));  // reduce col by 4 for rows 3 and 4
    start = j*16;                  // 16 characters per row
    for (int i=0; i<16; i++) lcd.print(char(i+start));
  }
}                             // display characters by row
```

The calculation *j%4* is j modulus 4 or the remainder when *j* is divided by 4.

A character is displayed on the LCD with the lcd.print(char(N)) instruction, where *N* is the binary, decimal, or hexadecimal character code. For example, the character T has binary, decimal, and hexadecimal character codes of B01010100, 84, and 0x54, respectively. Tables of character sets (see Table 4-4) are often formatted with the columns and rows containing the upper and lower four bits of the character code. For example, the letter T has upper and lower four bits equal to 0101 and 0100, respectively. ASCII codes with upper bits equal to 0001 are for non-printing characters and are not included in Table 4-4.

Table 4-4. *Upper and Lower Bits of Character Codes*

	Upper Four Bits					
Lower four Bits	0010	0011	0100	0101	0110	0111
0000	space	0	@	P	'	p
0001	!	1	A	Q	a	q
0010	"	2	B	R	b	r
0011	#	3	C	S	c	s
0100	$	4	D	T	d	t
0101	%	5	E	U	e	u
0110	&	6	F	V	f	v
0111	'	7	G	W	g	w
1000	(	8	H	X	h	x
1001	)	9	I	Y	i	y
1010	*	:	J	Z	j	z
1011	+	;	K	[	k	{
1100	,	<	L	\	l		
1101	-	=	M	]	m	}
1110	.	>	N	^	n	~
1111	/	?	O	_	o	DELETE

Additional Characters

An additional eight characters can be created for display on the LCD. The pixel pattern for a character is defined by an 7×5 array. The columns are allocated the value of 2^4, 2^3, 2^2, 2^1, and 2^0, from left to right, with the seven row totals equal to the sum of the five columns. Figure 4-4 illustrates creating the additional characters of a clock and a tick. The row totals are included in an eight byte array labelled with the additional character

name, for example byte clock[8] = {0, 14, 21, 23, 17, 14, 0}.
In the void setup() function, the additional character is allocated a
character number from 0 to 7, for example lcd.createChar(0, clock)
with the additional character displayed with the lcd.write(number)
instruction. The additional characters of a clock, a tick, and a cross are
created and displayed in Listing 4-8.

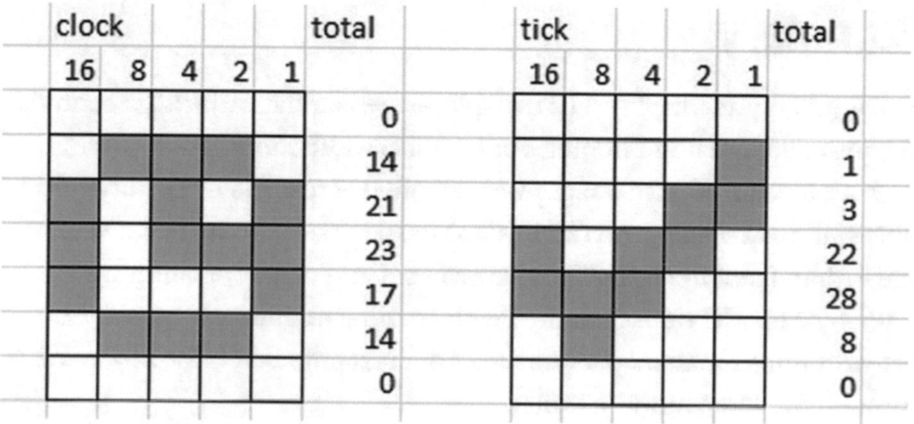

clock					total	tick					total
16	8	4	2	1		16	8	4	2	1	
					0						0
					14						1
					21						3
					23						22
					17						28
					14						8
					0						0

Figure 4-4. *Additional characters*

Listing 4-8. Additional Characters

```
#include <Wire.h>                          // include Wire library
#include <LiquidCrystal_I2C.h>             // include LCD with I2C library
int I2Caddress = 0x3F;                     // I2C address of I2C bus
LiquidCrystal_I2C lcd(I2Caddress,16,4);    // I2C address and LCD size
byte clock[8] = {0, 14, 21, 23, 17, 14, 0}; // clock pixel pattern
byte tick[8] = {0, 1, 3, 22, 28, 8, 0};     // tick pixel pattern
byte cross[8] = {0, 27, 14, 4, 14, 27, 0};  // cross pixel pattern

void setup()
{
  lcd.init();                              // initialise LCD
  lcd.createChar(0, clock);                // create character 0 named clock
  lcd.createChar(1, tick);                 // create character 1 named tick
```

```
  lcd.createChar(2, cross);          // create character 2 named cross
  lcd.setCursor(0,0);                // position cursor
  for (int i=0;i<3;i++) lcd.write(i); // display new characters
}
void loop()                          // nothing in void loop()
{}
```

Summary

The liquid crystal display (LCD) displayed sensor data. The LCD contrast is controlled by a potentiometer or by pulse width modulation (PWM) with a capacitor. Text messages were scrolled across the LCD, rather than only static text display. An I2C bus was used to communicate between the Arduino and the LCD. The character set and cursor positioning of a 16×4–pixel LCD were described with creating additional characters. Programming included parsing data from text entered on the keyboard through the serial monitor buffer.

Components List

- Arduino Uno and breadboard

- LCD display: 16×4pixels

- I2C bus for LCD

- Potentiometer: 10kΩ

- Capacitor: 100μF

- Temperature sensors: LM35DZ and BMP280

- Logic level converter

CHAPTER 5

7-Segment LED Display

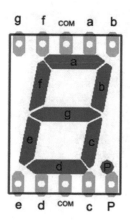

Numbers and characters displayed on electronic devices use modules of seven LEDs with an eighth LED for the decimal point. Conventions for labelling the LEDs are *a, b, ... g* or *A, B, ... G*, with the decimal point denoted *P* or *DP*. There are 10 pins on the 7-segment display with pins 1 to 5 corresponding to LEDs *e, d, common, c,* and *P* with pins 6 to 10 mapping to LEDs *b, a, common, f,* and *g.* The two common pins, 3 and 8, are connected to a common cathode or common anode (see Figure 5-1).

Figure 5-1. *7-segment LED display*

To determine if a 7-segment display has a common cathode or common anode, the negative center of a lithium battery can be held against the common pin and the positive top of the battery to another pin. If one of the LEDs turns on, the 7-segment display has a common cathode. The Chapter uses 7-segment displays with a common cathode, so that an LED is on when the signal to the LED is *HIGH*.

Basic Schematic

Each LED is connected to an Arduino pin, which is set to *HIGH* or *LOW*. The number *two* is displayed by setting the pins that control LEDs *a, b, d, e,* and *g* to *HIGH* with the pins for LEDs *c* and *f* set to *LOW*. As an example, the sketch (see Listing 5-1) alternately displays the numbers *two* and *six*. The blue-yellow color-coding of the connecting wires in Figure 5-2 is only to aid following connections between Arduino pins and the 7-segment display. The instructions at the start of Listing 5-1 detail connections between the Arduino pins and the 7-segment display, with Arduino GND connected to a 220Ω resistor and then to the common pin of the 7-segment display.

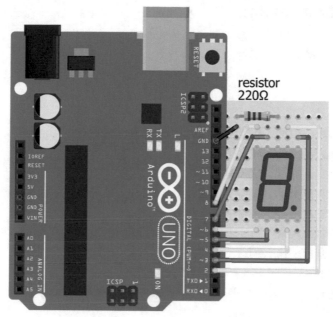

Figure 5-2. *7-segment LED display*

Listing 5-1. *7-Segment LED Display*

```
int pinA = 2;                        // yellow wire to display LED a
int pinB = 3;                        // blue wire to display LED b
int pinC = 4;                        // yellow wire to display LED c
int pinD = 5;                        // blue wire to display LED d
int pinE = 6;                        // yellow wire to display LED e
int pinF = 7;                        // blue wire to display LED f
int pinG = 8;                        // yellow wire to display LED g

void setup()
{
  pinMode (pinA, OUTPUT);            // define LED pins as output
  pinMode (pinB, OUTPUT);
  pinMode (pinC, OUTPUT);
  pinMode (pinD, OUTPUT);
```

103

```
  pinMode (pinE, OUTPUT);
  pinMode (pinF, OUTPUT);
  pinMode (pinG, OUTPUT);
}
void loop()
{
  digitalWrite(pinA, HIGH);      // display number two
  digitalWrite(pinB, HIGH);
  digitalWrite(pinC, LOW);
  digitalWrite(pinD, HIGH);
  digitalWrite(pinE, HIGH);
  digitalWrite(pinF, LOW);
  digitalWrite(pinG, HIGH);
  delay(1000);
  digitalWrite(pinA, HIGH);      // display number six
  digitalWrite(pinB, LOW);
  digitalWrite(pinC, HIGH);
  digitalWrite(pinD, HIGH);
  digitalWrite(pinE, HIGH);
  digitalWrite(pinF, HIGH);
  digitalWrite(pinG, HIGH);
  delay(1000);
}
```

Defining each LED pin, each LED pinMode as *OUTPUT*, the state of each LED pin and each digitalWrite() in separate instructions is not necessary. The LED pins and their states, 1 or 0 instead of *HIGH* or *LOW*, can be defined in arrays with for() loops to set the LED states and the digitalWrite() instructions. Listing 5-2 is substantially shorter and easier to understand than Listing 5-1.

Listing 5-2. *7-Segment LED Display*

```
int LEDs[] = {2,3,4,5,6,7,8};        // define LED pins
int two[] = {1, 1, 0, 1, 1, 0, 1}; // LED states to display number two
int six[] = {1, 0, 1, 1, 1, 1, 1}; // LED states to display number six

void setup()
{                                      // define LED pins as OUTPUT
  for (int i = 0; i<7; i++) pinMode (LEDs[i], OUTPUT);
}

void loop()
{                                      // display number two
  for (int i = 0; i<7; i++) digitalWrite(LEDs[i], two[i]);
  delay(1000);                         // display number six
  for (int i = 0; i<7; i++) digitalWrite(LEDs[i], six[i]);
  delay(1000);                         // delay 1s
}
```

PWM and LED Brightness

When an LED is turned on, the 220Ω resistor between ground and the common pin of the 7-segment display (see Figure 5-2) restricts the current to less than 20mA, given the forward voltage drop of 2V across an LED, as discussed in Chapter 1. When displaying numbers, the current per LED is the total current divided by the number of LEDs that are turned on, as the LEDs are in parallel. To display the number *one*, the current through both LEDs will be greater than the current through all the LEDs used to display the number *eight* and so the number *one* will be brighter. To ensure similar brightness for each number, one option is a resistor in series with each LED.

Alternatively, PWM can control the LED brightness of numbers *one* and *seven*, which have only a few LEDs turned on, with analogWrite() instead of digitalWrite(). The brightness levels of LEDs in the LED state arrays, *one* and *seven*, have the values 0 or 255 × *N*/7, where *N* is the number of LEDs to be turned on. The 7-segment display LEDs *a*, *b* and *c* are now connected to PWM pins 9, 10 and 11 for the analogWrite() instruction of numbers *one* and *seven*, with LED brightness levels of 73 or 109, respectively. The other numbers are displayed using digitalWrite(), given that most of the LEDs are turned on. When an analogWrite() follows a digitalWrite() instruction, then all the LEDs must be turned off before the analogWrite() instruction. The sketch (see Listing 5-3) combines digitalWrite() with analogWrite() and PWM to display numbers *one*, *two*, *seven*, and *zero*, with the numbers displayed having similar brightness.

Listing 5-3. *Display Numbers Zero, One, Two, and Seven*

```
int LEDpin[] = {9,10,11,5,6,7,8}; // LED pins with PWM for LEDs a, b and c
int one[] =    {0,72,72,0,0,0,0};   // LED brightness to display number one
int two[] = {1,1,0,1,1,0,1};        // LED states to display number two
int three[] = {1,1,1,1,0,0,1};
int four[] = {0,1,1,0,0,1,1};
int five[] = {1,0,1,1,0,1,1};
int six[] = {1,0,1,1,1,1,1};
int seven[] = {109,109,109,0,0,0,0};// LED brightness to display number seven
int eight[] = {1,1,1,1,1,1,1};
int nine[] = {1,1,1,1,0,1,1};
int zero[] = {1,1,1,1,1,1,0};

void setup()
{                                   // define LED pins as OUTPUT
  for (int i = 0; i<7; i++) pinMode (LEDpin[i], OUTPUT);
}
```

```
void loop()
{                                        // turn off all LEDs
  for (int i = 0; i<7; i++) digitalWrite(LEDpin[i],0);
  delay(10);                             // display number one
  for (int i = 0; i<3; i++) analogWrite(LEDpin[i], one[i]);
  delay(1000);                           // display number two
  for (int i = 0; i<7; i++) digitalWrite(LEDpin[i], two[i]);
  delay(1000);                           // turn off all LEDs
  for (int i = 0; i<7; i++) digitalWrite(LEDpin[i],0);
  delay(10);                             // display number seven
  for (int i = 0; i<3; i++) analogWrite(LEDpin[i], seven[i]);
  delay(1000);                           // display number zero
  for (int i = 0; i<7; i++) digitalWrite(LEDpin[i], zero[i]);
  delay(1000);                           // delay 1s
}
```

Shift Register

A shift register, such as a 74HC595, loads a byte, consisting of eight bits,

 of data, one bit at a time. An 8-bit number can represent the status of all LEDs in the 7-segment display, rather than individually declaring the status of each LED. For example, the number *five* is displayed by turning on LEDs *a, c, d, f,* and *g* and turning off LEDs *b* and *e*. If an LED turned off is represented by 0 with 1 for an LED turned on, then the sequence of 0s and 1s to display the number *five* is 1101101 for LEDs *g* to *a*, which is equivalent to the binary number B1101101 or decimal 109 or hexadecimal 0x6D. The second advantage of the shift register is that only three, rather than eight, Arduino pins are required to communicate the LED states for the LEDs (see Figure 5-3 and Table 5-1).

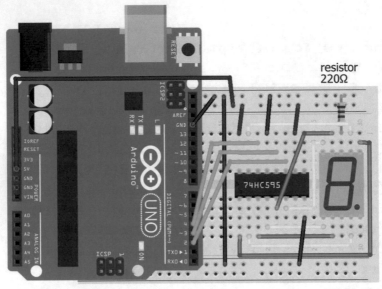

Figure 5-3. *7-segment display and shift register*

Table 5-1. *74HC595 Shift Register Pin Layout*

Symbol	Description	Connect to
QB	shift register output for LED b	7-segment display pin b
QC	shift register output for LED c	7-segment display pin c
QD	shift register output for LED d	7-segment display pin d
QE	shift register output for LED e	7-segment display pin e
QF	shift register output for LED f	7-segment display pin f
QG	shift register output for LED g	7-segment display pin g
QH	shift register output for LED P	
GND	ground	Arduino GND
QH'	output if more than one register	

(*continued*)

Table 5-1. (*continued*)

Symbol	Description	Connect to
$\overline{SRCLR}$	clear the register when LOW	Arduino 5V
SRCLK	storage register clock	Arduino pin 2 CLOCK
RCLK	shift register clock	Arduino pin 3 LATCH
$\overline{OE}$	output enabled when ground	Arduino GND
SER	serial input for next pin	Arduino pin 4 DATA
QA	shift register output for LED a	7-segment display pin a
VCC	5V supply	Arduino 5V

The line above the $\overline{SRCLR}$ and $\overline{OE}$ symbols indicate that the pin is active *LOW*, rather than the pin being active when the pin state is *HIGH*. The shift register pins are numbered 1 to 16, with pins 1, 8, 9 and 16 corresponding to *QB, GND, QH'*, and *VCC*. Note that the cut-out at the end of the 74HC595 shift register indicates the end with pins 1 and 16 or QB and VCC.

To display the number *five*, the states of LEDs *P* and *g* to *a* map to the binary number B01101101 equal to decimal 109.

LED P   LED g   LED f   LED e   LED d   LED c   LED b   LED a
$$(0{\times}2^7) + (1{\times}2^6) + (1{\times}2^5) + (0{\times}2^4) + (1{\times}2^3) + (1{\times}2^2) + (0{\times}2^1) + (1{\times}2^0) = 109$$

or hexadecimal conversion

$$2^4 \times [(0 \times 2^3) + (1 \times 2^2) + (1 \times 2^1) + (0 \times 2^0)] + [(1 \times 2^3) + (1 \times 2^2) + (0 \times 2^1) + (1 \times 2^0)]$$
$$= 2^4 \times 6 + 13, \text{ which is hexadecimal 0x6D.}$$

Hexadecimal is a 2-digit 4-bit representation of an 8-bit binary number, which is split into upper and lower 4-bit numbers. In the preceding example, the upper 4-bit binary number is B0110 and the lower 4-bit binary number is B1101. The upper and lower 4-bit numbers are equal to decimal 6 and 13, respectively, which is denoted as hexadecimal 0x6D, since decimal values 10, 11, 12, 13, 14, and 15 have hexadecimal representations of A, B, C, D, E, and F. The advantages of hexadecimal are that numbers up to 256 are represented by two alphanumeric characters and that an 8-bit binary number can easily be split into two hexadecimal components.

The shift register loads the state of the first LED, then the state of the next LED until the states all the LED have been loaded. While the shift register clock (RCLK or LATCH) is set *LOW*, the LED states (*HIGH* or *LOW*) for LEDs *P* and *g* to *a* are loaded via the data pin (SER or DATA) into the shift register, one LED state at a time, controlled by the storage register clock (SRCLK or CLOCK). After all eight LED states are loaded, the shift register clock (RCLK or LATCH) is set *HIGH* and the updated LED states are implemented simultaneously. Figure 5-4 illustrates the shift register sequentially loading the LED states to display the number *five* on a 7-segment display.

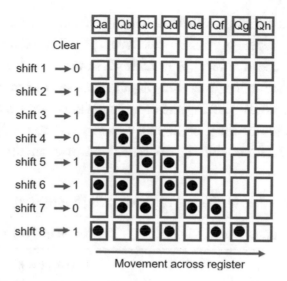

Figure 5-4. *Shift register loading*

The instructions to pass data through the shift register are

```
digitalWrite(latchPin, LOW);                    // set the latch to LOW
shiftOut(dataPin, clockPin, MSBFIRST, number);  // LED states as a number
digitalWrite(latchPin, HIGH);                   // set the latch to HIGH
```

MSBFIRST indicates that the most significant bit is loaded first, which is the state of LED *P*, the LED for the decimal point, which has binary multiple of 2^7. For example, the decimal representations of the numbers *one, two,* and *three* with the most significant bit first are 6, 91, and 79, with binary representations of B00000110, B01011011, and B01001111, respectively. The least significant bit, which is the state of LED *a*, has a binary multiple of 2^0. If the least significant bit was loaded first, then *LSBFIRST* would be used in the shiftOut() instruction. For example, the decimal representations of the

111

numbers *one, two,* and *three* with the least significant bit first are 96, 218, and 242, with binary representations of B01100000, B11011010, and B11110010, respectively. So use of *MSBFIRST* or *LSBFIRST* must be defined.

A sketch with a shift register to display the numbers *zero* to *nine* compared to the sketch without a shift register only displaying numbers *two* and *six* demonstrates the advantage of the shift register (see Table 5-2). Note that in Figure 5-3, the 74HC595 shift register pins 1 and 16 are on the left-hand side.

Table 5-2. *Sketches with and Without a Shift Register*

Numbers zero to nine	Numbers two and six, only
int clockPin = 2;	int pins[ ] = {2,3,4,5,6,7,8,9};
int latchPin = 3;	int two[ ] = {1, 1, 0, 1, 1, 0, 1 };
int dataPin = 4;	int six[ ] = {1, 0, 1, 1, 1, 1, 1};
int num[ ] = {63,6,91,79,102,109,125,7,127,111};	
void setup()	void setup()
{	{
pinMode (clockPin, OUTPUT);	for (int i=0; i<7; i++)
pinMode (latchPin, OUTPUT);	pinMode (pins[i], OUTPUT);
pinMode (dataPin, OUTPUT);	
}	}

(*continued*)

Table 5-2. (*continued*)

Numbers zero to nine	Numbers two and six, only
void loop()	void loop()
{	{
for (int i=0; i<10; i++)	for (int i=0; i<7; i++)
{	digitalWrite(pins[i], two[i]);
digitalWrite(latchPin, LOW);	delay(1000);
shiftOut(dataPin,clockPin,MSBFIRST,num[i]);	for (int i=0; i<7; i++)
digitalWrite(latchPin, HIGH);	digitalWrite(pins[i], six[i]);
delay(1000);	delay(1000);
}	
}	}

The shiftOut() instruction can use binary, decimal or hexadecimal numbers to represent the LED states in the 7-segment display. For example, the three instructions to display the number *five* are equivalent to

```
     shiftOut(dataPin, clockPin, MSBFIRST, B01101101}
or   shiftOut(dataPin, clockPin, MSBFIRST, 109)
or   shiftOut(dataPin, clockPin, MSBFIRST, 0x6D)
```

Shift Register, PWM, and LED Brightness

The shift register output enable pin, $\overline{OE}$, is normally connected to ground. If the shift register output enable pin is connected to a PWM pin (see Figure 5-5), then the brightness of the 7-segment display can be controlled with PWM.

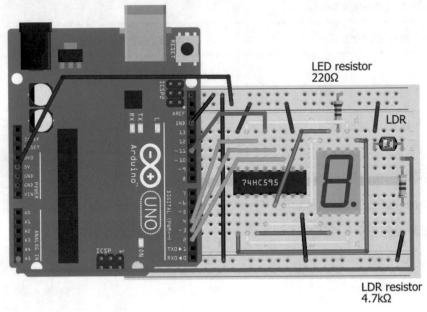

Figure 5-5. *7-segment display with PWM control*

For example, defining the PWM pin with int PWMpin = 11 and in the
void loop() function, inserting the analogWrite(PWMpin, 250 - i*25)
instruction increases the 7-segment display brightness as the display
number increases. The reason for the 7-segment display brightness
increasing as the value of (250 - i*25) in the analogWrite() function
decreases, is that the $\overline{OE}$ shift register pin is active *LOW* rather than *HIGH*.

An application of the display brightness being dependent on incident
light, with a brighter display in lighter conditions, is a digital clock that is
brighter during daylight than at night, as used in Listing 5-4 when numbers
are displayed. The output from a voltage divider with a light dependent
resistor controls the brightness of the seven segment display (see Figure 5-5).
The bright = map(reading, 0, 1023, 255, 0) instruction reverses the

effect of the $\overline{OE}$ shift register pin. The schematic is the same as in Figure 5-4 with the addition of a voltage divider and light dependent resistor, with the additional connections given in Table 5-3.

Table 5-3. *Connections for Shift Register, Voltage Divider, and Light Dependent Resistor*

Component	Connect to	and to
LDR right leg	Arduino A5	
LDR right leg	4.7kΩ resistor	Arduino GND
LDR left leg	Arduino 5V	
74HC595 $\overline{OE}$ pin 13	Arduino pin 11	

Listing 5-4. Display Brightness Dependent on Incident Light

```
int clockPin = 2;              // shift register CLOCK pin
int latchPin = 3;              // shift register LATCH pin
int dataPin = 4;               // shift register DATA pin
int num[] = {63,6,91,79,102,109,125,7,127,111};  // binary for numbers 0 to 9
int Vdivid = A5;               // voltage divider pin
int PWMpin = 11;               // shift register OE pin used for PWM
int reading, bright;

void setup()
{                              // define
  pinMode (clockPin, OUTPUT);  // shift register CLOCK pin as output
  pinMode (latchPin, OUTPUT);  // shift register LATCH pin as output
  pinMode (dataPin, OUTPUT);   // shift register DATA pin as output
}
```

```
void loop()
{
  for (int i=0; i<10; i++)          // for each number 0 to 9
  {
    reading = analogRead(Vdivid); // voltage divider reading
    bright = map(reading, 0, 1023, 255, 0); // map reading to LED brightness
    analogWrite(PWMpin, bright);   // change LED brightness
    digitalWrite(latchPin, LOW);   // set the latch to LOW
    shiftOut(dataPin,clockPin,MSBFIRST,num[i]); // LED states as a number
    digitalWrite(latchPin, HIGH); // change number pattern
    delay(1000);                    // delay 1s
  }
}
```

Alphanumeric Characters

Decimal representations to display alphanumeric characters for a
7-segment display with a common cathode and the most significant bit
first are given in Table 5-4.

Table 5-4. *Decimal Representations of Alphanumeric Characters*

Character	Number	Character	Number	Character	Number	Character	Number
0	63	A	119	J	30	S	109
1	6	B	124	K	112	T	120
2	91	C	57	L	56	U	62
3	79	D	94	M	21	V	28

(continued)

Table 5-4. (*continued*)

Character	Number	Character	Number	Character	Number	Character	Number
4	102	E	121	N	84	W	42
5	109	F	113	O	63	X	118
6	125	G	111	P	115	Y	110
7	7	H	118	Q	103	Z	91
8	127	I	6	R	80		
9	111					DP	128

Decimal representations of alphanumeric characters can be determined from an Excel spreadsheet with conditionally formatted cells representing LEDs set to *HIGH* or *LOW* and cell values equal to 1 or 0. For example, in Figure 5-6, the LEDs turned on to display the number *three* are *a, b, c, d,* and *g,* with LEDs *e* and *f* turned off.

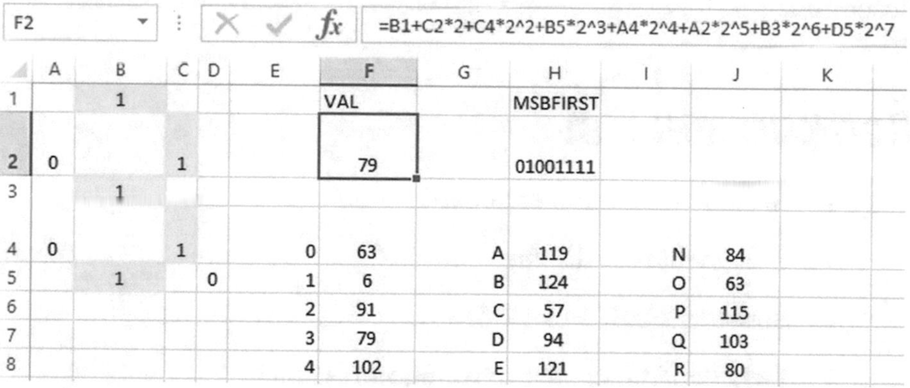

Figure 5-6. *Numeric values of characters with Excel*

The decimal representation of a pattern is calculated from

$$(S_P \times 2^7) + (S_g \times 2^6) + (S_f \times 2^5) + (S_e \times 2^4) + (S_d \times 2^3) + (S_c \times 2^2) + (S_b \times 2^1) + (S_a \times 2^0)$$

and S_a, S_b, S_c, S_d, S_e, S_f, S_g, and S_P are the eight LED states in the 7-segment display, including the decimal point.

If the 7-segment display has a common anode, then the decimal representation to display an alphanumeric character is 127 minus the value in Table 5-4. The decimal representation of the decimal point is 127 when the 7-segment display has a common anode.

Summary

Numbers and characters are displayed on the 7-segment LED display. LED brightness can be controlled with pulse width modulation, for characters only requiring a few LEDs. A shift register controlled the LEDs, reduced the connections to the Arduino Uno and simplified the sketch. Decimal, hexadecimal, and binary representations of characters are described.

Components List

- Arduino Uno and breadboard
- 7-segment LED display
- Resistors: 220Ω and 4.7kΩ
- Light dependent resistor (or photoresistor)
- Shift register: 74HC595

CHAPTER 6

4-Digit 7-Segment Display

 The 4-digit 7-segment display is an extension of the 1-digit 7-segment display discussed in Chapter 5. As with the 1-digit 7-segment display, there are seven LED segments on the 4-digit display, labelled *a, b, … g* and *P or DP*. There are an additional four pins controlling the 4-digit displays. The pin layout on the 4-digit 7-segment display is illustrated in Figure 6-1 and the order of the digits from the left-hand side is 1, 2, 3, and 4. The 4-digit 7-segment display has a common cathode and a digit display is on when the digit pin state is *LOW*, which is equivalent to the common pin connected to ground for the 1-digit 7-segment display.

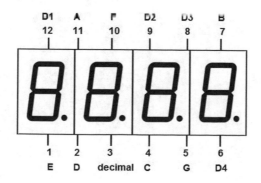

Figure 6-1. *Pin layout of 4-digit 7-segment display*

N. Cameron, *Arduino Applied*, https://doi.org/10.1007/978-1-4842-3960-5_6

Listing 6-1 uses a 4-digit 7-segment display as a timer counting seconds. Two functions are used with the digit() function turning on the appropriate digit and the number() function splitting the number of seconds into units, tens, hundreds, and thousands. The delay of 5ms between displaying digits prevents flicker, but changing the delay to 250ms illustrates the digit display pattern of displaying one digit at a time. In Figure 6-2, the wire colored yellow is to aid following the circuit, with connections in Table 6-1.

Listing 6-1 demonstrates control of the 4-digit 7-segment display. Inclusion of shift registers reduces the repeated instructions to define LED states and the digitalWrite() instructions for each number, which is described later in the chapter.

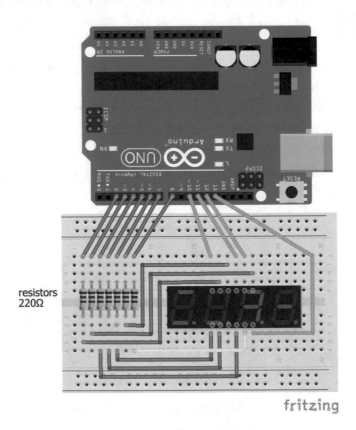

Figure 6-2. *4-digit 7-segment display as timer*

Table 6-1. *Connections for 4-Digit 7-Segment Display As Timer*

Component	Connect to	and to
4 digit 7 seg pin 1	220Ω resistor	Arduino pin 6
4 digit 7 seg pin 2	220Ω resistor	Arduino pin 5
4 digit 7 seg pin 3		
4 digit 7 seg pin 4	220Ω resistor	Arduino pin 4
4 digit 7 seg pin 5	220Ω resistor	Arduino pin 8
4 digit 7 seg pin 6	Arduino pin 13	
4 digit 7 seg pin 7	220Ω resistor	Arduino pin 3
4 digit 7 seg pin 8	Arduino pin 12	
4 digit 7 seg pin 9	Arduino pin 11	
4 digit 7 seg pin 10	220Ω resistor	Arduino pin 7
4 digit 7 seg pin 11	220Ω resistor	Arduino pin 2
4 digit 7 seg pin 12	Arduino pin 10	

Listing 6-1. 4-Digit 7-Segment Display As Timer

```
int pins[] = {2,3,4,5,6,7,8};        // LED pins
int digits[] = {10,11,12,13};        // digit control pins
int zero[] = {1,1,1,1,1,1,0};        // LED states for zero
int one[] = {0,1,1,0,0,0,0};         // LED states for one
int two[] = {1,1,0,1,1,0,1};
int three[] = {1,1,1,1,0,0,1};
int four[] = {0,1,1,0,0,1,1};
int five[] = {1,0,1,1,0,1,1};
int six[] = {1,0,1,1,1,1,1};
int seven[] = {1,1,1,0,0,0,0};
int eight[] = {1,1,1,1,1,1,1};
int nine[] = {1,1,1,1,0,1,1};
```

```
int time, n;
int del = 5;                        // time delay (ms)

void setup()
{                                   // define pins and digits as output
  for (int i = 0; i<7; i++) pinMode (pins[i], OUTPUT);
  for (int i = 0; i<4; i++) pinMode (digits[i], OUTPUT);
}

void loop()
{
  time = millis()/1000;             // time is number of seconds
  digit(0);                         // digit D1 for thousands
  number(time/1000);                // number to be displayed
  delay(del);
  digit(1);                         // digit D2 for hundreds
  number((time%1000)/100);          // modulus(time, 1000)/100
  delay(del);
  digit(2);                         // digit D3 for tens
  number((time%100)/10);            // modulus(time, 100)/10
  delay(del);
  digit(3);                         // digit D4 for units
  number(time%10);                  // modulus(time, 10)
  delay(del);
}

void digit(int d)                   // function to set digit states
{                                   // turn all digits off
  for (int i = 0; i<4; i++) digitalWrite(digits[i], 1);
  digitalWrite(digits[d], 0);       // digit pin state is LOW, display is on
}
```

```
void number(int n)                    // function to display numbers
{
  if      (n==0) for (int i = 0; i<7; i++)
     digitalWrite(pins[i], zero[i]);
  else if (n==1) for (int i = 0; i<7; i++)
     digitalWrite(pins[i], one[i]);
  else if (n==2) for (int i = 0; i<7; i++)
     digitalWrite(pins[i], two[i]);
  else if (n==3) for (int i = 0; i<7; i++)
     digitalWrite(pins[i], three[i]);
  else if (n==4) for (int i = 0; i<7; i++)
     digitalWrite(pins[i], four[i]);
  else if (n==5) for (int i = 0; i<7; i++)
     digitalWrite(pins[i], five[i]);
  else if (n==6) for (int i = 0; i<7; i++)
     digitalWrite(pins[i], six[i]);
  else if (n==7) for (int i = 0; i<7; i++)
     digitalWrite(pins[i], seven[i]);
  else if (n==8) for (int i = 0; i<7; i++)
     digitalWrite(pins[i], eight[i]);
  else if (n==9) for (int i = 0; i<7; i++)
     digitalWrite(pins[i], nine[i]);
}
```

Functions

The digit() and number() functions in Listing 6-1 are prefixed void as
the functions return no value to the main sketch. If a function returns an
integer or a real number, y, to the main sketch, then the function is prefixed
with int or float, respectively, and the instruction return y is included
in the function. If a function is passed a string, an integer, or a real number,

then the instruction includes the variable type with the variable name, as in void digit(int d). For example, Listing 6-2 shows the double function, which is passed an integer, x, and returns a real number, y.

Listing 6-2. Function to Pass an Integer and Return a Float

```
float double(int x)
{
  float y = 2.0*x;
  return y;
}
```

In Listing 6-1, the number() function uses the modulus of time divided by 10, 100, or 1000, where *modulus (x, y)* is the remainder when integer x is divided by integer y. For example, if *time* is 1234, the number of tens is *modulus(1234, 100) = 34*, which is then divided by 10 to obtain the result of 3, as the divisor uses integer arithmetic.

The combination of if else instructions is more efficient for multiple mutually exclusive tests, rather than a series of if() instructions, as the tests can be run simultaneously rather than sequentially. An alternative to if else instructions is switch case instructions, where the switch instruction compares the test variable to values in the case instruction and the corresponding code is carried out. Use of switch case instructions can be clearer to interpret when there are several instructions within a case; otherwise, use of if else instructions is sufficient. Note that each case instruction is closed with a break instruction. The switch case equivalent of the if else instructions of Listing 6-1 is given in Listing 6-3.

Listing 6-3. Example of Switch Case

```
switch(n)
{
  case 0:
    for (int i = 0; i<7; i++) digitalWrite(pins[i], zero[i]);
  break;
  case 1:
    for (int i = 0; i<7; i++) digitalWrite(pins[i], one[i]);
  break;
  case 3:
    for (int i = 0; i<7; i++) digitalWrite(pins[i], three[i]);
  break;
}
```

When only one of two options is to be activated, then an if() instruction, such as if(x>7) y = y+1, is sufficient. When both options are required, the following pair of instructions has the same outcome, but the left-hand side set of instructions is more efficient.

```
if(x>7) y = y+1;        if(x>7) y = y+1;
else y = y-1;           if(x<=7) y = y-1;
```

In contrast to the if() instruction, which operates once, the while() instruction repeats the *outcome* continuously as long as the *condition* is satisfied, so while(condition) outcome is a loop. For example, the instruction if(1 == 1) Serial.println("test") displays "*test*" on the serial monitor once, but while(1 == 1) Serial.println("test") displays "*test*" on the serial monitor repeatedly. The if(condition) break instruction is used to exit from within a while() loop.

One Shift Register

A shift register can load the LED states in the 4-digit 7-segment display, which reduces the number of connecting wires to the Arduino from eight to three (see Figure 6-3), just as with the 1-digit 7-segment display (see Figure 5-5). Connections to the shift register and 4-digit 7-segment display are given in Tables 6-2 and 6-3, respectively.

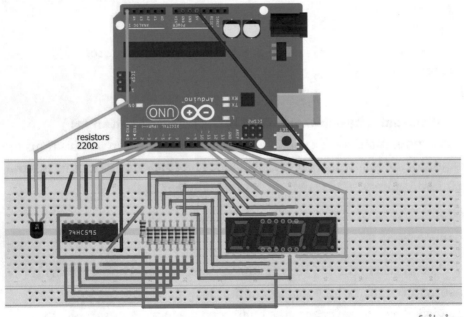

Figure 6-3. *4-digit 7-segment display with shift register and temperature sensor*

Table 6-2. *Connections to 74HC595 Shift Register*

Pin	Symbol	Description	Connect to
1	QB	shift register output for LED b	4-digit 7-segment display b
2	QC	shift register output for LED c	4-digit 7-segment display c
3	QD	shift register output for LED d	4-digit 7-segment display d
4	QE	shift register output for LED e	4-digit 7-segment display e
5	QF	shift register output for LED f	4-digit 7-segment display f
6	QG	shift register output for LED g	4-digit 7-segment display g
7	QH	shift register output for LED P	4-digit 7-segment display P
8	GND	ground	Arduino GND
9	QH'	output if more than one register	
10	$\overline{SRCLR}$	clear the register when LOW	Arduino 5V
11	SRCLK	storage register clock	Arduino pin 4 CLOCK
12	RCLK	shift register clock	Arduino pin 3 LATCH
13	$\overline{OE}$	output enabled when ground	Arduino GND
14	SER	serial input for next pin	Arduino pin 2 DATA
15	QA	shift register output for LED a	4-digit 7-segment display a
16	VCC	5V supply	Arduino 5V

Table 6-3. *Connections to 4-Digit 7-Segment Display and Temperature Sensor*

Symbol	Description	Connect to	and to
E	LED e	220Ω resistor	74HC595 pin 4
D	LED d	220Ω resistor	74HC595 pin 3
P or DP	LED P or DP	220Ω resistor	74HC595 pin 7
C	LED c	220Ω resistor	74HC595 pin 2
G	LED g	220Ω resistor	74HC595 pin 6
D4	Digit 4	Arduino pin 13	
B	LED b	220Ω resistor	74HC595 pin 1
D3	Digit 3	Arduino pin 12	
D2	Digit 2	Arduino pin 11	
F	LED f	220Ω resistor	74HC595 pin 5
A	LED a	220Ω resistor	74HC595 pin 15
D1	Digit 1	Arduino pin 10	
	LM35DZ GND	Arduino GND	
	LM35DZ OUT	Arduino pin A5	
	LM35DZ VCC	Arduino 5V	

A temperature sensor, LM35DZ, can be combined with the time display (see Figure 6-3). The sketch (see Listing 6-4) alternately displays, for a duration of 5 seconds, the temperature and number of seconds elapsed. The decimal point for the temperature is incorporated in the digit function by adding 128 to the value of the number to be displayed. For example, to display the number *two* without and with a decimal point, the binary representations are B01011011 and B11011011, corresponding to decimal values 91 and 219. In Figure 6-3, the brown wire is the connection between the shift register and the 4-digit 7-segment display for the decimal point.

Listing 6-4. Temperature and Time Display

```
int dataPin = 2;                    // shift register DATA pin
int latchPin = 3;                   // shift register LATCH pin
int clockPin = 4;                   // shift register CLOCK pin
int digits[ ] = {10,11,12,13};      // 4 digit pins and "values" of numbers 0 to 9
int numbers[ ] = {63,6,91,79,102,109,125,7,127,111};
int del = 5;                        // delay after turning digit on
int tempPin = A5;                   // temperature sensor pin
int duration = 5000;                // display duration
unsigned long start;
int time, n, temp, reading;

void setup()
{
  pinMode (dataPin, OUTPUT);     // define shift register DATA pin as output
  pinMode (latchPin, OUTPUT);    // define shift register LATCH pin as output
  pinMode (clockPin, OUTPUT);    // define shift register CLOCK pin as output
  for (int i = 0; i<4; i++) pinMode (digits[i], OUTPUT);
  analogReference (INTERNAL); // set ADC voltage to 1.1V rather than 5V
}

void loop()
{
  start = millis();                  // milliseconds elapsed
  while (millis()-start<duration)    // display time
  {
    time = millis()/1000;            // time in elapsed seconds
    digit(0, time/1000, 0);          // digit D1 for thousands
    digit(1, (time%1000)/100, 0);    // digit D2 for hundreds
    digit(2, (time%100)/10, 0);      // digit D3 for tens
    digit(3, time%10, 0);            // digit D4 for units
  }
```

```
reading = analogRead(tempPin);    // temperature reading
temp = 10.0*(reading*110.0)/1023.0; // multiplier to get decimal place
                                   // display temperature
while (millis()-start>duration && millis()-start<2*duration)
{
  digit(1, (temp%1000)/100, 0);        // digit D2 for tens
  digit(2, (temp%100)/10, 1);          // digit D3 for units 1 for DP
  digit(3, temp%10, 0);                // digit D4 for decimal places
}
}

void digit(int d, int n, int DP)
{                               // turn all digits off, digit states are HIGH
  for (int i = 0; i<4; i++) digitalWrite(digits[i], 1);
  digitalWrite(latchPin, LOW);         // add 128 for decimal point
  shiftOut(dataPin, clockPin, MSBFIRST, numbers[n]+DP*128);
  digitalWrite(latchPin, HIGH);        // change display pattern
  digitalWrite(digits[d], 0);          // turn digit on, digit state LOW
  delay(del);                          // delay del (ms)
}
```

The order of the instructions in the digit() function is important to ensure no ghosting of numbers from the previous display. All digits are turned off before the new display pattern is loaded. If the relevant digit is turned on before the new number pattern is loaded, then for a small period of time, the old number pattern is displayed, resulting in the ghosting of numbers from the previous display.

Two Shift Registers

With two shift registers, the first shift register controls the LED segments and the second shift register controls the digits, with the second shift register connected to the first shift register. To display a number on a given digit of the 4-digit 7-segment display, bit data on the digit to be turned on and the LED segment pattern of the number to be displayed is loaded into the storage register of the first shift register. The bit data consists of more than eight bits, so the additional bits are moved into the second shift register. Figures 6-4 and 6-5 illustrate loading the bit data to display on the third digit, B00010110, the number *five*, with LED segment pattern of B01101101.

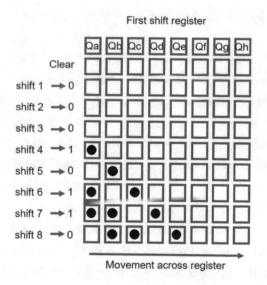

Figure 6-4. *4-digit data loaded into first shift register*

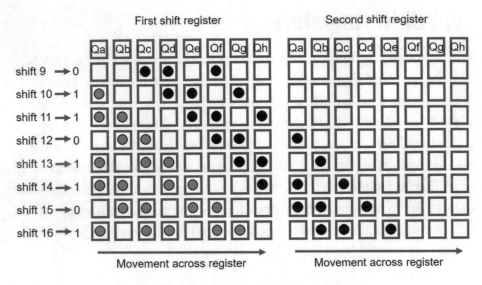

Figure 6-5. *4-digit data "shifted" into shift registers*

In Figure 6-6, digits of the 4-digit 7-segment display are connected to pins *QB, QC, QD,* and QE of the second shift register and a digit is turned on when the corresponding shift register pin is *LOW*. Bit data to only turn on the third digit is B00010110, as the third digit is connected to pin *QD*, set to *LOW*, and digits *1, 2,* and *4,* which are connected to pins *QB, QC,* and *QE,* are set to *HIGH*. The decimal representations of the bit data to turn on digits, *D1, D2, D3,* and *D4* are 28 (or B11100), 26 (or B11010), 22 (or B10110), and 14 (or B01110), respectively. Note that in Figure 6-6, the second shift register is turned upside down to make the schematic more interpretable, so that the cutout at end of the 74HC595 shift register, which indicates the end with pins 1 and 16 or *QB* and *VCC,* is on the right-hand side.

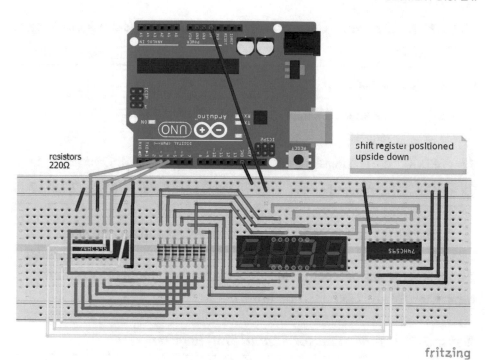

Figure 6-6. *4-digit 7-segment display with two shift registers*

The two shift registers are "daisy chained" together, so that only three connections are required to the Arduino, rather than the initial 12 when no shift registers were included. The serial output pin of the first shift register, pin *QH'*, is connected to the serial input pin of the second shift register, pin *SER*. The storage register clock pins, *SRCLK*, and the shift register clock pins, *RCLK*, of both shift registers are connected together. Figure 6-6 does not include provision for displaying the decimal point. The changes to connections for the first 74HC595 shift register, when a second shift register is included, are given in Table 6-4.

Table 6-4. *Change in Connections of First Shift Register Given Second Shift Register*

Pin	Symbol	Description	Connect to
9	QH'	output if more than one register	74HC595 (2) pin 14
11	SRCLK	storage register clock	Arduino CLOCK pin, 74HC595 (2) pin 11
12	RCLK	shift register clock	Arduino LATCH pin, 74HC595 (2) pin 12

74HC595 (1) and 74HC595 (2) refer to the first and second shift register, respectively. The second shift register is connected to the 4-digit 7-segment display and to the first shift register, but not to the Arduino, other than 5V and GND (see Table 6-5).

Table 6-5. *Connections for Second Shift Register*

Pin	Symbol	Description	Connect to
1	QB	shift register output for digit 1 (D1)	4-digit 7-segment display pin D1
2	QC	shift register output for digit 2 (D2)	4-digit 7-segment display pin D2
3	QD	shift register output for digit 3 (D3)	4-digit 7-segment display pin D3
4	QE	shift register output for digit 4 (D4)	4-digit 7-segment display pin D4
8	GND	ground	Arduino GND
10	$\overline{SRCLR}$	clear the register when LOW	Arduino 5V
11	SRCLK	storage register clock	74HC595 (1) pin 11
12	RCLK	shift register clock	74HC595 (1) pin 12
13	$\overline{OE}$	output enabled when ground	Arduino GND
14	SER	serial input for next pin	74HC595 (1) pin 9
16	VCC	5V supply	Arduino 5V

In Listing 6-4, the int digits[] = {10,11,12,13} instruction is replaced with int digits[] = {28,26,22,14}, which are the decimal representations of the bit data to turn on digits, *D1, D2, D3,* and *D4.* The digit() function is changed by deleting instructions to turn digits off and on and a new shiftOut() instruction (in bold) for the second shift register is included (see Listing 6-5).

Listing 6-5. Second Shift Register Control of Digits

```
void digit(int d, int n, int DP)
{
  for (int i = 0; i<4; i++) digitalWrite(digits[i], 1);
  digitalWrite(latchPin, LOW);
  shiftOut(dataPin, clockPin, MSBFIRST, digits[d]);
  shiftOut(dataPin, clockPin, MSBFIRST, numbers[n]+DP*128);
  digitalWrite(latchPin, HIGH);
  digitalWrite(digit[d], 0)
  delay(del);
}
```

Summary

The 4-digit 7-segment LED display presented the time and temperature, as an extension of the 1-digit 7-segment LED display. Shift registers were introduced, with one shift register controlling the four digits with the second shift register controlling the seven LED segments. Functions were introduced to improve programming efficiency.

Components List

- Arduino Uno and breadboard

- 4-digit 7-segment LED display

- Resistor: 8× 220Ω

- Shift register: 2× 74HC595

- Temperature sensor: LM35DZ

CHAPTER 7

8×8 Dot Matrix Display

The 8×8 dot matrix consists of 64 LEDs with 16 pins corresponding to eight columns of anodes and eight rows of cathodes. The label on one side of an 8×8 dot matrix display usually indicates the side containing pins 1 to 8 (left to right) with the other side containing pins 9 to 16 (right to left), as shown in Figure 7-1.

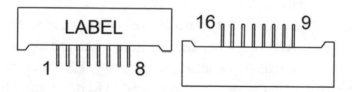

Figure 7-1. *Pin numbering of 8x8 dot matrix display*

Each 8×8 dot matrix has a specific column-row pin combination, such as in Figure 7-2. For example, pin 1 of the dot matrix used in the chapter controls LEDs in row 5. The orientation of the pin layout is determined with a multimeter on the diode setting. Mark a left-hand end pin as pin 1 (there are only two possibilities). Connect the multimeter COM (black) to pin 1 and the multimeter anode (red) to pin 16. If the LED in row 5 column 8 is turned on, then the 8×8 dot matrix has a common cathode; otherwise, connect the multimeter anode to pin 1 and the cathode to pin 16. If the LED in row 5 column 8 is turned on, then the 8×8 dot matrix has a common anode.

© Neil Cameron 2019
N. Cameron, *Arduino Applied*, https://doi.org/10.1007/978-1-4842-3960-5_7

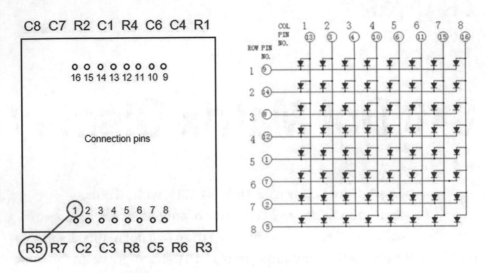

Figure 7-2. *Pin layout of an 8×8 dot matrix*

The letter *K* (see Figure 7-3) illustrates displaying an alphanumeric character with an 8×8 dot matrix. An 8-bit binary number represents the LED states in a row, with a one corresponding to an LED being turned on. The sixth row of the letter *K* is represented as B11011100, which has a decimal value of 220. For an 8×8 dot matrix with a common cathode, an LED is on when the column (anode) state is *HIGH* and the row (cathode) state is *LOW*.

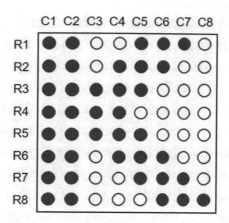

Figure 7-3. *LED display of letter K*

A pattern is displayed on an 8×8 dot matrix by updating each LED state in a row, with a short delay between updating each LED and then the next row is updated, which is termed *row scanning*. The short delay of 200μs, for example, is faster than the eye can detect and gives the impression that all the LEDS are on simultaneously. A delay of 200μs is equivalent to a display frequency of 5kHz and the human eye can detect flicker of up to 400Hz. For the letter K, the LED in row 6 column 3 is off, as the binary representation of row 6 is B11011100 and the value in the third column of the binary representation is zero. The rows and columns are numbered from the top left-hand corner ($R1$, $C1$), with rows parallel to the pins of the 8×8 dot matrix.

To display a character, the binary representation of the LED pattern is replaced by the corresponding decimal value. For example, in the third row of the letter A, LEDs in the first and fifth column are on and the binary representation of the LED pattern, B10001, has decimal value 17 (see Table 7-5 at the end of the chapter). The bitRead(binary number, c) instruction reads the *cth* bit of the binary number, starting at the least significant bit (rightmost), which is bit zero. If the bit is equal to one, then to turn on the LED, Arduino pins controlling the corresponding column (anode) and row (cathode) of the 8×8 dot matrix display are set to *HIGH* and *LOW*, respectively. Note that if the 8×8 dot matrix display has a common anode, then an LED is turned on when the corresponding cathode and anode of the LED are set to *HIGH* and *LOW*, respectively. A time lag of one second is required for each letter to be displayed, which is achieved with the while (millis() < start+1000) instruction with *start* equal to the start time that the character is first displayed.

In Figure 7-4, connections to Arduino pins (see Table 7-1) controlling rows of the 8×8 dot matrix are colored yellow and connections to pins controlling columns in blue or orange, to aid interpretation of the schematic. The 220Ω resistors are connected to each column pin (anode) of the 8×8 dot matrix display, as the rows are scanned. Arduino pins *A0, A1, A2,* and *A3* are referenced as pins 14, 15, 16, and 17, respectively. The 8×8 dot matrix rows (*R*) and columns (*C*) are referenced in Figure 7-2.

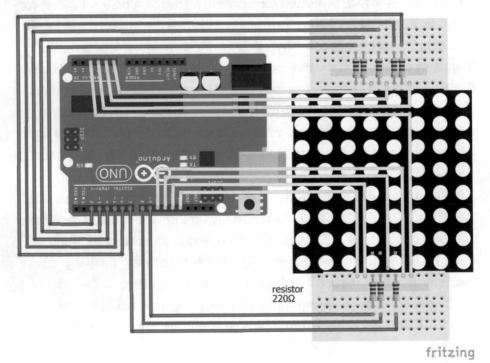

Figure 7-4. *8×8 dot matrix display*

Table 7-1. *Connections to 8×8 Dot Matrix Display*

8×8 Dot Matrix Pin	1	2	3	4	5	6	7	8	9	10	11	12	13	14	15	16
8×8 dot matrix		R5	R7	C2	C3	R8	C5	R6	R3	R1	C4	C6	R4	C1	R2	C7	C8
Arduino pin		13	12	9	8	11	7	10	17	16	6	5	15	4	14	3	2

In Listing 7-1, to display the three letters: *A, B,* and *C,* the LED patterns are defined in the matrix val[3][8], which has three rows, one for each letter, and eight columns, one for each row of the 8×8 dot matrix display. In the sketch, pin[] defines the 16 Arduino pins connected to the 8×8 dot matrix display. In the C programming language, numbering of matrix elements starts at zero, such that pin[1] refers to the second element of the pin[] matrix. The term matrix, a two-dimensional array, includes the term vector, which is a one-dimensional array. To aid consistency between the sketch and the 8×8 dot matrix data sheet, the first element of pin[] is set to 19, Arduino pin *A5*, to shift the other values by one element. For example, in Figure 7-4, Arduino pin 13 is connected to pin 1 of the 8×8 dot matrix display, which refers to row 5 of the 8×8 dot matrix display. Therefore, pin[1] is set equal to Arduino pin 13 and the fifth element of the row[] matrix refers to pin[1].

Listing 7-1. Display Letters A, B, and C

```
                              // Arduino display pins
int pin[] = {19,13,12,9,8,11,7,10,17,16,6,5,15,4,14,3,2};
                              // dot matrix display columns
int col[] = {pin[13],pin[3],pin[4],pin[10],pin[6],pin[11],pin[15],pin[16]};
                              // dot matrix display rows
int row[] = {pin[9],pin[14],pin[8],pin[12],pin[1],pin[7],pin[2],pin[5]};
byte val[3][8] = {4,10,17,17,31,17,17,0,  // decimal representation of letter A
                  15,17,17,15,17,17,15,0,  // decimal representation of letter B
                  14,17,1,1,1,17,14,0};   // decimal representation of letter C
unsigned long start;
bool pixel;
```

```
void setup()
{
  for (int i=1; i<18; i++) pinMode(pin[i], OUTPUT); // display pins as output
  for (int i=0;i<8;i++) digitalWrite(col[i], LOW); // set anodes LOW, turn off
  for (int i=0;i<8;i++) digitalWrite(row[i], HIGH); // set cathodes HIGH,
}                                                    // turn off

void loop()
{
  for (int n=0; n<3; n++)                  // display the letters A, B, C
  {
    start = millis();                      // milliseconds elapsed
    while (millis() < start+1000)          // display time for each letter
    for (int r=0; r<8; r++)
    {
      digitalWrite(row[r], LOW);           // set cathodes to LOW for each row
      for (int c=0; c<8; c++)
      {
        pixel = bitRead(val[n][r], c);    // read cth bit in rth row of nth letter
        if(pixel == 1) digitalWrite(col[c], HIGH);   // set anode HIGH, LED on
          delayMicroseconds(200);          // delay between LEDs in a row
          digitalWrite(col[c], LOW);       // reset anode to LOW, LED off
      }
      digitalWrite(row[r], HIGH);          // reset cathode to HIGH
    }
  }
}
```

A total of 16 Arduino pins are required to display patterns on the 8×8 dot matrix display, if shift registers are not used (see Figure 7-4). Just as with the 4-digit 7-segment display (see Chapter 6), one shift register can control the columns of the 8×8 dot matrix display with a second shift register to control the rows of the 8×8 dot matrix display.

One Shift Register

Connection information between an Arduino pin and an 8×8 dot matrix display pin, which was contained in the col[] matrix of Listing 7-1, is now incorporated in the shift register connections (see Figure 7-5 and Table 7-2). Only the pin[] and row[] matrices are now required in Listing 7-2.

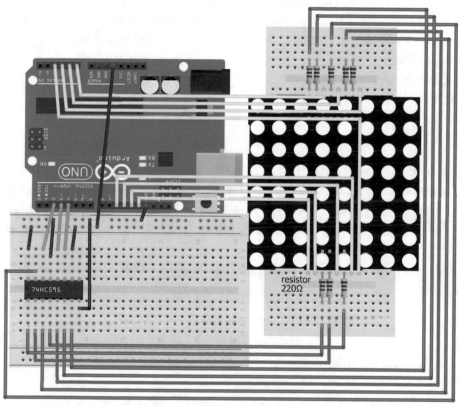

Figure 7-5. *8×8 dot matrix display and shift register*

Listing 7-2. Display Letters A, B, and C with Shift Register

```
                                         // Arduino display pins
int pin[] = {19,13,12,9,8,11,7,10,17,16,6,5,15,4,14,3,2};
                                         // dot matrix display rows
int row[] = {pin[9],pin[14],pin[8],pin[12],pin[1],pin[7],pin[2],pin[5]};
byte val[3][8] = {4,10,17,17,31,17,17,0,   // decimal representation of letter A
                 15,17,17,15,17,17,15,0,   // decimal representation of letter B
                 14,17,1,1,1,17,14,0};     // decimal representation of letter C
int dataPin = 2;                         // shift register DATA pin
int latchPin = 3;                        // shift register LATCH pin
int clockPin = 4;                        // shift register CLOCK pin
unsigned long start;

void setup()
{
  pinMode (dataPin, OUTPUT);     // define shift register DATA pin as output
  pinMode (latchPin, OUTPUT);    // define shift register LATCH pin as output
  pinMode (clockPin, OUTPUT);    // define shift register CLOCK pin as output
  for (int i=1; i<17; i++) pinMode(pin[i], OUTPUT);    // display pins as
                                                        // output
  for (int i=0; i<8; i++) digitalWrite(row[i], HIGH); // set cathodes
}                                                       // HIGH, turn off

void loop()
{
  for (int n=0; n<3; n++)                 // display the letters A, B, C
  {
    start = millis();                     // milliseconds elapsed
    while (millis()<start+1000)           // display time for each letter
    for (int r=0; r<8; r++)               // for each row of a letter
    {
      digitalWrite(latchPin,LOW);
      shiftOut(dataPin, clockPin, MSBFIRST,val[n][r]); // change display
                                                        // pattern
```

```
digitalWrite(latchPin,HIGH);
digitalWrite(row[r], LOW);      // set cathodes LOW, turn LED on
delayMicroseconds(200);         // delay between LEDs in a row
digitalWrite(row[r], HIGH);     // reset cathodes to HIGH, LED off
    }
  }
}
```

Table 7-2. *Connections with 8×8 Dot Matrix and Shift Register*

Pin	Symbol	Description	Connect to
1	QB	shift register output for column 2	8×8 dot matrix pin 3
2	QC	shift register output for column 3	8×8 dot matrix pin 4
3	QD	shift register output for column 4	8×8 dot matrix pin 10
4	QE	shift register output for column 5	8×8 dot matrix pin 6
5	QF	shift register output for column 6	8×8 dot matrix pin 11
6	QG	shift register output for column 7	8×8 dot matrix pin 15
7	QH	shift register output for column 8	8×8 dot matrix pin 16
8	GND	ground	Arduino GND
9	QH'	output if more than one register	
10	$\overline{SRCLR}$	clear the register when LOW	Arduino 5V
11	SRCLK	storage register clock	Arduino pin 4 CLOCK
12	RCLK	shift register clock	Arduino pin 3 LATCH
13	$\overline{OE}$	output enabled when ground	Arduino GND
14	SER	serial input for next pin	Arduino pin 2 DATA
15	QA	shift register output for column 1	8×8 dot matrix pin 13
16	VCC	5V supply	Arduino 5V

Two Shift Registers

A second 74HC595 shift register controls the rows of the 8×8 dot matrix display, which reduces the number of required Arduino pins to three (see Figure 7-6). Changes in connections to the first 74HC595 shift register, when a second shift register is included, are given in Table 7-3.

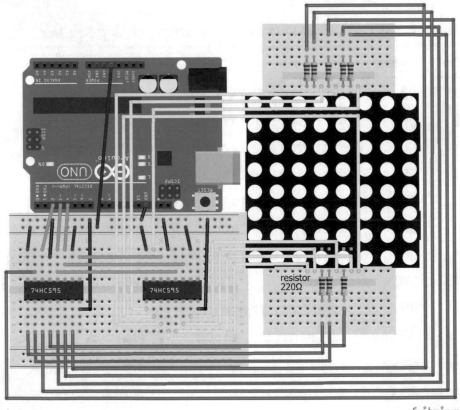

Figure 7-6. *8×8 dot matrix display and two shift registers*

Table 7-3. *Change in Connections of First Shift Register Given Second Shift Register*

Pin	Symbol	Description	Connect to
9	QH'	output if more than one register	74HC595 (2) pin 14
11	SRCLK	storage register clock	Arduino CLOCK pin, 74HC595 (2) pin 11
12	RCLK	shift register clock	Arduino LATCH pin, 74HC595 (2) pin 12

74HC595 (1) and 74HC595 (2) refer to the first and second shift register, respectively. The second shift register is connected to the 4-digit 7-segment display and to the first shift register, but not to the Arduino other than 5V and GND (see Table 7-4).

Table 7-4. *Connections with 8×8 Dot Matrix and Shift Register*

Pin	Symbol	Description	Connect to
1	QB	shift register output for row 2	8×8 dot matrix pin 14
2	QC	shift register output for row 3	8×8 dot matrix pin 8
3	QD	shift register output for row 4	8×8 dot matrix pin 12
4	QE	shift register output for row 5	8×8 dot matrix pin 1
5	QF	shift register output for row 6	8×8 dot matrix pin 7
6	QG	shift register output for row 7	8×8 dot matrix pin 2
7	QH	shift register output for row 8	8×8 dot matrix pin 5
8	GND	ground	Arduino GND
9	QH'	output if more than one register	
10	$\overline{SRCLR}$	clear the register when LOW	Arduino 5V

(continued)

Table 7-4. (*continued*)

Pin	Symbol	Description	Connect to
11	SRCLK	storage register clock	74HC595 (1) pin 11
12	RCLK	shift register clock	74HC595 (1) pin 12
13	$\overline{OE}$	output enabled when ground	Arduino GND
14	SER	serial input for next pin	74HC595 (1) pin 9
15	QA	shift register output for row 1	8×8 dot matrix pin 9
16	VCC	5V supply	Arduino 5V

In Listing 7-2, references to pin[ ] and row[ ] are not required, so the instructions in Listing 7-3 are deleted from Listing 7-2.

Listing 7-3. Deleted Instructions from Listing 7-2

```
int pin[] = {19,13,12,9,8,11,7,10,17,16,6,5,15,4,14,3,2}
int row[] = {pin[9],pin[14],pin[8],pin[12],pin[1],pin[7],pin[2],pin[5]}

for (int i=1; i<17; i++) pinMode(pin[i], OUTPUT)
for (int i=0; i<8; i++) digitalWrite(row[i], HIGH)

digitalWrite(row[r], LOW)
delayMicroseconds(200)
digitalWrite(row[r], HIGH)
```

The shiftOut(dataPin, clockPin, MSBFIRST, ~(1<<r)) instruction is added, before the shiftOut(dataPin, clockPin, MSBFIRST,val[n][r]) instruction.

The shiftOut() instruction of Listing 7-2 loads row information into the first shift register, the added shiftOut() instruction now shifts the row information from the first shift register to the second shift register and the column information is then loaded into the first shift register.

The shiftOut(dataPin, clockPin, MSBFIRST, ~(1<<r)) instruction controls the rows of the 8×8 dot matrix display. Row r is turned on by setting the corresponding cathode to *LOW* when the shift register loads the binary representation for the row. For example, to turn on the fifth row, the binary number B11101111 is loaded into the shift register. However, it is easier when coding to load the binary value B00010000, which is the "inverse" of B11101111, and then change bits from *one* to *zero* and from *one* to *zero* with the symbol ~. The symbol << moves a bit with value one to position r with the term (1<<r).

In summary, the shiftOut(dataPin, clockPin, MSBFIRST, ~(1<<r)) instruction generates the inverse of 2^r in binary and loads the value, with the most significant bit first, into the shift register.

With two shift registers, changing the shiftOut(dataPin, clockPin, MSBFIRST, ~(1<<r)) instruction can transform characters. A reflection, top to bottom, is obtained by changing MSBFIRST to LSBFIRST.

Characters can be repositioned by adding the loop for (int t=0; t<8; t++) before start = millis() in the updated Listing 7-2 and changing the shiftOut(dataPin, clockPin, MSBFIRST, ~(1<<r)) instruction to

shiftOut(dataPin, clockPin, LSBFIRST, ~(1<<r)) reflection top to bottom

or shiftOut(dataPin, clockPin, MSBFIRST, ~(1<<r+t)) step-shift down
or shiftOut(dataPin, clockPin, MSBFIRST, ~(1<<r-t)) step-shift up
with the if(r-t+1>0) instruction included before the digitalWrite(latchPin,LOW) instruction.

Replacing `MSBFIRST` with `LSBFIRST` in the `shiftOut(dataPin, clockPin, MSBFIRST,val[n][r])` instruction reflects a character left to right, when either one or two shift registers are used.

Scrolling Text

In Listings 7-1, 7-2, and 7-3, a row is activated and then the column LEDs, within the row, are turned on or off, which is *row scanning*. A 220Ω resistor in series with each column of the 8×8 dot matrix display restricts the current to control the LED brightness, as with *row scanning* only one LED in a column is on at any time. To display a scrolling message with the 8×8 dot matrix display, the characters must be shifted from right to left rather than shifted up or down. Therefore, columns, rather than rows, are activated and the LEDs, within a column, are turned on or off, which is *column scanning*. The 220Ω resistors are now connected in series with each row of the 8×8 dot matrix display (see Figure 7-7). When shifting characters with *column scanning*, the `shiftOut(dataPin, clockPin, MSBFIRST, (1<<7+c-t))` instruction does not include the symbol ~, as discussed in the previous paragraph, as a column is activated by setting the anode to *HIGH*, in contrast to *row scanning* when the cathode was set to *LOW*.

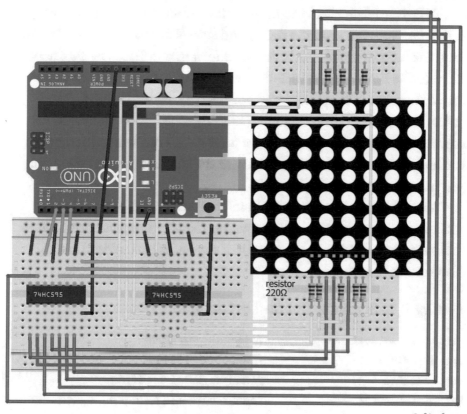

Figure 7-7. *8×8 dot matrix display with column scanning*

Listing 7-4 displays a message on the 8×8 dot matrix display with the characters moving from right to left and the message entered into the serial monitor buffer with the `Serial.available()>0` instruction, as described in Chapter 4. The `Serial.read()` instruction reduces the buffer by one character at a time.

Decimal representations of the uppercase and lowercase characters are loaded into a data file, rather than the main sketch to aid interpretation of the main sketch.

To create a data file in the Arduino IDE, select the triangle below the serial monitor button on the right-hand side of the IDE. Choose *New Tab* from the drop-down menu. Enter the title: *letters.h*. The New Tab, now titled *letters.h*, is edited to include the matrices letters[ ], containing the alphanumeric characters, and val[63][8], which includes the character decimal representations (see Table 7-5). The character decimal representations in the val[63][8] matrix have a row orientation, which is changed to a column orientation with the bitRead() instruction and results stored in the cols[ ] matrix.

When an additional file is included in a sketch, the #include "filename.h" instruction uses quotation marks rather than the angle brackets when a library is included in a sketch, as in the #include "letters.h" instruction.

Listing 7-4. Scrolling Text on 8×8 Dot Matrix Display

```
#include "letters.h"          // include letter data
int dataPin = 2;              // shift register DATA pin
int latchPin = 3;             // shift register LATCH pin
int clockPin = 4;             // shift register CLOCK pin
byte cols[8];
char data;
int n;
unsigned long start;

void setup()
{
  Serial.begin(9600);              // define Serial output baud rate
  pinMode (dataPin, OUTPUT);    // define shift register DATA pin as output
  pinMode (latchPin, OUTPUT);   // define shift register LATCH pin as output
  pinMode (clockPin, OUTPUT);   // define shift register CLOCK pin as output
}
```

```
void loop()
{
  while (Serial.available()>0)         // message read from Serial Monitor
  {
    data=Serial.read();                // message read one letter at a time
    Serial.print(data);

                                       // decimal representation of letter
    for (int lett=0; lett<63 ;lett++) if(data == letters[lett]) n=lett;
    for (int i=0; i<8;i++)             // convert row to column orientation
    {
      cols[i]=0;                       // change to column orientation
      for (int j=0; j<8; j++) cols[i]= cols[i] + (bitRead(val[n][j],i)<<j);
    }
    for (int t=0;t<12;t++)             // move character through 12 shifts
    {                                  // across the 8×8 dot matrix display
      start = millis();                // elapsed time (ms)
      while (millis() - start <60)     // 60 ms to display character
      for (int c=0; c<8; c++)          // display with column scanning
      {
        if(8+c-t>0)
        {
          digitalWrite(latchPin,LOW);   // change display pattern
          shiftOut(dataPin, clockPin, MSBFIRST,~cols[c]); // shift by one
                                                          // column
          shiftOut(dataPin, clockPin, MSBFIRST, (1<<7+c-t));
          digitalWrite(latchPin,HIGH);
        }
      }
    }
  }
}
```

Matrices with alphanumeric characters and their decimal representations are contained in the *letters.h* file (see Listing 7-5).

Listing 7-5. Loading Character Data

```
char letters[] =
{'A','B','C','D','E','F','G','H','I','J','K','L','M','N','O','P','Q',
 'R','S','T','U','V','W','X','Y','Z',
 'a','b','c','d','e','f','g','h','i','j','k','l','m','n','o','p','q',
 'r','s','t','u','v','w','x','y','z',
 '0','1','2','3','4','5','6','7','8','9',' '};

byte val[63][8] ={4,10,17,17,31,17,17,0 ... 0,0,0,0,0,0,0,0};
```

Note that the matrix val[63][8] consists of columns 1 and 3 of Table 7-5 for alphabetic characters, and column 1 of Table 7-6 for number characters.

Table 7-5. *Decimal Representations of Alphabetic Characters*

Decimal Representation	Character	Decimal Representation	Character
4,10,17,17,31,17,17,0,	// A	0,0,6,8,14,9,14,0,	// a
15,17,17,15,17,17,15,0,	// B	1,1,13,19,17,19,13,0,	// b
14,17,1,1,1,17,14,0,	// C	0,0,6,9,1,9,6,0,	// c
7,9,17,17,17,9,7,0,	// D	16,16,22,25,17,25,22,0,	// d
31,1,1,15,1,1,31,0,	// E	0,0,6,9,7,1,14,0,	// e
31,1,1,15,1,1,1,0,	// F	4,10,2,7,2,2,2,0,	// f
14,17,1,13,17,25,22,0,	// G	0,0,6,9,9,6,8,7,	// g
17,17,17,31,17,17,17,0,	// H	1,1,13,19,17,17,17,0,	// h
7,2,2,2,2,2,7,0,	// I	1,0,1,1,1,1,2,0,	// i
28,8,8,8,8,9,6,0,	// J	4,0,6,4,4,4,4,3,	// j
17,9,5,3,5,9,17,0,	// K	1,1,9,5,3,5,9,0,	// k

(*continued*)

Table 7-5. (*continued*)

Decimal Representation	Character	Decimal Representation	Character
1,1,1,1,1,1,15,0,	// L	3,2,2,2,2,2,2,0,	// I
17,27,21,21,17,17,17,0,	// M	0,0,21,43,41,41,41,0,	// m
17,19,19,21,25,25,17,0,	// N	0,0,13,19,17,17,17,0,	// n
14,17,17,17,17,17,14,0,	// O	0,0,6,9,9,9,6,0,	// o
15,17,17,15,1,1,1,0,	// P	0,0,13,19,19,13,1,1,	// p
14,17,17,17,21,9,22,0,	// Q	0,0,22,25,25,22,16,16,	// q
15,17,17,15,5,9,17,0,	// R	0,0,13,19,1,1,1,0,	// r
14,17,1,14,16,17,14,0,	// S	0,0,14,1,6,8,7,0,	// s
31,4,4,4,4,4,4,0,	// T	0,2,7,2,2,2,4,0,	// t
17,17,17,17,17,17,14,0,	// U	0,0,17,17,17,25,22,0,	// u
17,17,17,17,10,10,4,0,	// V	0,0,17,17,17,10,4,0,	// v
17,17,17,21,21,27,17,0,	// W	0,0,17,17,21,21,10,0,	// w
17,17,10,4,10,17,17,0,	// X	0,0,17,10,4,10,17,0,	// x
17,17,17,10,4,4,4,0,	// Y	0,0,9,9,9,14,8,6,	// y
31,16,8,4,2,1,31,0,	// Z	0,0,15,8,6,1,15,0,	// z

Table 7-6. *Decimal Representations of Numeric Characters*

Decimal Representation	Number
14,17,25,21,19,17,14,0,	// 0
4,6,4,4,4,4,14,0,	// 1
14,17,16,12,2,1,31,0,	// 2
14,17,16,12,16,17,14,0,	// 3
8,12,10,9,31,8,8,0,	// 4
31,1,1,14,16,17,14,0,	// 5
12,2,1,15,17,17,14,0,	// 6
31,16,8,4,2,2,2,0,	// 7
14,17,17,14,17,17,14,0,	// 8
14,17,17,30,16,8,6,0,	// 9
0,0,0,0,0,0,0,0};	// space

Summary

Alpha-numeric characters were displayed on the 8×8 dot matrix display, with LEDs activated in rows (row scanning). Message scrolling required LEDs to be activated in columns (column scanning). Two shift registers were included to control the row and column LEDs.

Components List

- Arduino Uno and breadboard

- 8×8 dot matrix display

- Resistors: 8× 220Ω

- Shift registers: 2× 74HC595

CHAPTER 8

Servo and Stepper Motors

Servo and stepper motors are used in a variety of applications, such as robotics, tracking systems, and positioning devices. Servo motors are used for fast movement to a given angle, while the stepper motors move at a controlled speed in either continuous rotation or to a specific position. The servo motor has a feedback mechanism to determine location in contrast to the stepper motor that is moved incrementally. Servo motors are included in projects in Chapters 13, 22, and 24 with the stepper motor used in Chapter 9.

Servo Motors

 Servo motors, or servomechanism, are used to move an armature by a fixed angle. A servo motor is precisely controlled by the width of a pulsed signal corresponding to the angle that the servo motor is rotated. The SG90 servo rotates to angles between 0° and 180° given signals with pulse widths between 0.5ms and 2.5ms, at intervals of 20ms between pulses. The pulsed signal is similar to pulse width modulation, described in Chapter 2.

The servo motor has three connections normally colored red for power, brown or black for ground and orange or white for signal (see Figure 8-1). A servo motor runs at 5V and can use hundreds of milliamps during a few milliseconds that the rotor is turning, which is more than

© Neil Cameron 2019
N. Cameron, *Arduino Applied*, https://doi.org/10.1007/978-1-4842-3960-5_8

the 40mA maximum output of the Arduino pins. Therefore, a servo motor requires an external power supply, such as a 9V battery. In a circuit with two power supplies, the 9V battery and the Arduino 5V output, the grounds of both supplies must be connected together.

An L4940V5 voltage regulator reduces the voltage from 9V to 5V and the energy converted to heat is lost through the metal surface at the rear of the voltage regulator. Decoupling capacitors, on both sides of the voltage regulator, smooth both the voltage supply and the voltage demand.

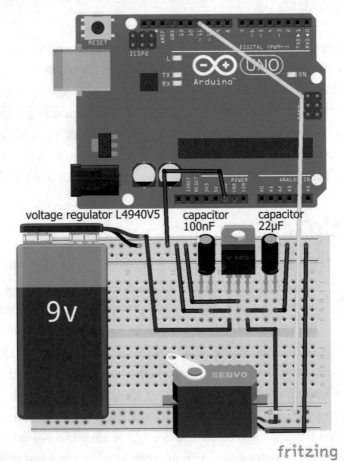

Figure 8-1. *Servo motor*

 If electrolytic capacitors are used as decoupling capacitors, then the negative terminal of the capacitor, indicated by a silver strip on the side of the capacitor, is connected to ground, as the capacitors are polarized. The schematic in Figure 8-1 uses a L4940V5 voltage regulator and the datasheet recommends a 0.1µF capacitor, which is 100nF, on the 9V (supply) side and a 22µF capacitor on the 5V (demand) side (see Table 8-1). The schematic in Figure 8-1 shows the decoupling capacitors either side of the voltage regulator to make the layout clearer. In practice, ground pins of the voltage regulator and decoupling capacitors are aligned to reduce wiring and space (see Figure 8-2). Note that for the negative pins to align with the central ground pin of the voltage regulator, the decoupling capacitors face opposite directions.

In general, motors requiring high current should not be powered directly by the Arduino, but by an external power source. The maximum current from Arduino Uno output pins is 40mA, with a maximum current from all output pins of 200mA. The Arduino Uno 5V pin is not connected through the microcontroller, so 400mA can be supplied by the 5V pin when the Arduino is powered by USB, given the limit of 500mA through the USB interface. The 3.3V pin can supply 150mA, which is the limit of the Arduino Uno voltage regulator.

Table 8-1. *Connections for Servo Motor*

Component	Connect to	and to
Servo VCC	L4940V5 demand	Capacitor 22µF positive
Servo GND	Arduino GND	
Servo signal	Arduino pin 11	
9V battery positive	L4940V5 supply	Capacitor 0.1µF positive
9V battery negative	Arduino GND	
Potentiometer VCC	Arduino 5V	
Potentiometer signal	Arduino pin A1	
Potentiometer GND	Arduino GND	
Capacitor 0.1µF negative	Arduino GND	
Capacitor 22µF negative	Arduino GND	

The *Servo* library by Michael Margolis is built-in to the Arduino IDE, so does not need to be uploaded. The *Servo* library utilizes *Timer1*, which uses Arduino pins 9 and 10, so these pins cannot be used in a sketch requiring pulse width modulation. The sketch (see Listing 8-1) rotates a servo motor to angle $x°$ with the servo.write(x) instruction. Some servo motors can stick at 0° or at 180°, so a range of angles from 5° to 175° may be more robust.

Listing 8-1. Servo motor

```
#include <Servo.h>        // include Servo library
Servo servo;              // associate servo with Servo library
int servoPin = 11;        // servo motor pin

void setup()
{
  servo.attach(servoPin);    // define servo motor pin to Servo library
}
```

```
void loop()
{
  for (int i=0; i<19; i++)
  {
    servo.write(10 * i);      // rotate to angles 0, 10, 20 ... 180
    delay(500);               // delay 500ms between movements
  }
  for (int i=8; i>=0; i--)
  {
    servo.write(20 * i);      // rotate to angles 160, 140 ... 0
    delay(500);               // delay 500ms between movements
  }
}
```

Servo Motor and a Potentiometer

A potentiometer is used to rotate the servo motor to a specific angle, with the potentiometer output voltage converted to a digital reading by the Arduino analog-to-digital converter (ADC) (see Figure 8-2). The map() instruction relates the digital reading from 0 to 1023 to the corresponding angle between 5° to 175°. The direction of the servo motor rotation can be changed, with respect to the direction of the potentiometer dial, by the swapping the voltage supply and ground connections of the potentiometer. Listing 8-2 shows the updated void loop() function of Listing 8-1, with the sketch updated by also including definition of the potentiometer pin, int potPin = A1, and declaring the integer variables *reading* and *angle*.

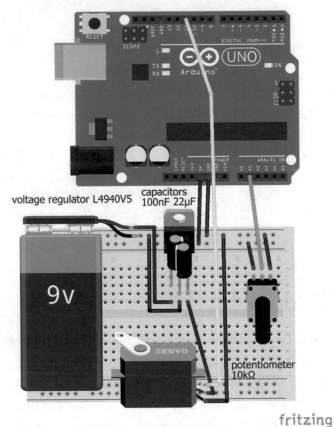

Figure 8-2. *Servo motor with potentiometer*

Listing 8-2. Updated void loop()

```
void loop()
{
  reading = analogRead(potPin);              // potentiometer voltage
  angle = map(reading, 0, 1023, 5, 175); // map voltage to angle
  servo.write(angle);                        // move servo to angle
  delay(10);                                 // delay 10ms
}
```

The delay of 10ms after the `servo.write()` instruction allows the servo motor time to rotate to required position before the next input from the potentiometer.

A light source can be detected by attaching a light dependent resistor (LDR), described in Chapter 3, to the rotor arm of the servo motor and scanning through 180°, with the LDR measuring the light intensity at each point on the semicircle (see Listing 8-3). Figure 8-3 shows the connections of the LDR to an Arduino, based on Figure 8-2, with the light dependent resistor attached to the rotor arm on top of the servo motor and not a breadboard. An application of a light sourcing sensor is the orientation of a solar panel to maximize power generation.

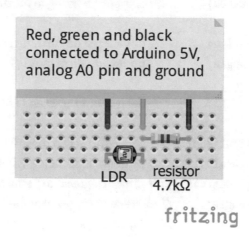

Figure 8-3. *Connection for LDR*

Listing 8-3. Servo Motor with LDR

```
#include <Servo.h>          // include servo library
Servo servo;                // associate servo with Servo library
int servoPin = 11;          // servo motor pin
int LDRpin = A0;            // LDR on analog pin A0
int maxLDR = 0;             // maximum LDR reading
int reading, maxAngle;
```

```
void setup()
{
  servo.attach(servoPin);     // define servo motor pin to servo library
  Serial.begin(9600);         // define Serial output baud rate
}

void loop()
{                             // scan from angle 0° to 180°
  for (int angle=0; angle<190; angle = angle + 10)
  {
    servo.write(angle);       // rotate servo motor
    reading = analogRead(LDRpin);     // read light dependent resistor
    if (reading>maxLDR)       // compare reading to maximum
    {
      maxLDR = reading;       // update maximum light reading
      maxAngle = angle;       // update angle of max light reading
    }
    delay(50);                // delay 50ms between LDR readings
  }
  Serial.print("Light source at ");   // print text to Serial Monitor
  Serial.print(maxAngle);     // print angle of incident light
  Serial.println(" degrees"); // print " degrees" to Serial Monitor
  servo.write(maxAngle);      // rotate servo to point at the light source
  delay(1000);                // delay while pointing at light source
  maxLDR=0;                   // reset maximum light reading
  servo.write(0);             // rotate to 0°
  delay(500);                 // delay 500ms
}
```

Stepper Motor

A stepper motor is also precisely controllable, but unlike a servo motor, a stepper motor can revolve continuously and the rotation speed can be controlled. For a stepper motor, the number of steps that the motor has to move is defined rather than the angle of movement. The 28BYJ-48 stepper motor is used in this chapter (see Figure 8-4).

A unipolar stepper motor consists of two pairs of coils, with a common center connected to 5V, and a coil is activated by connecting the coil to ground. The coil connecting wires are generally colored blue and yellow for one coil pair, pink and orange for the other coil pair, and red for the common center. The stepper motor connecting board includes a ULN2003 chip, to control the coil activation sequence, with four LEDs: *A, B, C,* and *D,* to indicate when the blue, pink, yellow, and orange coils are activated.

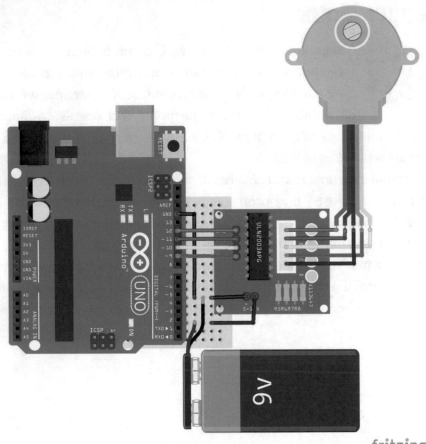

Figure 8-4. *Stepper motor*

To control a stepper motor, there are three coil activation sequences: wave driving, full-step and half-step. Wave driving activates each coil individually: blue, pink, yellow then orange, and the internal motor shaft turns by 1/32 of a revolution, as each of the four coils is associated with eight internal motor positions. Full-step activates two coils simultaneously: blue and pink, pink and yellow, yellow, and orange, and then orange and blue, which provides more torque to the stepper motor. The internal motor shaft again turns by 1/32 of a revolution. Both wave driving and full-step have four coil activation stages. Given the stepper motor's internal gearing of 63.68:1, the internal motor shaft rotates 2038 = 4 (coil activation stages) × 8 (internal motor positions) × 63.68 (gearing) times with wave driving or full-step for each rotation of the stepper motor rotor.

Half-step alternately activates one or two coils: blue, blue and pink, pink, pink and yellow, yellow, and so forth. Half-step provides intermediate torque compared to wave driving and full-step and the internal motor shaft turns by 1/64 of a revolution on each of eight coil activation stages. With half-step, the internal rotor shaft rotates 4076 = 8 × 8 × 63.68 times for each rotation of the stepper motor rotor. Wave drive and full step require at least 2ms between steps with at least 1ms between steps for half-step.

As with a servo motor, an external power supply is recommended for the stepper motor and the grounds of the external supply and the Arduino must be connected. The jumper next to the DC 5-12V power supply on the stepper motor connecting board can be used to turn on or off the stepper motor (see Table 8-2).

Table 8-2. *Connections for Stepper Motor*

Component	Connect to	and to
Stepper blue wire	ULN2003 IN1	Arduino pin 12
Stepper pink wire	ULN2003 IN2	Arduino pin 11
Stepper yellow wire	ULN2003 IN3	Arduino pin 10
Stepper orange wire	ULN2003 IN4	Arduino pin 9
9V battery positive	ULN2003 positive	
9V battery negative	ULN2003 negative	Arduino GND
Potentiometer VCC	Arduino 5V	
Potentiometer signal	Arduino pin A1	
Potentiometer GND	Arduino GND	
LED long leg	220Ω resistor	Arduino pin 6
LED short leg	Arduino GND	

The *Stepper* library originally by Tom Igoe is built-in to the Arduino IDE, so does not need to be uploaded. The *Stepper* library supports full-step. The order of pins on the stepper motor connecting board is IN1, IN2, IN3, and IN4, which are the connections for the blue and yellow coil pair and the pink and orange coil pair. In contrast, the ULN2003 stepper motor driver board configures the pins in coil activation order: blue, pink, yellow, and orange. The different coil connection and activation orders are defined in Listing 8-4. This sketch illustrates rotating the stepper motor half a revolution, then reversing the direction and increasing the motor speed. The stepper motor rotates at speed S rpm for N steps with the stepper.setSpeed(S) and stepper.step(N) instructions, where S is the number of revolutions per minute (rpm) and N is the number of steps, which is negative when the motor direction is reversed. For example, the stepper.step(50) and stepper.step(-50) instructions move the stepper motor 50 steps clockwise and 50 steps counterclockwise, respectively.

Listing 8-4. Stepper Motor with Stepper Library

```
#include <Stepper.h>          // include Stepper library
int blue = 12;
int pink = 11;                // coil activation order on ULN2003
int yellow = 10;              // blue, pink, yellow, orange
int orange = 9;
int steps = 2038;             // steps per revolution
            // associate stepper with Stepper library and coil pairing order
Stepper stepper(steps, blue, yellow, pink, orange);
int direct = 1;               // direction of rotation
int revTime;
float secs, revs;

void setup()
{
  Serial.begin(9600);                  // define Serial output baud rate
  Serial.println("rpm time(s) revs");  // print header to Serial Monitor
}
```

```
void loop()
{
  for (int i = 2; i<19; i=i+2)        // motor speed from 2 to 18 rpm
  {
    stepper.setSpeed(i);              // set motor speed (rpm)
    direct = -direct;                 // change direction of rotation
    revTime = millis();               // sct start time (ms)
    stepper.step(direct * steps/2);   // move number of steps
    revTime = millis()-revTime;       // time for half revolution (ms)
    delay(500);                       // delay 0.5s
    secs = revTime/1000.0;            // time (s) to move steps
    revs = i*secs/60.0;               // check number of revolutions
    Serial.print(i);Serial.print("\t");  // print speed on Serial Monitor
    Serial.print(secs);Serial.print("\t"); // print time
    Serial.println(revs,3);           // print number of revolutions
  }
}
```

The *Accelstepper* library, by Mike McCauley, is recommended for sketches with a stepper motor as it has more functionality than the *Stepper* library, such as control of the stepper motor acceleration rate and use of both half-step and full-step. The *Accelstepper* library is installed within the Arduino IDE, using installation method 3, as outlined in Chapter 3. The stepper motor's initial speed, acceleration rate and maximum speed can be set along with the target position.

The *Accelstepper* library requires the number of coil activation stages to be defined when initializing the stepper motor, which is four for full-step and eight for half-step. Listing 8-5 rotates the stepper motor for one revolution and then reverses the direction to demonstrate control of the acceleration rate. A rotation is defined as moving from position $+P$ to position 0 and then to position $-P$, where P is half the number of steps in a revolution, which is 1019 for full-step and 2038 for half-step. The maximum rotor speeds for full-step and half-step are set at 700 and 1400 steps per second, respectively, which results in the same rpm, given that half-step has double the number

169

of steps per revolution than full-step. Note that motor speed with the
AccelStepper library is measured in steps/s, but in rpm with the *Stepper*
library. To convert rpm to motor speed, in steps/s, use the formula: $rpm \times steps = 60 \times motor\ speed$, where *steps* is the number of steps per revolution.
In the example, an acceleration rate of 600 steps/s^2 maximized the time of
constant acceleration/deceleration with full-step, but with half-step, the
required acceleration rate was 1200 steps/s^2, given double the number of
steps per revolution.

Listing 8-5. Stepper Motor with Accelstepper Library

```
#include <AccelStepper.h>       // include Accelstepper library
int blue = 12;
int pink = 11;                   // coil activation order on ULN2003
int yellow = 10;                 // blue, pink, yellow, orange
int orange = 9;
int fullstep = 4;                // number of coil activation stages
int halfstep = 8;                // with full-step and half-step
int coil = fullstep;             // set to full-step or to half-step
        // associate stepper with AccelStepper library and coil pairing order
AccelStepper stepper(coil, blue, yellow, pink, orange);
int steps = (coil/4)*2038;       // number of steps per revolution
long last = 0;
int lag = 500;                   // time (ms) interval for display
int direct = 1;                  // direction of rotation
float rpm, speed, oldspeed, accel;
int nsteps;

void setup()
{
  Serial.begin(9600);                      // define Serial output baud rate
  stepper.setMaxSpeed((coil/4)*700);  // max speed 700 or 1400 steps/s
  stepper.setAcceleration(600);         // acceleration rate (steps/s²)
  Serial.println("steps rpm accel"); // print header to Serial Monitor
}
```

```
void loop()
{
  stepper.moveTo(direct*steps/2);    // move to position ±1019 or ±2038
                                     // change direction of rotation
  if(stepper.distanceToGo()==0) direct = -direct;
  if(millis()>last + lag)            // lag time elapsed since last print
  {
    speed = stepper.speed();         // current motor speed (steps/s)
    nsteps = speed*lag/pow(10,3);    // steps/s taken during lag time
    Serial.print(nsteps);Serial.print("\t");  // display number
                                     // of steps and a tab
    rpm = 60.0*speed/steps;          // derive rpm
    Serial.print(rpm,2);Serial.print("\t");   // display rpm to 2DP
    accel = (speed - oldspeed)*1000.0/lag;  // derived acceleration
                                     // rate (steps/s²)
    Serial.println(accel,0);         // display acceleration
    oldspeed = speed;                // update speed value
    last = millis();                 // update last print time
  }
  stepper.run();                     // move to new position
}
```

In Listing 8-5, the `stepper.run()` instruction moves the motor to a new position, but if the motor has to move at a different speed then the `stepper.runSpeed()` instruction is required. The following are other Accelstepper instructions.

`stepper.currentPosition()`	determine the current position
`stepper.move(N)`	move N steps, with N positive or negative
`stepper.moveTo(N)`	move to position N
`stepper.distanceToGo()`	determine number of steps to target position
`stepper.runToPosition()`	update motor to move to target position
`stepper.setSpeed(N)`	set constant speed (steps/s)
`stepper.runSpeed()`	update motor to run at new speed (steps/s)

To move the stepper motor for a fixed time, the `stepper.setSpeed()` and `delay()` instructions are required. To move the stepper motor a number of steps requires the `stepper.move()` or `stepper.moveTo()` and the `stepper.run()` instructions. Listing 8-6 provides the replacement `void setup()` and `void loop()` functions of Listing 8-5 to move the stepper with an initial speed and acceleration to a given position and back again.

Listing 8-6. Move Stepper Motor

```
void setup()
{
  stepper.setSpeed(200);
  stepper.setAcceleration(600);
  stepper.moveTo(512);
}

void loop()
{
  if (stepper.distanceToGo() == 0)
    stepper.moveTo (-stepper.currentPosition());
  stepper.run();
}
```

Stepper Motor and a Potentiometer

A potentiometer can be used to rotate the stepper motor at a specific speed, while the brightness of an LED is also changed (see Figure 8-5, Table 8-2, and Listing 8-7). The potentiometer output voltage is converted by the Arduino ADC to a digital value, which is mapped to the motor speed. The internal motor shaft is moved 256 steps to allow almost continuous response to changes in the potentiometer output voltage, rather than responding at the end of a revolution. Every 2038 steps, which is a complete revolution of the stepper motor rotor with full-step, the revolution time, rpm, and stepper motor speed are displayed on the serial monitor. The minimum and maximum stepper motor rotor speeds, as defined in rpm, are defined in the sketch and then converted to rotor speeds in terms of steps/s using the map() function.

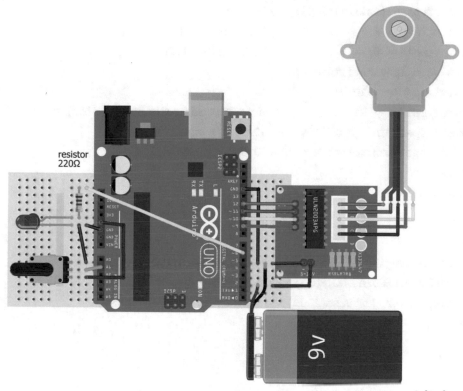

Figure 8-5. *Stepper motor and potentiometer*

Listing 8-7. Stepper Motor with Potentiometer

```
#include <AccelStepper.h>     // include Accelstepper library
int blue = 12;
int pink = 11;                // coil activation order on ULN2003
int yellow = 10;              // blue, pink, yellow, orange
int orange = 9;
```

```
int fullstep = 4;                 // number of coil activation stages
int coil = fullstep;              // set number of coil activation stages
    // associate stepper with AccelStepper library and coil pairing order
AccelStepper stepper(coil, blue, yellow, pink, orange);
int steps = (coil/4)*2038;     // number of steps per revolution
int potPin = A1;                  // potentiometer pin
int LEDpin = 6;                   // LED on PWM pin
unsigned long revTime = 0;
float rpmMin = 10.0;
float rpmMax = 21.0;            // minimum and maximum speed in rpm
float speedMin = rpmMin*steps/60.0;   // and in steps/s
float speedMax = rpmMax*steps/60.0;
float rpm;
int reading, speed, bright;

void setup()
{
  Serial.begin(9600);          // define Serial output baud rate
  pinMode(LEDpin, OUTPUT);     // LED pin as output
  stepper.setMaxSpeed(1500);   // set maximum speed (step/s)
}

void loop()
{
  reading = analogRead(potPin); // potentiometer voltage
                                // map voltage to speed (step/s)
  speed = map(reading, 0, 1023, speedMin, speedMax);
  bright = map(reading, 0, 1023, 0, 255);   // map voltage to LED
                                            // brightness
  analogWrite(LEDpin, bright);   // set LED brightness with PWM
  stepper.move(256);             // move the internal motor 256 steps
  stepper.setSpeed(speed);       // set the internal motor speed
  stepper.runSpeed();            // run the stepper motor
  if((stepper.currentPosition() % steps)==0) // on each complete
                                             // revolution
```

```
{
    revTime = millis()-revTime;          // time (ms) for one revolution
    rpm = stepper.speed()*60.0/steps;    // stepper motor rpm
    Serial.print(revTime);               // print revolution time
    Serial.print(" ms\t\t");             // print "ms " and two tabs
    Serial.print(rpm, 2);                // print rpm with 2DP
    Serial.print(" rpm\t");              // print "rpm" and a tab
    Serial.print(stepper.speed(),0);     // print motor speed with 0DP
    Serial.println(" steps/s");          // print " steps/s" and a new line
    delay(2);                            // delay 2ms to prevent duplicates
    revTime=millis();                    // update revolution start time
  }
}
```

Stepper Motor Gear Ratio

The often quoted gear ratio of 64:1 for the 28BYJ-48 stepper motor approximates the actual ratio of 63.684:1. The internal gearing consists of five cogs with gear ratios: motor shaft 31:1, internal A 26:10, internal B 22:9, internal C 32:11, and rotor shaft 1:9. The overall gear ratio is the product of the individual gear ratios. The number of steps per revolution with full-step or with half-step is the overall gear ratio multiplied by the number of coil activation stages (4 or 8) and the number of internal motor positions (8), which is 2038 and 4076 steps, respectively.

There are many stepper motors available and the 28BYJ-48 stepper motor is an example of a unipolar stepper motor, while the NEMA 17 is an example of a bipolar stepper motor. For unipolar stepper motors, the coils are activated the same way with the common center always negative, so at most only half of the coils can be activated at any one time. With bipolar stepper motors, an H-bridge circuit changes the direction of current at each coil activation stage, so that all coils can be activated at one time. Bipolar stepper motors have more torque than unipolar stepper motors, due to the higher number of activated coils.

Summary

The angle of rotation of a servo motor was controlled by a potentiometer and by a light dependent resistor to detect a light source. The speed and target position of a stepper motor was also controlled with a potentiometer. The map() function was used to convert the potentiometer output to motor speed or motor target position.

Components List

- Arduino Uno and breadboard

- Servo motor: SG90

- Stepper motor: 28BYJ-48

- Stepper motor connecting board with ULN2003 chip

- Battery: 9V

- Voltage regulator: L4940V5

- Capacitors: 0.1µF and 22µF

- Potentiometer: 10kΩ

- LED

- Resistor: 220Ω

CHAPTER 9

Rotary Encoder

A rotary encoder is used to finely control an output, such as the rotation of a motor, the cursor position on a screen or simply the brightness of an LED. Rotary encoders are used as control switches, such as on audio equipment. The rotary encoder has 20 positions, but the rotor can be continuously rotated either forward or backward to increase or decrease a control variable.

There are three pins inside a rotary encoder: a common pin and two pins, termed A and B, which are offset. As the rotor turns, pins A and B each make contact with the common pin or are disconnected with the common pin, which generates square waves of the same frequency, but a quarter of a cycle, or 90°, out of phase (see Figure 9-1). The number of pulses of the square waves indicates the extent of the rotation, which can be measured on either pin A or pin B.

The square wave positions on pins A and B determine the direction of rotation. If the rotation is clockwise, then pin A makes contact with the common pin before pin B, so the square wave on pin B will be *HIGH* at the falling edge of the square wave on pin A (see Figure 9-1) with the black vertical line indicating the falling edge of pin A. In contrast, if the square wave on pin B is *LOW* at the falling edge of the square wave of pin A, then the rotation is counterclockwise. The rising edge of the square wave on pin A can also be used as the time reference point, in which case a *LOW* value of the square wave on pin B indicates a clockwise rotation.

© Neil Cameron 2019
N. Cameron, *Arduino Applied*, https://doi.org/10.1007/978-1-4842-3960-5_9

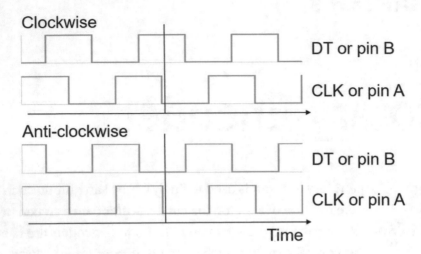

Figure 9-1. *Rotary encoder square wave*

The sequence of pin B and pin A states at a falling edge of the square wave on pin B with clockwise rotation of the rotary encoder is (*LOW, LOW*), (*LOW, HIGH*), (*HIGH, HIGH*) and (*HIGH, LOW*) or 00, 01, 11 and 10. Such a sequence is Gray code, with two successive values differing by one bit. An increasing binary sequence 00, 01, 10 and 11 can also be generated by two square waves (*LOW, LOW*), (*LOW, HIGH*), (*HIGH, LOW*) and (*HIGH, HIGH*), but the two waves are in phase and the frequency of the second wave is double that of the first wave (see Figure 9-2).

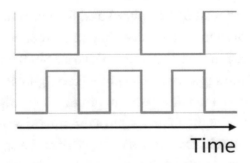

Figure 9-2. *Square waves for binary counting*

The switch on the rotary encoder, activated by pressing down on the stem of the rotary encoder, can be used to change the state of a binary variable. In the sketch (see Listing 9-1), pressing the switch turns off an LED. Pins A and B of the rotary encoder are referenced as the clock (CLK) and data (DT) pins. The switch (SW) pin of the rotary encoder uses an internal pull-up resistor, attached to each input pin of the Arduino Uno, rather than including a separate resistor in the circuit. An internal pull-up resistor is activated with the `digitalWrite(pin, INPUT_PULLUP)` instruction, but the pin is active *LOW* rather than active *HIGH*. The rotary encoder module, KY-040, used in this chapter, includes 10kΩ pull-up resistors on the clock (CLK) and data (DT) pins. An LED is connected to an Arduino PWM pin for the rotary encoder to control the level of LED brightness.

The rotary encoder clock (CLK), data (DT), and switch (SW) pins are connected to Arduino pins A0, A1, and A2 only for convenience of the schematic (see Figure 9-3 and Table 9-1), as a stepper motor is connected to the Arduino in Figure 9-4 and Listing 9-2. The Arduino analog pins A0 to A5 can be utilized as digital pins with the `digitalRead(pin)` instruction, with pins A0 to A5 corresponding to pin numbers 14 to 19.

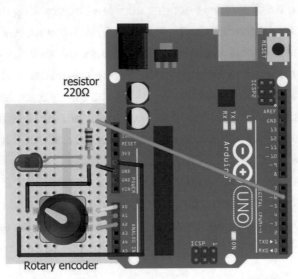

Figure 9-3. *Rotary encoder and LED*

Table 9-1. *Connections for Rotary Encoder and LED*

Component	Connect to	and to
Rotary encoder CLK	Arduino pin A0	
Rotary encoder DT	Arduino pin A1	
Rotary encoder SW	Arduino pin A2	
Rotary encoder VCC	Arduino 5V	
Rotary encoder GND	Arduino GND	
LED long leg	Arduino pin 6	
LED short leg	220Ω resistor	Arduino GND

In Listing 9-1, the encoder() function returns the direction of rotation, with a value of one for clockwise and minus one for counterclockwise rotation. The encoder() function waits for a falling edge on pin A with the if (oldA == HIGH && newA == LOW) instruction. The LED brightness is incremented by the fade amount, which is multiplied by the direction of rotation of the rotary encoder to increase or decrease the LED brightness. Pressing the rotary encoder switch turns the LED off by resetting the LED brightness to zero.

Listing 9-1. Rotary Encoder and LED

```
int CLKpin= A0;                      // pin A or clock pin
int DTpin= A1;                       // pin B or data pin
int SWpin= A2 ;                      // switch pin
int LEDpin = 6;                      // LED on PWM pin
int bright = 120;                    // initial LED value
int fade = 10;                       // amount to change LED
int rotate = 0;                      // number of rotary turns
int oldA = HIGH;                     // status of pin A
int change, result, newA, newB;

void setup()
{
  Serial.begin(9600);               // define Serial output baud rate
  pinMode(LEDpin, OUTPUT);          // LED pin as output
  pinMode(SWpin, INPUT_PULLUP);     // switch pin uses internal pull-up resistor
}

void loop()
{
  if(digitalRead(SWpin) == LOW) bright = 0; // switch, active LOW,
                                            // turns off LED
  change = encoder();               // function for direction of rotation
  rotate = rotate + abs(change);    // number of turns of rotary encoder
  bright = bright + change*fade;    // change LED brightness
  bright = constrain(bright, 0, 255);   // constrain LED brightness
```

```
  if(change != 0)
  {                                        // display number
    Serial.print(rotate);Serial.print("\t");   // of rotary turns
    Serial.println(bright);         // and LED brightness
  }
  analogWrite(LEDpin, bright);     // update LED brightness
}
int encoder()                      // function to determine direction
{
  result = 0;
  newA = digitalRead(CLKpin);      // state of (CLK) pin A
  newB = digitalRead(DTpin);       // state of (DT) pin B
                                   // falling edge on (CLK) pin A
  if (oldA == HIGH && newA == LOW) result = 2*newB - 1;
  oldA = newA;                     // update state of (CLK) pin A
  return result;
}
```

If the void loop() function contains several tasks or delays, then the microcontroller may miss turns of the rotary encoder by not detecting all the falling edges on pin A or the CLK pin. For example, inserting the delay(100) instruction within the void loop() function is sufficient for the microcontroller to miss turns of the rotary encoder. Implementing an interrupt resolves the problem of the microcontroller not detecting a change in state of a device, when there are several tasks or delays in the void loop() function. The subject of interrupts is discussed in Chapter 20.

Rotary Encoder and Stepper Motor

The rotary encoder can be used to control a stepper motor, which was outlined in Chapter 8. In the sketch (see Listing 9-2 and Table 9-2), the stepper motor first moves to an initial position, and then to a target position determined by the rotary encoder's direction and number of turns. When the stepper motor reaches the target position, the direction of rotation is reversed and the stepper motor moves to the "negative" target position. The rotary encoder switch resets the stepper motor target to zero. The maximum speed of the stepper motor is set at 700 steps per minute, which is equivalent to 20.6 rpm with full-step. An LED is connected to an Arduino PWM pin, so the rotary encoder controls the level of LED brightness in parallel with changes to the stepper motor target.

***Table 9-2.** Connections for Rotary Encoder and Stepper Motor*

Component	Connect to	and to
Stepper blue wire	ULN2003 IN1	Arduino pin 12
Stepper pink wire	ULN2003 IN2	Arduino pin 11
Stepper yellow wire	ULN2003 IN3	Arduino pin 10
Stepper orange wire	ULN2003 IN4	Arduino pin 9
9V battery positive	ULN2003 positive	
9V battery negative	ULN2003 negative	Arduino GND
Rotary encoder CLK	Arduino pin A0	
Rotary encoder DT	Arduino pin A1	
Rotary encoder SW	Arduino pin A2	
Rotary encoder VCC	Arduino 5V	
Rotary encoder GND	Arduino GND	
LED long leg	220Ω resistor	Arduino pin 6
LED short leg	Arduino GND	

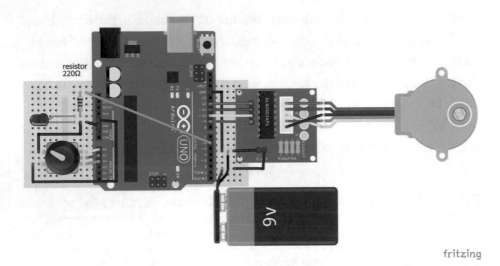

resistor
220Ω

fritzing

Figure 9-4. *Rotary encoder, LED, and stepper motor*

Listing 9-2. Rotary Encoder and Stepper Motor

```
#include <AccelStepper.h>     // include AccelStepper library
int blue = 12;                // coil activation order on ULN2003
int pink = 11;                // blue, pink, yellow, orange
int yellow = 10;
int orange = 9;
int fullstep = 4;             // number of coil activation stages
int halfstep = 8;             // with full-step and half-step
int coil = fullstep;          // set number of coil activation stages
     // associate stepper with AccelStepper library and coil pairing order
AccelStepper stepper(coil, blue, yellow, pink, orange);
int stepperTarget = 500;      // initial position for stepper motor
int stepperChange = 200;      // number of steps to move stepper motor
int CLKpin= A0;               // rotary encoder pin A
int DTpin= A1;                // and pin B
int SWpin= A2 ;               // switch pin
```

```
int rotate = 0;              // number of rotary encoder turns
int oldA = HIGH;             // status of pin A
int direct = 1;              // direction of rotation
int LEDpin = 6;              // LED on PWM pin
int bright = 60;             // initial LED value
int fade = 25;               // amount to change LED
int change, result, newA, newB;

void setup()
{
  Serial.begin(9600);               // define Serial output baud rate
  pinMode(SWpin, INPUT_PULLUP);     // switch pin uses internal pull-up resistor
  stepper.setMaxSpeed(700);         // maximum speed of stepper motor
  stepper.setAcceleration(600);     // acceleration rate (steps/s²)
}

void loop()
{
  if(digitalRead(SWpin) == LOW)
  {
    stepperTarget = 0;       // switch repositions stepper motor
    bright = 0;              // and turns off the LED
  }
  change = encoder();        // determine direction of rotary encoder
  rotate = rotate + abs(change);   // number of rotary encoder turns
                    // move stepper motor to new position
  stepperTarget = stepperTarget + change * stepperChange;
  stepperTarget = constrain(stepperTarget, 0, 2037);   // constrain position
  bright = bright + change*fade;        // change LED brightness
  bright = constrain(bright, 0, 255);  // constrain LED brightness
```

```
if(change != 0)
{
  Serial.print(rotate);Serial.print("\t");  // display rotary turn number
  Serial.print(bright);Serial.print("\t");  // display LED brightness
  Serial.println(stepperTarget);            // and new target position
}
analogWrite(LEDpin, bright);                // update LED brightness
stepper.moveTo(direct*stepperTarget/2);  // move to target position
if (stepper.distanceToGo() == 0) direct=-direct; // reverse direction
stepper.run();                            // move stepper motor
}
int encoder()                            // function to determine direction
{
  result = 0;
  newA = digitalRead(CLKpin);       // state of (CLK) pin A
  newB = digitalRead(DTpin);        // state of (DT) pin B
                                    // falling edge on (CLK) pin A
  if (oldA == HIGH && newA == LOW) result = 2*newB - 1;
  oldA = newA;                      // update state of (CLK) pin A
  return result;
}
```

Summary

The direction and extent of rotation of a rotary encoder is used to control devices, with an LED and a stepper motor as example devices.

Components List

- Arduino Uno and breadboard

- Rotary encoder: KY-040

- Stepper motor: 28BYJ-48

- Stepper motor connecting board with ULN2003 chip

- Battery: 9V

- LED

- Resistor: 220Ω

CHAPTER 10

Infrared Sensor

 Infrared (IR) remote controls operate devices, such as domestic appliances and office machinery, wirelessly by transmitting a signal consisting of pulses of infrared light. When a remote control button is pressed, the infrared sensor receives a signal, which is decoded to implement the appropriate action corresponding to the remote control button. For example, if the "power on" button signal has binary representation B011101, the pulsed infrared signal would be as shown in Figure 10-1. The infrared wavelength is not visible to the human eye, but a remote control signal can be observed when viewed through the camera of a mobile phone.

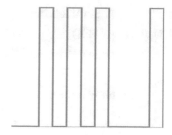

Figure 10-1. *Pulsed signal*

The *IRremote* library by Ken Shirriff is recommended for sketches with an IR sensor. The *IRremote* library is available within the Arduino IDE and is installed using installation method 3, as outlined in Chapter 3. Connections for the IR sensor are given in Table 10-1.

Listing 10-1 reads an infrared signal and displays the hexadecimal signal code associated with each button of an infrared remote control to illustrate use of the VS1838B IR sensor.

Listing 10-1. Infrared Signal

```
#include <IRremote.h>          // include IRremote library
int IRpin = 6;                 // IR sensor pin
IRrecv irrecv(IRpin);          // associate irrecv with IRremote library
decode_results reading;        // IRremote reading

void setup()
{
  Serial.begin(9600);          // set baud rate for Serial Monitor
  irrecv.enableIRIn();         // initialise the IR receiver
}

void loop()
{
  if(irrecv.decode(&reading))  // read the infrared signal
  {
    Serial.print("0x");               // print leading 0x for hexadecimal
    Serial.println(reading.value, HEX); // print HEX code to Serial Monitor
    irrecv.resume();                  // receive the next infrared signal
  }
  delay(1000);                 // delay before next remote control input
}
```

Once the pulsed infrared signals for the buttons have been determined, each button can be associated with a particular function. In the sketch (see Listing 10-2), three buttons are mapped to turning on one of three LEDs (see Figure 10-2). Note that the hexadecimal signal codes are just examples.

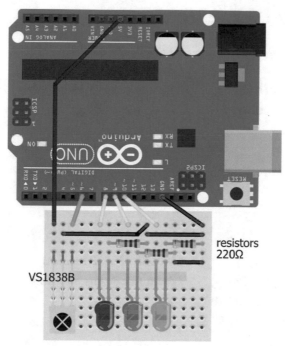

Figure 10-2. *Infrared sensor and LEDs*

Table 10-1. *Connections for IR Sensor and LEDs*

Component	Connect to	and to
IR sensor VCC	Arduino 5V	
IR sensor OUT	Arduino GND	
IR sensor GND	Arduino pin 6	
LED long legs	Arduino pins 8, 9, 10	
LED short legs	220Ω resistors	Arduino GND

191

Listing 10-2. IR Signal and LEDs

```
#include <IRremote.h>        // include IRremote library
int IRpin = 6;               // IR sensor pin
IRrecv irrecv(IRpin);        // associate irrecv with IRremote library
decode_results reading;      // IRremote reading
int redLED = 8;
int amberLED = 9;            // LED pins
int greenLED = 10;
int color;

void setup()
{
  irrecv.enableIRIn();       // initialise the IR receiver
  pinMode(redLED, OUTPUT);   // define LED pins as output
  pinMode(amberLED, OUTPUT);
  pinMode(greenLED, OUTPUT);
}

void loop()
{
  if(irrecv.decode(&reading))   // read the IR signal
  {
    switch(reading.value)       // switch ... case for button signals
    {                           // associate IR codes with LED pins
      case 0xFF30CF: color = redLED; break;
      case 0xFF18E7: color = amberLED; break;
      case 0xFF7A85: color = greenLED; break;
    }
    digitalWrite(color,HIGH);   // turn on and off corresponding LED
    delay(1000);
    digitalWrite(color,LOW);
  }
  irrecv.resume();              // receive the next infrared signal
  delay(1000);                  // delay before next remote control input
}
```

The IR sensor can also be used to display specific text on an LCD, based on a remote control button, with the LCD connected to an I2C bus, as described in Chapter 4. Figure 10-3 is the same as Figure 4-3, with an infrared sensor replacing the temperature sensor, with connections given in Table 10-2. The display string in Listing 10-3 is a combination of text and a number converted to a string using the String(number) function. The infrared signal is displayed in hexadecimal (HEX) or decimal (DEC) format, as an illustration.

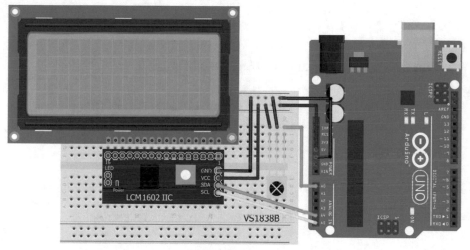

Figure 10-3. Infrared sensor and LCD with I2C bus

Listing 10-3. IR Sensor and Text Display

```
#include <Wire.h>                   // include Wire library
#include <LiquidCrystal_I2C.h>      // include LiquidCrystal_I2C library
#include <IRremote.h>               // include IRremote library
int I2Caddress = 0x3F;              // address of I2C bus
int LCDcol = 16;                    // define the number of LCD columns
int LCDrow = 4;                     // define the number of LCD rows
   // associate lcd with LiquidCrystal_I2C library, define LCD address and size
```

```
LiquidCrystal_I2C lcd(I2Caddress,LCDcol,LCDrow);
int IRpin = A0;              // IR sensor pin
IRrecv irrecv(IRpin);       // associate irrecv with IRremote library
decode_results reading;     // IRremote reading

void setup()
{
  lcd.init();               // initialise LCD
  irrecv.enableIRIn();      // initialise the IR receiver
}

void loop()
{
  if(irrecv.decode(&reading))   // read the IR signal
  {
    translateIR();          // function to map signal to display string
    irrecv.resume();        // receive the next infrared signal
    delay(1000);            // delay before next IR signal
  }
}

void translateIR()          // function to determine display string
{
  switch(reading.value) // switch case rather than a series of if else instructions
  {                         // string equal to text plus elapsed time
    case 0xFF6897: displ("Outcome "+String(millis()/1000)); break;
                            // string equal to signal in hexadecimal
    case 0xFF30CF: displ("Result "+String(reading.value,HEX)); break;
                            // string equal to signal in decimal
    case 0xFF18E7: displ("Event "+String(reading.value,DEC)); break;
    default: displ("Not valid");    // default display
  }
}
```

```
void displ(String s)      // function to display string on LCD
{
  lcd.print(s);      // display string on LCD
  delay(2000);       // delay 2000ms
  lcd.clear();       // clear LCD display and move cursor to zero position
}
```

Table 10-2. *Connections for IR Sensor and LCD with I2C Bus*

Component	Connect to	Component	Connect to
I2C bus GND	Arduino GND	*IR sensor VCC*	Arduino 5V
I2C bus VCC	Arduino 5V	*IR sensor OUT*	Arduino pin A0
I2C bus SDA	Arduino A4	*IR sensor GND*	Arduino GND
I2C bus SCL	Arduino A5		

Infrared Emitter and Sensor

Infrared signals can be sent with an IR emitter LED and received by an infrared sensor, VS1838B, exactly as if the IR signal was generated by a remote control device. The IR emitter LED must be connected to Arduino PWM pin 3, when using the *IRremote* library (see Figure 10-4). Note that the top of the IR emitter LED must be facing the IR receiver with no obstruction between the emitter and receiver (see Table 10-3). Information on the signal to be sent, in a Sony format, and the length of the signal is included in the irsend.sendSony(signal, signal length) instruction. The example signal *0xFF30CF* in hexadecimal format has a signal length of 24 bits, given 4 bits per integer. The sketch (see Listing 10-4) uses the sendSony() function as an example format to transmit signals, but other signal formats, such as NEC, JVC, RC5, and RC6, are included in the *IRremote* library. More information on IR codes is available at www.sbprojects.net/knowledge/ir/index.php.

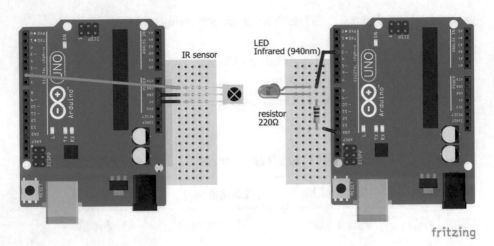

Figure 10-4. *IR emitter and receiver*

Table 10-3. *Connections for IR Emitter and Receiver*

Component	Connect to	and to
IR sensor VCC	Arduino 5V	
IR sensor OUT	Arduino pin 6	
IR sensor GND	Arduino GND	
IR emitter LED long leg	Arduino pin 3	
IR emitter LED short leg	220Ω resistor	Arduino GND

The sketch for the IR transmitter to accompany the IR receiver (see Listing 10-4) uses either the first sketch of the chapter (see Listing 10-1) or the infrared receiver VS1838B sketch (see Listing 3-10) in Chapter 3. Note that the hexadecimal signal codes are just examples.

Listing 10-4. IR Transmitter

```
#include <IRremote.h>        // include IRremote library
long signal[ ] = {0xFF6897, 0xFF30CF, 0xFF18E7, 0xFF7A85, 0xFF10EF};
IRsend irsend;                   // associate irsend with IRremote library
```

```
void setup()                    // nothing in void setup function
{}

void loop()
{
  for (int i=0; i<5; i++)   // transmit each of the five signals
  {
    irsend.sendSony(signal[i], 24);  // transmit signal with 24 bit length
    delay(1000);                     // delay 1s between signals
  }
}
```

Infrared Emitter and Receiver

 Infrared distance sensor modules contain an infrared emitter and receiver (see Figure 10-5), as well as signal processing circuits, such as the TCRT500 module that was outlined in Chapter 3. The infrared emitter is an LED that emits an infrared signal with a wavelength of 980nm and the infrared receiver is a photo-diode. Specific distance sensor modules can measure distances between 10cm and 80cm, while the IR emitter and receiver pair form a simple distance measure for distances between 10cm to 40cm. The IR receiver has a black casing to block visible light, while the IR emitter has a clear casing. The long legs of the IR emitter and receiver are the anodes and the flat side is on the cathode side, as with an LED. Note the cathode of the IR receiver is connected to 5V, as a reverse-biased photodiode conducts with incident light, while a forward-biased LED emits light. The 10kΩ resistor connected to the IR receiver functions as a pull-down resistor, as the IR receiver or photo diode does not conduct when no infrared light is detected (see Table 10-4).

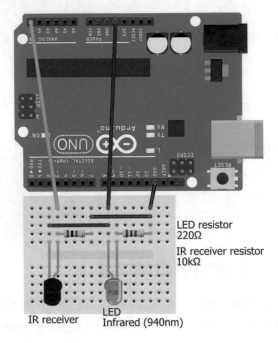

fritzing

Figure 10-5. IR emitter and receiver

The output voltage from the IR receiver is converted by the Arduino ADC to a digital reading. When the tops of the IR emitter and receiver are facing, the IR receiver reading can provide an estimate of the distance between them, with the IR receiver reading increasing, non-linearly, from 0 to 1000 with decreasing distance (see Figure 10-6). If the IR emitter and receiver are positioned close together and parallel, then the IR emitter signal bounces off the target object onto the IR receiver and the IR receiver reading is a measure of the double the distance to a target object.

Note that in Listing 10-5, the equations for converting the digital reading to a distance are empirically derived for an IR emitter and receiver pair. Different equations may be required for an IR emitter and receiver pair from other manufacturers.

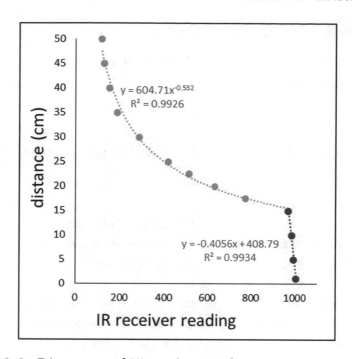

Figure 10-6. *Distance and IR receiver readings*

Table 10-4. *Connections for IR Emitter and Receiver*

Component	Connect to	and to
IR receiver short leg	Arduino 5V	
IR receiver long leg	Arduino A5	
IR receiver long leg	10kΩ resistor	Arduino GND
IR emitter LED long leg	Arduino 5V	
IR emitter LED short leg	220Ω resistor	Arduino GND

Listing 10-5. IR Emitter and Receiver

```
int IRpin = A5;                    // IR receiver pin
int reading, dist;

void setup()
{
  Serial.begin(9600);             // set Serial Monitor baud rate
}

void loop()
{                                  // reading from IR receiver
  reading = analogRead(IRpin);    // convert reading to distance
  if (reading < 970) dist = 605*pow(reading, -0.53);
  else dist = 409 - 0.406 * reading;
  Serial.print(reading);Serial.print("\t");   // print reading, tab and
  Serial.println(dist);           // distance to Serial Monitor
  delay(100);                     // delay between readings
}
```

The IR emitter and receiver pair can be used to detect an object moving between the IR emitter and receiver, as a moving object results in a change to the IR receiver reading. IR receiver modules for remote control systems, such as the TSOP382 contain a photo-detector and an amplifier with operational distances of 45m when powered with just 5V. The change in an IR receiver signal can trigger an alarm, which is how some movement detectors function.

Summary

An infrared sensor detected infrared signals from a remote control, displayed the corresponding signal codes on an LCD, controlled LEDs, and displayed text according to the transmitted signals. An infrared emitter LED and infrared sensor were used to transmit and receive infrared signals. An infrared emitter LED and receiver pair formed a motion detector by measuring the distance between the emitter and receiver.

Components List

- Arduino Uno and breadboard

- Infrared sensor: VS1838B

- Infrared remote control

- Infrared emitter LED

- Infrared receiver

- LCD display: 16×4

- I2C bus for LCD display

- Resistors: 2× 220Ω and 1×10kΩ

- LED: 3×

CHAPTER 11

Radio Frequency Identification

 Radio frequency identification, RFID, uses electromagnetic fields to transfer data wirelessly. Common uses of RFID are entry passes to secure sites, library book logging, or tracking component parts in a production process. Passive RFID tags consist only of an antenna and a microchip, whose shadow can be seen by holding an RFID card up to a light. Passive RFID tags are powered by the RFID reader's electromagnetic field to receive messages from the RFID reader and transmit messages to the RFID reader.

The MFRC522 RFID reader operates at a frequency of 13.56MHz and reads MIFARE Classic contactless cards and tags, which have to be within 2cm of the RFID reader to be read. The 1kB card has 1024 bytes of data storage, with 16 sectors of four blocks, each containing 16 bytes of data. The block structure is 6 bytes for data or Key A, and 4 access bytes and 6 bytes for data or Key B. The 4kB card has 4096 bytes of data storage, with 32 sectors of 4 blocks, and 8 sectors of 16 blocks, each containing 16 bytes of data. The first block of a 1kB or 4kB card contains the following:

- Unique Identifier (UID): stored in 4 bytes of block 0

- Select Acknowledge (SAK) HEX code: 08 and 18 for MIFARE Classic

- Proximity Integrated Circuit Card (PICC) type: MIFARE 1K or 4K

N. Cameron, *Arduino Applied*, https://doi.org/10.1007/978-1-4842-3960-5_11

The MFRC522 RFID reader uses the Serial Peripheral Interface bus (SPI) for communication. SPI has a master-slave framework, requiring the three lines: master-out slave-in (MOSI), master-in slave-out (MISO), and serial clock (SCK), with a separate slave select (SS) line for each device (see Figure 11-1). The terminology is, unfortunately, the current convention.

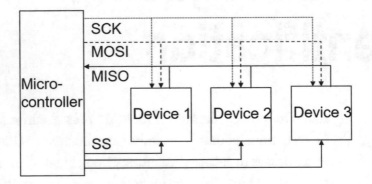

Figure 11-1. *SPI layout*

All devices share the MOSI, MISO, and SCK lines, but the SS line determines which device communicates with the microcontroller. The Arduino SPI pins are 10, 11, 12, and 13 for SS, MOSI, MISO, and SCK. Other Arduino pins can be used as the SS line, when there is more than one SPI device. The SS pin on the MFRC522 RFID reader is marked SDA, for serial data, and the interrupt pin (IRQ) is not connected to the Arduino. The MFRC522 RFID reader must be connected to 3.3V and not to 5V.

For comparison with SPI, the layout of the I2C bus, outlined in Chapter 4, uses the two bidirectional lines, SCK and SDA (see Figure 11-2). The microcontroller communicates with all devices, but the message includes the address of the device to be communicated with, so that only the relevant device responds to the microcontroller. I2C communication is slower than SPI communication, as the lines are bi-directional. I2C is used when outputting low amounts of data, such as with sensors, while SPI communication is used for high volumes of data.

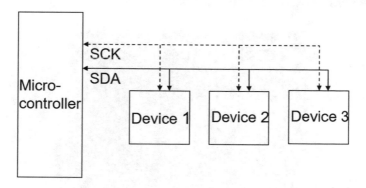

Figure 11-2. *I2C layout*

There are differences between SPI modules in the naming of module pins, such as CS or SS or LOAD, MOSI or DATA or DIN, and SCK or CLK. In sketches with SPI modules, the SPI pin naming of the module is used in the sketch.

The *MFRC522* library by Miguel Balbao is recommended for sketches with RFID. The *MFRC522* library is installed within the Arduino IDE, using installation method 3, as outlined in Chapter 3.

Display Content of MIFARE Classic 1K and 4K

Connections for the MFRC522 RFID reader (see Figure 11-3) are shown in Table 11-1. A sketch (see Listing 11-1) to display the content of a MIFARE Classic 1K or 4K RFID contactless card requires only the mfrc522.PICC_DumpToSerial(&(mfrc522.uid)) instruction. The rest of the sketch defines the pin connections to the Arduino, initializes hardware, and waits for the contactless card to be presented to the RFID reader. The mfrc522.PICC_IsNewCardPresent() and mfrc522.PICC_ReadCardSerial() instructions determine if a contactless card has been presented and read by the RFID reader.

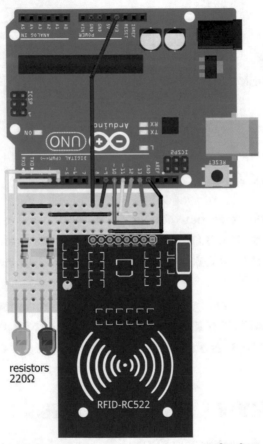

Figure 11-3. *RFID card reader*

Table 11-1. *Connections for RFID Card Reader*

Component	Connect to	and to
RFID reader 3.3V	Arduino 3.3V	
RFID reader RST	Arduino pin 9	
RFID reader GND	Arduino GND	
RFID reader IRQ	not connected	
RFID reader MISO	Arduino pin 12	
RFID reader MOSI	Arduino pin 11	
RFID reader SCK	Arduino pin 13	
RFID reader SDA	Arduino pin 10	
LED long legs	Arduino pins 3, 4	
LED short legs	220Ω resistors	Arduino GND

Listing 11-1. Content of MIFARE Contactless Card

```
#include <SPI.h>                      // include SPI library
#include <MFRC522.h>                  // include MFRC522 library
int RSTpin = 9;                       // reset pin for MFRC522
int SDApin = 10;                      // serial data pin
MFRC522 mfrc522(SDApin, RSTpin);      // associate mfrc522 with MFRC522 library

void setup()
{
  Serial.begin(9600);                 // Serial output at 9600 baud
  SPI.begin();                        // initialise SPI bus
  mfrc522.PCD_Init();                 // initialise card reader
}
```

```
void loop()
{
  if(!mfrc522.PICC_IsNewCardPresent()>0) return;    // wait for a new card
  if(!mfrc522.PICC_ReadCardSerial()>0) return;      // read card content
  mfrc522.PICC_DumpToSerial(&(mfrc522.uid));        // print to Serial Monitor
}
```

Mimic RFID and Secure Site

To mimic use of RFID for accessing a secure site, Listing 11-2 identifies which contactless cards are valid or are not valid and turns on a green LED or a red LED accordingly. Rather than turning on an LED, the rotor of a servo motor can be rotated to open a lock, when simulating use of RFID in a security scenario. The sketch uses two functions, cardID() and cardResult(), to read the card UID from the buffer one character at a time and to print on the serial monitor if the card is valid or invalid.

As with Listing 11-1, much of the sketch (see Listing 11-2) declares variables and prints to the serial monitor. The details of the *MFRC522* library instructions, such as mfrc522.PICC_GetType(mfrc522.uid.sak), were obtained from *MFRC522>Examples* in the *MFRC522* library within the Arduino IDE.

Listing 11-2. RFID for Accessing a Secure Site

```
#include <SPI.h>                        // include SPI library
#include <MFRC522.h>                    // include MFRC522 library
int RSTpin = 9;                         // reset pin for MFRC522
int SDApin = 10;                        // serial data pin
MFRC522 mfrc522(SDApin, RSTpin);        // associate mfrc522 with MFRC522 library
int redLED = 4;                         // red LED pin
int greenLED = 3;                       // green LED pin
```

```
int nuid = 1;                          // number of valid cards
String uids[20];                       // list of valid UIDs – maximum 20
String uid;
int cardOK, pin, piccType;
int cardRead;                          // ** for add/delete card Listing 11-3

void setup()
{
  Serial.begin(9600);                  // define Serial output baud rate
  SPI.begin();                         // initialise SPI bus
  mfrc522.PCD_Init();                  // initialise MFRC522
  pinMode (redLED, OUTPUT);            // define LED pins as output
  pinMode (greenLED, OUTPUT);
  uids[0] = "c049275";                 // UIDs of valid cards
}

void loop()
{
  if(!mfrc522.PICC_IsNewCardPresent()>0) return; // wait for a new card
  if(!mfrc522.PICC_ReadCardSerial()>0) return; // read new card content
  cardID(mfrc522.uid.uidByte, mfrc522.uid.size); // function to
                                               // read card UID
  Serial.print("\nCard UID\t");        // print "card UID" and a tab
  Serial.println(uid);                 // print card UID
  piccType = mfrc522.PICC_GetType(mfrc522.uid.sak); // card PICC type
  Serial.print("PICC type\t");         // print PICC type
  Serial.println(mfrc522.PICC_GetTypeName(piccType)); // card SAK code
  Serial.print("SAK code\t");          // print "SAK code" and a tab
  Serial.println(mfrc522.uid.sak);     // print SAK HEX code
  cardOK = 0;
  pin = redLED;
```

```
for (int i=0; i<nuid; i++)
{
  if(uid == uids[i])          // check if card on valid list
  {
    cardOK = 1;
    pin = greenLED;           // set relevant LED pin
  }
}                             // function to turn on LED and print SAK
cardResult(mfrc522.uid.uidByte, mfrc522.uid.size);
                              // *** INSERT Listing 11-3 HERE
}

void cardID(byte * buffer, byte bufferSize) // function to read card UID
{
  uid="";                              // increment uid with buffer
  for (int i=0; i<bufferSize; i++) uid=uid+String(buffer[i], HEX);
}

void cardResult(byte * buffer, byte bufferSize)
{                                      // function to turn on LED, print SAK
  digitalWrite(pin, HIGH);            // turn on and off relevant LED
  delay(1000);
  digitalWrite(pin, LOW);
  for (int i = 0; i < bufferSize; i++) // print to Serial Monitor SAK code
  {                                              // with leading "0" for
    if(buffer[i] <16) Serial.print("0"); // HEX values
    else Serial.print(" ");
    Serial.print(buffer[i], HEX);
  }                                              // print message to
  if (cardOK == 1) Serial.println("\tValid"); // Serial Monitor
  else Serial.println("\tInvalid");    // depending on card validity
}
```

Master Card Validation

In a contactless card security system, new cards must be defined as valid and old cards must be classed as invalid. Listing 11-3 is incorporated within Listing 11-2 to include the facility to update the list of validated cards. A master card is used to validate a card or to remove a card from the set of validated cards. The master card is the first card in the uid[ ] array. When the master card is detected, the UID of the next card read is checked against the list of valid cards and is added to the list, if not currently on the list, or deleted from the list, if currently on the list. The set of instructions in Listing 11-3 is inserted as the penultimate line of the void loop() function in Listing 11-2. An additional function, readUID() in Listing 11-4, is required to determine if the card has been read or not, is included at the end of the sketch.

Listing 11-3. Inclusion of Master Card

```
if(uid -= uids[0])                // read card is the master card
{
  Serial.println("\nMaster card"); // print "Master card" on a new line
  digitalWrite(redLED, HIGH);     // turn on the red and green LEDs
  digitalWrite(greenLED, HIGH);
  delay(1000);
  digitalWrite(redLED, LOW);      // turn off the red and green LEDS
  digitalWrite(greenLED, LOW);
  Serial.println("Scan card to be deleted or added"); // print message
  int cardRead=0;
  while(!cardRead >0)             // wait for a card to be read
  {
    cardRead = readUID();         // function to detect card
    if(cardRead == 1)             // card detected
```

```
  {
    cardID(mfrc522.uid.uidByte, mfrc522.uid.size); // read card UID
    cardOK = 0;
    for (int i=0; i<nuid; i++) if(uid == uids[i]) cardOK = i;
    if(cardOK !=0)              // card already validated, delete from list
    {
      Serial.print("Card ");    // print to Serial Monitor that card deleted
      Serial.print(uid);        // from validated list
      Serial.println(" deleted");
      uids[cardOK] = "";        // delete card from list of valid cards
    }
    else
    {
      Serial.print("Card ");    // print to Serial Monitor that card added
      Serial.print(uid);        // to validated list
      Serial.println(" added");
      nuid = nuid+1;            // increment valid cards
      uids[nuid-1] = uid;       // add card to list of valid cards
    }
  }
  }
  delay(500);                   // delay so card details are not shown again
}
```

The first two instructions in the readUID() function are the similar to the first two instructions in the void loop() function, with the addition of *0* after return (see Listing 11-4). If a card has not been presented to or read by the card reader, then the readUID() function returns *0* to the main sketch. After the card has been read, the readUID() function returns *1* to the main sketch. The exclamation mark before a variable in the readUID() function denotes the "opposite value," as in *0* and *1* or in *HIGH* and *LOW*. The instruction if(!mfrc522.PICC_IsNewCardPresent()>0) is equivalent to

if(mfrc522.PICC_IsNewCardPresent()<1).

Listing 11-4. Inclusion of Master Card: readUID Function

```
int readUID()
{
  if(!mfrc522.PICC_IsNewCardPresent()>0) return 0;  // wait for a new card
  if(!mfrc522.PICC_ReadCardSerial()>0) return 0;     // read card content
  return 1;
}
```

Read and Write to Classic 1KB Card

The MFRC522 reader can also write to a MIFARE Classic 1K card or tag. Each sector of the card has a sector trailer, which is the fourth block in a sector, containing security and access keys, which should not be over-written. The first three blocks in a sector are for data storage, with the exception of the first block of the first sector, which contains manufacturer data.

The sketch (see Listing 11-5) writes data to a user entered block and then displays the content of the data storage blocks. Again, the majority of the sketch is for declaring variables and printing to the serial monitor. In the sketch, the text *ABCDEFGHIJKLMNOP* is written to the required block as defined in byte blockData[16] and setting blockData[16] to {0,0,0,0 ,0,0,0,0,0,0,0,0,0,0,0,0} restores the block to the default null value.

In the void loop() function, the while() functions are used to wait on a card being presented and to wait for a block number to be entered on the serial monitor. Given that no action is required while waiting, there are no instructions for the while() functions, as indicated in the while(Serial.available() == 0) {} instruction. The block = Serial.parseInt()instruction extracts the block number from the serial buffer, as described in Chapter 4. After a block number is entered, the block number is checked to ensure it is not a sector trailer block. Information in *blockData* is then written to the required block with the writeBlock(block, blockData) function. Then for each block, the data content of the contactless card is read using the readBlock(block, blockRead) function and the card content is displayed on the serial monitor. Finally, communication with the contactless card is closed with the mfrc522.PCD_StopCrypto1() instruction.

The two functions, readBlock() and writeBlock(), have similar structure. Validation checks are made prior to reading or writing to a block with the mfrc522.PCD_Authenticate() function and the MFRC522::STATUS_OK status of the check is returned. The readBlock() function reads data in each block, except for the fourth block in each sector, which is the sector trailer containing security and access keys.

The mfrc522.PICC_DumpMifareClassicSectorToSerial(&(m frc522.uid),&key,sector) instruction reads and displays on the serial monitor all the data within a specified sector, while the mfrc522. PICC_DumpToSerial(&(mfrc522.uid)) instruction reads and displays on the serial monitor all the data on the MIFARE Classic 1K or 4K RFID contactless card.

Listing 11-5. Read and Write to Contactless Card

```
#include <SPI.h>        // include SPI library
#include <MFRC522.h>    // include MFRC522 library
int RSTpin = 9;         // reset pin for MFRC522
int SDApin = 10;        // serial data pin
MFRC522 mfrc522(SDApin, RSTpin);  // associate mfrc522 with MFRC522 library
MFRC522::MIFARE_Key key;          // access key
byte blockData[16] = {"ABCDEFGHIJKLMNOP"};  // data to be written
                                  // reset block to default value
//byte blockData[16] ={0,0,0,0,0,0,0,0,0,0,0,0,0,0,0,0};
byte blockRead[18];               // to hold the read data
byte blocksz = sizeof(blockRead);
int block, sectorTrail, check;
```

```
void setup()
{
  Serial.begin(9600);                    // define Serial output baud rate
  SPI.begin();                           // initialise SPI bus
  mfrc522.PCD_Init();                    // initialise mfrc522
  for (byte i=0; i<6; i++) key.keyByte[i] = 0xFF; // access key set to HEX 0xFF
}

void loop()
{                          // print message to Serial Monitor
  Serial.println("Place card or tag beside MFRC522 reader");
  while (!mfrc522.PICC_IsNewCardPresent())
  {};                      // do nothing but wait for a new card
  mfrc522.PICC_ReadCardSerial();         // read card content
  Serial.println("Enter block number");  // print message
  while(Serial.available() == 0){}       // no action until entry in serial buffer
  while(Serial.available() >0) block = Serial.parseInt(); // get block number
  if((block+1)%4==0 || block == 0)   // check if block is sector trailer block
  {                                        // print message to
    Serial.print("Cannot write to block "); // Serial Monitor
    Serial.println(block);         // return to start of void loop()
    return;
  }
  writeBlock(block, blockData); // function to write data
  Serial.print("\nFinished writing to block ");    // print message
  Serial.println(block);
  for (block=0; block<64; block++)   // display content of non-sector
  {                                  // trailer blocks
    if((block+1) % 4 !=0 && block !=0)  // non-sector trailer blocks
```

```
    {
       readBlock(block, blockRead);        // function to read data
       Serial.print("\nBlock  ");          // print block number
       Serial.print(block);Serial.print("\t");
       for (int i=0 ; i<16 ; i++) Serial.write(blockRead[i]);
    }                                       // print block data
  }
  Serial.println("\n\nFinished reading blocks"); // print message
  Serial.println("Enter 1 to continue writing to a card or tag");
  while(Serial.available() == 0) { }  // no action until entry to serial buffer
                                      // extract integer from serial buffer
  while(Serial.available()>0) check=Serial.parseInt();
  mfrc522.PCD_StopCrypto1();   // stop communication to card or tag
}

void writeBlock (int block, byte blockData[])   // function to write to block
{
  sectorTrail = 3+4*(block/4);
  check = mfrc522.PCD_Authenticate(MFRC522::PICC_CMD_MF_AUTH_KEY_A,
    sectorTrail, &key, &(mfrc522.uid));
  if (check != MFRC522::STATUS_OK)
    Serial.println(mfrc522.GetStatusCodeName(check));
  check = mfrc522.MIFARE_Write(block, blockData, 16);
  if (check != MFRC522::STATUS_OK)
    Serial.println(mfrc522.GetStatusCodeName(check));
}

void readBlock (int block, byte blockRead[])    // function to read block
{
  sectorTrail = 3+4*(block/4);
  check = mfrc522.PCD_Authenticate(MFRC522::PICC_CMD_MF_AUTH_KEY_A,
    sectorTrail, &key, &(mfrc522.uid));
```

```
if (check != MFRC522::STATUS_OK)
   Serial.println(mfrc522.GetStatusCodeName(check));
check =  mfrc522.MIFARE_Read(block, blockRead, &blocksz);
if (check != MFRC522::STATUS_OK)
   Serial.println(mfrc522.GetStatusCodeName(check));
}
```

Summary

The MFRC522 RFID reader was used to read and write to MIFARE contactless cards, with a master card validation process to emulate a security system by adding and deleting contactless cards from a validation list. SPI and I2C communication protocols were compared.

Components List

- Arduino Uno and breadboard
- RFID reader: MFRC522
- MIFARE Classic 1 contactless cards: ×3
- LED: ×2
- Resistor: 2× 220Ω

CHAPTER 12

SD Card Module

GND MISO SCK
VCC MOSI CS

SD (Secure Digital) cards can be used for data storage and data logging. Examples include data storage on digital cameras or mobile phones and data logging to record information from sensors. Micro SD cards can store 2GB of data and should be formatted as FAT32 (File Allocation Table) format. The micro SD card operates at 3.3V, so only micro SD card modules with a 5V to 3.3V voltage level shifter chip and a 3.3V voltage regulator can be connected to the Arduino 5V supply.

The micro SD module communicates with the Arduino using Serial Peripheral Interface (SPI), as outlined in Chapter 11. The SPI connecting pins on the micro SD module include the MOSI, MISO, SCK pins and the SS pin denoted chip select (CS), which are connected to Arduino pins 11, 12, 13, and 10, respectively. Data is stored in a *.csv* file (comma-separated values), which can be directly loaded into Excel. File names must have FAT 8.3 format, with no more than eight characters in the file name followed by a dot and a three-character extension, such as *File1234.csv*. If a *.csv* file is created on the micro SD card with Excel, then Excel should be closed before ejecting the SD card from the computer or laptop.

Alphanumeric data, in a *.csv* file written to an SD card, must be formatted as a string with commas separating each data value. The following instruction concatenates into the *data* string the *light*, *temp*, and *humid* values, separated by commas.

```
data = String(light) + "," + String(temp) + "," + String(humid)
```

N. Cameron, *Arduino Applied*, https://doi.org/10.1007/978-1-4842-3960-5_12

Data is only written to the file on the SD card following the `file.close()` instruction; therefore, every `file.println(data)` instruction must be followed by a `file.close()` instruction and be preceded by an `SD.open("filename", FILE_WRITE)` instruction. The `SD.open()` function has default setting of `FILE_READ`, so the option `FILE_WRITE` is required to write to a file.

The sequence of instructions required every time to write to an SD card is

```
SD.open("filename", FILE_WRITE);
file.println(data);
file.close();
```

Temperature and Light Intensity Logging

Storing temperature and light intensity measurements on a micro SD card illustrates use of the micro SD module (see Figure 12-1). When the light dependent resistor (LDR) and LM35DZ sensors operate separately, the LDR signal has a sinusoidal pattern, while the LM35DZ signal is essentially flat (see Figure 12-2). When the two sensors operate together, there can be interference from the LDR signal on the LM35DZ signal, which can be removed with a bypass capacitor (see Figure 12-2). Electrolytic capacitors are polarized and the cathode, which has a "–" marking and a colored strip on the side, is connected to GND. Connections for Figure 12-1 are given in Table 12-1.

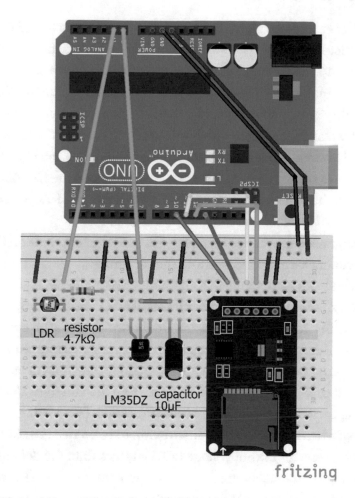

Figure 12-1. *Micro SD card module with sensors*

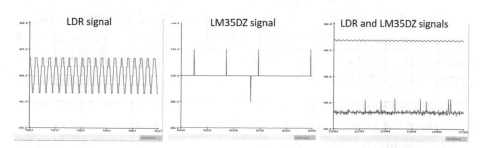

Figure 12-2. *Signals from LDR and LM35DZ sensors*

221

Another example of signal noise is the alternating current (AC) ripple effect, particularly in the 50Hz-60Hz frequency, which is the frequency of domestic AC power supplies. With alternating current, a capacitor's reactance is analogous to a resistor's resistance and is equal to $1/(2\pi fC)$, where f is the signal frequency and C the capacitance. A bypass capacitor has high reactance to signals with low frequency, such as the LM35DZ signal, and low reactance to signals with high frequency, such as the LDR signal. When a bypass capacitor is connected between the LM35DZ signal and ground, the high-frequency noise will go to ground, leaving a clean LM35DZ signal available for the microcontroller.

The required capacitance of the bypass capacitor depends on the lower limit of frequencies to be blocked and the reactance of the capacitor has to be significantly lower than the output impedance of the LM35DZ sensor. The LM35DZ sensor has an output current of 60µA and an output voltage of 200mV with a temperature measurement of 20°C, giving an output impedance of 3.3kΩ. Setting the capacitor's reactance to one tenth of the LM35DZ output impedance (Z), with a frequency threshold of 50Hz, then the required capacitance of 10µF is derived from the equation $C = 1/(2\pi fZ)$.

In Chapter 3, the temperature-recording sketch (see Listing 3-1) used the analogReference(INTERNAL) instruction to reference the LM35DZ temperature sensor's output voltage to 1.1V rather than the default 5V. The output voltage of the light dependent resistor is referenced to 5V, so when the temperature sensor and light dependent resistor are used together, the analogReference(INTERNAL) option is not available.

The sketch (see Listing 12-1) to write measurements of light intensity and temperature to an SD card checks for the presence of the SD card and that the SD card can be written to. Measurement of light intensity with a LDR in conjunction with a voltage divider was described in Chapter 3. The *SD* library is included in the Arduino IDE and is used to write to the micro SD card. In the sketch, the existing file, *data.csv*, is effectively overwritten by first deleting the file and then creating a new file. Later in the chapter, file names are incremented, so that overwriting files is not required.

Table 12-1. *Connections for Micro SD Card Module with Sensors*

Component	Connect to	and to
SD card GND	Arduino GND	
SD card VCC	Arduino 5V	
SD card MISO	Arduino pin 12	
SD card MOSI	Arduino pin 11	
SD card SCK	Arduino pin 13	
SD card SCS	Arduino pin 10	
LDR right	Arduino 5V	
LDR left	Arduino pin A0	
LDR left	4.7kΩ resistor	Arduino GND
LM35DZ GND	Arduino GND	
LM35DZ signal	Arduino pin A1	10µF capacitor positive
LM35DZ VCC	Arduino 5V	
10µF capacitor negative	Arduino GND	

Listing 12-1. Micro SD Card Module With Sensors

```
#include <SPI.h>                        // include SPI library
#include <SD.h>                         // include SD library
File file;                             // associate file with SD library
String filename = "data.csv";          // filename
int CSpin = 10;                        // chip select pin
int lightPin = A0;                     // LDR light intensity pin
int tempPin = A1;                      // temperature sensor pin
int i = 0;                             // data record counter
int light;
float temp;
String data;
```

```
void setup()
{
  Serial.begin(9600);                      // define Serial output baud rate
  Serial.println("checking SD card");   // print message to Serial Monitor
  if(SD.begin(CSpin) == 0)                 // check for presence of SD card
  {
    Serial.println("Card fail");   // return to void setup() if SD card not found
    return;
  }
  Serial.println("Card OK");
  if(SD.exists(filename)>0) SD.remove(filename); // delete existing file
  file = SD.open(filename, FILE_WRITE);      // create new file
  if(file == 1)                              // file opened
  {
    String header = "i, light, temp";   // create column headers
    file.println(header);               // write column header to SD card
    file.close();                       // close file after writing to SD card
  }
  else Serial.println("Couldn't access file");   // file not opened
}

void loop()
{
  i++;                      // increase data record counter
  Serial.print("record ");Serial.println(i);   // print record number
  light = analogRead(lightPin);                 // light reading
  temp = (500.0*analogRead(tempPin))/1023;      // temp reading
                          // referenced to 5V create string from readings
  data = String(i) + "," + String(light) + "," + String(temp);
  file = SD.open(filename, FILE_WRITE);   // open data file before writing
  file.println(data);     // write data string to file
  file.close();           // close file after writing to SD card
  delay(5000);            // delay 5s before next reading
}
```

Information on an SD card can be read and the contents displayed
on the serial monitor. The `Serial.print()` and `Serial.write()`
instructions differ as the former displays the ASCII (American Standard
Code for Information Interchange) code for an alphanumeric character,
while the latter converts the ASCII code to display the alphanumeric
character. In Listing 12-2, `Serial.write()` is used to display the
content of the *data.csv* file.

Listing 12-2. Display Contents Of File

```
#include <SPI.h>              // include SPI library
#include <SD.h>               // include SD library
File file;                    // associate file with SD library
String filename = "data.csv"; // filename
int CSpin = 10;               // chip select pin

void setup()
{
  Serial.begin(9600);         // define Serial output baud rate
  if(SD.begin(CSpin) == 0)    // check for presence of SD card
  {
    Serial.println("Card fail");
    return;                   // return to void setup() if SD card not found
  }
  Serial.println("Card OK");
  file = SD.open(filename);   // open file to read display contents of file
  while (file.available()>0) Serial.write(file.read());
  file.close();               // close file after reading
}

void loop()
{}                            // nothing in void loop() function
```

Date and Time Logging

 The date and time of a sensor measurement or of a data record can be included when writing data to an SD card using a real-time clock (RTC) module, such as the DS3231. The real-time clock can provide seconds, minutes, hours, day, date, month, and year information. The DS3231 can be powered with 3.3V or 5V and a CR2032 lithium button-cell battery powers the RTC when not connected to the Arduino. The DS3231 also has an inbuilt temperature sensor. The DS3231 uses I2C communication with the two bidirectional lines: serial clock (SCL) and serial data (SDA) (see Figure 12-3). Connections for the DS3231 are given in Table 12-2.

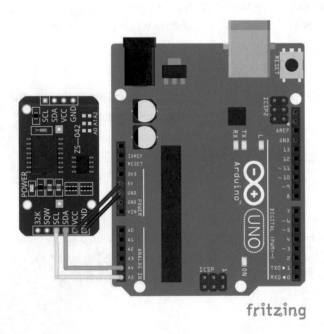

Figure 12-3. *DS3231 real-time clock*

The *DS3231* library by Henning Karsen is recommended, due to the quality of the manual and ease of accessing time components with the *DS3231* library. A *.zip* file containing the *DS3231* library can be downloaded from `www.rinkydinkelectronics.com`. Chapter 3 included details on installing a downloaded library *.zip* file using either installation method 1 or method 2.

When the DS3231 RTC is first used, the date and time must be included and then the sketch is re-run, with the date and time setting instructions commented out, as in Listing 12-3. When setting the time, use the 24-hour time format without leading zeros with uppercase for the weekday. Compiling and loading takes 10 seconds, so set the time forward by 10 seconds. The sketch displays the weekday, date and time, followed by the components of the date and time and then the temperature in Celsius.

Table 12-2. *Connections for Real-Time Clock Module*

Component	Connect to
DS3231 GND	Arduino GND
DS3231 VCC	Arduino 5V
DS3231 SDA	Arduino pin A4
DS3231 SCL	Arduino pin A5

Listing 12-3. Real-time Clock Module

```
#include <DS3231.h>          // include DS3231 library
DS3231 rtc(SDA, SCL);        // associate rtc with DS3231 library
Time t;

void setup()
{
  Serial.begin(9600);        // define Serial output baud rate
  rtc.begin();               // start rtc
```

```
//  rtc.setDOW(WEDNESDAY)       // set weekday
//  rtc.setTime(10, 23, 20);   // set the time to hh mm ss
//  rtc.setDate(22, 8, 2018);   // set the date to dd mm yyyy
}

void loop()
{
  Serial.print(rtc.getDOWStr());Serial.print(" "); // day of week
  Serial.print(rtc.getDateStr());Serial.print(" "); // date
  Serial.print(rtc.getTimeStr());Serial.print("\t"); // time
  t = rtc.getTime();                    // components of date and time
  Serial.print(t.date);Serial.print(" ");  // day
  Serial.print(rtc.getMonthStr());            // month as text
  Serial.print(" (month ");
  Serial.print(t.mon);Serial.print(") ");  // month
  Serial.print(t.year);Serial.print("\t"); // year
  Serial.print(t.hour);Serial.print(":");  // hour
  Serial.print(t.min);Serial.print(":");   // minute
  Serial.print(t.sec);Serial.print("\t");  // second
  Serial.print(rtc.getTemp(),1);              // temperature to 1DP
  Serial.println(" C");
  delay (1000);
}
```

Logging Weather Station Data

Listing 12-3 extends Listing 12-1, which stored temperature and light intensity measurements on an SD card, by including humidity measurements and recording the date and time of measurement (see Figure 12-4 and Table 12-3).

The sketch has four phases: (1) load libraries for the SD card, the real-time clock (RTC), and the DHT11 sensor; define the Arduino connection pins; initialize the real-time clock and DHT11 sensor; and define variables (2) check the presence of the SD card; create a new *data.csv* file; and write a header to the file (3) read the light intensity, temperature, and humidity sensors; get the date and time components from the real-time clock; create a data string of the date and time and the sensor measurements to be written to the data file and (4) write data to the file on the SD card.

There are several libraries for the DHT11 sensor and the *dht* library (DHTlib) by Rob Tilllaart is recommended. The *dht* library is contained within a *.zip* file available at `https://github.com/RobTillaart/Arduino`. Use installation method 1 or method 2 to install the *dht* library, as outlined in Chapter 3.

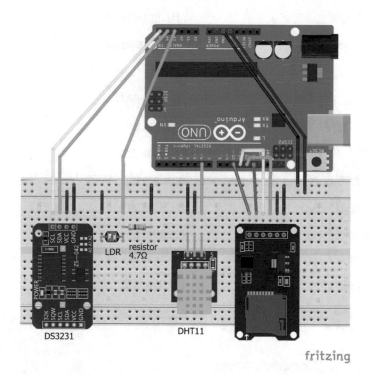

Figure 12-4. *SD card, RTC with sensors*

Table 12-3. *Connections for SD Card, RTC with Sensors*

Component	Connect to
DS3231 GND	Arduino GND
DS3231 VCC	Arduino VCC
DS3231 SDA	Arduino pin A4
DS3231 SCL	Arduino pin A5
LDR left	Arduino 5V
LDR right	Arduino pin A3
LDR right	4.7kΩ resistor
4.7kΩ resistor	Arduino GND
PCB DHT11 GND	Arduino GND
PCB DHT11 VCC	Arduino 5V
PCB DHT11 OUT	Arduino pin 6
SD card SCS	Arduino pin 10
SD card SCK	Arduino pin 13
SD card MOSI	Arduino pin 11
SD card MISO	Arduino pin 12
SD card VCC	Arduino 5V
SD card GND	Arduino GND

Listing 12-4. Weather Station

```
#include <SD.h>                      // include SD library
File file;                          // associate file with SD library
String filename = "data.csv";       // filename
#include <DS3231.h>                 // include DS3231 library
```

```
DS3231 rtc(SDA, SCL);        // associate rtc with DS3231 library
#include <dht.h>             // include dht library
dht DHT;                     // associate DHT with dht library
int CSpin = 10;              // chip select pin for SD card
int lightPin = A3;           // light dependent resistor pin
int PCBpin = 6;              // PCB mounted DHT11 pin
int i = 0;                   // data record counter
int check, light, temp, humid;
String data, date, time;

void setup()
{
  Serial.begin(9600);        // define Serial output baud rate
  rtc.begin();               // start rtc
  Serial.println("checking SD card"); // check for presence of SD card
  if(SD.begin(CSpin) == 0)
  {
    Serial.println("Card fail");   // return to void setup() if SD card not found
    return;
  }
  Serial.println("Card OK");
  if(SD.exists(filename)>0) SD.remove(filename);    // delete old file
  file = SD.open(filename, FILE_WRITE);             // create new file
  if(file == 1)
  {                              // column headers
    String header = "record, time, light, temp, humid, on ";
    header = header + String(rtc.getDateStr());        // date
    file.println(header);    // write column headers to file
    file.close();            // close file after writing to SD card
  }
  else Serial.println("Couldn't access file");   // file not opened
}
```

```
void loop()
{
  i++;                            // increase data record counter
  Serial.print("record ");Serial.println(i);  // print record number
  light= analogRead(lightPin);    // light intensity reading
  check = DHT.read11(PCBpin);
  temp = DHT.temperature;         // temperature reading
  humid = DHT.humidity;           // humidity reading
  time = rtc.getTimeStr();        // time stamp
                                  // combine measurements into a string
  data = String(i) + "," + String(time) + "," + String(light);
  data = data + "," + String(temp)+ "," + String(humid);
  file = SD.open(filename, FILE_WRITE);   // open data file before writing
  file.println(data);             // write data string to file
  file.close();                   // close file after writing to SD card
  delay(1000);                    // delay 1s before next reading
}
```

Increment File Name for Data Logging

A file name for writing data to an SD card can be incremented within a sketch to create a new file, rather than deleting the existing file. For example, a new file *data4.csv* is created if the file *data3.csv* already exists. Listing 12-5 illustrates incrementing the file name and then writing to the new file on the SD card. In the sketch, the base file name is *data.csv*, which is incremented to *data1.csv, data2.csv*, and so forth, with the following instruction.

```
filename = basefile + String(filecount) + ".csv"
```

filecount increments the file name.

Listing 12-5. Incrementing File Name

```
#include <SPI.h>                // include SPI library
#include <SD.h>                 // include SD library
File file;                      // associate file with SD library
```

```
int CSpin = 10;                   // chip select pin for SD card
String filename;
String basefile = "data";    // default filename is data.csv
bool filefound = false;
int filecount = 0;                // for incrementing filename
int count = 0;
String data;                      // data to write to SD card

void setup()
{
  Serial.begin(9600);             // define Serial output baud rate
  if(SD.begin(CSpin) == 0)
  {
    Serial.println("Card fail");    // return to void loop() if SD card not found
    return;
  }
  Serial.println("Card OK");
  filename=basefile + ".csv";      // generate filename
  while (filefound == 0)           // search for file with filename
  {
    if(SD.exists(filename)>0)      // if filename exists on SD card,
    {                              // then increment filename counter
      filecount++;                 // generate new filename
      filename = basefile + String(filecount) + ".csv";
    }
    else filefound = true; // flag file with filename located on SD card
  }
  file = SD.open(filename, FILE_WRITE);    // open file on SD card
  if(file == 1)
  {
    Serial.print(filename);Serial.println(" created");
    data = "Count";                // column header
```

233

```
    file.println(data);            // write column header to file
    file.close();                  // close file after writing to SD card
  }
  else Serial.println("Couldn't access file"); // file not opened
}

void loop()
{
  count = count + 1;              // incremental counter
  data = String(count);           // convert counter to string
  File file = SD.open(filename, FILE_WRITE); // open file on SD card
  if(file == 1) file.println(data);    // write data string to file on SD card
  file.close();                   // close file on SD card
  delay(1000);                    // delay 1s before next count
}
```

Listing Files on an SD Card

Details of the file names and sizes, in bytes, on an SD card are displayed
with Listing 12-6. The list() function checks if a file is a directory and
displays the directory name, and if the file is not a directory, then details of
the files within the directory are displayed.

Listing 12-6. Display Contents of SD Card

```
#include <SPI.h>              // include SPI library
#include <SD.h>               // include SD library
File file;                    // associate file with SD library
int CSpin = 10;               // chip select pin

void setup()
{
  Serial.begin(9600);         // define Serial output baud rate
```

```
  if(SD.begin(CSpin) == 0)  // check for presence of SD card
  {
    Serial.println("Card fail");   // return to void setup() if SD card not found
    return;
  }
  Serial.println("Card OK");
  file = SD.open("/");              // open SD directory of file information
  list(file, 0);                    // function to display file information
}

void loop()                         // nothing in void loop() function
{}

void list(File direct, int nfiles)  // function to display file information
{
  while (1)                         // list function only runs once
  {
    File entry = direct.openNextFile();  // next file in directory
    if (entry == 0) break;                // stop at end of directory
    if (entry.isDirectory())              // check is file is a directory
    {
      Serial.print(entry.name());         // display directory name
      Serial.println("\tis a directory");
      list(entry, nfiles+1);      // only list details of files
    }
    else
    {
      Serial.print(entry.name());Serial.print("\t"); // display file name
      Serial.println(entry.size());       // display file size (bytes)
    }
    entry.close();
  }
}
```

Summary

Data from a real-time clock module and sensors was written to an SD card for date-stamped data logging. File names were automatically incremented rather than overwriting files. The content of a given file and information on the file structure of the SD card were displayed.

Components List

- Arduino Uno and breadboard

- Micro SD card module

- Real-time clock module: DS3231

- Temperature sensors: LM35DZ and DHT11

- Light dependent resistor (or photoresistor)

- Resistor: 4.7kΩ

- Capacitor: 10µF

CHAPTER 13

Screen Displays

 Displaying information on the serial monitor has limitations on mobility with the Arduino connected to a computer screen, and the LCD screen displays only 16×4 characters and does not display images. The TFT (thin-film transistor) LCD screen offers both mobility and flexibility in a display.

TFT LCD Screen

The ST7735 1.8-inch TFT LCD screen with resolution 160×128 pixels used in this chapter has an SD card module for reading files to display.

The two rows of pins on the ST7735 are connections to the TFT LCD screen, eight pins, and to an SD card, four pins (see Figure 13-1 and Table 13-1). The ST7735 display screen communicates with the Arduino using the Serial Peripheral Interface (SPI), as outlined in Chapter 11.

© Neil Cameron 2019

N. Cameron, *Arduino Applied*, https://doi.org/10.1007/978-1-4842-3960-5_13

SPI requires the three lines: MOSI, MISO, and serial clock (SCK). The TFT
LCD screen does not use MISO, as the TFT LCD screen does not transmit
to the Arduino. The SD card module also uses MOSI, MISO, and SCK, as
information from the SD card can be transmitted to the Arduino to display
an image on the TFT LCD screen. MOSI, MISO, and SCK connections are
to Arduino pins 11, 12, and 13, with the SD card module CS connection
generally to Arduino pin 10. In Chapter 19, Arduino pin 8 must be used
for GPS transmission, so the ST7735 TFT CS, RESET, and DC (data or
instruction) pins are connected to Arduino pins 6, 7, and 9, respectively.
Note that the ST7735 A0 pin does not refer to Arduino analog pin A0.

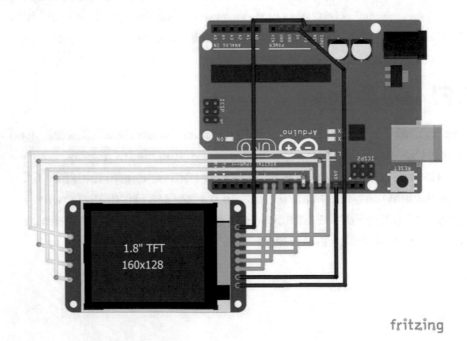

Figure 13-1. *ST7735 TFT LCD screen*

Table 13-1. *Connections for the ST7735 TFT LCD Screen with an SD Card Module*

TFT screen	VCC	GND	TFT CS	RESET	DC or A0	MOSI or SDA	SCK	LED
Arduino pin	5V	GND	6	7	9	11	13	3.3V
SD card	**SD CS**	**MOSI**	**MISO**	**SCK**				
Arduino pin	10	11	12	13				

Connection of the TFT LCD screen VCC pin to Arduino 5V is only required when the SD card module is required, as the TFT LCD screen LED connection to Arduino 3.3V is sufficient for the ST7735 TFT LCD screen.

Two libraries: *Adafruit ST7735* and *Adafruit GFX* must be installed using the Arduino IDE, as outlined in Chapter 3 using installation method 3. When using example sketches from the *Adafruit ST7735* library, pin connections for ST7735 TFT CS, RESET, and DC pins should be changed from Arduino pins 10, 9, and 8 to Arduino pins 6, 7, and 9, respectively.

The ST7735 1.8-inch TFT LCD screen has 160 rows and 128 columns of pixels. The top-left corner of the screen is position (0,0). The cursor is moved to position (x, y) by the setCursor(x, y) instruction. The default font size is 5×8 pixels per character, which can be increased to 5N×8N with the setTextSize(N) instruction for N equal to 1, 2, 3, and so forth. Text color is defined as setTextColor(color), where *color* is the HEX code for a color, with default values given in Listing 13-1. Text is printed with the print(text) instruction.

Rectangles are defined by the position of the top-left corner, the width, and the height of the rectangle, with the drawRect(x, y, width, height, color) instruction or fillRect(x, y, width, height, color) instruction when the rectangle is to be filled in.

Circles are defined by the position of the center and radius of the circle, with the drawCircle(x, y, radius, color) instruction and the corresponding fillCircle(x, y, radius, color) instruction to fill-in the circle.

Triangles are defined by the three corner points from left to right, with the drawTriangle(x0, y0, x1, y1, x2, y2, color) instruction or to fill-in the triangle by fillTriangle(x0, y0, x1, y1, x2, y2, color).

A point and line are defined by drawPixel(x, y, color) and drawLine(x0, y0, x1, y1, color), respectively.

The screen orientation can be set as portrait or landscape with the setRotation(N) instruction with values of 0 or 1, respectively, or the values of 2 or 3 to rotate the image by 180° for portrait and landscape, respectively.

The setTextColor(text_color, background_color) instruction ensures that new text overwrites existing text, so it is not necessary to draw a background rectangle over the existing text.

To illustrate positioning the cursor, printing text, and drawing shapes on the ST7735 TFT LCD screen, Listing 13-1 prints the names of colors and draws rectangles, circles, and triangles in each color.

Listing 13-1. Display Shapes and Colors

```
#include <Adafruit_ST7735.h>        // include ST7735 library
#include <Adafruit_GFX.h>           // include GTX library
int TFT_CS = 6;                     // screen chip select pin
int DCpin = 9;                      // screen DC pin
int RSTpin = 7;                     // screen reset pin
                            // associate tft with Adafruit_ST7735 library
Adafruit_ST7735 tft = Adafruit_ST7735(TFT_CS, DCpin, RSTpin);
unsigned int BLACK = 0x0000;
unsigned int BLUE = 0x001F;
unsigned int RED = 0xF800;
unsigned int GREEN = 0x07E0;
unsigned int CYAN = 0x07FF;         // HEX codes for colors
unsigned int MAGENTA = 0xF81F;
unsigned int YELLOW = 0xFFE0;
unsigned int WHITE = 0xFFFF;
unsigned int GREY = 0xC618;
```

```
String texts[ ] =
  {"BLUE","RED","GREEN","CYAN","MAGENTA","YELLOW","WHITE","GREY"};
String text;
unsigned int colors[ ] =
  {BLUE, RED, GREEN, CYAN, MAGENTA, YELLOW, WHITE, GREY};
unsigned int color;

void setup()
{
  tft.initR(INITR_BLACKTAB);          // initialize screen
  tft.fillScreen(BLACK);              // fill screen in black
  tft.drawRect(0,0,128,160,WHITE);    // draw white frame line
  tft.drawRect(1,1,126,158,WHITE);    // and second frame line
  tft.setTextSize(2);                 // set text size
}

void loop()
{
  tft.fillRect(2,2,124,156,BLACK);    // clear screen apart from frame
  for (int i=0; i<8; i++)             // for each color
  {
    color = colors[i];               // set color
    text = texts[i];                 // set text
    tft.setTextColor(color);         // set text color
    tft.setCursor(20, 20 * i + 2);   // position cursor
    tft.print(text);                 // print color name
    delay(250);                      // delay 250ms between colors
  }
  delay(500);
  for (int i=0; i<8; i++)            // for each color
  {
    tft.fillRect(2,2,124,156,BLACK); // clear screen apart from frame
    color = colors[i];
    text = texts[i];
```

```
    tft.setCursor(20,25);              // move cursor position to (20, 25)
    tft.setTextColor(color);           // set text color
    tft.print(text);                   // print color name
    if ((i+1) % 3 == 0)                // draw filled-in triangle
      tft.fillTriangle(20,134,64,55,107,134,color);
                                       // draw open rectangle
    else if ((i+1) % 2 == 0) tft.drawRect(20,55,88,80,color);
    else tft.fillCircle(64,95,39,color);   // draw filled-in circle
    delay(500);
  }
  tft.fillRect(2,2,124,156,BLACK);   // clear screen apart from frame
  tft.drawLine(2,78,125,78,RED);     // draw horizontal line (x₀,y) to (x₁, y)
  tft.drawLine(2,80,125,80,RED);
  tft.drawLine(62,2,62,157,RED);     // draw vertical line (x,y₀) to (x, y₁)
  tft.drawLine(64,2,64,157,RED);
  delay(500);
}
```

Displaying Images from an SD Card

Images stored on an SD card, formatted with file system FAT32, can be displayed on the ST7735 1.8-inch TFT LCD screen, with images saved as 160×128 pixels in Bitmap format of bit depth 24 and the file extension *.bmp*. The ST7735 TFT LCD screen VCC and LED pins are connected to Arduino 5V and 3.3V pins, respectively, to power the SD card module and the LCD screen.

The *spitftbitmap* sketch in the *Adafruit ST7735* library displays, on the ST7735 TFT LCD screen, images stored on an SD card. To retain the same pin connections between the ST7735 TFT LCD screen and the Arduino as in Listing 13-1, the pin numbers of the following lines must be changed:

```
#define TFT_CS 10    // Chip select line for TFT display        change to 6
#define TFT_RST 9    // Reset line for TFT (or see below...)    change to 7
#define TFT_DC 8     // Data/command line for TFT               change to 9
#define SD_CS 4      // Chip select line for SD card            change to 10
```

In the void setup() function of the *spitftbitmap* sketch, after the tft.initR(INITR_BLACKTAB) instruction, add the tft.setRotation(1) instruction for landscape orientation. For each image to be displayed with the file name *image_filename.bmp*, add the following instructions.

```
bmpDraw("image_filename.bmp", 0, 0); // display image_filename.bmp
delay(5000)                          // time delay to view image
```

Screen, Servo Motor, and Ultrasonic Distance Sensor

An HC-SR04 ultrasonic distance sensor can be secured to the top of a servo motor for scanning distances through a 180° arc. The scanned image, which is analogous to a "radar" effect, but using sound waves rather than radio waves, can be displayed on the ST7735 TFT LCD screen (see Figure 13-2), with the green points indicating the positions of two objects perpendicular to each other. Listing 13-2 uses Listing 3-5 for the HC-SR04 ultrasonic distance sensor from Chapter 3, Listing 8-1 for the servo motor from Chapter 8, and Listing 13-1 for the screen from this chapter. The schematic in Figure 13-3 has the ultrasonic distance scanner on a breadboard to illustrate connection to the Arduino, but for the project, the ultrasonic distance scanner is secured to the top of the servo motor. As noted in Chapter 8, the servo motor requires an external power supply. The L4940V5 voltage regulator reduces the external 9V supply to 5V for the servo motor. The ST7735 TFT LCD screen is connected to Arduino 3.3V with the LED connection, as the SD card module is not required (see Table 13-2). Note that the GND connections for all devices must be connected together.

Figure 13-2. *ST7735 TFT screen "radar"*

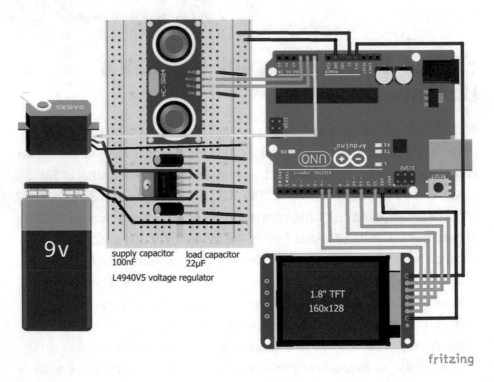

Figure 13-3. *Screen, servo motor, and ultrasonic scanner*

Table 13-2. *Connections for Screen, Servo Motor, and Ultrasonic Scanner*

Component	Connect to	and to
ST7735 TFT GND	Arduino GND	
ST7735 TFT CS	Arduino pin 6	
ST7735 TFT RESET	Arduino pin 7	
ST7735 TFT A0	Arduino pin 9	
ST7735 TFT SDA	Arduino pin 11	
ST7735 TFT SCK	Arduino pin 13	
ST7735 TFT LED	Arduino 3.3V	
HC-SR04 scanner VCC	Arduino 5V	
HC-SR04 scanner Trig	Arduino pin A1	
HC-SR04 scanner Echo	Arduino pin A2	
HC-SR04 scanner GND	Arduino GND	
Servo VCC	L4940V5 output	22µF capacitor positive
Servo GND	Arduino GND	
Servo signal	Arduino pin A0	
9V battery positive	L4940V5 input	100nF capacitor positive
9V battery negative	Arduino GND	
22µF capacitor negative	Arduino GND	
100nF capacitor negative	Arduino GND	

Listing 13-2 sets up the screen image with text and scan arcs in the setup() and radar1() functions, measures the distance to an object in the scan() function, and calculates the scan line and the points indicating an object to draw on the screen in the radar2() function (see Figure 13-2). The majority of the sketch is defining variables and setting up the "radar" screen with instructions for scanning and calculating the scan line only accounting for a small part of the sketch.

The maximum measureable scanning distance, *maxdist*, the incremental change in scan angle, *increment*, and the time interval between scans, *speed*, can be readily changed in the first section of the sketch. The interval between scans should be at least 20ms to allow the servo motor time to move to the new position. Distances displayed in the screen are scaled based on the radius of the large scan arc of the ST7735 TFT LCD screen and the maximum scanning distance.

The scan line from the middle of the bottom of the screen to the end point (x, y) is calculated from the scan angle, θ, and the radius of the scan arc, r. Formula for the horizontal, x, and vertical, y, components of the scan line are given in Figure 13-4. When drawing a scan line on the ST7735 TFT LCD screen, the angle is defined in radians, so the angle, measured in degrees, is converted to radians by the formula: radian = angle$\times\pi$/180. In the sketch, the *PI* variable is predefined in the Arduino IDE with the value of $\pi = 3.14159$. The vertical component of the scan line, *128-y*, moves the end point of the scan line up the screen with increasing distance.

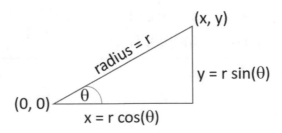

Figure 13-4. *Calculating the scan line*

There are several libraries for the HC-SR04 ultrasonic distance sensor and the *NewPing* library by Tim Eckel is recommended. The *NewPing* library can be installed within the Arduino IDE using installation method 3, as outlined in Chapter 3.

Listing 13-2. Screen, Servo Motor, and Ultrasonic Scanner

```
#include <Adafruit_ST7735.h>      // include the ST7735 library
#include <Adafruit_GFX.h>         // include the GFX library
int TFT_CS = 6;                   // screen chip select pin
int DCpin = 9;                    // screen DC pin
int RSTpin = 7;                   // screen reset pin
                                  // associate tft with Adafruit_ST7735 library
Adafruit_ST7735 tft = Adafruit_ST7735(TFT_CS, DCpin, RSTpin);
#include <NewPing.h>              // include ultrasonic sensor library
int trigPin = A1;                 // ultrasonic sensor pins
int echoPin = A2;
int maxdist = 50;                 // maximum scanning distance in cm
NewPing sonar(trigPin, echoPin, maxdist);  // associate sonar with
                                           // NewPing library
#include <Servo.h>                // include the servo motor library
Servo servo;                      // associate servo with Servo library
int servoPin = A0;                // servo motor pin
float radius = 110.0;             // radius of displayed scan arc
int increment = 3;                // incremental change of scan angle
int speed = 30;                   // interval (ms) between scans
unsigned int BLACK  = 0x0000;
unsigned int YELLOW = 0xFFE0;
unsigned int LITEYEL = 0xFFF5;    // HEX codes for colors
unsigned int GREEN  = 0x07E0;
unsigned int WHITE  = 0xFFFF;
int angle, x, y, distance, duration;
```

```
void setup()
{
  servo.attach(servoPin);              // initialize servo motor
  tft.initR(INITR_BLACKTAB);           // initialize ST7735 TFT LCD screen
  tft.fillScreen(BLACK);               // clear screen
  tft.setRotation(3);                  // orientate ST7735 TFT LCD screen
  tft.setTextColor(WHITE, BLACK);      // text color with over-write
  tft.drawRect(0,0,160,128,WHITE);     // draw white frame line
  tft.drawRect(1,1,158,126,WHITE);     // and second frame line
  tft.setTextSize(1);                  // set text size
  tft.setCursor(3,3);                  // move cursor to position (3, 3)
  tft.print("Distance");               // print text on screen
  tft.setCursor(95,3);
  tft.print("Radius ");
  tft.setCursor(135,3);
  tft.print(maxdist);                   // display value of large arc
}

void loop()
{
  radar1();                   // set up screen with anti-clockwise scan
  for (int angle=10; angle<170; angle=angle+increment) radar2(angle);
  radar1();                   // set up screen with clockwise scan
  for (int angle=170; angle>10; angle=angle-increment) radar2(angle);
}

void radar1()
{
  tft.fillRect(2,12,156,114,BLACK); // clear screen apart from frame
  tft.drawCircle(80,128,radius/2,YELLOW);    // draw arc to assist reading
  tft.drawCircle(80,128,radius,YELLOW);      //image and second arc
}
```

```
void radar2(int angle)
{
  servo.write(angle);                 // move servo motor to angle
  scan();                             // function to measure distance
  delay(speed);                       // interval between scans
  x = radius*cos(angle*PI/180);       // calculate scan line
  y = radius*sin(angle*PI/180);
  tft.drawLine(80,128,80+x,128-y,LITEYEL);   // draw line from baseline to arc
  x = x*distance/maxdist;                     // calculate position of object
  y = y*distance/maxdist;
  tft.fillCircle(80+x,128-y,2,GREEN);   // draw circle when object detected
}

void scan()
{
  duration = sonar.ping();            // duration of echo
  distance = (duration/2)*0.0343;     // distance measured in cm
  char printOut[4];                   // array of characters
  String dist = String(distance);     // convert distance to string
  if(distance<10) dist = " " + dist;  // leading a space for values < 10
  dist.toCharArray(printOut, 4);      // convert string to characters
  tft.setCursor(60,3);                // move cursor
  tft.print(printOut);                // display distance on screen
}
```

OLED Display

 OLED (organic-light emitting diode) displays contain an organic carbon-based film that emits light in response to a current. OLED displays do not require a backlight and are low power devices. OLED displays are used in mobile phones, digital cameras, and laptops. There are many varieties of OLED displays and a 128×32–pixel display based on the SSD1306 chip is used in this chapter. The OLED display logic operates at 3.3V.

The *Adafruit SSD1306* and *Adafruit GFX* libraries are used in this chapter, although there are several libraries for OLED displays. The libraries are installed in the Arduino IDE with installation method 3, as outlined in Chapter 3. The hexadecimal I2C address of the OLED display is required by the microcontroller for communication with the OLED display. With the *Adafruit SSD1306* library, the I2C address is *0x3C* or *0x3D* for 128×32 or 128×64 OLED displays, respectively. Listing 4-3 of Chapter 4, scans for I2C devices and provides the I2C addresses. OLED connections are given in Table 13-3.

If the OLED display has a Reset pin, then the Reset pin is defined as

```
int OLED_RESET = 4;              // OLED reset pin = 4
Adafruit_SSD1306 oled(OLED_RESET);
```

Otherwise, the Reset pin is not defined as in the Adafruit_SSD1306 oled(-1) instruction.

Table 13-3. *Connections for an OLED Screen*

Component	Connect to
OLED GND	Arduino GND
OLED VCC	Arduino3.3V
OLED SCK	Arduino pin A5
OLED SDA	Arduino pin A4

A character and spacing requires 6×8 pixels and a text size of N requires $6N×8N$ pixels, so four, two or one lines of text are possible with text sizes 1, 2, or 4 on a 128×32 pixel OLED display screen.

Listing 13-3 illustrates some OLED display instructions that must be followed with the oled.display() instruction to activate the display instructions.

Listing 13-3. OLED Display

```
#include <Adafruit_GFX.h>        // include Adafruit GFX library
#include <Adafruit_SSD1306.h>    // include Adafruit SSD1306 library
                                 // associate oled with Adafruit_SSD1306 library
Adafruit_SSD1306 oled(-1);       // no need to define Reset pin

void setup()
{
  oled.begin(SSD1306_SWITCHCAPVCC, 0x3C);   // OLED display and I2C address
  oled.clearDisplay();               // clear OLED display
  oled.setTextColor(WHITE);          // set font color
  oled.setTextSize(2);               // set font size (1, 2, 3 or 4)
  oled.setCursor(0,0);               // position cursor at (0, 0)
  oled.println("Arduino");           // print text with carriage return
  oled.print("Applied");             // starting on new line print text
  oled.display();                    // start display instructions
  delay(2000);                       // delay 2s
  oled.clearDisplay();
  oled.setTextSize(1);               // font size 1 characters 6×8 pixels
  oled.setCursor(0,0);
  oled.println("Arduino");
  oled.print("Applied");
  oled.setCursor(45,16);             // position cursor at (x, y)
  oled.print("Arduino");             // at top left hand corner of text
  oled.setCursor(45,24);
  oled.print("Applied");
  oled.display();
  delay(2000);
```

```
  oled.clearDisplay();
  oled.setTextSize(3);      // font size 3 characters 18×24 pixels
  oled.setCursor(0,8);      // maximum of 7 characters per row
  oled.print("1234567");
  oled.display();
}

void loop()                 // nothing in void loop() function
{}
```

Touch Screen

 The 2.4-inch ILI9341 SPI TFT LCD touch screen with 240×320 pixels enables text and shapes to be drawn with different colors on the screen. The ILI9314 TFT LCD screen operates at 3.3V, so an 8-channel or two 4-channel logic level converters should be used to reduce the voltage of the transmitted signal from the Arduino, which operates at 5V (see Figure 13-5 and Table 13-4). Logic level converters were outlined in Chapter 4.

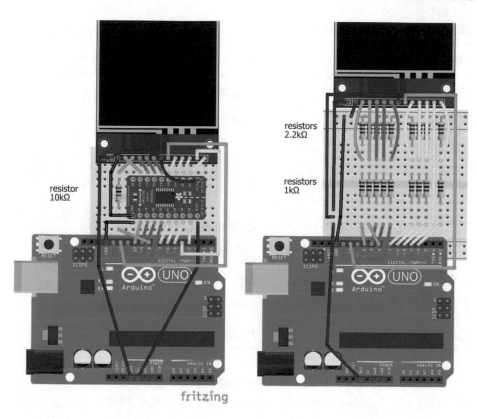

Figure 13-5. *ILI9341 TFT LCD screen with 8-channel logic level converter and voltage dividers*

Table 13-4. *Connections for ILI9341 TFT LCD Screen with Logic Level Converter*

ILI9314 TFT Screen		Connect with	Arduino Uno
VCC	3.3V		3.3V
GND			GND
CS	chip select	logic level	Pin 10
RESET	reset	10kΩ resistor	Pin 8
DC	data command	logic level	Pin 9

(continued)

Table 13-4. (*continued*)

ILI9314 TFT Screen		Connect with	Arduino Uno
MOSI		logic level	Pin 11
SCK	serial clock	logic level	Pin 13
LED			3.3V
MISO			Pin 12
"touch"			
T_CLK	serial clock	logic level	Pin 7
T_CS	chip select	logic level	Pin 6
T_DIN	data input	logic level	Pin 5
T_DO	data output		Pin 4
T_IRQ	interrupt	logic level	Pin 3

An alternative to logic level converters is voltage dividers based on 1kΩ and 2.2kΩ resistors between the Arduino and the ILI9314 TFT LCD screen, with the reduced voltage at the junction between the two resistors (see Figure 13-5). A logic level converter is preferable to a voltage divider, as the signal capacitance and the voltage divider resistors form a resistor-capacitor filter (outlined in Chapter 2) that rounds the edge of the digital signal, which can impact performance of the device receiving the signal.

If 1kΩ and 2.2kΩ resistors are used voltage dividers, then Arduino pins 3, 5 to 11 and 13 are each connected to a 1kΩ resistor, which is connected to a 2.2kΩ resistor, which is connected to GND. The junction between the 1kΩ and 2.2kΩ resistors is connected to the corresponding pin on the ILI9314 TFT LCD screen (see Figure 13-5).

The *Adafruit_ILI9341* and *Adafruit_GFX* libraries are required, which are available from the Arduino IDE and installed using installation method 3, as outlined in Chapter 3. The *URTouch* library by Henning Karlsen is required for the touch functionality, which can be downloaded from www.rinkydinkelectronics.com and installed using installation method 1.

The screen orientation can be set as portrait or landscape with the setRotation(N) instruction with values of 0 or 1, respectively, or the values of 2 or 3 to rotate the image by 180° for portrait and landscape. The setRotation(N) instruction is contained in the *Adafruit_GFX* library, which impacts coordinate referencing by the *URTouch* library, so the (*x*,*y*) coordinates of the touch screen must be transformed, depending on the screen orientation. Table 13-5 shows the transformation of the (*x*,*y*) coordinates for each setRotation(N) setting, with the orientation of the ILI9341 TFT LCD screen relative to the screen pins.

Table 13-5. *ILI9341 TFT LCD Screen Orientation*

		Coordinates		Transformation	
setRotation(N)	Screen Pins	Top-Left	Top-Right	x	y
0	bottom	(320,240)	(320,0)	240 - y	320 - x
1	right	(320,0)	(0,0)	320 - x	y
2	top	(0,0)	(0,240)	y	x
3	left	(0,240)	(320,240)	x	240-y

Listing 13-4 enables drawing on the ILI9341 TFT LCD screen with a palette of colors. The screen is cleared by clicking the bottom-left corner of the screen. The precision options of the *URTouch* library are *PREC_LOW*, *PREC_MEDIUM*, *PREC_HI*, and *PREC_EXTREME*, with the last two taking longer to read, which can impact drawing with a fast-moving cursor.

Color codes available in the *Adafruit ILI9341* library are *BLACK, NAVY, DARKGREEN, DARKCYAN, MAROON, PURPLE, OLIVE, LIGHTGREY, DARKGREY, BLUE, GREEN, CYAN, RED, MAGENTA, YELLOW, WHITE, ORANGE, GREENYELLOW,* and *PINK*. Colors are defined by prefixing with *ILI9341_*, such as *ILI9341_GREEN*, which is more convenient than defining HEX codes for each color, as listed in the *Adafruit_ILI9341.h* file.

After defining variables, the sketch calls the clear() function to clear the screen and display the available colors in the palette, which are selected by touching the screen within a specified region, such as else if(ty>100 && ty<120) color = ILI9341_YELLOW for the yellow color.

When the screen is touched outside the palette area, a point is displayed in the chosen color by the if(tx>20) tft.fillCircle(tx, ty, radius, color) instruction. Note that the coordinates (tx, ty) refer to the transformed coordinates after taking account of the screen orientation, due to the different coordinate referencing of the *Adafruit_GFX* and *URTouch* libraries.

Listing 13-4. Drawing on ILI9341 TFT LCD Screen

```
#include <Adafruit_GFX.h>          // include Adafruit GFX library
#include <Adafruit_ILI9341.h>      // include Adafruit ILI9341 library
#include <URTouch.h>               // include URTouch library
int tftCLK  = 13;                  // clock (SCL)
int tftMISO = 12;                  // MISO (SDA/SDO - serial data output)
int tftMOSI = 11;                  // MOSI  (SDI - serial data input)
int tftCS = 10;
int tftDC = 9;
int tftRST = 8;
              // associate tft with Adafruit ILI9341 library and define pins
Adafruit_ILI9341 tft =
  Adafruit_ILI9341(tftCS, tftDC, tftMOSI, tftCLK, tftRST, tftMISO);
int tsCLK = 7;
int tsCS = 6;
int tsDIN = 5;                      // data input (~MOSI)
int tsDO = 4;                       // data output (~MISO)
int tsIRQ = 3;
URTouch ts(tsCLK, tsCS, tsDIN, tsDO, tsIRQ);// associate ts with
                                            // URTouch library
int radius = 2;                    // radius of "paintbrush"
```

```
int setRot = 3;                          // portrait 0 or 2, landscape = 1 or 3
unsigned int color;
int x, y, tx, ty;

void setup()
{
  tft.begin();                           // initialise TFT LCD screen
  tft.setRotation(setRot);               // set touch screen orientation
  ts.InitTouch();                        // initialise touch screen
  ts.setPrecision(PREC_MEDIUM);          // set touch screen precision
  clear();                               // function to clear screen
}

void loop()
{
  while(ts.dataAvailable())              // when touch screen pressed
  {
    ts.read();                           // read (x,y) co-ordinates
    x = ts.getX();
    y = ts.getY();
    if(x != -1 && y != -1)               // when contact with screen (-1 is no contact)
    {                                    // transform (x,y) co-ordinates
          if(setRot == 0) {tx = 240-y; ty = 320-x;}
      else if(setRot == 1) {tx = 320-x; ty = y;}
      else if(setRot == 2) {tx = y; ty = x;}
      else if(setRot == 3) {tx = x; ty = 240-y;}
      if(tx<20 && tx>0)                  // choose color from palette
      {
            if(ty>75 && ty<95)   color = ILI9341_RED;
        else if(ty>100 && ty<120) color = ILI9341_YELLOW;
        else if(ty>125 && ty<145) color = ILI9341_GREEN;
        else if(ty>150 && ty<170) color = ILI9341_BLUE;
        else if(ty>175 && ty<195) color = ILI9341_WHITE;
```

```
        else if(ty>215) clear();        // clear screen
                                         // display chosen color
        if(ty>75 && ty<195) tft.fillCircle(10, 50, 10, color);
      }                                  // paint color on touch screen
    if(tx>20) tft.fillCircle(tx, ty, radius, color);
  }
 }
}

void clear()
{                      // available colors listed in Adafruit_ILI9341.h
  tft.fillScreen(ILI9341_BLACK);
  tft.setTextColor(ILI9341_GREEN);     // set text color
  tft.setTextSize(2);                  // set text size
  tft.setCursor(110,5);                // position cursor middle-top
  tft.print("Paintpot");
  tft.fillRect(0,75,20,20,ILI9341_RED);   // display color palette
  tft.fillRect(0,100,20,20,ILI9341_YELLOW);
  tft.fillRect(0,125,20,20,ILI9341_GREEN);
  tft.fillRect(0,150,20,20,ILI9341_BLUE);
  tft.fillRect(0,175,20,20,ILI9341_WHITE);
  tft.drawCircle(10,225,10,ILI9341_WHITE); // draw "clear" circle
  tft.setCursor(25,217);
  tft.setTextColor(ILI9341_WHITE);
  tft.print("clear");
  color = ILI9341_WHITE;                    // default color
}
```

Summary

The TFT LCD screen was used to display shapes and digital images stored on an SD card. An ultrasonic distance sensor and servo motor were combined to create a "radar" image of surrounding objects. Images were displayed on an OLED screen, which uses I2C communication. Images were drawn on the SPI TFT LCD touch screen with a screen-pen.

Components List

- Arduino Uno and breadboard

- TFT LCD screen: ST7735 1.8-inch

- OLED display: 128×32pixels or 128×64 pixels

- SPI TFT LCD touch screen: ILI9341 2.4-inch

- Ultrasonic distance sensor: HC-SR04

- Servo motor: SG90

- Voltage regulator: L4940V5

- Battery: 9V

- Logic level converter: 1×8 channel or 2×4 channel

- Capacitors: 0.1µF and 22µF

- Resistor: 1×10kΩ or 9×1kΩ and 9×2.2kΩ

CHAPTER 14

Sensing Colors

A color can be defined as a combination of red, green, and blue components, as shown in Figure 14-1. One byte or 8 bits is used to store each of the red, green, and blue values with $2^8 = 256$ possible values for each of the red (R), green (G), and blue (B) components of the compound color. For example, magenta has a (255, 0, 255) RGB format.

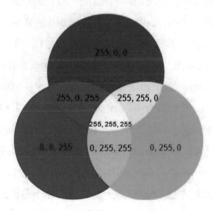

Figure 14-1. *RGB color values*

N. Cameron, *Arduino Applied*, https://doi.org/10.1007/978-1-4842-3960-5_14

Red Green Blue (RGB) LED

Red
Common   Blue
Green

An RGB LED consists of three combined LEDs: a red, a green, and a blue LED. An RGB LED is activated with the analogWrite(pin, value) instruction with *pin* defined as the Arduino pulse width modulation (PWM) pin for the red, green, or blue LEDs and *value* is the light intensity. The RGB LED used in Listing 14-1 has a common cathode, which has the longest leg.

Listing 14-1 defines the RGB combinations for each of 14 colors, ranging from white to navy. For example, the RGB combination for magenta is (255, 0, 255). A color is then randomly selected by the random(14) instruction, for a number between 0 and 13, inclusive. The number of increments, 63, corresponds to step sizes 2 or 4, which minimizes the difference between the pixel value of one color and any other color in the R, G, and B matrices. The magnitude of the incremental change, for each of the RGB components, between the current and new color is the RGB component difference divided by number of increments. The delay() determines the rate of change in color. To best visualize the color change, place a ping-pong ball on top of the RGB LED.

The three instructions at the start of Listing 14-1 detail connections between the Arduino pins and an RGB LED (see Figure 14-2), with the Arduino GND connected the common pin of the RGB LED. A 220Ω resistor is connected between each of the RGB LEDs and the Arduino PWM pins. The RGB LED module includes a 150Ω resistor for each LED, so no additional resistors are required.

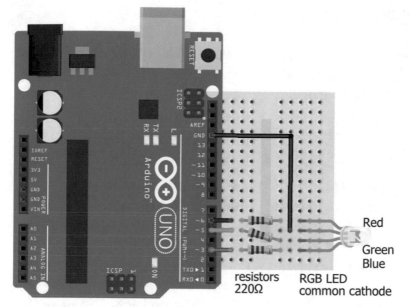

Figure 14-2. *RGB LED*

Listing 14-1. RGB LED

```
int redLED = 6;                 // LEDs on PWM pins
int greenLED = 5;
int blueLED = 3;
int steps = 63;                 // number of increments
int oldR = 0;                   // pixel value difference = 255 or 128
int oldG = 0;                   // so steps of size 4 or 2
int oldB = 0;
int incR, incG, incB;           // incremental changes
String color[ ] =
  {"White","Red","Lime","Blue","Yellow","Cyan","Magenta","Grey",
  "Maroon","Olive","Green","Purple","Teal","Navy"};
int R[] = {255,255, 0, 0,255, 0,255,128,128,128, 0,128, 0, 0};
int G[] = {255, 0,255, 0,255,255, 0,128, 0,128,128, 0,128, 0};
int B[] = {255, 0, 0,255, 0,255,255,128, 0, 0, 0,128,128,128};
```

```
void setup()
{
  pinMode(redLED, OUTPUT);      // define LED pins as output
  pinMode(greenLED, OUTPUT);
  pinMode(blueLED, OUTPUT);
}

void loop()
{
  int i = random(14);          // select next color, between 0 and 13
  incR = (R[i]-oldR)/steps;    // calculate the incremental amount
  incG = (G[i]-oldG)/steps;
  incB = (B[i]-oldB)/steps;
  for (int n = 0; n<steps; n++)  // for each incremental change
  {
    analogWrite(redLED, oldR + n*incR); // change the LED intensity
    analogWrite(greenLED, oldG + n*incG);
    analogWrite(blueLED, oldB + n*incB);
    delay(5000/steps);         // time delay between color increments
  }
  oldR = R[i];                 // update the current color
  oldG = G[i];
  oldB = B[i];
}
```

565 Color Format

Each R, G, and B component has $2^8 = 256$ possible values as a component is stored as an 8 bit number, so the number of possible RGB colors is about 17 million ($= 256^3$). Color liquid crystal display (LCD) screens, such as the ST7735 TFT LCD screen described in Chapter 13, use 16-bit color definition, with the R, G, and B components converted from three 8 bit numbers into a single 16-bit number, resulting in $2^{16} = 65536$ possible colors. The last three bits of the R and B components are dropped, but only the last two bits of the G component are dropped, as the human eye is more sensitive to graduations of green compared to red and blue. The 16-bit number has 5 bits for the red component, 6 bits for the green component, and 5 bits for the blue component—the 565 format.

For example, the pale green color in Figure 14-3 has RGB format of (95, 153, 66). The 8-bit binary representation for the R component of 95 is 01011111. When the last three bits of the R component are dropped, the remaining 5-bit representation is 01011. Similarly, the last three bits of the B component of 01000010 are dropped resulting in the 5-bit binary number of 01000. Only the last two bits of the G component are dropped leaving 100110. When the 5-, 6-, and 5-bit R, G, and B components are combined into a 16-bit number, the combined value is 0101110011001000.

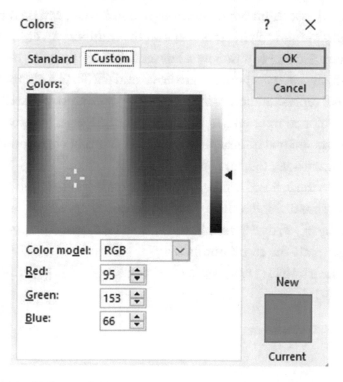

Figure 14-3. *Color palette*

The decimal representation of the 16-bit 565-formatted RGB number is 23752 equal to

$$2^8 \times [(0 \times 2^7) + (1 \times 2^6) + (0 \times 2^5) + (1 \times 2^4) + (1 \times 2^3) + (1 \times 2^2) + (0 \times 2^1) + (0 \times 2^0)]$$
$$+ [(1 \times 2^7) + (1 \times 2^6) + (0 \times 2^5) + (0 \times 2^4) + (1 \times 2^3) + (0 \times 2^2) + (0 \times 2^1) + (0 \times 2^0)]$$
$$= 2^8 \times 92 + 200$$
$$= 2^8 \times [(5 \times 2^4) + 12] + [(12 \times 2^4) + 8]$$

Given that the numbers 10, 11, 12, 13, 14 and 15 have hexadecimal representation of A, B, C, D, E and F, then the 16 bit 565 formatted RGB number corresponds to a hexadecimal representation of 0x5CC8.

A color is generally represented in 565 format as hexadecimal with the example of the *Adafruit_ILI9341.h* file in the *Adafruit ILI9341* library, as noted in Chapter 13. An advantage of the hexadecimal system is that a color, defined as a 16-bit binary number in 565 format, can be represented by four alphanumeric characters and that the number can easily be split into two hexadecimal components. For example, in the pale green color in Figure 14-3, the two components are 0x5C and 0xC8. As a comparison, the hexadecimal representation of the original 24-bit number describing the three RGB color components in Figure 14-3 is 0x5F9942, consisting of the three hexadecimal numbers—5F, 99, and 42—that correspond to the decimal numbers 95, 153, and 66.

To obtain the 5, 6 and 5-bit values, the three 8-bit R, G, and B components are divided by 2^3, 2^2, and 2^3, respectively, which are then multiplied by 2^{11}, 2^5, and 2^0 to shift the values 11, 5, and 0 places "to the left" and generate the 16-bit number.

The instruction is ((r/8) << 11) | ((g/4) << 5) | (b/8), as used in Listing 14-1.

Color-Recognition Sensor

 The color-recognition sensor TCS230 has an array of 64 photodiodes with red, blue, green, and clear color filters. There are 16 photodiodes for each color filter and the color-recognition sensor produces a square wave with the frequency proportional to the light intensity of the relevant color.

The color-recognition sensor has two pairs of control pins with pin states *HIGH* or *LOW* that determine which filter is activated and the scaling of the output frequency (see Table 14-1). The output frequency scaling can be set to 100% by connecting color-recognition sensor control pins S0 and S1 to 5V (see Table 14-2). The status of color-recognition sensor control pins S2 and S3 to activate a color filter is determined in the sketch.

Table 14-1. *Control Pins of the Color-Recognition Sensor*

Control Pins			Control Pins		
S2	S3	Photodiode Filter	S0	S1	Output Scalar
LOW	LOW	Red	LOW	LOW	Power down
LOW	HIGH	Blue	LOW	HIGH	2%
HIGH	LOW	Clear	HIGH	LOW	20%
HIGH	HIGH	Green	HIGH	HIGH	100%

Table 14-2. *Connections of the Color-Recognition Sensor*

Color Sensor Pin		Arduino Pin	Color Sensor Pin		Arduino Pin
GND	ground	GND	S3	Photodiode	A5
OE	output enable	not connected	S2	Photodiode	A4
S1	Output freq.	5V	OUT	Output	A3
S0	Output freq.	5V	VCC		5V

In Listing 14-2, the color-recognition sensor is calibrated by scanning a white object and then a black object. Entering a *<carriage return>* at the serial monitor signifies when each of the two calibration scans are made. The color-recognition sensor output values, with the red, green, or blue filters, for a white and a black image are of the order of 5 and 50, respectively. An object is then scanned using the scan() function and the color-recognition sensor output values with the red, green, and blue filters are scaled to the range (0, 255) based on the calibration values. The three scaled RGB components are combined and converted into a 16-bit number representing the RGB compound color in the convertRGB() function. A rectangle is then displayed on the ST7735 TFT LCD screen filled with the RGB color (see Figure 14-4 and Table 14-3).

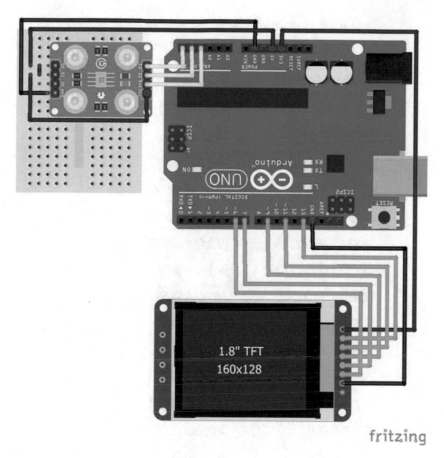

Figure 14-4. *Color-recognition sensor and TFT LCD screen*

Table 14-3. *Connections for Color-recognition Sensor and TFT LCD Screen*

Component	Connect to
ST7735 TFT GND	Arduino GND
ST7735 TFT CS	Arduino pin 6
ST7735 TFT RESET	Arduino pin 7
ST7735 TFT A0	Arduino pin 9
ST7735 TFT SDA	Arduino pin 11
ST7735 TFT SCK	Arduino pin 13
ST7735 TFT LED	Arduino 3.3V
TCS230 GND	Arduino GND
TCS230 S1	Arduino 5V
TCS230 S0	Arduino 5V
TCS230 S3	Arduino pin A5
TCS230 S2	Arduino pin A4
TCS230 OUT	Arduino pin A3
TCS230 VCC	Arduino 5V

Listing 14-2. Color-recognition Sensor

```
#include <Adafruit_ST7735.h>    // include ST7735 library
#include <Adafruit_GFX.h>       // include GFX library
int TFT_CS = 6;                 // screen chip select pin
int DCpin = 9;                  // screen DC pin
int RSTpin = 7;                 // screen reset pin
                                // associate tft with Adafruit_ST7735 library
```

```
Adafruit_ST7735 tft = Adafruit_ST7735(TFT_CS, DCpin, RSTpin);
unsigned int BLACK = 0x0000;      // HEX code for black color
int S2 = A4;                      // color sensor pins
int S3 = A5;
int OUT = A3;
int calibrate = 0;
byte R, G, B, Rlow, Rhigh, Glow, Ghigh, Blow, Bhigh;

void setup()
{
  Serial.begin(9600);            // set baud rate for Serial Monitor
  pinMode(S2, OUTPUT);           // sensor pins S2 and S3 as output
  pinMode(S3, OUTPUT);
  pinMode(OUT, INPUT);           // sensor pin OUT as input
  tft.initR(INITR_BLACKTAB);     // initialize screen
  tft.fillScreen(BLACK);         // fill screen in black
                                 // print instructions to Serial Monitor
  Serial.println("Select Newline option on Serial Monitor");
  Serial.println("Calibrate WHITE, <enter> when ready");
}

void loop()
{
  if (calibrate == 0)                // calibrate white image
  {
    while (Serial.available()>0)     // wait for <enter> to be pressed
    {
      if(Serial.read() == '\n')      // white calibration on <enter>
      {
        Rlow = scan(LOW, LOW);       // red filter scan of white image
        Glow = scan(HIGH, HIGH);     // green filter scan of white image
        Blow = scan(LOW, HIGH);      // blue filter scan of white image
```

```
      Serial.println("WHITE calibration complete");
      Serial.println("to calibrate BLACK, <enter> when ready");
      calibrate = 1;                // flag WHITE has been calibrated
    }
  }
}
else if (calibrate == 1)          // calibrate black image
{
  while (Serial.available()>0)    // wait for <enter> to be pressed
  {
    if(Serial.read() == '\n')     // black calibration on <enter>
    {
      Rhigh = scan(LOW, LOW);     // red filter scan of black image
      Ghigh = scan(HIGH, HIGH);   // green filter scan of black image
      Bhigh = scan(LOW, HIGH);    // blue filter scan of black image
      Serial.println("BLACK calibration complete");
      calibrate = 2;              // flag BLACK has been calibrated
      Serial.println("<enter> when ready for color scan");
    }
  }
}
else if(calibrate == 2)
{
  while (Serial.available()>0)       // wait for <enter> to be pressed
  {
    if(Serial.read() == '\n')        // start scan on <enter>
    {
      R = scan(LOW, LOW);                   // red filter scan of image
      R = map(R, Rlow, Rhigh, 255, 0);  // scale red filter scan to
                                            // low-high range
      G = scan(HIGH, HIGH);                 // green filter scan of image
      G = map(G, Glow, Ghigh, 255, 0);  // scale green filter scan to
                                            // low-high range
```

```
        B = scan(LOW, HIGH);                    // blue filter scan of image
        B = map(B, Blow, Bhigh, 255, 0); // scale blue filter scan to
                                                // low-high range
      unsigned int RGB = convertRGB(R,G,B);   // convert to 16bit color
      tft.fillRect(20,60,88,80,RGB); // fill screen rectangle with scanned color
                                      // *** INSERT Listing 14-3 HERE

    }

  }

 }

}
int scan(int level2, int level3)    // function to scan image
{
  digitalWrite(S2, level2);               // set color sensor pins
  digitalWrite(S3, level3);
  unsigned int val = 0;                   // 1000 scans of image
  for (int i=0; i<1000; i++) val = val + pulseIn(OUT, LOW);
  val = val/1000.0;                       // average of 1000 scans
  return val;
}

unsigned int convertRGB(byte r, byte g, byte b)
{                        // convert three 8 bit numbers to 16 bit number
  return ((r / 8) << 11) | ((g / 4) << 5) | (b / 8);
}
```

The sketch can be extended by displaying the calibration values on the serial monitor and using the scaled RGB components to activate an RGB LED to reproduce the scanned color, with the following instructions:

```
analogWrite(redLED, R);
analogWrite(greenLED, G);
analogWrite(blueLED, B);
```

The color name of the scanned object can be predicted based on the RGB components of the scanned image, and displayed on the ST7735 TFT LCD screen with an appropriately filled rectangle. For example, if the RGB components satisfied the following condition:

```
if (R>200 && G>200) {color = 0xFFE0; text = "YELLOW";}
tft.setTextColor(color);
tft.print(text);
```

Then, the text "YELLOW" in a yellow color is displayed beside a yellow-filled rectangle on the ST7735 TFT LCD screen. The `unsigned int color` and `String text` variables are defined at the start of the sketch. HEX codes for colors were listed in Chapter 13. Listing 14-3 contains instructions for predicting colors that are included in Listing 14-1 after the instruction.

```
tft.fillRect(20,60,88,80,RGB); // fill screen rectangle with scanned color.
```

Listing 14-3. Predicting Color with the Color-Recognition Sensor

```
     if (R>220 && G<150) {color = 0xF800; text = "RED      ";}
else if (G>120 && R<100) {color = 0x07E0; text = "GREEN    ";}
else if (B>170 && R<150) {color = 0x001F; text = "BLUE     ";}
else if (R>200 && G>170) {color = 0xFFE0; text = "YELLOW   ";}
else if (R>200 && B>200) {color = 0xF81F; text = "MAGENTA  ";}
else if (G>170 && B>200) {color = 0x07FF; text = "CYAN     ";}
else {color = 0xFFFF; text = "no color";}
tft.setTextSize(2);
tft.setCursor(20,20);
tft.setTextColor(color, BLACK);
tft.print(text);
```

The `setTextColor(text_color, background_color)` instruction ensures that new text overwrites existing text, so it is not necessary to draw a background rectangle over the existing text before writing the new text, which must be at least as long as the existing text.

The angle of a servo motor can be based on the predicted color, so that a pointer moves to indicate the color on a color arch. For example, the color names and corresponding angles can be defined in the arrays texts[] and angles[], respectively, and the angle that the servo motor moves through is determined by the predicted color (see Listing 14-4).

Listing 14-4. Move Servo According to Predicted Color

```
String texts[] = {"RED","GREEN","BLUE","YELLOW","MAGENTA","CYAN"};
int angles[] = {0, 36, 72, 108, 144, 180};
for (int i=0; i<6; i++)
  {
    if(text == texts[i]) servo.write(angles[i]);
  }
```

Summary

Red, green, and blue components of color are described and illustrated with a RGB LED. The color-recognition sensor was used to scan a pattern and reproduce the color of the pattern. The scanned color was categorized by the sensor as belonging to one of a range of standard colors.

Components List

- Arduino Uno and breadboard
- RGB LED module
- Color-recognition sensor: TCS230
- TFT LCD screen: ST7735 1.8-inch

CHAPTER 15

Camera

 The Arduino can support a camera, such as the OV7670 module, and display images on an ST7735 TFT LCD screen (see Figure 15-1) with a frame transfer rate of 10 frames per second (fps). The resolutions of the OV7670 camera and ST7735 TFT LCD screen are 640×480 and 160×128 pixels, respectively.

This chapter uses the *LiveOV7670* library by Indrek Luuk. To access the library, download the *.zip* file from github.com/indrekluuk/LiveOV7670. Unzip the file and copy the *LiveOV7670-master* ➤ *src* ➤ *lib* ➤ *LiveOV7670Library* folder to the default Arduino libraries folder. The *Adafruit GFX* library must be also installed using the Arduino IDE, as outlined in Chapter 3, with installation method 3.

A sketch to capture digital images is accessed by copying the *LiveOV7670-master* ➤ *src* ➤ *LiveOV7670* folder to the desktop. Within the Arduino IDE, compile and load the *Desktop* ➤ *LiveOV7670* ➤ *LiveOV7670.ino* sketch to display OV7670 camera images at 10fps on the ST7735 TFT LCD screen. Prior to displaying the camera images, a green screen indicates correct connections between the OV7670 camera module and the Arduino; otherwise, a red screen is displayed.

© Neil Cameron 2019
N. Cameron, *Arduino Applied*, https://doi.org/10.1007/978-1-4842-3960-5_15

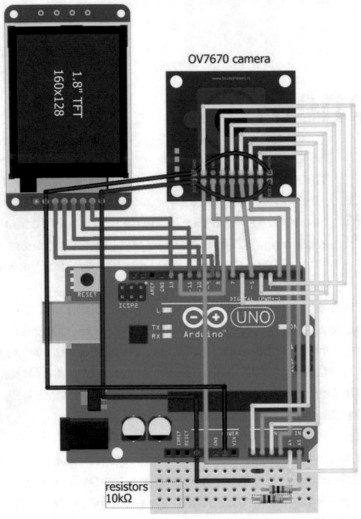

Figure 15-1. *OV7670 camera and ST7735 TFT LCD screen*

Magnified OV7670 camera images at 1fps can be displayed with the sketch *LiveOV7670* after a change to the tab *setup.h*. To locate the tab *setup.h*, select the triangle below the serial monitor button, on the right-hand side of the Arduino IDE to reveal a drop-down list of tabs. On line 31 of *setup.h*, change #define EXAMPLE 1 to #define EXAMPLE 2, then compile and load the sketch *LiveOV7670*.

Pin connections of the OV7670 camera module to the Arduino are given in Table 15-1. Note that the OV7670 camera module and the ST7735 TFT LCD screen are both connected to 3.3V. The *HREF* (horizontal reference) pin on the OV7670 camera module is not connected, as *VSYNC* (vertical synchronized output) indicates the start of a new frame and the number of pixels depends on the image resolution. The OV7670 camera module *SIOD* (I2C data) and *SIOC* (I2C clock) pins are connected to Arduino I2C pins A4 (SDA) and A5 (SCL) with 10kΩ pull-up resistors to 3.3V.

Table 15-1. *Connections for OV7670 Camera Module*

Arduino		OV7670 camera module		Arduino
3.3V		3V3 ● ● GND	GND	
A5 – 10kΩ	I2C clock	SIOC ● ● SIOD	I2C data	A4 – 10kΩ
Pin 2	Vertical sync	VSYNC ● ● HREF	Horizon ref	
Pin 12	Pixel clock	PCLK ● ● XCLK	System clock	Pin 3
Pin 7		D7 ● ● 6		Pin 6
Pin 5	Video parallel	D5 ● ● D4	Video parallel	Pin 4
Pin A3	Output	D3 ● ● D2	Output	Pin A2
Pin A1		D1 ● ● D0		Pin A0
3.3V	Reset	RESET ● ● PWDN	Power down	GND

Pin connections between the ST7735 TFT LCD screen and the Arduino depend on the particular ST7735 TFT LCD screen. The ST7735 TFT LCD screen used in this chapter and in Chapter 13 is denoted the red screen in Table 15-2. Connections between another ST7735 TFT LCD screen (denoted the blue screen in Figure 15-2) and the Arduino are also shown in Table 15-2. The pin layout of the blue TFT LCS screen is given in Table 15-3.

Figure 15-2. *Red and blue ST7735 TFT LCD screens*

Table 15-2. *Connections for Red and Blue ST7735 TFT LCD Screens*

Arduino	Red Screen	Arduino	Blue Screen
		GND	LED-
3.3V	LED	3.3V	LED+
		Pin 9	CS
Pin 13	SCK	Pin 13	SCK
Pin 11	SDA	Pin 11	SDA
Pin 8	A0 or DC	Pin 8	A0 or DC
Pin 10	RESET	Pin 10	RESET
Pin 9	CS		
GND	GND		
---	VCC		

Table 15-3. *Pin Layout of the Blue TFT LCD Screen*

	SD Card								
LED-	LED+	CS	MOSI	MISO	SCK				
ST7735 TFT LCD Screen									
CS	SCK	SDA	A0	RESET	NC	NC	NC	VCC	GND

Camera Image Capture Setup

The sketch *LiveOV7670* has an image capture function, but a larger image can be captured with code available at https://github.com/Kanaris/OV7670. Both approaches require Java, with the 32-bit Java version used by the *github.com/Kanaris/OV7670* code and the 64-bit Java version used by *LiveOV7670*. It is important not to mix 32-bit and 64-bit software.

To determine if a computer has a 32-bit or a 64-bit operating system, select *Control Panel* ➤ *System and Security* ➤ *System*. The system type is displayed. Note that 32-bit programs are stored in *C:* ➤ *Program Files (x86)*, while 64-bit programs are stored in *C:* ➤ *Program Files*.

In the setup instructions for the 32-bit version of Java, the Java version number was 192, which was released in October 2018 (see Release Notes on `www.oracle.com/technetwork/java/javase/documentation/index.html`). If a different Java version number is installed, then replace the 192 version number in file names with the appropriate version number.

Download and install the Java SE Development Kit for Windows x86 from `www.oracle.com/technetwork/java/javase/downloads/jdk8-downloads-2133151.html`.

The extracted files are saved in *C:* ➤ *Program Files (x86)* ➤ *Java* ➤ *jdk1.8.0_192* and in *C:* ➤ *Program Files (x86)* ➤ *Java* ➤ *jre1.8.0_192*.

Download the *.zip* file from `github.com/Kanaris/OV7670`. The *grabber* folder contains the *win32com.dll* file. The *src* and *lib* folders contain the *comm.jar* and *javax.comm.properties* files, respectively.

Copy *win32com.dll* to *C:* ➤ *Program Files (x86)* ➤ *Java* ➤ *jdk1.8.0_192* ➤ *jre* ➤ *bin*.

Copy *comm.jar* to *C:* ➤ *Program Files (x86)* ➤ *Java* ➤ *jdk1.8.0_192* ➤ *jre* ➤ *lib* ➤ *ext*.

Copy *javax.comm.properties* to *C:* ➤ *Program Files (x86)* ➤ *Java* ➤ *jdk1.8.0_192* ➤ *jre* ➤ *lib*.

The *src* folder contains the *com* ➤ *epam* folders, which contain *BMP.java* and *SimpleRead.java*. Paste the *com* folder to the desktop. The default communication (COM) port in *SimpleRead.java* is set at *COM9* and must be changed to the appropriate port.

The COM port can be determined in the Arduino IDE by selecting *Tools* ➤ *port*.

Or from the computer,

1. Select *Control Panel* ➤ *Hardware and Sound* ➤ *Device Manager* under *Ports (COM & LPT)*.

2. Open the *Desktop* ➤ *com* ➤ *epam* ➤ *SimpleRead.java* file with a text editor.

3. On line 32,

   ```
   if (portId.getName().equals("COM9")) {
   ```

   change COM9 to the appropriate port; for example COM3.

4. Save the file.

The *SimpleRead.java* file is compiled in the Windows instruction environment.

1. Right-click the Windows symbol at the bottom left-hand side of the screen and select *Run*.

2. Enter *cmd* in the instruction line.

3. Select *OK*.

4. In the Window instruction environment, enter *cd c:*.

5. Enter the desktop address; for example,

   cd c:\Users\username\Desktop.

6. Enter *javac com\epam\SimpleRead.java*. This creates the *BMP.class* and *SimpleRead.class* files in the *com* ➤ *epam* folder.

7. Save the *com* folder in *C:* ➤ *Program Files (x86)* ➤ *Java* ➤ *jdk1.8.0_192* ➤ *bin*.

8. Create a folder named *new* on the C drive to store images.

Table 15-4 illustrates differences in the connections between the OV7670 camera module and the Arduino if images are viewed on an ST7735 TFT LCD screen (see Figure 15-1) or if images are stored in the *new* folder on the C drive of the connected computer (see Figure 15-3).

Table 15-4. *Connections Between the OV7670 Camera Module and Arduino*

OV7670 Camera Module	Images on Screen	Images Stored
	Connect to Arduino	*Connect to Arduino*
VSYNC	Pin 2	Pin 3
PCLK	Pin 12	Pin 2
HREF	---	Pin 8
XCLK	Pin 3	Pin 11

A 4.7kΩ pull-down resistor is also required for the system clock, XCLK, with a second 4.7kΩ resistor between the system clock and Arduino pin 11. In Figure 15-3, changes to connections between the OV7670 camera module and the Arduino, relative to Figure 15-1 are colored orange.

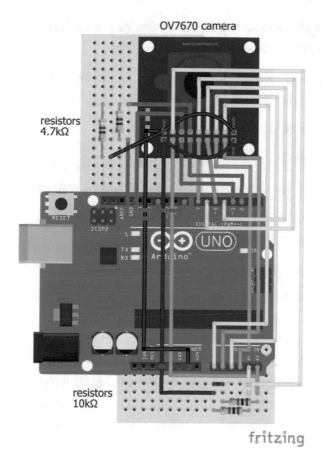

Figure 15-3. *Image capture with OV7670 camera*

Capturing Camera Images

The *.zip* file downloaded from https://github.com/Kanaris/OV7670
contains the *OV7670 ➤ arduino* folder with the *arduino_uno_ov7670.ino*
sketch by Siarhei Charkes. Compile and load the *arduino_uno_ov7670*
sketch. The built-in LED on pin 13 is turned on. After a short delay, the
Arduino TX LED flickers in pulses.

Image captures from the OV7670 camera is managed by the Windows instruction environment.

1. Right-click the Windows symbol at the bottom left-hand side of the screen. Select *Run*.

2. Enter *cmd* in the instruction line.

3. Select *OK*.

4. In the Window instruction environment, enter *cd c:*.

5. Next, enter *cd C:\Program Files (x86)\Java\jdk1.8.0_192\bin*.

6. Then, enter *java com.epam.SimpleRead*.

The Arduino TX LED is turned off, then after a short delay, the Arduino TX LED is turned on in pulses, as images are captured.

Open the *new* folder on the C drive, which was created to store images. The 240×320 pixel images with 24-bit depth are available to view as they are captured. The first few images can be disregarded as the OV7670 camera module adjusts to the surrounding light. Figure 15-4 shows the Windows commands to save images on the C drive, with an example image shown in Figure 15-5.

```
C:\WINDOWS\system32\cmd.exe - java com.epam.SimpleRead
Microsoft Windows [Version 10.0.17134.407]
(c) 2018 Microsoft Corporation. All rights reserved.

C:\Users\neil>cd Desktop

C:\Users\neil\Desktop>javac com\epam\SimpleRead.java

C:\Users\neil\Desktop>cd C:\Program Files (x86)\Java\jdk1.8.0_192\bin

C:\Program Files (x86)\Java\jdk1.8.0_192\bin>java com.epam.SimpleRead
Port name: COM3
Looking for image
Found image: 0
Saved image: 1
Looking for image
Found image: 1
Saved image: 2
Looking for image
Found image: 2
Saved image: 3
Looking for image
Found image: 3
Saved image: 4
Looking for image
Found image: 4
-
```

Figure 15-4. *Capturing OV7670 camera images*

Figure 15-5. *Example image*

287

Two changes to the *arduino_uno_ov7670* sketch may improve the quality of the captured images. On line 602 of the sketch, `wrReg(0x11, 12)`, the second parameter can be changed from 12 to 9, 10, 11, or 13. Also, on line 549, increasing the time delay between image captures from 3000ms to 5000ms can improve the quality of captured images.

Summary

Digital images at 10 frames per second were displayed on a TFT LCD screen using the OV7670 camera module. Digital images from the camera module were stored on a computer connected to the Arduino, which required the installation of Java files.

Components List

- Arduino Uno and breadboard

- Camera module: OV7670

- TFT LCD screen: ST7735 1.8-inch

- Resistors: 2× 4.7kΩ and 2× 10kΩ

CHAPTER 16

Bluetooth Communication

Bluetooth is a wireless technology for short distance communication between devices with short wavelength radio waves and operating at 2.4GHz. Bluetooth is used for hands-free car phones, streaming audio to headphones, data transfer, and communication between devices. The HC-05 Bluetooth module mounted on a breakout board is recommended, as the module itself does not have connecting pins. The HC-05 module communicates by Bluetooth Serial Port Profile (SPP) with a coverage distance of up to 10m.

The HC-05 Bluetooth module can be powered from 3.6V to 6V, given the HC-05's 5V to 3.3V voltage regulator, but the transmit (TXD) and receive (RXD) serial data communication function at 3.3V. The Arduino receiver pin (RX) interprets a voltage of 3.3V as *HIGH*, so the HC-05 TXD pin can be directly connected to the Arduino RX pin. The Arduino transmit pin (TX) has a 5V output, so a logic level converter or a voltage divider, as outlined in Chapter 3 using 4.7kΩ and 10kΩ resistors, reduces the voltage to the HC-05 RXD pin to 3.4V. Both options, a logic level converter or a voltage divider, are displayed in Figure 16-1 and given in Tables 16-1 and 16-2. A logic level converter is preferable to a voltage divider, as the signal capacitance and the

N. Cameron, *Arduino Applied*, https://doi.org/10.1007/978-1-4842-3960-5_16

voltage divider resistors form a resistor-capacitor filter that rounds the edge of the digital signal, which can impact performance of the device receiving the signal.

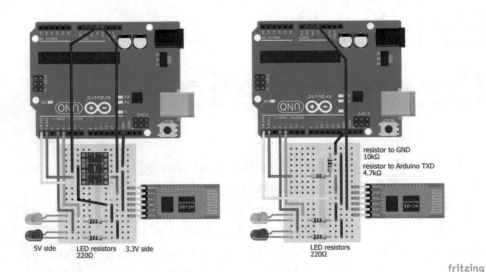

Figure 16-1. *HC-05 Bluetooth module, logic level converter, and voltage divider*

The Arduino uses serial communication to upload a compiled sketch. During uploading, the Arduino RX pin must be disconnected, or uploading fails and the An error occurred while uploading the sketch message is displayed.

Remember to reconnect the Arduino RX pin after the sketch has compiled.

Table 16-1. *Connections for Bluetooth Module with Logic Level Converter (LLC)*

Component	Connect to	High side LLC	Connect to
Bluetooth VCC	Arduino 3.3V		
Bluetooth GND	Arduino GND		
Bluetooth TXD	LLC low voltage TX	LLC high voltage TX	Arduino pin 0 RX
Bluetooth RXD	LLC low voltage RX	LLC high voltage RX	Arduino pin 1 TX
LLC low voltage	Arduino 3.3V		
LLC high voltage	Arduino 5V		
LLC GND	Arduino GND		
LED long legs	Arduino pins 3, 4		
LED short legs	220Ω resistors		Arduino GND

Table 16-2. *Connections for Bluetooth Module with Voltage Divider*

Component	Connect to	and to
Bluetooth VCC	Arduino 5V	
Bluetooth GND	Arduino GND	
Bluetooth TXD	Arduino pin 0 RX	
Bluetooth RXD	4.7kΩ resistor	Arduino pin 1 TX
Bluetooth RXD	10kΩ resistor	Arduino GND
LED long legs	Arduino pins 3, 4	
LED short legs	220Ω resistors	Arduino GND

There are several Bluetooth communication applications that can be downloaded from Google Play for an Android tablet to communicate with an Arduino using Bluetooth. The *Bluetooth Terminal HC-05* app, by Memighty, and the *ArduDroid* app, by Hazim Bitar, are both recommended. The two apps have similar functions, with the *ArduDroid* app also having a PWM facility. Examples are given of the two apps to control LEDs and display text on the tablet or serial monitor, with the *ArduDroid* app also controlling LED brightness with PWM.

After compiling a sketch, the HC-05 module LED flashes five times a second, waiting to be paired to a device. Turn on the Android tablet's Bluetooth, open the *Bluetooth Terminal HC-05* or *ArduDroid* app and scan for new devices. Pair the HC-05 module with the Android tablet, using the password of either *1234* or *0000*. When paired with the Android tablet, the HC-05 module's LED flashes every two seconds, indicating that the module is paired with a device.

Bluetooth Terminal HC-05 App

In the *Bluetooth Terminal HC-05* app, button settings can be configured with a long press to enter the *Button Name* and the corresponding ASCII Command letter. For example, *Button names of Red LED on*, *Green LED on*, and *Both LEDs off* can be configured with Command letters *R*, *G*, and *O*, respectively (see Figure 16-2). Pressing a *Bluetooth Terminal HC-05* app button turns LEDs on or off, with a corresponding message displayed on the *Bluetooth Terminal HC-05* app. If the serial monitor is open, then the message is also displayed on the serial monitor. Command letters can also be typed into the *Enter ASCII Command* box followed by *Send ASCII*. The *Send ASCII* button (see Figure 16-3) must be configured, with a long press, to end the *sent data* with a line feed, \n, character, so that text can be entered with the *Send ASCII* button.

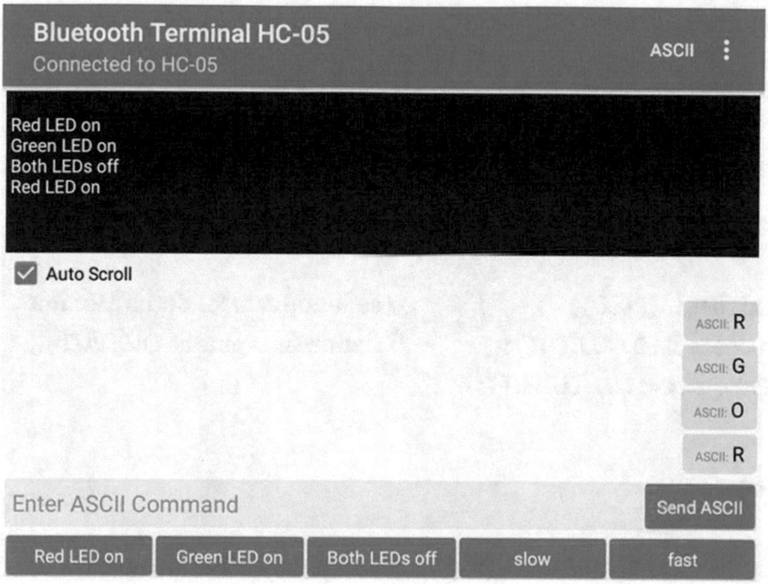

Figure 16-2. *Bluetooth Terminal HC-05*

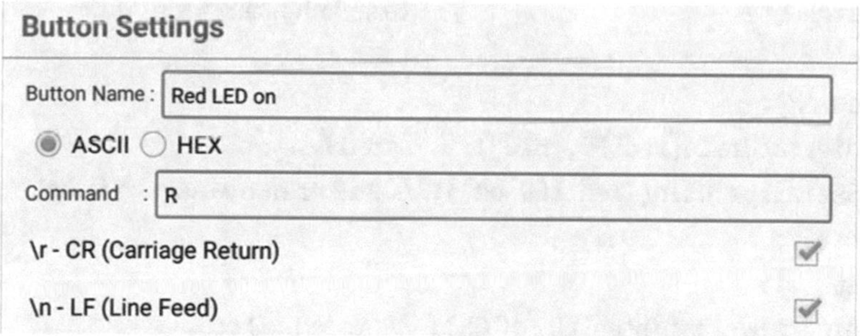

Figure 16-3. *Bluetooth Terminal HC-05 button setup to control LEDs*

Listing 16-1 turns LEDs on or off using Bluetooth communication between an Android tablet with the *Bluetooth Terminal HC-05* app and the Arduino. Use of switch case instructions rather than if else instructions is outlined in Chapter 6. The default case is included for Command letters other than *R*, *G*, and *O*.

Listing 16-1. Bluetooth Terminal HC-05 App

```
int redLED = 3;                    // LED pins
int greenLED = 4;
char c;                            // command letter input

void setup()
{
  Serial.begin(9600);             // set baud rate for Serial Monitor
  pinMode(redLED, OUTPUT);        // define LED pins as OUTPUT
  pinMode(greenLED, OUTPUT);
}

void loop()
{
  while (Serial.available()>0)    // when data in Serial buffer
  {
    c = Serial.read();            // read character from Serial buffer
    switch (c)                    // use switch...case for options
    {
    case 'R':
      digitalWrite(redLED, HIGH);    // red LED on
      Serial.println("red LED on"); // and print message to Serial
      break;
    case 'G':
      digitalWrite(greenLED, HIGH); // green LED on
      Serial.println("green LED on");
      break;
    case 'O':
      digitalWrite(redLED, LOW);    // both LEDs off
      digitalWrite(greenLED, LOW);
      Serial.println("both LEDs off");
      break;
```

```
    default: break;                 // instruction letter not R, G or O
    }
  }
}
```

ArduDroid App

The *ArduDroid* app has 12 buttons consistent with Arduino digital pins 2 to 13 and six sliders matching Arduino PWM pins 3, 5, 6, 9, 10, and 11. The SEND DATA and GET DATA panels allow alphanumeric characters to be sent from or received by the *ArduDroid* app (see Figure 16-4). A baseline sketch accompanying the *ArduDroid* app can be downloaded from www.techbitar.com.

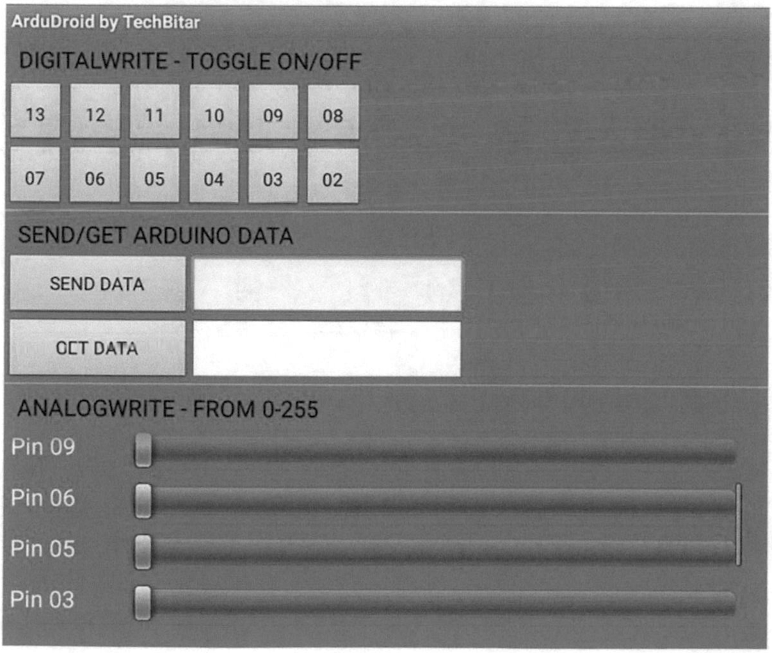

Figure 16-4. *ArduDroid*

When an *ArduDroid* app button is pressed, or a slider is changed, or the SEND DATA button pressed, a control sequence is sent by the *ArduDroid* app to the Arduino using Bluetooth communication (see Table 16-3). The control sequence is the command number, prefixed by the * character, the Arduino pin number, the pin value, the alphanumeric text and the end character #. Control variables are separated by the | character. For example, pressing the *ArduDroid* app button 03 has the control sequence *10|03|02# or *10|03|03#, changing the *ArduDroid* app slider for PWM pin 06 to position 125 has the control sequence *11|06|125# and sending the text "*ABC123*" with SEND DATA has control sequence *12|99|99|ABC123#.

Listing 16-2 displays the control sequences of the ArduDroid app and has a 5ms delay between reading character input, so the sliders should be "pressed" rather than "slid."

Table 16-3. *Control Sequence of ArduDroid App*

ArduDroid App	Command	Arduino Pin	Value	Alphanumeric
Button	10	Digital pin	2 or 3	
Slider	11	PWM pin	0-255	
SEND DATA	12	99	99	Text

Listing 16-2. Control Sequence of ArduDroid App

```
int val[3];               // command, Arduino pin and pin value
const int bufferSz = 30;  // const int required to define array size
char data[bufferSz];      // alphanumeric data including | and #
char c;
int flag = 0;
int index;
```

```
void setup()
{
  Serial.begin(9600);            // set baud rate for Serial Monitor
}

void loop()
{
  readSerial();                  // function to read control sequence
  if(flag == 1)                  // if control sequence read
  {
    for (int i=0; i<3; i++)
    {                            // display three control variables
      Serial.print(val[i]);Serial.print(" ");
    }                            // display alphanumeric data
    for (int i=0; i<bufferSz; i++) Serial.print(data[i]);
    Serial.println("");
  }
  flag = 0;                      // resct flag for new control sequence
                                 // overwrite data with null character
  for (int i=0; i<bufferSz; i++) data[i]='\0';
  index = 0;                     // reset data index to zero
}

void readSerial()                // function to read control sequence
{
  while (Serial.available()>0) // when character in Serial buffer
  {
    if(flag == 0)                // new control sequence
    {
      c = Serial.read();         // read character from Serial buffer
                                 // parse three control variables
      for (int i=0; i<3; i++) val[i]=Serial.parseInt();
      flag = 1;                  // control sequence read
    }
```

```
c = Serial.read();    // read character from Serial buffer
delay(5);             // delay 5ms between characters
                      // increment data and add next character
if(c != '|' && c != '#') data[index++] = c;
  }
}
```

The *ArduDroid* app is used to control the brightness of the LED on pin Arduino 3 using *ArduDroid* slider 3 and control the LEDs on Arduino pins 3 and 4 using the *ArduDroid* app buttons or alphanumeric text (*R* for red LED on, *G* for green LED on and *O* for both LEDs off). The sketch builds on Listing 16-2, with the LED pins defined at the start of the sketch.

```
int redLED = 3;              // red and green LED pins
int greenLED = 4;
```

The LED pin OUTPUT status in the void setup() function.

```
pinMode(redLED, OUTPUT);      // define LED pins as output
pinMode(greenLED, OUTPUT);
```

Listing 16-3 contains the updated void loop() function.

Listing 16-3. ArduDroid App (2)

```
void loop()
{
  readSerial();            // function to read control sequence
  if(flag == 1)            // if control sequence read
  {
    switch (val[0])        // switch ... case based on instruction
    {
      case 10:             // turn red or green LED on or off
        digitalWrite(val[1],!digitalRead(val[1]));
        break;
```

```
   case 11:                                  // change red LED brightness
     analogWrite(val[1],val[2]);
     break;
   case 12:                                  // R: turn red LED on
     if(data[0] == 'R') digitalWrite(redLED, HIGH);
                                             // G: turn green LED on
     else if (data[0] == 'G') digitalWrite(greenLED, HIGH);
     else if (data[0] == 'O')          // O: turn both LEDs off
     {
        digitalWrite(redLED, LOW);
        digitalWrite(greenLED, LOW);
     }
     break;
    default: break;                          // default case
   }
  }
  flag = 0;                                  // reset flag to zero
  for (int i=0; i<10; i++) data[i]='\0';    // overwrite previous data
  index = 0;                                 // reset data index to zero
}
```

Additional functionality can be allocated to the *ArduDroid* app pins by editing the relevant switch case section of the sketch. For example, to flash the green LED several times when the *ArduDroid* app pin 5 is pressed, Listing 16-4 includes the changes to case 10 of Listing 16-3.

Listing 16-4. ArduDroid App (3)

```
case 10:
  if(val[1] == 3 || val[1] == 4)    // turn LED 3 or 4 on or off
    digitalWrite(val[1],!digitalRead(val[1]));
  else if(val[1] == 5)
  {
    for (int i=0;i<10;i++)
    {                                // turn green LED on and off five times
```

```
    digitalWrite(greenLED, !digitalRead(greenLED));
    delay(500);                 // delay 500ms
  }
 }
 break;
```

Message Scrolling with MAX7219 Dot Matrix Module

 The MAX7219 dot matrix module manages the 8×8 dot matrix display for turning LEDs on and off to display alphanumeric characters and scroll messages. Displaying and scrolling characters on an 8×8 dot matrix display with two 74HC595 shift registers was described in Chapter 7. Several MAX7219 dot matrix modules can be daisy-chained to make longer LED displays, while still only requiring three connections between the 8×8 dot matrix displays and the Arduino. The MAX7219 module uses Serial Peripheral Interface (SPI), outlined in Chapter 11, and modules are daisy chained by connecting the Chip Select (CS or SS or LOAD), MOSI (DATA or DIN), and serial clock (SCK or CLK) pins at the *OUT* end of one module to the *IN* end of the next module. Two daisy-chained MAX7219 modules are shown in Figure 16-5, with connections in Table 16-4.

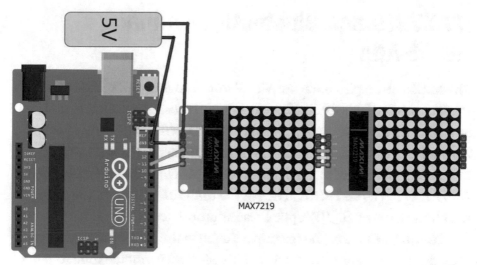

Figure 16-5. *MAX7219 modules*

Table 16-4. *Connections for MAX7219 Modules*

Component	Connect to
MAX7217 VCC	External 5V
MAX7219 GND	Arduino GND
MAX7219 DIN	Arduino pin 11
MAX7219 CS	Arduino pin 10
MAX7219 CLK	Arduino pin 13

The MAX7219 module contains a 10kΩ SMD (surface-mounted device) resistor to restrict LED brightness. Displaying text and patterns on four MAX7219 modules requires currents of at least 140mA, so MAX7219 modules must be powered by an external power source and not by the Arduino. In Figure 16-5, the MAX7219 modules are externally powered with 5V. The L4940V5 voltage regulator, as described in Chapter 8, reduces the external 9V supply from a battery to 5V to power the MAX7219 modules. Alternatively, a 5V powerbank can be used as the external 5V supply.

MAX7219 and Bluetooth Terminal HC-05 App

The MAX7219 display libraries: *MD_Parola* and *MD_MAX72XX* by Majic Designs are available through the Arduino IDE, using installation method 3, as outlined in Chapter 3. *MD_Parola* and *MD_MAX72XX* library version 3.0.0 were used in the sketches. The MAX7219 display module must be defined in a sketch, with the options being *PAROLA_HW*, *GENERIC_HW*, *ICSTATION_HW*, and *FC16_HW*. For the MAX7219 display module used in the chapter, the *FC16_HW* option was appropriate.

The *MD_MAX72xx_Test* example sketch in the *MD_MAX72X* library provides a comprehensive display of the MAX7219 module functionality. Before compiling the sketch, the hardware type and number of MAX7219 modules must be defined in lines 25 and 26.

```
#define HARDWARE_TYPE MD_MAX72XX::FC16_HW
#define MAX_DEVICES 4
```

Listing 16-5 scrolls a message on four daisy-chained 8×8 dot matrix displays with the message transferred from the *Bluetooth Terminal HC-05* app to the Arduino with Bluetooth communication. The *Send ASCII* button must be configured, with a long press, to end the *sent data* with a line feed, \n, character, so that text can be entered with the Send ASCII button (see Figure 16-3). When a new message is available, the current message is replaced with the null character, \0, to avoid a shorter new message including the non-overlapping part of the current message. The *tidyUp* variable ensures that new messages are updated, but not when a change display speed character is received by the Arduino.

Note that in Listings 16-5 and 16-7, characters are bracketed with a single apostrophe ('), while strings have a double apostrophe (").

The display speed is the inverse of the frame delay time, with a longer frame delay time resulting in a slower message display speed. The message display speed is changed using buttons on the *Bluetooth Terminal HC-05* app configured with button names *slow* and *fast* to send characters - and + with no carriage return nor line feed characters selected (see Figure 16-6).

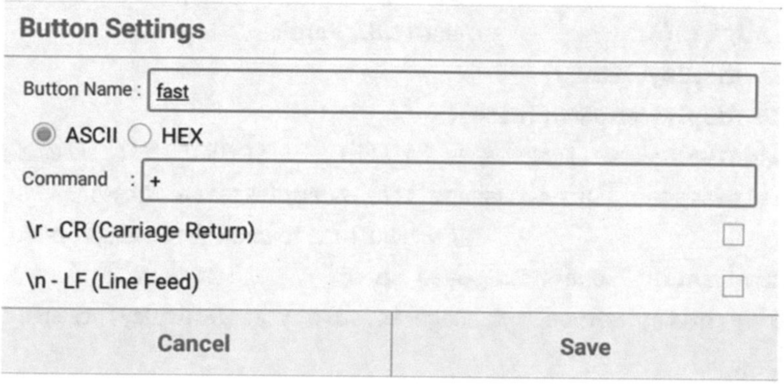

Button Settings	
Button Name :	fast
● ASCII ○ HEX	
Command :	+
\r - CR (Carriage Return)	☐
\n - LF (Line Feed)	☐
Cancel	Save

Figure 16-6. *Bluetooth Terminal HC-05 button setup to control display speed*

Listing 16-5. Message Scrolling with MAX7219 Modules and Bluetooth Terminal HC-05 App

```
#include <SPI.h>                 // include SPI library
#include <MD_Parola.h>           // include MD_Parola library
#include <MD_MAX72xx.h>          // include MAX72xx library
#define HARDWARE_TYPE MD_MAX72XX::FC16_HW   // MAX7219 module type
int devices = 4;                 // number of MAX7219 modules
int CSpin = 10;                  // chip select pin for SPI
                                 // associate parola with MD_Parola library
MD_Parola parola = MD_Parola(HARDWARE_TYPE, CSpin, devices);
int frameDelay = 20;             // initial frame speed
const int bufferSz = 60;         // array must be sized with a const
char message[bufferSz];          // message currently displayed
```

```
char newMessage[bufferSz];   // new message to be displayed
char c;                      // character input
int index;                   // number of characters in message
int flag = 0;

void setup()
{
  Serial.begin(9600);        // set baud rate for Serial Monitor
  parola.begin();            // start MD_Parola
  parola.displayClear();
  parola.displaySuspend(false);
  parola.displayScroll(message, PA_LEFT, PA_SCROLL_LEFT, frameDelay);
  strcpy(message, "Enter message");   // copies text to message
                             // use buttons to change message speed
  Serial.println("Send + to speed up or - to slow down");
  Serial.println("\nType a message to scroll"); // display message on Serial
}

void loop()
{
  readSerial();              // function to get new message
  if(flag == 1)              // new message
  {                          // replace with null character
    for (int i=index;i<bufferSz-1;i++) newMessage[i]= '\0';
    strcpy(message, newMessage);   // copy newMessage to message
    Serial.print("Message: ");Serial.println(message); // display message
    flag = 0;                // reset flag and index
    index = 0;
  }                          // scroll message
  if (parola.displayAnimate()) parola.displayReset();
}
```

```
void readSerial()                        // function to get new message
{
  while (Serial.available()>0)     // when data in Serial buffer
  {
    c = Serial.read();     // read character from Serial buffer
                           // new line at end of new message
    if ((c == '\n') || (index >= bufferSz-2)) flag = 1;
    else if(c == '+')
    {                             // increase speed by reducing frame delay
      frameDelay=parola.getSpeed()-5;
      if(frameDelay < 20) frameDelay = 20;
      Serial.print("Reduce delay to ");  // display faster "speed"
      Serial.println(frameDelay);
      parola.setSpeed(frameDelay);       // change display speed
      flag = 0;                          // message unchanged
    }
    else if(c == '-')
    {                             // decrease speed by increasing frame delay
      frameDelay=parola.getSpeed()+5;
      Serial.print("Increase delay to ");  // display slower "speed"
      Serial.println(frameDelay);
      parola.setSpeed(frameDelay);
      flag = 0;
    }
    else
    {
      delay(5);                   // delay 5ms between characters
      newMessage[index++] = c;    // save next char to new message
      flag = 0;
    }
  }
}
```

Message Speed and Potentiometer

An alternative to controlling the speed of the display with a command from the *Bluetooth Terminal HC-05* app is to use the output voltage from a potentiometer. The newSpeed() function is called from within the void loop() function and the potentiometer pin declared as int potPin = A0, for example. Listing 16-6 includes the newSpeed() function for controlling display speed with a potentiometer.

The two else sections of the readSerial() function in Listing 16-5, else if(c == '+') and else if(c == '-') are deleted. The potentiometer signal pin is connected to Arduino pin A0, with the other potentiometer pins connected to Arduino 5V and GND (see Figure 16-7).

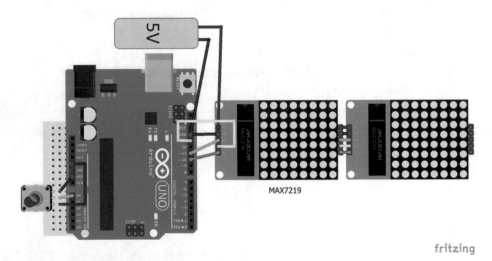

Figure 16-7. *MAX7219 speed and potentiometer*

Listing 16-6. MAX7219 Speed and Potentiometer

```
void newSpeed()                    // function to set the speed
{
  frameDelay = map(analogRead(potPin), 0, 1023, 20, 100);
  frameDelay = constrain(frameDelay, 20, 100); // constrain speed: 20 to 100
  parola.setSpeed(frameDelay);    // speed is the delay between frames
}
```

The `constrain()` function follows the `map()` function to ensure that the value of *frameDelay* is constrained within the limits of 20 and 100. If the value of *frameDelay* was less than 20 or greater than 100 following the `map()` function, then the `constrain()` function would set the value of *frameDelay* to 20 or 100, respectively.

MAX7219 and ArduDroid App

As noted at the start of the chapter, the *ArduDroid* app sends a control sequence to the Arduino by Bluetooth communication, which includes the message to be displayed. Listing 16-7 is similar to Listing 16-5 for the Bluetooth Terminal HC-05 sketch, with the main difference in the parsing of commands.

Listing 16-7. Message Scrolling with MAX7219 Modules and ArduDroid App

```
#include <SPI.h>              // include SPI library
#include <MD_Parola.h>        // include MD_Parola library
#define HARDWARE_TYPE MD_MAX72XX::FC16_HW
int devices = 4;              // number of MAX7219 modules
int CSpin = 10;               // chip select pin for SPI
                              // associate parola with MD_Parola library
MD_Parola parola = MD_Parola(HARDWARE_TYPE, CSpin, devices);
```

```
int val[3];
int frameDelay = 20;            // initial frame speed
const int bufferSz = 60;        // array must be sized with a const
char message[bufferSz];         // message currently displayed
char newMessage[bufferSz];      // new message to be displayed
char c;                         // character input
int index;                      // number of characters in message
int flag = 0;

void setup()
{
  Serial.begin(9600);           // set baud rate for Serial Monitor
  parola.begin();               // start MD_Parola
  parola.displayClear();
  parola.displaySuspend(false);
  parola.displayScroll(message, PA_LEFT, PA_SCROLL_LEFT, frameDelay);
  strcpy(message, "Enter message");       // copies text to message
                                // use buttons to change message speed
  Serial.println("Send + to speed up or - to slow down");
                                // display message on Serial Monitor
  Serial.println("\nType a message to scroll");
}

void loop()
{
  readSerial();                 // function to get new message
  if(flag == 1)                 // new message
  {                             // replace with null character
    for (int i=index;i<bufferSz-1;i++) newMessage[i]= '\0';
    strcpy(message, newMessage);   // copy newMessage to message
                                // display message on Serial Monitor
    Serial.print("Message: ");Serial.println(message);
    flag = 0;                   // reset flag and index
    index = 0;
  }                             // scroll message
```

```
    if (parola.displayAnimate()) parola.displayReset();
}

void readSerial()                   // function to get new message
{
  while (Serial.available()>0)  // when data in Serial buffer
  {
    if(flag == 0)                   // new control sequence
    {
      c = Serial.read();            // read character in Serial buffer
                                    // parse 3 integers 12, 99 and 99
      for (int i=0;i<3;i++) val[i] = Serial.parseInt();
      flag = 1;                     // control sequence read
    }
    c = Serial.read();              // read character from Serial buffer
    delay(5);                       // delay 5ms between characters
    if(c == '+')                    // increase speed
    {
      c = Serial.read();            // read end of control sequence
      frameDelay=parola.getSpeed()-5;   // reduce frame delay
      if(frameDelay < 20) frameDelay = 20;
      Serial.print("Reduce delay to ");  // display faster "speed"
      Serial.println(frameDelay);
      parola.setSpeed(frameDelay);       // change display speed
      flag = 0;                          // message unchanged
    }
    else if(c == '-')               // decrease speed
    {
      c = Serial.read();                 // read end of control sequence
      frameDelay=parola.getSpeed()+5;    // increase frame delay
      Serial.print("Increase delay to ");  // display slower "speed"
      Serial.println(frameDelay);
      parola.setSpeed(frameDelay);
      flag = 0;
    }                                    // save next char to new message
```

```
    else if((c != '|') && (c != '#')) newMessage[index++] = c;
  }
}
```

Summary

The Bluetooth HC-5 module was used to communicate between the Arduino and an Android tablet using the *Bluetooth Terminal HC-05* and *ArduDroid* apps. Devices can be controlled through Bluetooth communication, such as controlling LEDs and changing the LED brightness. Text entered on the Android tablet was scrolled across several MAX7219 dot matrix modules, with the scrolling speed controlled as a command within the *Bluetooth Terminal HC-05* and *ArduDroid* apps or by converting the output voltage from a potentiometer to the scrolling speed.

Components List

- Arduino Uno and breadboard

- Bluetooth module: HC-05

- LED

- Resistor: 220Ω

- Potentiometer: 10kΩ

- Logic level converter

- Dot matrix 4-unit module: MAX7219

- Battery: 9V

- Voltage regulator: L4940V5

- Capacitors: 0.1µF and 22µF

CHAPTER 17

Wireless Communication

While Bluetooth communication is used between devices less than 10m apart, communication over longer distances is possible using wireless transceiver modules. The greater distance between wireless transceiver modules or between a wireless transceiver module and the Arduino enables access to remote sensors and control of remote devices. The nRF24L01 radio transceiver module operates at 2.4GHz, the same frequency as Bluetooth, with 126 available channels and baud rates of 250kbps, 1Mbps, and 2Mbps. The lower baud rate may be more suitable for longer distances.

The nRF24L01 transceiver module communicates with the Arduino using serial peripheral interface (SPI). The nRF24L01 module and connections to Arduino pins are shown in Figure 17-1, with the GND pin indicated by a square surround. The CE (transmit/receive) and CSN (standby/active mode) pins can be connected to any Arduino pin, but pins 7 and 8 are used in the sketches. The IRQ (interrupt) pin is not connected. The nRF24L01 module must be connected to 3.3V and not to 5V. Connections between the nRF24L01 module and the Arduino are also given in Table 17-2.

N. Cameron, *Arduino Applied*, https://doi.org/10.1007/978-1-4842-3960-5_17

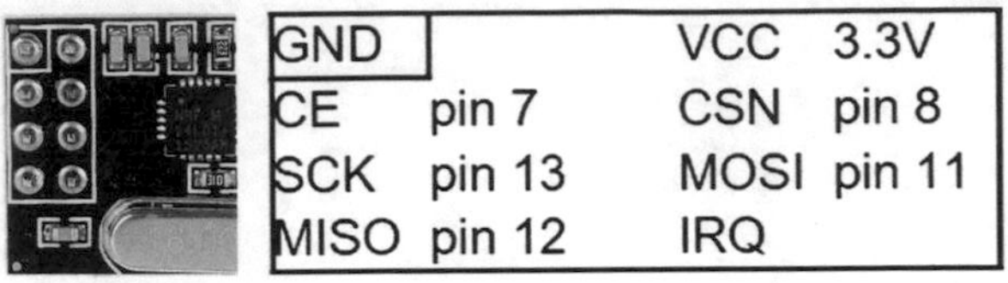

GND		VCC	3.3V
CE	pin 7	CSN	pin 8
SCK	pin 13	MOSI	pin 11
MISO	pin 12	IRQ	

Figure 17-1. *nRF24L01 pin connections*

The *RF24* library by J Coliz is required and installed using the Arduino IDE with installation method 3, as outlined in Chapter 3. Communication between nRF24L01 transceiver modules is through data pipes that require an address, such as "*Node1*" or "*12*" for each data pipe; a channel number between 0 and 125; and a baud rate of 250kbps, 1Mbps, or 2Mbps. The default address length is five characters, the default channel is 76, and the default baud rate is 1Mbps.

Reception of transmissions from an nRF24L01 radio transceiver module is improved if activity on the transmission channel is low. A low activity channel can be identified by scanning all available channels for carrier activity. In Listing 17-1, the carrier activity on each channel, over several scans, is displayed on the serial monitor. A low activity channel can then be selected with the setChannel() instruction, rather than using the default channel.

Listing 17-1. Channel Scanning

```
#include <SPI.h>            // include SPI library
#include <RF24.h>           // include RF24 library
RF24 radio(7, 8);           // associate radio with RF24 library
const int nChan = 126;      // 126 channels available
int chan[nChan];            // store counts per channel
int nScan = 100;            // number of scans per channel
int scan;
```

```
void setup()
{
  Serial.begin(9600);              // define Serial output baud rate
  radio.begin();                   // start radio
}

void loop()
{
  for (int i=0;i<nChan;i++)    // for each channel
  {
    chan[i] = 0;                   // reset counter
    for (scan=0; scan<nScan; scan++)      // repeat scanning
    {
      radio.setChannel(i);     // define channel
      radio.startListening();
      delayMicroseconds(128);  // listen for 128µs
      radio.stopListening();
      if(radio.testCarrier()>0) chan[i]=chan[i]+1;  // carrier on channel
    }
  }                              // format HEX for values <16 rather than <10
  for (int i=0; i<nChan; i++) Serial.print(chan[i], HEX);
  Serial.print("\n");        // carriage return
}
```

The channel number, baud rate, and power amplifier level are set using the following instructions.

setChannel()   channel number between 0 and 125 inclusive
setDataRate()   values RF24_250KBPS, RF24_1MBPS or RF24_2MBPS
setPALevel()   values RF24_PA_MIN, RF24_PA_LOW, RF24_PA_HIGH or
                  RF24_PA_MAX

The default power amplifier level is RF24_PA_MAX.

The default or currently set channel number, baud rate and power amplifier level are obtained using the following instructions.

313

getChannel()   channel number

getDataRate()   2, 0 or 1 for RF24_250KBPS, RF24_1MBPS or RF24_2MBPS

getPALevel()   0, 1, 2 or 3 for RF24_PA_MIN, RF24_PA_LOW, RF24_PA_HIGH
                or RF24_PA_MAX

On one channel, the nRF24L01 radio transceiver module can receive data simultaneously from up to six different transmitting nRF24L01 radio transceiver modules, with each data pipe having a different address.

Information transmitted by the nRF24L01 transceiver can be an integer, a real number, text or a data structure containing a combination of the three data types. To provide some generality, the sketches include a data structure. The maximum size of a data structure is 32 bytes, with an integer, real number or a character requiring 2, 4, and 1 bytes, respectively. The named components of a data structure are defined and the data structure is named.

For example, a data structure, named *test*, consists of two integers, a real number, and a character string. The character string can be up to 24 characters, as the two integers and the real number account for eight of the available 32 bytes. Listing 17-2 includes the instructions to define the example data structure.

Listing 17-2. Example Data Structure

```
typedef struct              // define data structure to include
{
  int count;                // an integer: count
  int level = 5;            // an integer: level defined as 5
  float value;              // a real number: value
  char text[24] = "text";   // a string defined as "text"
} dataStruct;
dataStruct test;            // name the data structure as test
```

Each component can be individually accessed in the main sketch, for example `test.value = 2.3`. The data structure is transmitted or received using the name of the data structure with the `radio.write(&test, sizeof(test))` or `radio.read(&test, sizeof(test))` instructions. The parameters are equal to the data structure reference, *&test*, and the size of the data structure.

Transmit or Receive

Table 17-1 contains two sketches—one for the transmitter and one for the receiver nRF24L01 module—to allow side-by-side comparison of the sketches. The sketches transceive a data structure with an incrementing integer and real number and a character string, to be displayed on the serial monitor. The two sketches are similar except for the `openWritingPipe()` and `openReadingPipe()` instructions, the `startListening()` instruction for the receiving module and the `write()` and `read()` instructions. Instructions in bold indicate the differences in transmission related instructions between the transmitter and receiver sketches. The maximum length of the character string is 26 characters, given that the integer and real number account for 6 bytes of the data structure, which has maximum size of 32 bytes.

Table 17-1. *Transmit or Receive*

Transmit nRF24L01	Receive nRF24L01

```
#include <SPI.h>
#include <RF24.h>
RF24 radio(7, 8);
byte addresses[ ][6] = {"12"};
typedef struct
{
 int number;
 float value;
 char text[26] = "Transmission";
} dataStruct;
dataStruct data;
void setup()
{


 radio.begin();
 radio.openWritingPipe(addresses[0]);


}
void loop()
{


 data.number = data.number+1;
 data.value = data.value+0.1;
 radio.write(&data, sizeof(data));
 delay(1000);




}
```

```
#include <SPI.h>
#include <RF24.h>
RF24 radio(7, 8);
byte addresses[ ][6] = {"12"};
typedef struct
{
 int number;
 float value;
 char text[26];
} dataStruct;
dataStruct data;
void setup()
{
 Serial.begin(9600);
 radio.begin();
 radio.openReadingPipe(0, addresses[0]);
 radio.startListening();

}
void loop()
{
 if(radio.available())


 {
  radio.read(&data, sizeof(data));
  Serial.print(data.text);Serial.print("\t");
  Serial.print(data.number);Serial.print("\t");
  Serial.println(data.value);
 }

}
```

Information about the transmitted data structure can be displayed on the serial monitor by defining the *printf* library, which is included in the *RF24* library, at the start of the sketch.

```
#include <printf.h>          // include the printf library
```

Initializing the *printf* library and serial monitor in the void setup() function.

```
printf_begin();              // initialise the printf library
Serial.begin(9600);          // set baud rate for Serial Monitor
```

With the print instruction included in the void loop() function.

```
radio.printDetails();        // display data structure information
```

Transmit and Receive

Bidirectional communication with nRF24L01 transceiver modules requires two data pipes and two addresses with one address for writing and reading on one nRF24L01 transceiver module and one address for reading and writing on the second nRF24L01 transceiver module. Prior to one nRF24L01 transceiver module writing, the stopListening() instruction must be issued and the startListening() instruction must be issued to the second nRF24L01 transceiver module prior to reading. The situation is reversed with the second nRF24L01 transceiver module writing and the first nRF24L01 transceiver module reading. An nRF24L01 transceiver with an LED is shown in Figure 17-2, with connections given in Table 17-2.

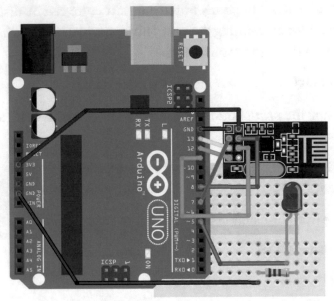

Figure 17-2. *nRF24L01 transceiver module with LED*

Table 17-2. *Connections nRF24L01 Transceiver Module with LED*

Component	Connect to	and to
nRF24L01 GND	Arduino GND	
nRF24L01 CE	Arduino pin 7	
nRF24L01 SCK	Arduino pin 13	
nRF24L01 MISO	Arduino pin 12	
nRF24L01 VCC	Arduino 3.3V	
nRF24L01 CSN	Arduino pin 8	
nRF24L01 MOSI	Arduino pin 11	
LED long leg	Arduino pin 5	
LED short leg	220Ω resistor	Arduino GND

The sketches included in Table 17-3 build on the sketches in Table 17-1. While the first nRF24L01 transceiver transmits the data structure, *data*, the second nRF24L01 transceiver module transmits an integer variable, *led*, with values 0 or 1, which the first nRF24L01 transceiver module uses to turn on or off the LED. Note that using *LED_BUILTIN* on pin 13 for the LED is not possible, as pin 13 is used by the Serial Clock (SCK) for SPI communication. Sketches to transmit and receive a data structure or only a variable by the two nRF24L01 transceiver modules are again presented side-by-side for comparison in Table 17-3, with instructions in bold indicating the transceiver related differences between the transmit then receive or the receive then transmit sketches.

Table 17-3. *Transmit and Receive*

Transmit then receive	Receive then transmit
#include <SPI.h>	#include <SPI.h>
#include <RF24.h>	#include <RF24.h>
RF24 radio(7, 8);	RF24 radio(7, 8);
byte addresses[ ][6] = {"12", "14"};	byte addresses[ ][6] = {"12", "14"};
typedef struct	typedef struct
{	{
int number;	int number = 1;
float value;	float value;
char text[26] = "Transmission";	char text[26];
} dataStruct;	} dataStruct;
dataStruct data;	dataStruct data;
int led;	int led = 1;
int ledPin = 5;	

(continued)

Table 17-3. (*continued*)

Transmit then receive	Receive then transmit
void setup()	void setup()
{	{
	Serial.begin(9600);
radio.begin();	radio.begin();
radio.openWritingPipe(addresses[0]);	**radio.openReadingPipe(1, addresses[0]);**
radio.openReadingPipe(1,	**radio.openWritingPipe(addresses[1]);**
addresses[1]);	
pinMode(ledPin, OUTPUT);	}
}	
void loop()	void loop()
{	{
radio.stopListening();	**radio.startListening();**
data.number = data.number+1;	**if(radio.available())**
data.value = data.value+0.1;	{
radio.write(&data, sizeof(data));	**radio.read(&data, sizeof(data));**
	Serial.print(data.text);Serial.print("\t");
	Serial.print(data.number);
	Serial.print("\t");
	Serial.println(data.value);
	}
delay(500);	delay(500);
radio.startListening();	**radio.stopListening();**
while(!radio.available());	led = 1 − led;
radio.read(&led, sizeof(led));	**radio.write(&led, sizeof(led));**
if(led == 1) digitalWrite(ledPin, HIGH);	
else digitalWrite(ledPin, LOW);	
delay(500);	delay(500);
}	}

A pair of nRF24L01 transceiver modules enable a sensor to be read by one Arduino with the reading transmitted to a second Arduino to display information on an LCD display or to activate a device. For example, internal and external temperature can be simultaneously monitored with one temperature sensor and the Arduino connected with an externally positioned transmitting nRF24L01 module, and a second temperature sensor and the Arduino connected to an internally positioned receiving nRF24L01 module.

A different type of example uses the output voltage from a potentiometer, which is converted to an angle and is transmitted to an nRF24L01 receiver module connected to an Arduino. This moves a servo motor through the required angle. The servo motor was described in Chapter 8 (see Figure 8-1, Table 8-1, and Listing 8-1). Extending the sketches in Table 17-3, the data structure incorporates the integer *angle*, which requires 2 bytes, so the maximum size of the character array in Table 17-3 is reduced by 2 bytes. The updated instructions to define the data structures are shown in Table 17-4.

Table 17-4. *Transmit and Receive (2)*

Transmit then receive	Receive then transmit
typedef struct	typedef struct
{	{
int number;	int number = 1;
int angle;	int angle;
float value;	float value;
char text[24] = "Transmission";	char text[24];
} dataStruct;	} dataStruct;
dataStruct data;	dataStruct data;

In the "transmit then receive" sketch, the potentiometer reading on Arduino pin A0 is mapped to the corresponding angle in the void loop() function.

```
int potent = analogRead(A0);              // read potentiometer value
data.angle = map(potent, 0, 1023, 0, 180); // convert to angle
data.angle = constrain(data.angle, 0, 180); // constrain angle value
```

In the "receive then transmit" sketch, the Servo library is installed, and the servo pin is defined at the start of the sketch.

```
#include <Servo.h>       // include the servo motor library
Servo servo;             // associate servo with Servo library
int servoPin = 11;       // servo motor pin = 11
```

The servo motor initialized in the void setup() function with the servo.attach(servoPin) instruction, and the servo motor rotated in the void loop() function with the servo.write(data.angle) instruction.

Summary

Wireless communication of numbers and text between transmitting and/ or receiving nRF24L01 modules was used to control devices, with the examples of turning on or off an LED or remotely moving a servo motor through an angle based on the transmitted output of a potentiometer.

Components List

- Arduino Uno and breadboard: 2×

- Wireless transceiver module: 2× nRF24L01

- LED

- Resistor: 220Ω

- Servo motor: SG90

- Potentiometer: 10kΩ

- Battery: 9V

- Voltage regulator: L4940V5

- Capacitors: 0.1µF and 22µF

CHAPTER 18

Build Arduino

In this chapter, we'll review the ATmega328P-PU 8-bit microcontroller. It has three types of memory: 32kB ISP (in-system programming) flash memory where sketches are stored, 1kB EEPROM (electrically erasable programmable read-only memory) for long-term data storage and 2kB SRAM (static random-access memory) for storing variables when a sketch is running. Information in flash memory and EEPROM is retained when power to the microcontroller is removed.

There are three communication modes: a serial programmable USART (universal synchronous and asynchronous receiver-transmitter), an SPI (Serial Peripheral Interface) serial port, and a two-wire serial interface. USART takes bytes of data and transmits the individual bits sequentially, which requires transmit (TX) and receive (RX) communication lines. SPI (outlined in Chapter 11) uses four communication lines: master-out slave-in (MOSI), master-in slave-out (MISO), and serial clock (SCK), with a separate slave select (SS) line for each device. The I2C communication (outlined in Chapter 11) Two Wire Interface (TWI) bus uses two signal lines: serial data (SDA) and serial clock (SCL).

The microcontroller has 13 digital general-purpose input/output (GPIO) lines and six 10-bit (values between 0 and $2^{10}-1 = 1023$) analogue to digital converter (ADC) GPIO lines to convert the voltage on a pin to a digital value. There are three timers with two 8-bit timers, with values between 0 and $2^8-1 = 255$, and one 16-bit timer, with values between 0 and $2^{16}-1 = 65535$, which are used by the delay() function in a sketch or by pulse width modulation (PWM), as outlined in Chapter 1.

The programmable watchdog timer with an internal oscillator (outlined in Chapter 20) checks that the microcontroller is active, and it resets the microcontroller if there is a malfunction. Internal and external interrupts allow the main sketch to stop, while the interrupt service routine (ISR) is completed, and then the main sketch continues.

There are five software selectable power-saving modes (outlined in Chapter 21) and the microcontroller operates between 1.8V and 5.5V.

ATmega328P Pin Layout

The pin layout of the ATmega328P-PU, shown in Figure 18-1, is available on the Arduino website (www.arduino.cc). There are three groups of ports: PB, PC, and PD with 8, 7, and 8 pins, respectively, (see Table 18-1) plus two ground (GND) pins, a 5V pin (VCC) with supply voltage (AVCC), and analog reference voltage (AREF) pins for the analog-to-digital converter (ADC).

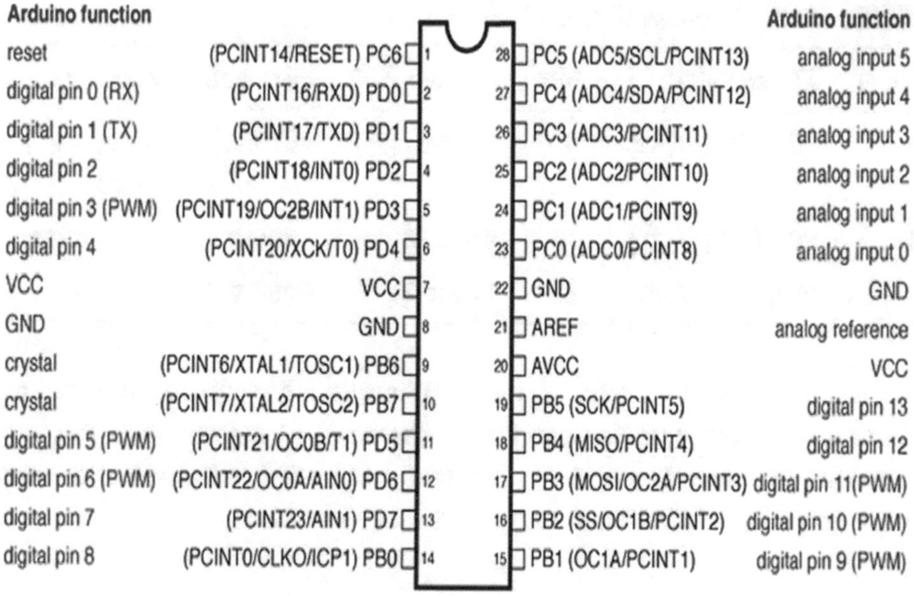

Arduino function				Arduino function
reset	(PCINT14/RESET) PC6 ☐ 1		28 ☐ PC5 (ADC5/SCL/PCINT13)	analog input 5
digital pin 0 (RX)	(PCINT16/RXD) PD0 ☐ 2		27 ☐ PC4 (ADC4/SDA/PCINT12)	analog input 4
digital pin 1 (TX)	(PCINT17/TXD) PD1 ☐ 3		26 ☐ PC3 (ADC3/PCINT11)	analog input 3
digital pin 2	(PCINT18/INT0) PD2 ☐ 4		25 ☐ PC2 (ADC2/PCINT10)	analog input 2
digital pin 3 (PWM)	(PCINT19/OC2B/INT1) PD3 ☐ 5		24 ☐ PC1 (ADC1/PCINT9)	analog input 1
digital pin 4	(PCINT20/XCK/T0) PD4 ☐ 6		23 ☐ PC0 (ADC0/PCINT8)	analog input 0
VCC	VCC ☐ 7		22 ☐ GND	GND
GND	GND ☐ 8		21 ☐ AREF	analog reference
crystal	(PCINT6/XTAL1/TOSC1) PB6 ☐ 9		20 ☐ AVCC	VCC
crystal	(PCINT7/XTAL2/TOSC2) PB7 ☐ 10		19 ☐ PB5 (SCK/PCINT5)	digital pin 13
digital pin 5 (PWM)	(PCINT21/OC0B/T1) PD5 ☐ 11		18 ☐ PB4 (MISO/PCINT4)	digital pin 12
digital pin 6 (PWM)	(PCINT22/OC0A/AIN0) PD6 ☐ 12		17 ☐ PB3 (MOSI/OC2A/PCINT3)	digital pin 11(PWM)
digital pin 7	(PCINT23/AIN1) PD7 ☐ 13		16 ☐ PB2 (SS/OC1B/PCINT2)	digital pin 10 (PWM)
digital pin 8	(PCINT0/CLKO/ICP1) PB0 ☐ 14		15 ☐ PB1 (OC1A/PCINT1)	digital pin 9 (PWM)

Figure 18-1. *ATmega328P pin layout*

The ATmega328P-PU pin nomenclature indicates the function of each pin (sec Figure 18-1). For example, pin change interrupts (PCINT0 to PCINT23) detect a change of pin state, as in a rising or a falling signal, interrupt pins (INT0 and INT1), analog-to-digital conversion pins (ADC0 to ADC5), serial communication (RXD and TXD), SPI communication pins (SS, MOSI, MISO, and SCK), I2C communication pins (SCL and SDA), timer0 (OC0A and OC0B), timer1 (OC1A and OC1B), and timer2 (OC2A and OC2B) (see Table 18-2), and Reset.

Table 18-1. *ATmega328P-PU pins and Mapped Arduino Pins by Port*

Port pins	ATmega328P-PU	Arduino pin	Function of Arduino pins
PB0 - PB7	14 to 19, 9, 10	Digital 8 to 13	PWM - 9, 10, 11, SPI - 10 to 13
PC0 - PC6	1, 23 to 28	Reset, A0 to A5	ADC - A0 to A5, I2C - A4, A5
PD0 - PD7	2 to 6, 11 to 13	Digital 0 to 7	PWM - 3, 5, 6, Serial - 0, 1, Interrupt 2, 3

Table 18-2. *ATmega328P-PU Timers*

Timer	ATmega328P	Bits	Arduino PWM	Frequency	Functions
0	PD5, PD6 (11, 12)	8	5 and 6	~976Hz	delay, millis, micros
1	PB1, PB2 (15, 16)	16	9 and 10	~490Hz	Servo library
2	PB3, PD3 (17, 5)	8	11 and 3	~490Hz	tone

From Tables 18–1 and 18–2, the dual functionality of some pins means that analogWrite() on Arduino PWM pins 9 and 10 is disabled by the *Servo* library, on Arduino PWM pins 10 and 11 by SPI communication and on Arduino PWM pins 3 and 11 by the tone() function.

Building an Arduino

Building an Arduino provides a portable microcontroller for projects not connected to a laptop and the low power consumption of the microcontroller ensures that a project can run for a long time on a battery. The required parts are an ATmega328P-PU microcontroller, two 22pF ceramic capacitors, a clock crystal with frequency 16MHz and a USB to serial UART (Universal Asynchronous Receiver Transmitter) interface, such as the FT232R FTDI, which has a switch to control the serial communication voltage to 3.3V or 5V.

The ATMega328P-PU microcontroller pin 1 has a semicircle indent on the end and a dot on the left-hand side. The 16MHz clock crystal is connected to the microcontroller with two 22pF ceramic capacitors, which enable the crystal to start oscillating and microcontroller circuitry converts the crystal into an oscillator (see Figure 18-2 and Table 18-3). A 10kΩ pull-up resistor is connected between microcontroller pin 1 and 5V to prevent the microcontroller resetting, as Reset is active *LOW*. A switch is also connected to microcontroller pin 1 for resetting the microcontroller.

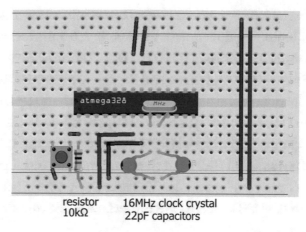

resistor   16MHz clock crystal
10kΩ   22pF capacitors

fritzing

Figure 18-2. *Microcontroller setup*

Table 18-3. *Connections for Building an Arduino*

Component	Connect to	and to
ATMega328P-PU pin 1	10kΩ resistor	Battery 5V
ATMega328P-PU pin 7	Battery 5V	
ATMega328P-PU pin 8	GND	
ATMega328P-PU pins 9, 10	16MHz clock crystal	
ATMega328P-PU pins 9, 10	22pF capacitor	GND
ATMega328P-PU pins 20, 21	Battery 5V	
ATMega328P-PU pin 22	GND	
Switch right leg	ATMega328P-PU pin 1	
Switch left leg	GND	

A USB to serial UART interface connects the microcontroller to a computer or laptop for downloading a sketch. A 0.1µF electrolytic capacitor is connected between the DTR (Data Terminal Ready) pin on the USB to serial UART interface and the microcontroller Reset, which resets the microcontroller to synchronize with the USB to serial UART interface. Microcontroller serial communication RX and TX pins are connected to the USB to serial UART interface TXD and RXD pins, respectively. USB to serial UART interface and microcontroller VCC and GND pins are connected (see Figure 18-3 and Table 18-4). The CTS (Clear to Send) pin on the USB to serial UART interface is not connected to the microcontroller.

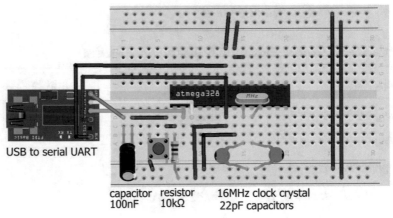

Figure 18-3. *Downloading a sketch*

Table 18-4. *Connections for Building an Arduino (2)*

Component	Connect to	and to
0.1µF capacitor positive	USB to serial UART DTR	
0.1µF capacitor negative	ATMega328P-PU pin 1	
USB to serial UART RXD	ATMega328P-PU pin 3	
USB to serial UART TXD	ATMega328P-PU pin 2	
USB to serial UART VCC	ATMega328P-PU pin 7	
USB to serial UART GND	ATMega328P-PU pin 22	
LED long leg	220Ω resistor	ATMega328P-PU pin 19
LED short leg	GND	

To download a sketch onto the microcontroller, in the Arduino IDE, from the *Tools* ➤ *Port* menu, select the relevant communication (COM) port and from the *Tools* ➤ *Board* menu select *Arduino/Genuino Uno*. The sketch is compiled in the Arduino IDE and then loaded to the microcontroller with the USB to serial UART interface. When the sketch is downloaded, the green and red LEDs of the USB-to-serial UART interface TXD and RXD flicker.

The USB to serial UART interface can be removed and a 5V power supply connected to the microcontroller (see Figure 18-4). An LED and 220kΩ resistor are connected to microcontroller pin 19, equivalent to Arduino pin 13, to run the blink sketch.

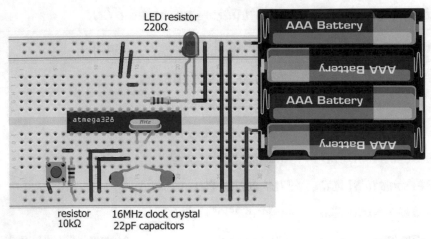

LED resistor
220Ω

AAA Battery

AAA Battery

AAA Battery

AAA Battery

atmega328

MHz

resistor
10kΩ

16MHz clock crystal
22pF capacitors

fritzing

Figure 18-4. *Stand-alone microcontroller with LED*

Installing the Bootloader

ATmega238P-PU microcontrollers require a bootloader for uploading and running sketches from the Arduino IDE. When power is applied to the microcontroller, the bootloader determines if a sketch is being uploaded, and then loads the sketch into the microcontroller memory. If a sketch is not being uploaded, then the bootloader instructs the microcontroller to run the loaded sketch.

If the ATmega328P-PU microcontroller is not supplied with a bootloader, then the bootloader must be uploaded. An Arduino can upload the bootloader using SPI communication (see Figure 18-5 and Table 18-5).

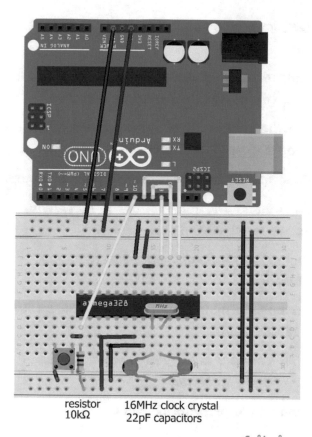

resistor
10kΩ

16MHz clock crystal
22pF capacitors

Figure 18-5. *Installing bootloader*

Table 18-5. *Connections for Installing a Bootloader*

Component	Connect to
Arduino pin 11	ATMega328P-PU pin 17
Arduino pin 12	ATMega328P-PU pin 18
Arduino pin 13	ATMega328P-PU pin 19
Arduino pin 10	ATMega328P-PU pin 1
Arduino 5V	ATMega328P-PU pin 7
Arduino GND	ATMega328P-PU pin 22

The *Atmega_Board_Programmer* by Nick Gammon is recommended.

1. Download the *arduino_sketches-master .zip* file from `github.com/nickgammon/arduino_sketches`.

2. Extract the *Atmega_Board_Programmer* folder to the desktop of a computer/laptop.

3. Connect an Arduino Uno to the computer or laptop.

4. In the Arduino IDE, from the *Tools* ➤ *Port* menu, select the relevant COM port.

5. From the *Tools* ➤ *Board* menu, select *Arduino/ Genuino Uno*.

6. Open the serial monitor and select *Both NL & CR* and *115200* baud.

7. Open the *Atmega_Board_Programmer* sketch and select *Compile and Load*.

The serial monitor displays the following.

> *Atmega chip programmer.*
>
> *Written by Nick Gammon.*
>
> *Version 1.38*
>
> *Compiled on May 22 2018 at 10:17:57 with Arduino IDE 10805.*
>
> *Attempting to enter ICSP programming mode ...*
>
> *Entered programming mode OK.*
>
> *Signature = 0x1E 0x95 0x0F*

Processor = ATmega328P

Flash memory size = 32768 bytes.

LFuse = 0xFF

HFuse = 0xDE

EFuse = 0xFD

Lock byte = 0xCF

Clock calibration = 0x9D

Type 'L' to use Lilypad (8 MHz) loader, or 'U' for Uno (16 MHz) loader …

Enter U and the serial monitor displays:

Using Uno Optiboot 16 MHz loader.

Bootloader address = 0x7E00

Bootloader length = 512 bytes.

Type 'Q' to quit, 'V' to verify, or 'G' to program the chip with the bootloader …

Enter G and the serial monitor displays:

Erasing chip …

Writing bootloader …

Committing page starting at 0x7E00

Committing page starting at 0x7E80

Committing page starting at 0x7F00

Committing page starting at 0x7F80

Written.

Verifying ...

No errors found.

Writing fuses ...

LFuse = 0xFF

HFuse = 0xDE

EFuse = 0xFD

Lock byte = 0xEF

Clock calibration = 0x9D

Done.

Programming mode off.

Type 'C' when ready to continue with another chip ...

The bootloader is now loaded onto the microcontroller, which is ready to receive a sketch after changing the COM port in the *Tools* ➤ *Port* menu.

Summary

The ATmega328P-PU microcontroller, which drives the Arduino Uno, is described. An Arduino is built and a sketch is downloaded to the microcontroller. Installation of the bootloader program to the microcontroller is described.

Components List

- Arduino Uno and breadboard

- Microcontroller: ATmega328P-PU

- USB to UART interface: FT232R FTDI

- Clock crystal: 16MHz

- Capacitor: 2× 22pF ceramic

- Resistor: 220Ω and 10kΩ

- Switch: tactile

- LED

CHAPTER 19

Global Navigation Satellite System

Longitude, latitude, and altitude can be determined from the global navigation satellite system (GNSS) using radio signals transmitted by line-of-sight satellites. GNSS includes the American GPS, Russian GLONASS, European Union Galileo, Chinese BeiDou, Japanese Quasi-Zenith, and satellite-based augmentation satellite systems. The u-blox NEO-7M module used in this chapter can receive signals from the GPS and GLONASS systems.

GNSS Messages on Serial Monitor

Signal reception by the u-blox NEO-7M module can be demonstrated by connecting the u-blox NEO-7M module to a computer or laptop with a USB to serial UART (Universal Asynchronous Receiver-Transmitter) interface (see Figure 19-1 and Table 19-1), with the output voltage of the USB to serial UART interface set at 3.3V for the u-blox NEO-7M module. After loading the Arduino IDE, select a communication (COM) port and open the serial monitor, at 9600 Baud, which displays the GNSS messages.

© Neil Cameron 2019
N. Cameron, *Arduino Applied*, https://doi.org/10.1007/978-1-4842-3960-5_19

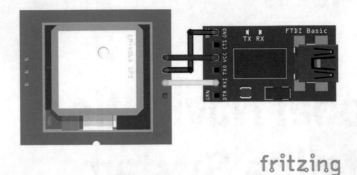

Figure 19-1. *GNSS receiver with USB to UART*

Table 19-1. *Connections for GNSS Receiver with USB to UART*

Component	Connect to
NEO-7M VCC	USB to UART VCC
NEO-7M GND	USB to UART GND
NEO-7M TX	USB to UART RXD
NEO-7M RX	USB to UART TXD

An example series of the National Marine Electronics Association (NMEA) GNSS messages is

```
$GPRMC,162436.00,A,5595.0000,N,00317.0000,W,0.378,,221017,,,A
$GPVTG,,T,,M,0.378,N,0.701,K,A
$GPGGA,162436.00, 5595.0000,N, 00317.0000,W,1,04,2.55,97.0,M,49.8,M,,
$GPGSA,A,3,09,06,07,05,,,,,,,,,6.66,2.55,6.16
$GPGSV,3,1,11,02,50,268,27,03,00,114,,05,24,290,27,06,43,203,33
$GPGSV,3,2,11,07,44,150,31,09,66,080,31,16,14,056,,23,34,071,14
$GPGSV,3,3,11,26,12,028,,29,16,326,18,30,20,176,11
$GPGLL, 5595.0000,,N, 00317.0000,W,162436.00,A,A
```

The example messages are prefixed with $GP followed by the message name—such as RMC, GGA, and GLL—to provide information on time, latitude, and longitude. The GSV message provides positional information on each satellite or space vehicle (SV). Speed over ground, altitude, and date are provided by the VTG, GGA, and RMC messages, respectively.

u-blox u-center

The u-blox u-center GNSS evaluation software provides real-time displays of GNSS message information. It can be downloaded from www.u-blox.com/en/product/u-center. The u-blox u-center GNSS evaluation display version 18.10 is illustrated in Figure 19-2. The position and signal strength of each satellite can be displayed along with speed over ground; 3D location of longitude, latitude, and altitude; and date and time. The u-blox u-center GNSS evaluation display identifies satellites from the GPS, GNSS, SBAS, and QZSS systems by the letters G, R, S, and Q, respectively. NMEA message names are prefixed by $GP for GPS, $GL for GLONASS, and $GN for a combination of GS and GLONASS.

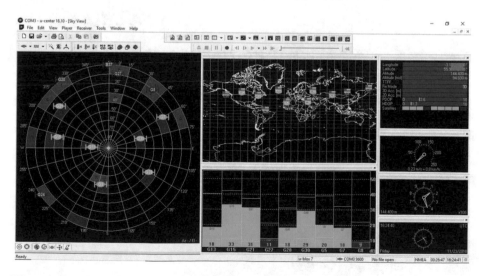

Figure 19-2. *u-blox u-center GNSS evaluation display*

A 2D or 3D location requires at least three or four satellites with position and motion data and a carrier to noise density ratio (C/N0) of 34dB-Hz to obtain a fix in 30 to 40 seconds. If the C/NO ratio is between 25 and 34dB-Hz, then it can take up to five minutes to obtain a valid 3D location.

To communicate between the u-blox u-center GNSS evaluation display and the GNSS receiver, the USB to serial UART interface TXD (transmit) must also be connected to u-blox NEO-7M module RX (receive) (see Figure 19-3). Close the Arduino IDE serial monitor. In the u-blox u-center GNSS evaluation display menu, select *Receiver* ➤ *Connection* ➤ *COMport* and select *View* ➤ *Sky View* to display satellite position.

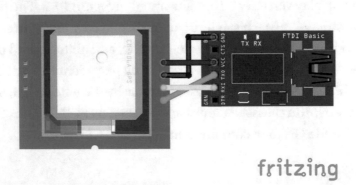

Figure 19-3. *GNSS receiver, USB to UART for u-blox u-center*

Information on the NMEA message content is available within the u-blox u-center GNSS evaluation display. From the *View* menu, select *Messages View* and click the required message.

Information from the GSS/QZSS or GLONASS satellite systems is obtained through the *View* menu.

1. Select *Messages View*.

2. Select *UBX*.

3. Select *CFG (Config)*.

4. Select *Enable* for either GPS and QZSS or GLONASS.

5. Select *Send* at the bottom left of the u-blox u-center
    GNSS evaluation display.

Instructions on the u-blox u-center GNSS evaluation software are available on the u-blox website at `www.u-blox.com/en/product/u-center`.

Arduino and GNSS

NMEA messages from the GNSS module can be displayed on the u-blox u-center GNSS evaluation display by selecting *View* ➤ *Text* console. The following is the order of messages.

- RMC – recommended minimum data

- VTG – course over ground

- GGA – global positioning data

- GSA – active satellites

- GSV – satellites in view

- GLL – latitude and longitude

Information on the NMEA 0183 message structure is available from several sources, such as `www.u-blox.com/en/product-resources`.

An example RMC message is

$GPRMC, 083559.00, A, 4717.11437, N, 00833.91522, E, 0.004, 77.52, 091202, , , A*57

It has a comma-separated structure (see Table 19-2).

Table 19-2. RMC Message Structure

Example	Description	Name	Format
$GPRMC	RMC message ID	xxRMC	
083559.00	UTC time	time	hhmmss.ss
A	Status (A:valid)	status	
4717.11437	Latitude (degrees and minutes)	lat	ddmm.mmmmm
N	North/South indicator	NS	
00833.91522	Longitude	long	ddmm.mmmmm
E	East/West indicator	EW	
0.004	Speed over ground	spd	knots
77.52	Course over ground	cog	degrees
091202	Date	date	ddmmyy
	blank	mv	
	blank	mvEW	
A	Mode indicator	posMode	
*57	Checksum	cs	
<CR><LF>	Carriage return and line feed		

The GNSS module is connected to the Arduino using software serial with GNSS module TX (transmit) and RX (receive) connected to Arduino pins 8 and 9, respectively. The library *AltSoftSerial* by Paul Stoffregen can be installed within the Arduino IDE using installation method 3, as outlined in Chapter 3.

The u-blox NEO-7M module operates at 3.3V and the module RX (receive) should not be connected to the Arduino TXD (transmit) pin, which operates at 5V. A logic level converter ensures that the GNSS

module TX signal has sufficient voltage for the Arduino RXD pin as
well as protecting the GNSS module (see Figure 19-4 and Table 19-3).
Alternatively, a voltage divider, with a 4.7kΩ and a 10kΩ resistor, between
the Arduino TXD and GNSS module RX as outlined in Chapter 3, would
suffice.

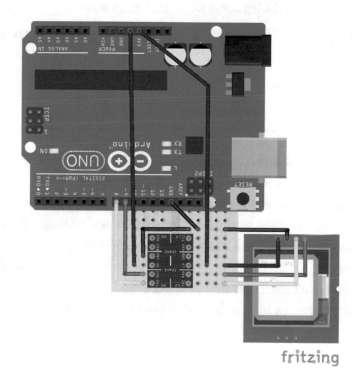

Figure 19-4. *Logic level converter and GNSS module*

Table 19-3. *Logic Level Converter and GNSS Module*

Component	Connect to	and to	and to
NEO-7M VCC	Arduino 3.3V		
NEO-7M GND	Arduino GND		
NEO-7M TX	LLC low voltage TX	LLC high voltage TX	Arduino pin 8
NEO-7M RX	LLC low voltage RX	LLC high voltage RX	Arduino pin 9
LLC high voltage	Arduino 5V		
LLC low voltage	Arduino 3.3V		
LLC GND	Arduino 5GND		

In Listing 19-1, information from two NMEA messages, RMC and GGA, is extracted, so the other NMEA messages are turned off by message settings. Within the u-blox u-center GNSS evaluation display, the *UTX–CFG–MSG* message settings are located by selecting the *View* menu ➤ *Messages View* ➤ *UBX* ➤ *CFG (Config)* ➤ *MSG (Messages)*. Choose the required message from the drop-down menu, for example *F0-04 NMEA GxRMC*, and deselect all options except UART1. At the bottom of the screen, the message setting is displayed (see Figure 19-5).

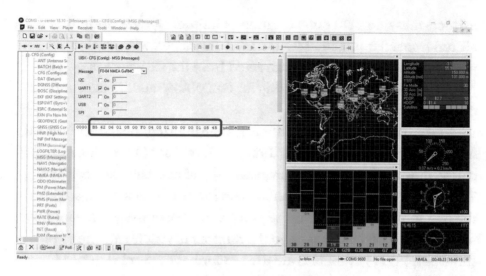

Figure 19-5. *UTX - CGF - MSG message settings*

For example, the message setting in HEX, but without the 0x prefix, for the NMEA-RMC message is

B5 62 06 01 08 00 F0 04 00 01 00 00 00 01 05 15 that can be converted to decimal, *181,98,6,1,8,0,240,4,0,1,0,0,0,1,5,69*

to make the message setting more manageable in the sketch.

The default setting of the u-blox NEO-7M module receives GPS satellite signals. The u-blox NEO-7M module can be set to receive GPS or GLONASS satellite signals, using the *UTX–CFG–GNSS (GNSS Config)* satellite settings in the same manner as the *UTX–CFG–MSG* message settings.

The *UTX–CFG–MSG* message settings indicate the message type, column eight in bold in Listing 19-1, and the message on/off state, column ten in bold in Listing 19-1. In the sketch, all messages are initially switched off and then the required messages are switched on, column 15 in bold in Listing 19-1.

Given the structure of NMEA messages, specific variables can be readily selected to record time, location, and speed, which can be subsequently input to *Google Maps* for route marking. The sketch

347

extracts measurement time; location of latitude, longitude, and altitude; speed from the RMC and GGA messages, with satellite position; and signal strength extracted from the GSV messages. The NMEA message labels and setting for GLONASS satellite data are commented out in the sketch.

The switch case function allocates the information to be extracted from each message, with the .toInt() and .toFloat() functions converting message text into integers and real numbers, respectively. The GSV message contains satellite data for up to four satellites, with the first three variables being the number of GSV messages, the number of the current GSV message, and the number of visible satellites. The three temp[1...3] variables are used to format the Serial.print() instructions. The replace() function is useful for replacing one character in a string with another, as in the void parseMessage() function.

Listing 19-1. Reading GNSS Messages

```
#include <AltSoftSerial.h> // include AltSoftSerial library
AltSoftSerial AltSoft;        // associate AltSoft with AltSoftSerial library
String NMEAdata, nmea, val[6], temp[19]; // define string to store data
int rec, lastRow;
  String message[3]={"$GPRMC","$GPGGA","$GPGSV"}; // GPS message labels
//String message[3]={"$GLRMC","$GLGGA","$GLGSV"}; // GLONASS
                                                  // message labels
                        // matrix of UTX – CFG – MSG message settings
const unsigned char ublox[ ] PROGMEM = {
181,98,6,1,8,0,240,0,0,0,0,0,0,1,0,36,     // GGA message off
181,98,6,1,8,0,240,1,0,0,0,0,0,1,1,43,     // GLL message off
181,98,6,1,8,0,240,2,0,0,0,0,0,1,2,50,     // GSA message off
181,98,6,1,8,0,240,3,0,0,0,0,0,1,3,57,     // GSV message off
181,98,6,1,8,0,240,4,0,0,0,0,0,1,4,64,     // RMC message off
181,98,6,1,8,0,240,5,0,0,0,0,0,1,5,71,     // VTG message off
```

```
181,98,6,1,8,0,240,0,0,1,0,0,0,1,1,41,          // GGA message set on
181,98,6,1,8,0,240,3,0,1,0,0,0,1,4,62,          // GSV message set on
181,98,6,1,8,0,240,4,0,1,0,0,0,1,5,69,          // RMC message set on
   181,98,6,62,36,0,0,0,22,4,0,4,255,0,0,0,0,1,1,1,3,  // GPS and
   0,0,0,0,1,5,0,3,0,0,0,0,1,6,8,255,0,0,0,0,1,163,9,  // GLONASS off
   181,98,6,62,36,0,0,0,22,4,0,4,255,0,1,0,0,1,1,1,3,  // GPS on
   0,0,0,0,1,5,0,3,0,0,0,0,1,6,8,255,0,0,0,0,1,164,37  // GPS on
//181,98,6,62,36,0,0,0,22,4,0,4,255,0,0,0,0,1,1,1,3,  // GLONASS on
//0,0,0,0,1,5,0,3,0,0,0,0,1,6,8,255,0,1,0,0,1,164,13  // GLONASS on
};

void setup()
{
  Serial.begin(9600);                  // baud rate for Serial Monitor
  AltSoft.begin(9600);                 // serial connection to GNSS module
  for(int i = 0; i < sizeof(ublox); i++)
  {
    AltSoft.write(pgm_read_byte(ublox+i));  // send message settings to GNSS
    delay(5);
  }                                          // column headers
  Serial.println("time, lat, long, altitude, speed, satellite data");
  delay(1000);
}

void loop()
{
  NMEAdata = AltSoft.readStringUntil('\n');  // read data until a carriage return
  nmea = NMEAdata.substring(0, 6);  // first 6 characters are message name
  if(nmea == message[0]) rec = 0;  // message name equals $GLRMC
  else if(nmea == message[1]) rec = 1;    // or $GLGGA
  else if(nmea == message[2])rec = 2;     // or $GLGSV
  switch (rec)                            // use switch ...case
```

```
{
   case 0:
     parseMessage(NMEAdata, 7);      // parse GPRMC message, 7 values
     val[0]=temp[0].toInt();                // time
     val[1]= temp[2].toFloat()/100.0;     // latitude
     val[2]= temp[4].toFloat()/100.0;     // longitude
     if(temp[5]="W") val[2]="-"+val[2];
     val[4]= String(temp[6].toFloat()*1.852); // convert speed in
                                                   // knots to kmph
   break;
   case 1:
     parseMessage(NMEAdata, 9);     // parse GPGGA message, 9 values
     val[3]=temp[8];                        // altitude (m)
     val[5]=temp[6];                        // number of satellites for fix
   break;
   case 2:
     parseMessage(NMEAdata,19);     // parse GLGSV message
     if(temp[1]=="1")
     {
       val[6]=temp[2];                     // number of visible satellites
       for (int i=0; i<6; i++)
         {Serial.print(val[i]);Serial.print(",");}
       Serial.println();
       for (int i=0;i<6;i++) val[i]="";
     }
     if(temp[1].toInt()<temp[0].toInt()) // not the last line of data
     {
       for (int i=3;i<19;i++)
         {Serial.print(temp[i]);Serial.print(",");}
       Serial.println();
     }
     else                                  // last line of data
```

```
    {
      lastRow = 4*(temp[2].toInt()-(temp[1].toInt()-1)*4)+3;
      for (int i=3;i<lastRow;i++)
        {Serial.print(temp[i]);Serial.print(",");}
      Serial.println();
    }
  break;
  default:    break;
  }
}

void parseMessage(String data, int nval) // function to parse message
{
  data.replace('*', ',');                // replace asterisk, *, with comma
  int istart, iend;
  iend = 0;
  for (int i=0; i<nval; i++)
  {
    istart = data.indexOf(",", iend); // istart is location before value
    iend = data.indexOf(",", istart+1); // iend is location after value
    temp[i] = data.substring(istart+1, iend);
  }
}
```

An alternative to extracting information directly from the NMEA
messages is to use a library, such as the *NeoGPS* library by Slash Devin,
which can be installed within the Arduino IDE using installation
method 3, as outlined in Chapter 3. Information about the *NeoGPS*
library and the structure of extracted data from the NMEA messages
is available at github.com/SlashDevin/NeoGPS. Version 4.2.9 of
the *NeoGPS* library uses *AltSoftSerial* as the default software serial
connection, so the u-blox NEO-7M module TX pin is connected to
Arduino pin 8.

The *NMEAorder* sketch, which is included in the *NeoGPS* library, checks the configuration of the LAST SENTENCE variable and displays the result on the serial monitor. The definition of LAST SENTENCE is changed by editing the *NMEAGPS_cfg.h* file located in the *NeoGPS* library. The default is the *Documents* ➤ *Arduino* ➤ *libraries* folder, with the location of the default library folder for the Arduino IDE confirmed by selecting *File* ➤ *Preferences* within the Arduino IDE.

1. Open the *Arduino* ➤ *libraries* ➤ *NeoGPS* ➤ *NMEAGPS_cfg.h* file to change line 48 from

   ```
   #define LAST_SENTENCE_IN_INTERVAL NMEAGPS::NMEA_RMC
   ```

   to have the required value; for example,

   ```
   #define LAST_SENTENCE_IN_INTERVAL NMEAGPS::NMEA_GLL
   ```

2. Save the *NMEAGPS_cfg.h* file and then re-run the sketch *NMEAorder* to ensure that the change is correctly incorporated and the serial monitor should display

   SUCCESS: LAST_SENTENCE_IN_INTERVAL is correctly set to NMEAGPS::NMEA_GLL

3. If information on individual satellites is required, then edit the *NMEAGPS_cfg* file, within the *src* folder of the *NeoGPS* library, and uncomment the lines in Listing 19-2.

Listing 19-2. Individual Satellite Settings

```
#define NMEAGPS_PARSE_GGA               // on line 33
#define NMEAGPS_PARSE_GLL               // on line 34
#define NMEAGPS_PARSE_GSV               // on line 36
#define NMEAGPS_PARSE_RMC               // on line 38
#define NMEAGPS_PARSE_SATELLITES        // on line 209
#define NMEAGPS_PARSE_SATELLITE_INFO    // on line 210
```

Listing 19-3, which uses the *NeoGPS* library, provides the same satellite information as Listing 19-1 without having to parse NMEA messages or define *UTX–CFG–MSG* message settings.

Listing 19-3. Reading GNSS Messages Using the NeoGPS Library

```
#include <AltSoftSerial.h>      // include AltSoftSerial library
AltSoftSerial AltSoft;       // associate AltSoft with AltSoftSerial library
#include <NMEAGPS.h>       // include NeoGPS library
NMEAGPS nmea;           // associate nmea with NMEAGPS library
gps_fix gps;           // associate gps with NMEAGPS library
int GPS, SBAS, Nsat, count;

void setup()
{
  Serial.begin(9600);          // define Serial output baud rate
  AltSoft.begin(9600);         // serial connection to GNSS module
  Serial.println("time, lat, long, altitude, speed, satellite data");
  delay(500);                  // column headers
}

void loop()
{
  if (nmea.available(AltSoft)) // GNSS data available
  {
    gps = nmea.read();         // latest satellite message
    if(gps.valid.time)         // validated time – every second
    {                                              // leading zeros for
      if(gps.dateTime.hours < 10) Serial.print("0"); // time
      Serial.print(gps.dateTime.hours); Serial.print(":");
      if(gps.dateTime.minutes < 10) Serial.print("0");
      Serial.print(gps.dateTime.minutes); Serial.print(":");
      if(gps.dateTime.seconds < 10) Serial.print("0");
      Serial.print(gps.dateTime.seconds); Serial.print(", ");
    }
```

```
if(gps.valid.location)        // validated location
{                             // latitude and longitude
  Serial.print(gps.latitude(), 3); Serial.print(", ");
  Serial.print(gps.longitude(), 3); Serial.print(", ");
}
if(gps.valid.altitude)       // altitude
  {Serial.print(gps.altitude(), 1);Serial.print(", ");}
if(gps.valid.speed)          // speed
  {Serial.print(gps.speed_kph(), 1);Serial.print(", ");}
if(gps.valid.satellites)
{
  Serial.print(gps.satellites);   // number of satellites for fix
  Serial.print(",");
  GPS = 0;
  SBAS = 0;
  Nsat = 0;
  for (int i=0; i<16; i++)         // max number of visible satellites
  {
    if (nmea.satellites[i].tracked)
    {
      Nsat++;                      // number of tracked satellites
      if (nmea.satellites[i].id <= 32) GPS++;
      else if (nmea.satellites[i].id >32 &&
              nmea.satellites[i].id <= 64) SBAS++;
    }
  }
  Serial.print(Nsat);Serial.print(",");   // display satellite numbers
  Serial.print(GPS);Serial.print(",");
  Serial.println(SBAS);
  count = 0;
  for (int i=0; i<16; i++)
```

```
//      if (nmea.satellites[i].tracked)    // display only tracked satellites
        if (nmea.satellites[i].id>0)       // display all visible satellites
        {
          Serial.print(nmea.satellites[i].id);Serial.print(",");
          Serial.print(nmea.satellites[i].elevation);
          Serial.print(",");
          Serial.print(nmea.satellites[i].azimuth);Serial.print(",");
          Serial.print(nmea.satellites[i].snr);Serial.print(",");
          count++;
          if(count%4==0) Serial.println();
        }
        if(count%4!=0) Serial.println();
    }
  }
}
```

If a sketch using the *NeoGPS* library (such as Listing 19-3) follows a sketch defining the *UTX–CFG–MSG* message settings (such as Listing 19-1), then message settings should be reset using Listing 19-4.

Listing 19-4. Reset GNSS Message Settings

```
#include <AltSoftSerial.h>        // include AltSoftSerial library
AltSoftSerial AltSoft; // associate AltSoft with AltSoftSerial library
                          // matrix of UTX – CFG – MSG message settings
const unsigned char ublox[ ] PROGMEM = {
181,98,6,1,8,0,240,0,0,0,0,0,0,1,0,36,    // GGA message off
181,98,6,1,8,0,240,1,0,0,0,0,0,1,1,43,    // GLL message off
181,98,6,1,8,0,240,2,0,0,0,0,0,1,2,50,    // GSA message off
181,98,6,1,8,0,240,3,0,0,0,0,0,1,3,57,    // GSV message off
181,98,6,1,8,0,240,4,0,0,0,0,0,1,4,64,    // RMC message off
181,98,6,1,8,0,240,5,0,0,0,0,0,1,5,71,    // VTG message off
```

```
181,98,6,1,8,0,240,0,0,1,0,0,0,1,1,41,      // GGA message on
181,98,6,1,8,0,240,1,0,1,0,0,0,1,2,48,      // GLL message on
181,98,6,1,8,0,240,2,0,1,0,0,0,1,3,55,      // GSA message on
181,98,6,1,8,0,240,3,0,1,0,0,0,1,4,62,      // GSV message on
181,98,6,1,8,0,240,4,0,1,0,0,0,1,5,69,      // RMC message on
181,98,6,1,8,0,240,5,0,1,0,0,0,1,6,76,      // VTG message on
  181,98,6,62,36,0,0,0,22,4,0,4,255,0,0,0,0,1,1,1,3,      // GPS and
  0,0,0,0,1,5,0,3,0,0,0,0,1,6,8,255,0,0,0,0,1,163,9,      // GLONASS off
  181,98,6,62,36,0,0,0,22,4,0,4,255,0,1,0,0,1,1,1,3,      // GPS on
  0,0,0,0,1,5,0,3,0,0,0,0,1,6,8,255,0,0,0,0,1,164,37,    // GPS on
//181,98,6,62,36,0,0,0,22,4,0,4,255,0,0,0,0,1,1,1,3,      // GLONASS on
//0,0,0,0,1,5,0,3,0,0,0,0,1,6,8,255,0,1,0,0,1,164,13      // GLONASS on
};

void setup()
{
  Serial.begin(9600);          // baud rate for Serial Monitor
  AltSoft.begin(9600);         // serial connection to GNSS module
  for(int i = 0; i < sizeof(ublox); i++)
  {
    AltSoft.write(pgm_read_byte(ublox+i)); // send message settings to GNSS
    delay(5);
  }
  Serial.println("NMEA messages all on");
}

void loop()                    // nothing in void loop function
{}
```

GNSS Data Logging to SD Card

Satellite data written to an SD card forms the basis of a mobile GNSS tracker (see Figure 19-6 and Table 19-4). Listing 19-5 builds on Listing 19-3 by including data logging with an SD card, as described in Chapter 12 in the "Logging Weather Station Data" and "Increment File Name for Data Logging" sections.

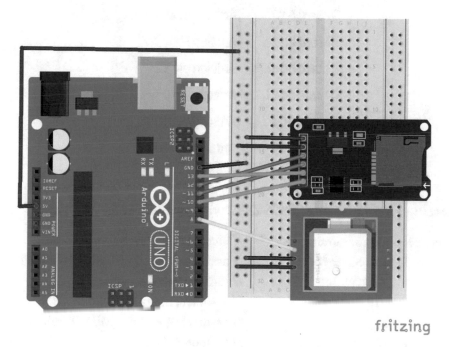

fritzing

Figure 19-6. *Logging GNSS data with an SD card*

Table 19-4. *Logging GNSS Data with an SD Card*

Component	Connect to
NEO-7M VCC	Arduino 5V
NEO-7M GND	Arduino GND
NEO-7M TX	Arduino pin 8
SD card GND	Arduino GND
SD card VCC	Arduino 5V
SD card MISO	Arduino pin 12
SD card MOSI	Arduino pin 11
SD card SCK	Arduino pin 13
SD card SCS	Arduino pin 10

Listing 19-5. Logging GNSS Data with an SD Card

```
#include <AltSoftSerial.h>        // include AltSoftSerial library
AltSoftSerial AltSoft;            // associate AltSoft with AltSoftSerial library
#include <NMEAGPS.h>              // include NeoGPS library
NMEAGPS nmea;                     // associate nmea with NMEAGPS library
gps_fix gps;                      // associate gps with NMEAGPS library
#include <SPI.h>                  // include SPI library
#include <SD.h>                   // include SD library
File file;                       // associate file with SD library
String filename = "data.csv";    // filename
int CSpin = 10;                  // chip select pin for SD card
int i = 0;                       // data record counter
String header, data, hr, mn, s;
```

```
void setup()
{
  Serial.begin(9600);                  // define Serial output baud rate
  if(SD.begin(CSpin) == 0)             // check for presence of SD card
  {
    Serial.println("Card fail");  // return if SD card not found
    return;
  }
  Serial.println("Card OK");
  if(SD.exists(filename)) SD.remove(filename); // delete existing file
  file = SD.open(filename, FILE_WRITE); // create new file
  if(file == 1)                         // file opened
  {                                     // column headers
    header = "Time, Latitude, Longitude, Altitude, Speed, Satellites";
    file.println(header);               // write column headers to SD card
    file.close();                       // close file after writing to SD card
  }
  else Serial.println("Couldn't access file"); // file not opened
  AltSoft.begin(9600);                  // serial connection to GNSS
}

void loop()
{
  while (nmea.available(AltSoft))    // GNSS data available
  {
    i++;                                 // increase data record counter
    Serial.print("record ");Serial.println(i); // print record number
    gps = nmea.read();                   // latest satellite message
    hr = String(gps.dateTime.hours);     // leading zeros for time
    if(gps.dateTime.hours<10) hr = "0"+hr;
    mn = String(gps.dateTime.minutes);
```

```
  if(gps.dateTime.minutes<10) mn="0"+mn;
  s = String(gps.dateTime.seconds);
  if(gps.dateTime.seconds<10) s="0"+s;
  data = hr + mn+ s;                          // create string of readings
  data =data+","+String(gps.latitude(),4)+","+
  String(gps.longitude(),4);
  data =data+","+String(gps.altitude(),1)+","+
  String(gps.speed_kph(), 1);
  data = data + "," + String(gps.satellites);
  file = SD.open(filename, FILE_WRITE);   // open file on SD card
  file.println(data);                         // write data to SD card
  file.close();                               // close file on SD card
 }
}
```

GNSS and ST7735 Screen

The mobile GNSS tracker is completed by including a ST7735 TFT LCD (Thin Film Transistor Liquid Crystal Display) screen to display current location and time, while simultaneously writing GNSS data to an SD card (see Figure 19-7 and Table 19-5). The ST7735 TFT LCD screen has an SD card module on the rear of the screen. Listing 19-6 uses code for the SD card from Chapter 12, for the ST7735 TFT LCD screen from Chapter 13, and for the GNSS module from this chapter. The stand-alone microcontroller is built and programmed as described in Chapter 18.

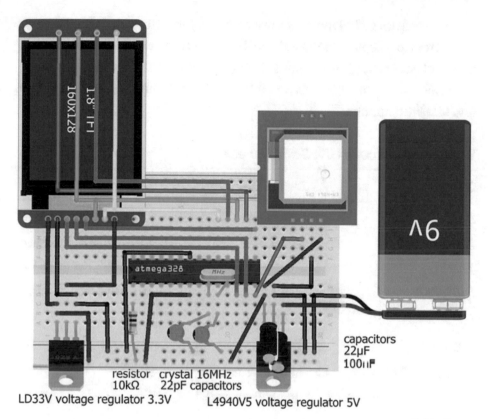

Figure 19-7. *Mobile GNSS with screen*

The sketch uses the *NeoGPS* library to access positional data rather than having to parse NMEA messages. The sketch first checks the status of the SD card and opens a new *dataN.csv* file with the file name incremented rather than overwriting the existing data file. The ST7735 TFT LCD screen is cleared and headers for the speed, location, and number of satellites are displayed on the screen. Every second, the ST7735 TFT LCD screen is updated with speed, satellite number, and location of altitude, latitude, and longitude, with satellite number and location only updated if there are new values. Every five seconds, data on the time, latitude, longitude, altitude, speed, and number of satellites is written to the SD card.

Values from GNSS messages are converted to strings and then to characters for display on the ST7735 TFT LCD screen with the `String()` and `.toCharArray()` functions. Prior to the valid NMEA messages being obtained, values of 96, 97, 98, and 99 are written to the SD card for location and satellite number.

Table 19-5. *Mobile GNSS with Screen*

Component	Connect to	and to
L4940V5 supply	Battery 9V	0.1µF capacitor positive
L4940V5 GND	GND rail	0.1µF capacitor negative 22µF capacitor negative
L4940V5 demand	5V rail	22µF capacitor positive
LD33V supply	5V rail	
LD33V GND	GND rail	
ATMega328P-PU pin 1	10kΩ resistor	5V rail
ATMega328P-PU pins 9, 10	16MHz clock crystal	
ATMega328P-PU pins 9, 10	16MHz clock crystal	
ATMega328P-PU pins 9, 10	22pF capacitor	GND
ATMega328P-PU pin 7	5V rail	
ATMega328P-PU pin 22	GND rail	
NEO-7M VCC	5V rail	
NEO-7M GND	GND rail	
NEO-7M TX	ATMega328P-PU pin 14	
ST7735 TFT VCC	5V rail	
ST7735 TFT GND	GND rail	
ST7735 TFT CS	ATMega328P-PU pin 12	

(continued)

Table 19-5. (*continued*)

Component	Connect to	and to
ST7735 TFT RESET	ATMega328P-PU pin 13	
ST7735 TFT A0	ATMega328P-PU pin 15	
ST7735 TFT SDA	ATMega328P-PU pin 17	SD card module MOSI
ST7735 TFT SCK	ATMega328P-PU pin 19	SD card module SCK
ST7735 TFT LED	LD33V output 3.3V	
SD card module CS	ATMega328P-PU pin 16	
SD card module MISO	ATMega328P-PU pin 18	

The schematic in Figure 19-7 starts with 9V from the battery reduced to 5V by the L4940V5 voltage regulator, which powers the NEO-7M module, the ATMega328P-PU microcontroller and the SD card module. The 5V output from the L4940V5 voltage regulator is reduced to 3.3V by the LD33V voltage regulator to supply the ST7735 TFT LCD screen. Note the voltage regulator pins are different with supply, GND and demand for the L4940V5 regulator and GND, demand and supply for the LD33V regulator.

The ATMega328P-PU microcontroller is connected to the NEO-7M module, ST7735 TFT LCD screen, and SD card module. Downloading the complied sketch with a USB to serial UART interface connected to the microcontroller was outlined in Chapter 18, with the USB to serial UART connections shown in Table 19-6.

Table 19-6. *USB to Serial UART Interface*

Component	Connect to
100nF capacitor positive	USB to serial UART DTR
100nF capacitor negative	ATMega328P-PU pin 1
USB to serial UART RXD	ATMega328P-PU pin 3
USB to serial UART TXD	ATMega328P-PU pin 2
USB to serial UART VCC	5V rail
USB to serial UART GND	GND rail

Listing 19-6. Mobile GNSS with Screen

```
#include <AltSoftSerial.h>      // include AltSoftSerial library
AltSoftSerial AltSoft;          // associate AltSoft with AltSoftSerial library
#include <NMEAGPS.h>            // include NeoGPS library
NMEAGPS nmea;                   // associate nmea with NMEAGPS library
gps_fix gps;                    // associate gps with NMEAGPS library
#include <SPI.h>               // include SPI library
#include <SD.h>                // include SD library
String filename;
String basefile = "data";      // default filename is data.csv
bool filefound = false;        // checks if filename exists
int filecount = 0;             // adds number to filename
int SDcount = 0;               // counter to write to SD card
int nsat = 0;                  // last number of satellites
float oldlat = 0;              // last latitude
float oldlong = 0;             // last longitude
#include <Adafruit_ST7735.h>   // include the ST7735 library
#include <Adafruit_GFX.h>      // include the GFX library
int TFT_CS = 6;                // screen chip select pin
int RSTpin = 7;                // screen reset pin
int DCpin = 9;                 // screen DC pin
```

```
int SD_CS = 10;                  // SD card chip select pin
                                 // associate tft with Adafruit_ST7735 library
Adafruit_ST7735 tft = Adafruit_ST7735(TFT_CS, DCpin, RSTpin);
String fill;
String data;                     // GNSS output converted to string
char text[6];                    // string converted to characters

void setup()
{
  tft.initR(INITR_BLACKTAB);       // initialize ST7735 TFT LCD screen
  tft.fillScreen(ST7735_BLACK);    // clear screen
  tft.setTextColor(ST7735_WHITE, ST7735_BLACK); // text colour with over-write
  AltSoft.begin(9600);             // serial connection to GNSS module
  if(SD.begin(SD_CS) == 0)         // check for presence of SD card
  {
    printScreen("Card fail", 10, 5, 2);      // return if SD card not found
    return;
  }
  printScreen("Card OK", 10, 5, 2);
  delay(1000);
  filename=basefile+".csv";    // option to delete and replace file
  //if(SD.exists(filename)>0) SD.remove(filename);
  while (filefound == 0)       // search for file with filename
  {
    if(SD.exists(filename))  // if filename already exists on SD card
    {
      filecount++;                 // then increment filename counter
      filename = basefile + String(filecount) + ".csv"; // new filename
    }
    else filefound = true;     // file with filename located on SD card
  }                              // column headers
```

```
  data = "Time, Latitude, Longitude, Altitude, Speed, Satellites";
  File file = SD.open(filename, FILE_WRITE); // open file on SD card
  if(file == 1) file.println(data);          // write header to SD card
  file.close();
  tft.fillScreen(ST7735_BLACK);                      // clear screen
  printScreen("Speed & satellites", 9, 5, 1);    // print fixed text
  printScreen("Altitude", 8, 50, 1);
  printScreen("Latitude & longitude", 8, 95, 1);
}

void loop()
{
  while (nmea.available(AltSoft))        // GNSS data available
  {
    gps = nmea.read();
    if(gps.valid.time) data = String(gps.dateTime.hours) + ":" +
                              String(gps.dateTime.minutes)+ ":" +
                              String(gps.dateTime.seconds);
    else data ="99:99:99";
    if(gps.valid.location) data = data + "," +
                                  String(gps.latitude(), 4) + "," +
                                  String(gps.longitude(), 4);
    else data = data +",,96"; // default values while waiting for position
    if(gps.valid.altitude) data = data +","+
                                  String(gps.altitude(), 1);
    else data = data +",97";
    if(gps.valid.speed) data = data +","+ String(gps.speed_kph(), 4);
    else data = data +",98";
    if(gps.satellites>0) data = data +","+ String(gps.satellites);
    else data = data +",99";
    SDcount++;
    if(SDcount>4)                        // write to SD card every 5 seconds
    {
      File file = SD.open(filename, FILE_WRITE); // write to SD card
```

```
  if(file) file.println(data);  // write data string to file on SD card
  file.close();                  // close file on SD card
  SDcount = 0;                   // reset counter
}
if(gps.speed_kph()<10)           // print speed (kmph)
{
  fill = " "+ String(gps.speed_kph(), 1);   // convert number to string
  fill.toCharArray(text,6);       // convert string to characters
}
else String(gps.speed_kph(), 1).toCharArray(text,6);
printScreen(text, 10, 20, 3);
if(nsat != gps.satellites)
{
  if(nsat<10) fill = " "+ String(gps.satellites);
  else fill = String(gps.satellites);   // print number of
                                         // satellites to screen
  fill.toCharArray(text,6);
  printScreen(text, 100, 20, 2);
  nsat = gps.satellites;          // current number of satellites
}
if(gps.altitude()<100)fill = " "+ String(gps.altitude(), 1);
else fill = String(gps.altitude(), 1); // print altitude to screen
fill.toCharArray(text,6);
printScreen(text, 10, 65, 3);
if(abs(oldlat-gps.latitude())>0.1 || abs(oldlat-gps.latitude())>0.1)
{                                 // update latitude and longitude
  String(gps.latitude(), 1).toCharArray(text,6);
  printScreen(text, 10, 110, 2);   // print latitude to screen
  String(gps.longitude(), 1).toCharArray(text,6);
  printScreen(text, 70, 110, 2);   // print longitude to screen
```

```
        oldlat = gps.latitude();          // current latitude
        oldlong = gps.longitude();        // current longitude
    }
  }
}

void printScreen(char *text, int x, int y, int textSize)
{                                         // function to print to screen
  tft.setCursor(x, y);
  tft.setTextSize(textSize);
  tft.print(text);
}
```

Displaying GNSS Data

The route for which GNSS data was stored on the SD card can be displayed
using *GPS Visualizer*, developed by Adam Schneider. To display the GNSS
data, upload the GNSS data file on www.gpsvisualizer.com and select
Choose an output format. Select *Google Maps*, and then click *Map it*.
Within the map, at the top right, there is a drop-down box for map types.
Four of several map types are *Google map*, *Google aerial*, *Google hybrid*,
and *Google terrain*, which are a street map, a satellite view, a combination
of street map and satellite view, and a map similar to an Ordnance Survey
map, respectively. The chosen map can be downloaded as an HTML
document, retaining the map format option, by selecting the download
option located above the map.

Route elevations can also be displayed using *GPS Visualizer*.

1. In the menu at the top of the *GPS Visualizer* home
   page, select *Look up elevations*.

2. Upload the GNSS data file and

3. Select *Draw elevation profile*.

4. The elevation profile can be saved as a *.png* file.

An example of a Google hybrid map and a route elevation using GPS Visualizer is shown in Figure 19-8.

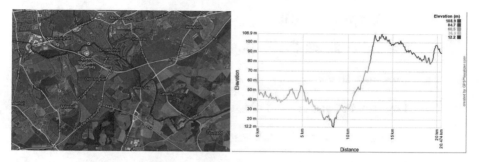

Figure 19-8. *Route maps from GNSS data*

Summary

The NEO-7M module accessed global navigation satellite system (GNSS) messages to determine position and speed. GNSS information was displayed using u-blox u-center software. Positional information was accessed directly from the GNSS messages and by using the *NeoGPS* library that parsed the NMEA message data. A battery-powered mobile GNSS tracker was built with the current position and speed information displayed on a TFT LCD screen and stored on an SD card. Positional data for a route was displayed using Google Maps to show the route and its elevation profile.

Components List

- Arduino Uno and breadboard

- u-blox GNSS module: NEO-7M

- TFT LCD screen: 1.8-inch ST7735

- Micro SD card module

- Microcontroller: ATmega328P-PU

- USB to UART interface: FT232R FTDI

- Clock crystal: 16MHz

- Capacitor: 2× 22pF ceramic, 0.1µF, and 22µF

- Resistor: 10kΩ

- Logic level converter: 4 channel

- Voltage regulator: LD33V and L4940V5

- Battery: 9V

CHAPTER 20

Interrupts and Timed Events

Interrupts allow the microcontroller to respond to an external signal, such as the change in state of a device, while performing another task. An interrupt pauses the sketch and implements the interrupt service routine (ISR), then the sketch continues from the point that it was interrupted.

There are at least three approaches for scheduling an event to occur after a certain period of time has elapsed. The simplest is the delay() function, which pauses the sketch for the required number of milliseconds. A second approach is to use the millis() function, which returns the number of milliseconds that the sketch has been running. A third approach is to use the microcontroller timers.

Interrupts

The two advantages of an interrupt are that the microcontroller does not have to constantly check the state of a device, known as polling, and when the change of state occurs, the ISR is immediately implemented.

A simple example of an interrupt is the sound on a mobile phone indicating that an email has arrived. The ISR is to read the email. The interrupt ensures that the email account does not have to be constantly checked to determine if an email has arrived. As noted in Chapter 9 on the

© Neil Cameron 2019
N. Cameron, *Arduino Applied*, https://doi.org/10.1007/978-1-4842-3960-5_20

rotary encoder, given several tasks or delays in the void loop() function, the microcontroller can miss detecting changes in the state of a device. Interrupts resolve the problem by being triggered from hardware, rather than from software, such that when a change in the state of a device occurs, the microcontroller responds accordingly.

The Arduino's interrupt pins are 2 and 3, which are referenced as *interrupt0* and *interrupt1* or *INT0* and *INT1*, respectively. An ISR should not pass or return variables, should be short and should not include the delay() instruction. Variables that are included both in the sketch and in the ISR must be declared in the sketch as volatile. The variable is then loaded from RAM, and not from the storage register.

An interrupt can be defined with the attachInterrupt(interrupt number, ISR, state change) instruction. Although the attachInterrupt(digitalPinToInterrupt(interrupt pin), ISR, state change) instruction is more portable across Arduino devices.

For example, if the interrupt, called ISR, is activated by a state change of a switch on Arduino pin 3, which corresponds to *interrupt 1*, then the two instructions that can be used are

attachInterrupt(1, ISR, CHANGE)

and

attachInterrupt(digitalPinToInterrupt (3),ISR,CHANGE).

An example illustrates the advantage of using an interrupt. The objective is to turn on or off an LED depending on a switch being pressed, while displaying, every second on the serial monitor, the number of milliseconds that the sketch has been running (see Figure 20-1 and Table 20-1). The sketch (see Listing 20-1) does not use an interrupt, and if the switch is pressed during the one-second delay after printing to the serial monitor, then the microcontroller will not detect a change in the switch state. The interval of one second between printing could be implemented with the millis() function, as outlined later in the chapter, which would also enable detection of changes in switch state.

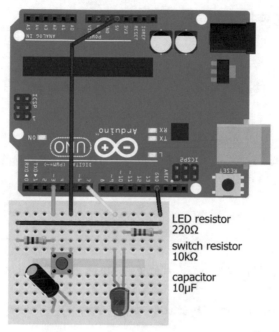

Figure 20-1. *Interrupt switch and LED*

Table 20-1. *Interrupt Switch and LED*

Component	Connect to	and to
Switch right	Arduino 5V	
Switch left	Arduino pin 3	
Switch left	10kΩ resistor	Arduino GND
Capacitor positive	Switch right	
Capacitor negative	Switch left	
LED long leg	Arduino pin 7	
LED short leg	220Ω resistor	Arduino GND

Listing 20-1. Switch and LED

```
int LEDpin = 7;                    // LED pin
int switchPin = 3;                 // switch pin
int switchState = LOW;             // initial switch state

void setup()
{
  Serial.begin(9600);              // define Serial output baud rate
  pinMode(LEDpin, OUTPUT);         // LED pin as output
}

void loop()
{
  Serial.println(millis());    // display time (ms) on Serial Monitor
  delay(1000);                     // delay 1s
  if(digitalRead(switchPin) != switchState) State(); // change of switch state
}

void State()                 // can't use switch as a function name
{
  switchState = digitalRead(switchPin);   // update switch state
  if(switchState == HIGH) digitalWrite(LEDpin, !digitalRead(LEDpin));
}                                    // turn LED on or off
```

The problem of not detecting a change in the switch state during
the one-second delay is resolved by attaching an interrupt that detects a
change in the switch state (see Listing 20-2). At the start of the sketch, the
switchState variable is defined as volatile as it is used in both the main
sketch and the interrupt. In the void setup() function, the interrupt is
defined as

```
attachInterrupt(1, State, CHANGE)
```

374

In the void loop() function, the following instruction is deleted.

```
if(digitalRead(switchPin) != switchState) Switch()
```

Changes to Listing 20-1 are indicated in bold.

Listing 20-2. Interrupt Switch and LED

```
int LEDpin = 7;                    // LED pin
int switchPin = 3;                 // switch pin
volatile int switchState = LOW;    // initial switch state

void setup()
{
  Serial.begin(9600);           // define Serial output baud rate
  pinMode(LEDpin, OUTPUT);      // LED pin as output
  attachInterrupt(1, State, CHANGE);    // define the interrupt
}

void loop()
{
  Serial.println(millis());      // display time (ms) on Serial Monitor
  delay(1000);                   // delay 1s
  if(digitalRead(switchPin) != switchState) State();
}

void State()                       // can't use switch as a function name
{
  switchState = digitalRead(switchPin);   // update switch state
  if(switchState == HIGH) digitalWrite(LEDpin, !digitalRead(LEDpin));
}                                     // turn LED on or off
```

When the switch is pressed, the interrupt is immediately triggered by hardware, the sketch pauses, and the interrupt service routine (ISR) is applied to turn on or off the LED. The sketch then returns to display, on the serial monitor, the number of milliseconds that the sketch has been running.

Types of Interrupt

An interrupt can be initiated by a state change on an interrupt pin from *LOW* to *HIGH* or from *HIGH* to *LOW* (CHANGE option), from *HIGH* to *LOW* (FALLING option), and from *LOW* to *HIGH* (RISING option). The interrupt can also be triggered by setting the interrupt pin to *LOW* (LOW option).

For example, in Listing 20-2, the switch is connected to Arduino pin 3 (see Figure 20-1), which is *interrupt1*. The ISR is the State() function and the interrupt is triggered with the CHANGE option on the switch state. The interrupt is defined by the attachInterrupt(1, State, CHANGE) instruction.

If the switch was connected to Arduino pin 2, *interrupt0*, and the interrupt only triggered when the switch state changed from *LOW* to *HIGH*, then the interrupt would be defined with the attachInterrupt(0, State, RISING) instruction.

The outcome of an interrupt depends on both the trigger option— CHANGE, FALLING, RISING or LOW—and on the state of the variable used in the ISR, such as a switch state. If the ISR turns on or off an LED when the switch state is *HIGH*, then the interrupt outcomes to the four trigger options are shown in Table 20-2.

Table 20-2. *Interrupt Triggers and State Changes*

Trigger	Press switch state changes from LOW to HIGH	Release switch state changes from HIGH to LOW
CHANGE	interrupt active	interrupt active
	switch state = HIGH	switch state = LOW
	turn LED on or off	no change to LED
FALLING	interrupt not active	interrupt active
		switch state = LOW
	no change to LED	no change to LED
RISING	interrupt active	interrupt not active
	switch state = HIGH	
	turn LED on or off	no change to LED
LOW	interrupt inactive while switch pressed	interrupt active
	if switch change occurs with digitalRead,	
	then switch state = HIGH	switch state = LOW
	turn LED on or off	no change to LED
	millis() function resumes	millis() function stops
	display to serial monitor resumes	no display to serial monitor

In Table 20-2, the outcomes of the CHANGE and RISING options are the same, while the FALLING option has no impact on the LED. With the LOW option, the interrupt is constantly active when the switch is not pressed, so the millis() function is halted and there is no output to the serial monitor.

Conversely, if the ISR turns on or off the LED when the switch state is *LOW*, the ISR outcomes are shown in Table 20-3.

Table 20-3. *Interrupt Triggers and State Changes (2)*

Trigger	Press switch state changes from LOW to HIGH	Release switch state changes from HIGH to LOW
CHANGE	interrupt active switch state = HIGH no change to LED	interrupt active switch state = LOW turn LED on or off
FALLING	interrupt not active no change to LED	interrupt active switch state = LOW turn LED on or off
RISING	interrupt active switch state = HIGH no change to LED	interrupt not active no change to LED
LOW	interrupt inactive while switch pressed if switch change does not occur with digitalRead, then switch state = LOW turn LED on or off millis() function resumes display to serial monitor resumes	interrupt active switch state = LOW LED turns on and off repeatedly with a 50% duty cycle millis() function stops

In Table 20-3, the CHANGE and FALLING options have the same outcome, while the RISING option has no impact on the LED. When the interrupt is triggered by the LOW option, the LED is repeatedly turned on and off, equivalent to a 50% duty cycle, as well as halting both the millis() function and display to the serial monitor.

Interrupts can be stopped and restarted with the noInterrupts() and interrupts() instructions, respectively. An example of stopping and restarting an interrupt is when copying a volatile variable to another variable for use in the void loop() function. If the interrupt is not stopped, then value of the volatile variable may change while being copied to the second variable.

Additional Interrupt Pins

The *PinChangeInterrupt* library by Nico Hood enables additional Arduino pins to be used as interrupt pins, rather than only the two *interrupt0* and *interrupt1* pins. The *PinChangeInterrupt* library can be installed within the Arduino IDE, using installation method 3, as outlined in Chapter 3. Two changes are required to a sketch to define an Arduino input pin as an additional interrupt pin.

The attachInterrupt(0 or 1, interrupt, trigger option) interrupt instruction is replaced with either attachPCINT(digital PinToPCINT(interPin), interrupt, trigger option) or attach PinChangeInterrupt(PCINT_interPin, interrupt, trigger option), where *interPin* is the Arduino pin to be used as an interrupt pin. *PCINT_interPin* is the corresponding pin change interrupt number for the Arduino pin.

For example, if Arduino digital pin 6 is to be used as an interrupt pin in Listing 20-2, rather than pin 3, then *interPin is 6* and *PCINT_interPin* is the *PCINT* number of Arduino pin 6, which is 22 (PCINT22) (see Figure 18-1). The interrupt instruction would be replaced by either attachPCINT(digital PinToPCINT(6), State, CHANGE) or attachPinChangeInterrupt(22, State, CHANGE).

The #include <PinChangeInterrupt.h> instruction must also be included in the updated sketch.

Interrupts and Rotary Encoder

Inclusion of an interrupt with a rotary encoder ensures that the microcontroller detects all turns on the rotary encoder, even with a delay included in the void loop() function (see Figure 20-2 and Listing 20-3). A few changes are required to the rotary encoder sketch of Chapter 9 (see Listing 9-1). The SW (switch) and CLK (pin A) pins are connected to *interrupt0* and *interrupt1* pins, which are Arduino pins 2 and 3. The interrupt ISRs turnOff() and encoder(), which detect a falling edge on the SW and CLK pins, as in Listing 9-1 are defined by:

```
attachInterrupt(0, turnOff, FALLING)
attachInterrupt(1, encoder, FALLING)
```

A three second delay is included in the void loop() function to demonstrate that the two interrupts detect all changes in the rotary encoder.

The turnOff() ISR sets the LED brightness to zero. The encoder() ISR requires the state of the DT pin (pin B) to determine the direction of the rotary encoder and as the interrupt is applied on a falling edge of the CLK pin, there is no need to check the status of the CLK pin.

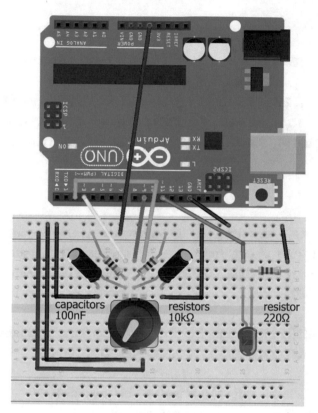

Figure 20-2. *Rotary encoder with LED and interrupt*

Listing 20-3. Rotary Encoder with LED and Interrupt

```
int DTpin= 9;                    // pin B or data pin
int SWpin= 2;                    // switch pin
int LEDpin = 11;                 // LED on PWM pin
volatile int bright = 120;       // initial LED value
int fade = 10;                   // amount to change LED
int rotate = 0;                  // number of rotary turns
volatile int SW = 0;
volatile int change;
```

```
void setup()
{
  Serial.begin(9600);                    // define Serial output baud rate
  pinMode(LEDpin, OUTPUT);               // LED pin as output
  pinMode(SWpin, INPUT_PULLUP);      // switch pin uses internal pull-up resistor
  attachInterrupt(1, encoder, FALLING); // detect change in rotary encoder
  attachInterrupt(0, turnOff, FALLING); // detect switch change
}

void loop()
{
  rotate = rotate + abs(change); // number of turns of rotary encoder
  bright = bright + change*fade;        // change LED brightness
  bright = constrain(bright, 0, 255);   // constrain LED brightness
  if(change != 0)
  {
    Serial.print(rotate);Serial.print("\t");   // display number of rotary
    Serial.println(bright);       // turns and LED brightness
  }
  analogWrite(LEDpin, bright); // update LED brightness
  change = 0;                   // reset change
  delay(3000);                  // delay to verify interrupt functioning
}

void encoder()                      // interrupt to detect rotations
{
  int newB = digitalRead(DTpin);      // state of (DT) pin B
  change = change + (2*newB - 1); // number of changes and direction of rotation
}

void turnOff()                          // interrupt for switch
{
  bright = 0;
  analogWrite(LEDpin, bright);
}
```

As discussed in Chapter 2, when a switch is pressed, the springy nature of the metal used in the contact points can cause the contact points to touch several times; in other words, to bounce before making a permanent contact. The Arduino clock speed of 16 MHz equates to 16 million operations per second; so after pressing the switch, the bouncing switch contact appears to the microcontroller as having opened and closed several times.

The hardware solution to switch bouncing is inclusion of a capacitor across the switch and a resistor in series with the switch. The rotary encoder CLK and DT pins are debounced by including 10kΩ (R) pull-up resistors with 10μF (C) capacitors connected between each of the CLK and DT pins and GND (see Figure 20-2 and Table 20-4). The debounce delay is 69ms, equal to RC×ln(2) seconds. Some rotary encoder modules include 10kΩ pull-up resistors on the CLK and DT pins, in which case only the additional capacitors are required for debouncing the rotary encoder CLK and DT pins.

Table 20-4. *Rotary Encoder with LED and Interrupt*

Component	Connect to	and to	and to
Rotary encoder CLK	Arduino pin 3	Capacitor positive	
Rotary encoder CLK		10kΩ resistor	Arduino 5V
Rotary encoder DT	Arduino pin 9	Capacitor positive	
Rotary encoder DT		10kΩ resistor	Arduino 5V
Rotary encoder SW	Arduino pin 10		
Rotary encoder VCC	Arduino 5V		
Rotary encoder GND	Arduino GND		
Capacitor negative	Arduino GND		
LED long leg	Arduino pin 11		
LED short leg		220Ω resistor	Arduino GND

Timed Events: delay()

In Chapter 1, the delay(1000) function followed a digitalWrite()
instruction to turn on or off an LED, such that the LED was on or off for
one second. The disadvantage of the delay() function is that virtually all
microcontroller activity is stopped, such as checking the state of input
pins, changing the state of output pins or data processing. The delay()
function argument is an unsigned long, with a maximum delay of $(2^{32} - 1)$
ms or 49.7 days.

Timed Events: millis()

As with the delay() function, the argument is an unsigned long, equal
to $(2^{32} - 1)$ms or 49.7 days. When the required time has elapsed since the
scheduled event last occurred, the scheduled event is again implemented.
For example, in Listing 20-4, the built-in LED blinks every second, which is
when the difference between the elapsed time, millis(), and the time that
the LED state was last changed, *LEDtime*, is equal to 1000ms.

Listing 20-4. Timed Event with millis()

```
int LEDpin = 7;                      // LED pin
unsigned long LEDtime = 0;           // event time

void setup()
{
  pinMode(LEDpin, OUTPUT);           // LED pin as OUTPUT
}

void loop()
{
  if(millis()-LEDtime > 1000)        // 1000ms since event time
  {
    digitalWrite(LEDpin, !digitalRead(LEDpin)); // turn LED on or off
```

```
    LEDtime = millis();              // reset time that event last occurred
  }
}
```

Two events can be scheduled with the millis() function, so that the LED is off for two seconds and on for 100ms. The condition determines if the required time has elapsed since the last event and implements the changeLED() function to change the LED state. For example, in Listing 20-5, the following instruction

```
if(timeNow >= (lastEvent + Atime) && digitalRead(LEDpin) == Aevent)
  changeLED(Bevent)
```

turns the LED on, the *Bevent*, if 2000ms, the *Atime*, have elapsed since the LED was off, the *Aevent*.

Listing 20-5. Timed Events with millis() and One LED

```
int Atime = 2000;               // time for event A: LED off
int Aevent = LOW;
int Btime = 100;                // time for event B: LED on
int Bevent = HIGH;
unsigned long lastEvent = 0;    // time event last occurred
unsigned long timeNow;          // elapsed time in ms
int LED = 7;                    // LED pin

void setup()
{
  pinMode(LED, OUTPUT);         // LED pin as output
}

void loop()
{
  timeNow = millis();           // turn LED on
  if(timeNow >= (lastEvent + Atime) && digitalRead(LED) == Aevent)
    changeLED(Bevent);
```

```
  else                             // turn LED off
  if(timeNow >= (lastEvent + Btime) && digitalRead(LED) == Bevent)
    changeLED(Aevent);
}

void changeLED(int event)        // function to turn LED on or off
{
  digitalWrite(LED, event);      // change LED state
  lastEvent = timeNow;           // reset time that event last occurred
}
```

Incorporation of a second LED (*Cevent* and *Devent*) with different timings (*Ctime* and *Dtime*) into the sketch (see Listing 20-6) is straight forward, with one LED briefly flashing on when the second LED turns on for the third time. Note that in the example *(Atime + Btime) = 3*(Ctime + Dtime)*, so turning the second LED on (*Devent*) occurs three times for every time the first LED is turned on (*Bevent*).

Listing 20-6. Timed Events with millis() and Two LEDs

```
int Atime = 2900;                        // time for event A: LED1 off
int Aevent = LOW;
int Btime = 100;                         // time for event B: LED1 on
int Bevent = HIGH;
int Ctime = 500;                         // time for event C: LED2 off
int Cevent = LOW;
int Dtime = 500;                         // time for event D: LED2 on
int Devent = HIGH;
unsigned long lastEvent[ ] = {0, 0};   // time event last occurred
unsigned long timeNow;                   // elapsed time in ms
int LED1 = 7;                            // LED pins
int LED2 = 8;
int LD;
```

```
void setup()
{
  pinMode(LED1, OUTPUT);              // define LED pins as output
  pinMode(LED2, OUTPUT);
}

void loop()
{
  timeNow = millis();                // turn first LED on
  if(timeNow >= (lastEvent[0] + Atime) && digitalRead(LED1) == Aevent)
    changeLED(Bevent, LED1, 1);
  else                               // turn first LED off
  if(timeNow >= (lastEvent[0] + Btime) && digitalRead(LED1) == Bevent)
    changeLED(Aevent, LED1, 1);
  else                               // turn second LED on
  if(timeNow >= (lastEvent[1] + Ctime) && digitalRead(LED2) == Cevent)
    changeLED(Devent, LED2, 2);
  else                               // turn second LED off
  if(timeNow >= (lastEvent[1] + Dtime) && digitalRead(LED2) == Devent)
    changeLED(Cevent, LED2, 2);
}

void changeLED(int event, int LED, int LD) // function to turn LED on or off
{
  digitalWrite(LED, event);      // change LED state
  lastEvent[LD-1] = timeNow;     // reset time that event last occurred
}
```

Timed Events: Timer1

The ATmega328P-PU microcontroller has two 8 bit timers, *Timer0* and *Timer2*, and a 16 bit timer, *Timer1*, as outlined in Chapter 18. *Timer0* is used by the delay(), millis() and micros() functions, so is not available for triggering interrupts. *Timer1* counts to 65535 ($= 2^{16} - 1$), resets to zero and starts counting again. *Timer1* takes 4.10 seconds, equal to $(2^{16} - 1)/(16 \times 10^6)$, to count to 65535, given the 16MHz clock speed. With the *TimerOne* library, a timer period can be defined, such that an interrupt is triggered when *Timer1* reaches the end of the timer period (see Table 20-5). The *TimerOne* library by Paul Stoffregen can be installed within the Arduino IDE using installation method 3, as outlined in Chapter 3.

***Table 20-5.** TimerOne Library Instructions*

Instruction	Explanation
`Timer1.initialize(period)`	define the time period in microseconds
`Timer1.pwm(pin, duty)`	generates a PWM signal on Arduino pins 9 or 10, with a duty value between 0 and 1023 for a duty cycle of 0% and 100% respectively. The instruction `analogWrite()` on Arduino pins 9 and 10 is disabled by the *TimerOne* library.
`Timer1.attachInterrupt(function)`	interrupt function triggered at the end of the time period

For example, Listing 20-7 defines a cycle period of 0.05 seconds, when the interrupt *interLED* is triggered to turn on or off an LED and the number of times the LED is turned on is displayed on the serial monitor. A square wave with frequency 20Hz, equal to the inverse of the cycle period, and a 50% duty cycle is generated on Arduino pin 9. To ensure that the interrupt has not incremented the number of counts, while the number of counts is being read for displaying on the serial monitor, the interrupt is stopped, a copy of the counter is made and then the interrupt is restarted. The number of counts is divided by two, as turning on and off the LED is equal to one event.

Listing 20-7. Timed Events with Timer1

```
#include <TimerOne.h>              // include TimerOne library
int LEDpin = 11;                   // LED pin
int PWMpin = 9;                    // must be pin 9 or 10
int freq = 20;                     // frequency of 20Hz
unsigned long sec = pow(10,6);     // setup one second
unsigned long interval;
volatile int count = 0;          // increment counter defined as volatile
int countCopy, oldCount;

void setup()
{
  Serial.begin(9600);              // define Serial output baud rate
  pinMode(LEDpin, OUTPUT);         // LED pin as output
  interval = sec/(2*freq);         // define time period
  Timer1.initialize(interval);     // initialize timer
  Timer1.pwm(PWMpin, 0.5*1024);    // PWM duty cycle (50%)
  Timer1.attachInterrupt(interLED); // ISR as timer overflow interrupt
}

void loop()
{
  noInterrupts();                  // stop the interrupt
  countCopy = count/2;             // make copy of counter
  interrupts();                    // restart the interrupt
  if(countCopy > oldCount) Serial.println(countCopy); // display count
  oldCount = countCopy;            // update count
}

void interLED()                    // interrupt function
{
  digitalWrite(LEDpin, !digitalRead(LEDpin)); // change LED status
  count = count + 1;               // increment counter
}
```

Timer Register Manipulation

The timer registers of the ATmega328P-PU microcontroller can be manipulated to generate square waves with frequencies up to 200kHz and a variable duty cycle. *Timer0* is used by the delay(), millis() and micros() functions, so is not used for generating square waves. *Timer2* is an 8-bit timer, so only counts to 255 ($2^8 - 1$) before resetting to zero. *Timer1* is a 16-bit timer, providing greater resolution than *Timer2*, and counts to 65535 ($= 2^{16} - 1$), overflows or resets to zero and starts counting again.

The time taken by *Timer1* to overflow, given the 16MHz clock speed is $\dfrac{2^{16}}{16 \times 10^6} = 4.10$ms. The count time can be increased by including a prescalar, $\dfrac{pre - scalar \times 2^{16}}{16 \times 10^6}$, with values between 1 and 1024. For example, a prescalar of 256 increases the time taken for *Timer1* to overflow to 1049ms. *Timer1* can start counting from an initial value, *TCNT1*, to alter the time, t, taken for *Timer1* to overflow. With a prescalar, the value of *TCNT1* associated with a time t for *Timer1* to overflow is $2^{16} - \dfrac{t \times (16 \times 10^6)}{pre - scalar}$.

When *TCNT1* = 3036 with a prescalar of 256, *Timer1* takes exactly one second to overflow and if an interrupt is triggered when *Timer1* overflows, then the interrupt would be triggered at one-second intervals.

To generate a square wave with frequency 50Hz requires *Timer1* to overflow every 10ms, equal to the inverse of double the frequency as the square wave has a high and low phase, which corresponds to TCNT1 values of 45536, 63036 or 64911 with prescalars of 8, 64, or 256, respectively.

There are two *Timer1* registers, *TCCR1A* and *TCCR1B*, which contain information on comparators, the prescalar and the waveform generation mode (see Table 20-6).

Table 20-6. *Timer1 Registers*

Register	Bit 7	Bit 5	Bit 4	Bit 3	Bit 2	Bit 1	Bit 0
TCCR1A	COM1A1	COM1B1				WGM11	WGM10
TCCR1B			WGM13	WGM12	CS12	CS11	CS10

The value of the prescalar is set by *CS12, CS11,* and *CS10,* with the waveform generation mode set by *WGM13, WGM12, WGM11,* and *WGM10,* as shown in Table 20-7.

Table 20-7. *Timer1 Prescalars and Waveforms*

Pre scalar	CS12	CS11	CS10	Waveform	WGM13	WGM12	WGM11	WGM10
1	0	0	1	*Normal*	0	0	0	0
8	0	1	0	*Clear timer on compare*	0	1	0	0
64	0	1	1					
256	1	0	0	*Fast PWM 8bit*	0	1	0	1
1024	1	0	1	*Fast PWM*	1	1	1	1

Listing 20-8 illustrates using the *Timer1* registers to turn on or off an LED at one-second intervals, with a prescalar of 256 and waveform generation in normal mode.

Listing 20-8. Timer1 Registers

```
int LEDpin = 11;              // LED pin

void setup()
{
  Serial.begin(9600);         // define Serial output baud rate
  pinMode(LEDpin, OUTPUT);    // LED pin as output
  TCCR1A = 0;                 // initialise register TCCR1A
  TCCR1B = 0;                 // initialise register TCCR1B
  TCNT1 = 3036;               // define TCNT1 in void setup() and ISR
  TCCR1B |= (1<<CS12);        // set pre-scalar to 256
  TIMSK1 |= (1<<TOIE1);       // enable Timer1 overflow interrupt
}

ISR(TIMER1_OVF_vect)                  // interrupt at Timer1 overflow
{
  TCNT1 = 3036;                       // define TCNT1 in setup and ISR
  if(millis()<9000) Serial.println(millis()); // print interrupt times (ms)
  digitalWrite(LEDpin, !digitalRead(LEDpin)); // turn LED on or off
}

void loop()                           // nothing in void loop() function
{}
```

Registers *TCCR1A* and *TCCR1B* are set to zero and the bit corresponding to *CS12*, register *TCCR1B* bit 2, is set to one as the prescalar equals 256.

The TCCR1B |= (1<<CS12) instruction is a compound bitwise OR operator, equivalent to TCCR1B = TCCR1B | (1<<CS12), which results in a bit value of 0 when bit 2 of *TCCR1B* and *CS12* are both 0 and a bit value of 1 otherwise. For example, the binary value of *B0011* | *B0101* is *B0111*.

The *TIMSK1* register enables interrupts, such as the *Timer1* overflow interrupt, *TOIE1*, and the compare match interrupts on *Timer1: OCIE1A* and *OCIE1B*.

In *clear timer on compare* (CTC) mode, an interrupt, *A*, is triggered when the *Timer1* counter reaches the value in the *OCR1A* register and then resets to zero. Another interrupt, *B*, is triggered when the counter matches the value in the *OCR1B* register (see Figure 20-3). The register value to trigger an interrupt at time *t* is $\dfrac{t \times (16 \times 10^6)}{pre - scalar}$, so *OCR1A* and *OCR1B* register values of 62,500 and 12,500 will trigger interrupts at one second and 200ms later, with a prescalar of 256.

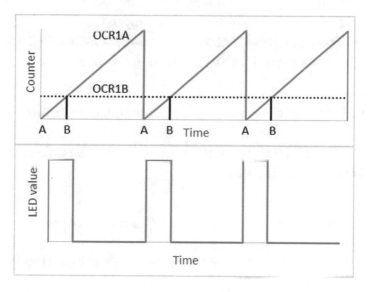

Figure 20-3. *Compare interrupts and square wave*

In Listing 20-9, an LED turns on at one-second intervals, interrupt *A*, and turns off 200ms later, interrupt *B*, with the waveform generation set at CTC mode. The LED value is *HIGH* when interrupt A is triggered and then *LOW* when interrupt B is triggered.

Listing 20-9. Timer1 Registers and Two Events

```
int LEDpin = 11;                 // LED pin

void setup()                     // interrupts at 1s and 0.2s later
{
  Serial.begin(9600);            // define Serial output baud rate
  pinMode(LEDpin, OUTPUT);       // LED pin as output
  TCCR1A = 0;                    // initialise register TCCR1A
  TCCR1B = 0;                    // initialise register TCCR1B
  OCR1A = 62500;                 // trigger interrupt A at 1s
  OCR1B = 12500;                 // trigger interrupt B 200ms
  TCCR1B |= (1<<CS12) | (1<<WGM12); // set pre-scalar 256 and CTC mode
  TIMSK1 |= (1<<OCIE1A) | (1<<OCIE1B);  // enable OCR1A and OCR1B
}

ISR(TIMER1_COMPA_vect)                       // interrupt at overflow A
{
  if(millis()<9000) {Serial.print("A ");Serial.println(millis());}
    digitalWrite(LEDpin, HIGH);
}

ISR(TIMER1_COMPB_vect)                       // interrupt at overflow B
{
  if(millis()<9000) {Serial.print("B ");Serial.println(millis());}
    digitalWrite(LEDpin, LOW);
}

void loop()                      // nothing in void loop() function
{}
```

Summary

Interrupts allow the microcontroller to immediately stop performing one task, and then perform a second task and return to the first task. An interrupt was illustrated by detecting all turns on a rotary encoder with a delay included in the sketch. Timed events were scheduled with the delay function, the elapsed time between events and by manipulating the microcontroller timer register.

Components List

- Arduino Uno and breadboard

- Rotary encoder

- LED

- Switch: tactile

- Capacitor: 2× 10µF

- Resistor: 220Ω and 10kΩ

CHAPTER 21

Power Saving

The power demands on the Arduino are the ATmega328P microcontroller, the ATmega16U2 microcontroller controlling the USB-to-serial interface, the 3.3V and 5V voltage regulators, and the three LEDs: power-on, transmit (TX), and receive (RX). There are several power-down options, but they only apply to the ATmega328P microcontroller.

The ATmega328P microcontroller has several functions that require power, including the three timers: *Timer0, Timer1,* and *Timer2,* and the three communication systems: Serial Peripheral Interface (SPI), Inter-Integrated Circuit (I2C), and serial communication (USART). The analog-to digital-converter (ADC) converts analog voltages to digital values. The brownout detector (BOD) monitors the microcontroller voltage supply and powers down the microcontroller when the voltage is too low. The watchdog timer (WDT) checks microcontroller activity and resets the microcontroller if there is a malfunction. The ADC and the two monitor functions: BOD and WDT also require power. If the microcontroller is to be battery powered, then some power can be saved by reducing microcontroller functionality, until the microcontroller is triggered by an interrupt to perform a specific task.

Of the six power-saving options for the microcontroller, the *Idle* option saves the least power, but retains most microcontroller functionality, while the *Power Down* option saves the most power, but retains the least functionality (see Table 21-1). All power-saving options maintain interrupt functionality and the watchdog timer. The difference between the *Standby*

N. Cameron, *Arduino Applied,* https://doi.org/10.1007/978-1-4842-3960-5_21

and *Power Down* options is in maintaining the oscillator, while retention of *Timer2* is the difference between the *Power Save* and *Power Down* options and between the *Extended Standby* and *Standby* options.

Table 21-1 illustrates differences in current requirements of the Arduino and of the ATmega328P microcontroller for the six power-saving options.

The current to a "non-power-saving" Arduino with the built-in LED turned off is 32.7mA, with a supply voltage of 5.18V from a laptop USB port and a sketch consisting of

```
void setup() {}
void loop() {}
```

With the power-saving *Power Down* option, the current requirement of the Arduino of 23.8mA indicates 27% power savings. The corresponding current requirements of the ATmega328P microcontroller were 18.2mA and 0.38mA, indicating a power saving of 98%.

Table 21-1. *Power-Saving Options*

			Retained Functionality				Current (mA)	
	I2C	SPI	USART	ADC	Oscillator	Timers	Arduino	ATmega
Power Down							23.8	0.38
Power Save						Timer2	24.7	1.6
Standby					On		24.1	0.87
Extended Standby					On	Timer2	24.7	1.6
ADC noise reduce				On	On	Timer2	25.2	9.6
Idle	On	On	On	On	On	All	32.1	18.2

The current requirements of the ATmega328P microcontroller with the six power-saving options can be determined with a stand-alone microcontroller (see Figure 21-1), as outlined in Chapter 18. The sketch (see Listing 21-1) sets the sleep mode and when the switch is pressed an interrupt is triggered for the microcontroller to leave sleep mode, as indicated by the LED flashing. *Interrupt0* on microcontroller pin 4 is connected to the switch (see Table 21-2). After the sketch is downloaded to the microcontroller, the USB to serial UART interface is disconnected.

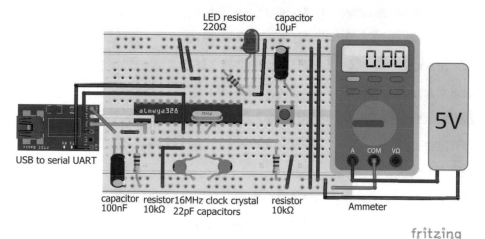

Figure 21-1. *ATMega328 current requirement with power-saving options*

Table 21-2. *ATMega328 Current Requirement with Power-Saving Options*

Component	Connect to	and to
ATMega328P-PU pin 1	10kΩ resistor	5V rail
ATMega328P-PU pin 7	5V rail	
ATMega328P-PU pins 9, 10	16MHz clock crystal	

(continued)

Table 21-2. (*continued*)

Component	Connect to	and to
ATMega328P-PU pins 9, 10	22pF capacitor	GND rail
ATMega328P-PU pins 20, 21	5V rail	
ATMega328P-PU pin 22	GND rail	
0.1µF capacitor positive	USB to serial UART DTR	
0.1µF capacitor negative	ATMega328P-PU pin 1	
USB to serial UART RXD	ATMega328P-PU pin 3	
USB to serial UART TXD	ATMega328P-PU pin 2	
USB to serial UART VCC	ATMega328P-PU pin 7	
USB to serial UART GND	ATMega328P-PU pin 22	
LED long leg	220Ω resistor	ATMega328P-PU pin 17
LED short leg	GND	
Switch left	10kΩ resistor	GND rail
Switch left	ATMega328P-PU pin 4	
Switch right	5V rail	
10µF capacitor negative	Switch left	
10µF capacitor positive	switch right	

An interrupt can be initiated with a *RISING* or a *FALLING* trigger. From the perspective of an interrupt named *wake,* a *RISING* trigger for the interrupt with a default *LOW* switch state seems more intuitive than a *FALLING* trigger with a default *HIGH* switch state. Schematics for both options are displayed in Figure 21-2. Initiating the interrupt with a *RISING* trigger requires a pull-down resistor connected to the switch for a *LOW* default switch state.

In contrast, a *HIGH* default switch state requires a pull-up resistor connected to the switch, if the interrupt is initiated with a *FALLING* trigger. The difference between the schematics in Figure 21-2 is connection of VCC and GND around the resistor-switch combination, noting that the orientation of the capacitor is also changed (see Table 21-3), with the different connections for the *RISING* and *FALLING* triggers highlighted in bold.

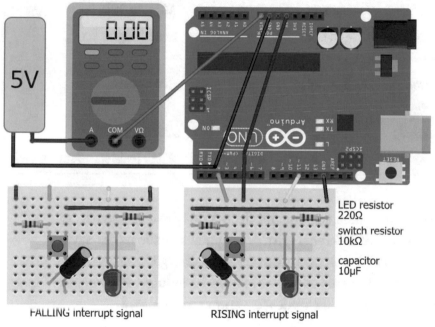

Figure 21-2. *Arduino current requirement with power-saving option*

Table 21-3. *Arduino Saving Current Requirement with Power Option*

Component	Rising trigger pull-down resistor		Falling trigger pull-up resistor	
	Connect to	**and to**	**Connect to**	**and to**
Switch left	10kΩ resistor	Arduino GND	10kΩ resistor	**Arduino 5V**
Switch left	Arduino pin 2		Arduino pin 2	
Switch right	**Arduino 5V**		**Arduino GND**	
Capacitor negative	**Switch left**		**Switch right**	
Capacitor positive	**Switch right**		**Switch left**	
LED long leg	Arduino pin 11		Arduino pin 11	
LED short leg	220Ω resistor	Arduino GND	220Ω resistor	Arduino GND

The power management and sleep mode are controlled by bit manipulation of different registers to obtain specific power-saving conditions. Further details are available at www.gammon.com.au/power. This chapter discusses use of the *avr/sleep* module and *LowPower* library to utilize different sleep modes for power management.

avr/sleep Module

AVR is a class of microcontrollers developed by Atmel, which includes the ATmega328P microcontroller of the Arduino. The AVR language is used to program Atmel microcontrollers and the *AVR* library includes the *avr/sleep* module for power management and sleep modes.

The *avr/sleep* module is enabled to put the microcontroller into sleep mode. The *avr/sleep* module can be deactivated (i.e., the microcontroller is woken up) with an external interrupt on pins *INT0* or *INT1*, as outlined in Chapter 20. The interrupt must be defined before the *avr/sleep* module is implemented; otherwise, the microcontroller will always be in sleep mode. A sketch (see Listing 21-1) incorporating the *avr/sleep* module includes two functions. The sleep() function attaches the interrupt, sets the sleep mode, puts the microcontroller in sleep mode and detaches the interrupt. The wake() function contains instructions for the microcontroller when leaving sleep mode, but before re-entering the void loop() function.

Listing 21-1. Sleep Mode with avr/sleep Module

```
#include <avr/sleep.h>            // include avr/sleep module
int LEDpin = 11;
int wakePin = 2;                  // pin connected to interrupt 0

void setup()
{
  pinMode(LEDpin, OUTPUT);        // LED pin as OUTPUT
  pinMode(LED_BUILTIN, OUTPUT);   // turn off built-in LED
}

void loop()
{
  delay(500);
  digitalWrite(LEDpin, LOW);      // turn LED off after sleep mode
  sleep();                        // function to set sleep mode
}

void sleep()
{
  attachInterrupt(0, wake, RISING);      // interrupt wake function
  set_sleep_mode(SLEEP_MODE_PWR_DOWN);   // define sleep mode
//sleep_enable();                 // set sleep enable bit
```

```
//sleep_cpu();            // initiate sleep
  sleep_mode();           // set sleep enable bit, initiate sleep and reset
                          // sketch resumes here on interrupt trigger
//sleep_disable();        // reset sleep enable bit
  detachInterrupt(0);     // effectively debounces switch interrupt
}

void wake()                      // wake interrupt function
{
  digitalWrite(LEDpin, HIGH);    // turn LED on
}
```

The sleep_mode() instruction effectively consists of the three instructions: sleep_enable(), sleep_cpu(), and sleep_disable(). The three separate instructions, are included in Listing 21-1, in bold but commented out, to illustrate the implicit order of the instructions. The sleep_enable() instruction sets the sleep enable bit in the Sleep Mode Control Register, sleep_cpu() puts the microcontroller into sleep mode, and sleep_disable() resets the sleep enable bit. The interrupt is attached before and detached after the microcontroller is put into sleep mode.

The following are the six sleep mode options.

SLEEP_MODE_PWR_DOWN

SLEEP_MODE_PWR_SAVE

SLEEP_MODE_STANDBY

SLEEP_MODE_EXT_STANDBY

SLEEP_MODE_ADC

SLEEP_MODE_IDLE

LowPower Library

The *Low-Power* library by Rocket Scream Electronics provides options for managing power to the microcontroller and the library can be installed within the Arduino IDE using installation method 3, as outlined in Chapter 3. Interrupts are used by the *LowPower* library to wake the microcontroller, just as with the *avr/sleep* module.

The *LowPower* library instruction is

```
LowPower.powerDown(SLEEP_FOREVER, ADC_OFF, BOD_OFF)
```

It essentially combines the two instructions of the *avr/sleep* module.

```
set_sleep_mode(SLEEP_MODE_PWR_DOWN)
sleep_mode()
```

The *LowPower* library also enables timed interrupts of 0.5, 1, 2, 4, and 8 seconds with the following instruction.

```
LowPower.powerDown (sleeptime, ADC_OFF, BOD_OFF)
```

sleeptime takes these values: *SLEEP_500MS, SLEEP_1S, SLEEP_2S, SLEEP_4S,* or *SLEEP_8S.*

If a longer sleep period than 8 seconds is required, then the LowPower.powerDown() instruction can be repeated with a for() instruction. For example, Listing 21-2 demonstrates using the void sleep() function to achieve a sleep period of one minute.

Listing 21-2. Sleep Mode with LowPower Library

```
void sleep()
{                                          // 7×8s = 56s
  for (int i = 0; i<7; i++) LowPower.powerDown(SLEEP_8S,
  ADC_OFF, BOD_OFF);
  LowPower.powerDown(SLEEP_4S, ADC_OFF, BOD_OFF); // plus 4s = 60s
  wake();
}
```

During the sleep period, the required current to the ATmega328P is 7µA (see Table 21-4), achieved with the LowPower.powerDown(SLEEP_8S, ADC_OFF, BOD_OFF) instruction, which is significantly lower than the current of 385µA when the *avr/sleep Power Down* module is implemented (see Table 21-1). The *LowPower* library has the facility to separately turn off the BOD and the ADC.

Table 21-4. *Current for BOD and ADC Combinations*

Current (µA)	Brownout Detector (BOD)	
Analog-to-digital converter (ADC)	**On**	**Off**
On	385	360
Off	49	7

The *avr/sleep Power Down* module is equivalent to the LowPower. powerDown(SLEEP_8S, ADC_ON, BOD_ON) instruction.

Further power savings can be obtained with the LowPower. powerDown(SLEEP_FOREVER, ADC_OFF, BOD_OFF) instruction, which reduces the current requirement to just 5µA.

Power Down and an Infrared Sensor

A practical example of combining interrupts (see Chapter 20) with power saving is using a passive infrared (PIR) sensor to turn on a light when movement is detected, as in a battery-powered security light (see Figure 21-3 and Table 21-5). Listing 21-3 uses an interrupt, which is triggered with a *RISING* signal from the PIR sensor, to wake the microcontroller from sleep mode and turn on an LED for 30 seconds.

The stand-alone ATmega328P microcontroller was outlined in Chapter 18 and the PIR sensor in Chapter 3.

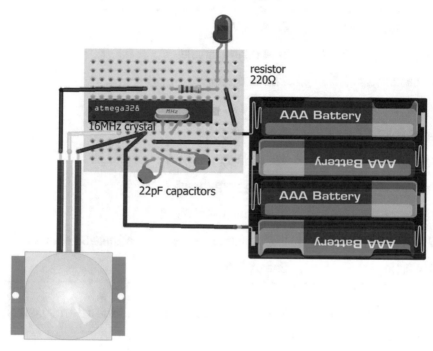

Figure 21-3. *Power saving with PIR sensor interrupt*

When movement is detected, the default *LOW* PIR signal changes to *HIGH* and triggers the interrupt. As the PIR signal is *RISING*, the microcontroller leaves sleep mode and the LED is turned on. An interrupt service routine (ISR) should not include the delay() function, as noted in Chapter 20, so a movement flag, *detect*, maintains the LED being on for the required time of 30 seconds within the void loop() function. After 30 seconds, the LED is flashed on and off to indicate that the microcontroller is again set to sleep mode. In sleep mode, the required current of only 75µA implies that the battery-operated security light can operate for a substantial time on a battery.

Table 21-5. *Power Saving with PIR Sensor Interrupt*

Component	Connect to	and to
ATMega328P-PU pin 7	Battery 5V	
ATmega328P pins 9, 10	16MHz clock crystal	
ATmega328P pins 8, 9	22pF capacitor	
ATmega328P pins 8, 10	22pF capacitor	
ATMega328P-PU pin 8	Battery GND	
PIR sensor VCC	ATmega328P-PU pin 7	
PIR sensor OUT	ATmega328P-PU pin 4	
PIR sensor GND	ATmega328P-PU pin 22	
LED long leg	220Ω resistor	ATmega328P-PU pin 17
LED short leg	Battery GND	

Note than ATmega328P pins 4 and 17 correspond to Arduino pins 2 (interrupt0) and 11 (LED), respectively.

Listing 21-3. Power saving with PIR Sensor Interrupt

```
#include <LowPower.h>          // include LowPower library
int LEDpin = 11;               // LED pin
int PIRpin = 2;                // interrupt on pin 2 (INT0)
int detect = 0;                // movement flag

void setup()
{
  pinMode(LEDpin, OUTPUT);     // LED pin as output
}
```

```
void loop()
{
  if(detect == 1)                    // if movement detected
  {
    delay(30000);                    // delay 30s as LED is ON
    digitalWrite(LEDpin, LOW);    // turn LED off
    delay(1000);                     // delay 1s
  }
  detect = 0;                        // reset movement flag
  digitalWrite(LEDpin, LOW);      // turn LED off
  for (int i = 0; i<4; i++)
  {                                  // four steps for turning LED
    digitalWrite(LEDpin, !digitalRead(LEDpin)); // on and off, twice
    delay(1000);
  }
  sleep();                           // call sleep function
}

void sleep()                    // sleep function
{
  attachInterrupt(0, wake, RISING); // interrupt pin, wake function and mode
  LowPower.powerDown(SLEEP_FOREVER, ADC_OFF, BOD_OFF); // power down
  detachInterrupt(0);                      // detach interrupt
}

void wake()                              // wake interrupt function
{
  digitalWrite(LEDpin, HIGH);         // turn LED on
  detect = 1;                         // set movement flag
}
```

Summary

Power-saving options with the *avr/sleep* module and the *LowPower* library are described with an interrupt used to wake the microcontroller from sleep mode. Current requirement of a stand-alone microcontroller in sleep mode can be reduced to just 5μA compared to 18mA in non-sleep mode. A battery-powered PIR sensor activating an interrupt to turn on an LED replicated a security light system, with the microcontroller normally in sleep mode to save power.

Components List

- Arduino Uno and breadboard

- Ammeter

- Microcontroller: ATmega328P-PU

- USB to UART interface: FT232R FTDI

- Clock crystal: 16MHz

- Capacitor: 2× 22pF ceramic, 0.1μF, and 10μF

- Resistor: 220Ω and 10kΩ

- Switch: tactile

- LED

- Passive infrared sensor: HR-SC501

CHAPTER 22

Sound and Square Waves

Sound is the vibration of air particles. If the vibration is continuous and regular, then the sound can be described by its frequency, as the number of waves per second, quantified in Hertz (Hz). For the time interval in Figure 22-1, the blue sound wave has two complete cycles, while the red sound wave has four complete cycles, so double the frequency and half the wavelength of the blue sound wave. For electromagnetic and sound waves, wavelength is the speed of light and sound, respectively, divided by the frequency.

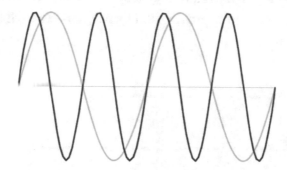

Figure 22-1. *Two different frequencies*

The human ear can hear sounds with frequencies of 20Hz to 20kHz and ultrasound has frequencies above 20kHz. FM radio stations broadcast with frequencies of 100MHz and wireless networks operate at 2.4GHz.

© Neil Cameron 2019
N. Cameron, *Arduino Applied*, https://doi.org/10.1007/978-1-4842-3960-5_22

The musical note A above middle C (see Figure 22-2) has a frequency of 440Hz and is the tuning standard for musical pitch, which is the perception that a note is higher or lower than another note. The frequency of a note above or below A above middle C is $440 \times 2^{n/12}$, where n is the number of notes above or below the note A above middle C. For example, D4 is seven notes below A above middle C, and it has a frequency of 294Hz.

Figure 22-2. *Note A above middle C*

The number of cycles of a sound is the sound duration multiplied by the frequency. For example, a sound with a frequency of 440Hz that lasts 50ms consists of 22 cycles. A Piezo transducer can approximate a regular, continuous sound wave by a square wave, with the transducer switched to *HIGH*, then to *LOW* repeatedly (see Figure 22-3). The Piezo transducer is *HIGH* or *LOW* for 1/(2×frequency) seconds. A sound wave with frequency 440Hz can be approximated by a square wave that is *HIGH* or *LOW* for 1136μs.

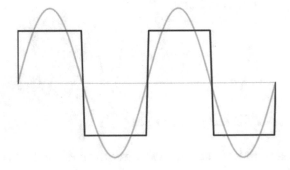

Figure 22-3. *Square wave approximation*

The Piezo transducer (see Figure 22-4) produces a repeating sound every second in Listing 22-1; it has a frequency of 440Hz and the sound lasts 50ms.

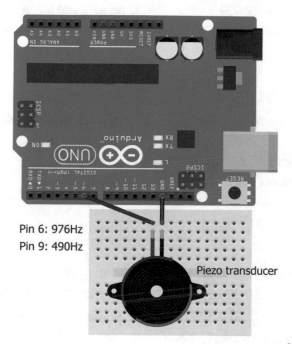

Pin 6: 976Hz
Pin 9: 490Hz

Piezo transducer

Figure 22-4. *Piezo transducer*

Listing 22-1. Piezo Transducer

```
int piezoPin = 6;                       // define PWM pin for piezo transducer
float freq = 440;                       // sound frequency (Hz)
int duration = 50;                      // duration of sound (ms)
int interval = 1000;                    // sound duration plus pause (ms)
int pause;
int cycles = (duration*freq)/pow(10,3); // number of cycles of sound duration
```

```
int timeHigh = pow(10,6)/(2.0*freq);    // time (µs) that square wave is HIGH

void setup()
{
  pinMode(piezoPin, OUTPUT);              // define piezo pin as output
  pause = interval-duration;              // pause between sounds
}

void loop()
{
  for (int i=0; i<cycles+1; i++)          // number of cycles per sound
  {                                       // square wave HIGH or LOW
    digitalWrite(piezoPin, !digitalRead(piezoPin));
    delayMicroseconds(timeHigh);
  }
  delay(pause);
}
```

Rather than having to calculate the number of cycles and the time that the square wave is *HIGH* or *LOW*, the tone(piezoPin, frequency) instruction generates sound of the required frequency. The tone() function is followed by a delay() equal to the sound duration, then the noTone(piezoPin) instruction is followed by a delay(), equal to the interval between sounds. The tone(piezoPin, frequency) function defines *piezoPin* as an *OUTPUT* pin, so the pinMode(piezoPin, OUTPUT) instruction is not required.

There are two alternatives for using the tone() function. The first is

```
tone(piezoPin, frequency);              // sound frequency
delay(duration);                        // sound duration
noTone(piezoPin);
delay(pause);                           // pause between sounds
```

The second alternative is the tone(piezoPin, frequency, duration) instruction and the delay() is the sound duration plus the pause between sounds, as the timers for the tone() and delay() functions run simultaneously.

```
tone(piezoPin, frequency, duration);  // sound frequency and duration
delay(duration + pause);     // time(ms) between start of sound repeats
```

The tone(piezoPin, frequency, duration) instruction can be used in the 4-digit 7-segment display timer sketch (see Listing 6-1) in Chapter 6 to produce a "clock ticking" effect with tone(piezoPin, 1000, 50) with the delay(1000) instruction in the void loop() function.

Another method of generating sound uses the analogWrite() instruction with Pulse Width Modulation (PWM) and a 50% duty cycle to replicate the square wave (see Listing 22-2). PWM operates on a frequency of 490.1961Hz on Arduino PWM pins 3, 9, 10 and 11 and a frequency of 976.5625Hz on Arduino PWM pins 5 and 6. The frequency values of 490Hz and 977Hz are equal to the microcontroller clock speed of 16MHz divided by the default scalar of 64 and a cycle length of 256 or 510 for *Timer0* or *Timer1* and *Timer2*, respectively. The tone() library uses *Timer2* on Arduino PWM pins 3 and 11, so those pins are not available for PWM when using the tone() library.

Listing 22-2. Piezo Transducer with PWM

```
for (int rep=0; rep<reps; rep++)   // number of cycles
{
  analogWrite(piezoPin, 128);      // analogWrite with 50% duty cycle
  delay(duration);                 // duration of sound
  analogWrite(piezoPin, 0);        // no sound
  delay(pause);                    // pause between sounds
}
```

The three methods—counting cycles, the `tone()` function, and `analogWrite()` on PWM pins—of generating sound give the same result for frequencies of 490Hz or 977Hz, with the appropriate Arduino PWM pin, but for other frequencies only the first two methods are applicable.

Piezo Transducer and Buzzer

 A Piezo (passive) transducer (image on left) requires a square wave to generate sounds of different frequencies, while a Piezo (active) buzzer (image on right) contains an internal oscillator with a single preset frequency. The Piezo transducer and buzzer look similar, but the buzzer is higher than the transducer, due to the internal oscillator, and has substantially greater resistance across the two pins than the transducer, 3MΩ compared to 15Ω. Applying power to the transducer or the buzzer produces a click or a sound, respectively. The volume of the Piezo transducer or buzzer can be reduced by connecting a 100Ω or a 220Ω resistor in series. Note the ⊕ symbol on the top of the Piezo buzzer and transducer indicating the positive pin.

Musical Notes

A series of musical notes can be "played" using an Piezo transducer with the `tone()` function. Information on a range of musical notes and the corresponding frequencies can be loaded into a separate tab in the Arduino IDE, rather than being included in the main sketch. In the Arduino IDE, a new tab is created by selecting the triangle below the serial monitor button in the right-hand side of the Arduino IDE and choosing *New Tab* from the drop-down menu. The new tab should be titled *notes.h* and frequencies are edited into the tab (see Listing 22-3). For example, the frequency of 262Hz for middle C is `int NOTE_C4 = 262`. The tone definition can also be written as `#define NOTE_C4 262`, which is the format used in the sketch at www.arduino.cc/en/Tutorial/ToneMelody, where details of musical notes and frequencies are available.

Listing 22-3. A Selection of Notes

```
int NOTE_C4 = 262;
int NOTE_D4  =294;
int NOTE_E4 = 330;
int NOTE_F4 = 349;
int NOTE_G4 = 392;
int NOTE_A4 = 440;
int NOTE_B4 = 494;
int NOTE_C5 = 523;
```

In Listing 22-4, the *notes.h* tab is referenced with quotation marks, as "notes.h" and not with angular brackets, which is for a library.

Listing 22-4. A Series of Notes

```
#include "notes.h"               // include reference to notes.h tab
int piezoPin = 12;               // Piezo transducer pin
int tune[] = {NOTE_C5, NOTE_G4, NOTE_G4, NOTE_A4,
                    NOTE_G4, 0, NOTE_B4, NOTE_C5};
int beats[] = {2, 1, 1, 2, 2, 2, 2, 2}; // length of note
int duration;

void setup()
{}                               // nothing in void setup() function

void loop()
{
  for (int i = 0; i < 8; i++)    // play the 8 notes
  {
    duration = 125*beats[i];     // duration of note = 125 or 250ms
    tone(piezoPin, tune[i], duration); // generate sound
```

```
    delay(duration*1.25);  // interval between notes 1.25×note duration
  }
  while(1);                       // stop the "tune" after being played once
}
```

Switches can be used to switch on sounds, as in a digital piano (see Figure 22-5 and Table 22-1), with the sound produced as long as the switch is pressed. Listing 22-5 uses the four notes: G4, A4, B4, and C5, from Listing 22-4.

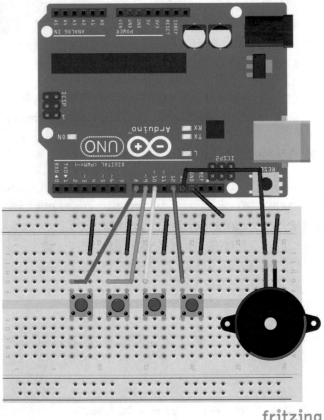

Figure 22-5. *Four-note piano*

Table 22-1. *Four-Note Piano*

Component	Connect to
Piezo trans VCC	Arduino pin 13
Piezo trans GND	Arduino GND
Switch left	Arduino pins 8, 9, 10, 12
Switch right	Arduino GND

Listing 22-5. Four-Note Piano

```
int Note_G = 392;                          // note frequencies (Hz)
int Note_A = 440;
int Note_B = 494;
int Note_C = 523;
int piezoPin = 13;                         // Piezo transducer pin
int switch_G = 8;
int switch_A = 9;                          // define switches
int switch_B = 10;
int switch_C = 12;

void setup()
{                                          // pins set HIGH
  for (int i = 8; i<13; i++) pinMode(i, INPUT_PULLUP);
}
void loop()
{                                          // sound on switch press
  while(digitalRead(switch_A) == LOW) tone(piezoPin, Note_A);
  while(digitalRead(switch_B) == LOW) tone(piezoPin, Note_B);
  while(digitalRead(switch_C) == LOW) tone(piezoPin, Note_C);
  while(digitalRead(switch_G) == LOW) tone(piezoPin, Note_G);
  noTone(piezoPin);                        // switch off sound
}
```

Associating the pressing of a switch with a *LOW* state seems intuitively incorrect, but it has the advantage that the switch pins can use the Arduino's built-in pull-up 20kΩ resistors, rather than connecting 10kΩ pull-up resistors to each switch. The `pinMode(pin, INPUT_PULLUP)` instruction sets the pin state to *HIGH*, while `pinMode(pin, INPUT)` sets the pin state to *LOW*. The internal pull-up resistors, on the pins for the four notes, are initialized with the instruction in the `void setup()` function.

```
for (int i = 8; i<13; i++) pinMode(i, INPUT_PULLUP)
```

Sensor and Sound

A sensor, such as a light dependent resistor (LDR), can be used to generate a sound with the frequency of the sound dependent on the sensor input, such as the light intensity. An LDR was used in Chapter 3 to control the brightness of an LED, as the basis of a night light. In the example (see Figure 22-6 and Table 22-2), the frequency of the Piezo speaker increases and the LED brightness decreases as the incident light increases. The `map()` function converts the LDR reading to a frequency for the Piezo transducer, with an analog reading of 0 to 900 corresponding to a frequency value of 262Hz to 494Hz, which are notes C4 to B4 (see Listing 22-6). The `map()` function also inversely converts the LED reading to an LED brightness value with the light intensity class, based on the threshold values: *Bright, Light, Dim,* and *Dark.* The LED is turned on only for low-light intensity, given an upper limit in the `map()` function. Each `map()` function is followed by a `constrain()` function to ensure that values remain within the boundary values of the `map()` function.

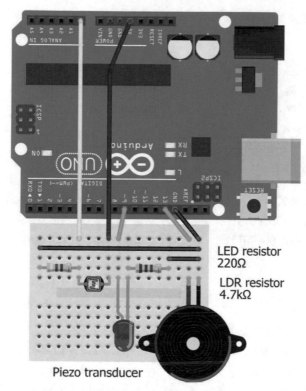

LED resistor
220Ω

LDR resistor
4.7kΩ

Piezo transducer

Figure 22-6. *Light sensor, sound, and LED*

Table 22-2. *Light Sensor, Sound, and LED*

Component	Connect to	and to
Piezo trans VCC	Arduino pin 13	
Piezo trans GND	Arduino GND	
LDR left	4.7kΩ resistor	GND
LDR left	Arduino pin A0	
LDR right	Arduino 5V	
LED long leg	Arduino pin 9	
LED short leg	220Ω resistor	GND

Listing 22-6. Light Sensor, Sound, and LED

```
int LDRpin = A0;                    // LDR voltage divider
int LEDpin = 9;                     // LED on PWM pin
int piezoPin = 13;                  // Piezo transducer pin
int duration = 100;                 // sound duration (ms)
int LED, LDR, freq;

void setup()
{
  Serial.begin(9600);              // define Serial output baud rate
  pinMode(LEDpin, OUTPUT);         // LED pin as output
  pinMode(piezoPin,OUTPUT);        // define Piezo pin as output
}

void loop()
{
  LDR = analogRead(LDRpin);             // read LDR
  LED = map(LDR, 0, 500, 255, 0);       // map LED brightness inversely to LDR
  LED = constrain (LED, 0, 255);        // constrain LED brightness
  freq = map(LDR, 0, 900, 262, 494);    // map sound frequency to LDR
  freq = constrain (freq, 262, 494);    // constrain sound frequency
  analogWrite(LEDpin, LED);             // set LED brightness
  tone (piezoPin, freq, duration);      // Piezo pin and frequency defined
  Serial.print("Light intensity is "); // message to Serial Monitor
  if(LDR >= 750) Serial.println("Bright");
  else if(LDR >= 500) Serial.println("Light"); // display light intensity class
  else if(LDR >= 250) Serial.println("Dim");
  else Serial.println("Dark");
  delay(1000);                          // delay 1s
}
```

The *toneAC* library by Tim Eckel with the `toneAC()` function controls both the frequency and volume of a sound. A *.zip* file containing the *toneAC* library can be downloaded from `https://playground.arduino.cc/Code/ToneAC`. Chapter 3 included details on installing a downloaded library *.zip* file using either installation method 1 or method 2.

When using the `toneAC()` function, the Piezo transducer is connected to Arduino PWM pins 9 and 10. The `toneAC(frequency, volume, duration)` instruction defines the sound frequency, the volume on a 0 (off) to 10 (high) scale, and the sound duration in milliseconds, with 0 corresponding to forever. The `noToneAC()` or `toneAC(0)` instructions stop the sound.

An electro-Theremin can be imitated by moving one hand above an LDR to change the light intensity and the associated sound frequency (see Figure 22-7). A second LDR and voltage divider pair are included in the circuit to control the sound volume, by moving the other hand above the second LDR (see Table 22-3 and Listing 22-7).

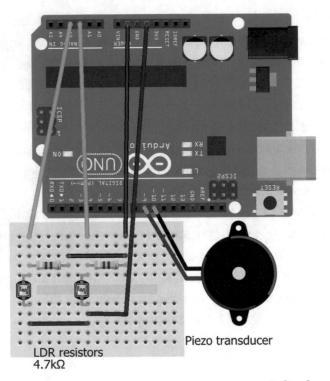

Figure 22-7. *Electro-Theremin*

Table 22-3. *Electro-Theremin*

Component	Connect to	and to
Piezo VCC	Arduino pin 9	
Piezo GND	Arduino pin 10	
LDR bottom	Arduino 5V	
LDR top	Arduino pin A2, A3	
LDR top	4.7kΩ resistor	Arduino GND

Listing 22-7. Electro-Theremin

```
#include <toneAC.h>                         // include toneAC library
int LDRFpin = A2;                           // LDR for frequency
int LDRVpin = A3;                           // LDR for volume
int LDRF, LDRV, freq, volume;

void setup()
{}                                          // nothing in void setup() function

void loop()
{
  LDRF = analogRead(LDRFpin);                    // LDR for frequency
  LDRV = analogRead(LDRVpin);                    // LDR for volume
  freq = map(LDRF, 0, 900, 523, 1047);  // map sound frequency C5 to C6
  freq = constrain (freq, 523, 1047);  // constrain sound frequency
  volume = map(LDRV, 0, 900, 0, 10);   // map volume to LDRV
  volume = constrain (volume, 0, 10);  // constrain volume
  toneAC (freq, volume, 0);                 // play sound
}
```

Generating Square Waves

Square waves with frequencies 490.1961Hz or 976.5625Hz can be generated by analogWrite() to Arduino PWM pins 3, 9, 10 and 11 or to pins 5 and 6, respectively. The duty cycle of the square wave is defined as a multiple of 256. For example, analogWrite(3, 128) and analogWrite(6, 64) produce square waves with frequencies 490 and 977Hz with 50% and 25% duty cycles, respectively.

The *PWM* library generates square waves with frequencies between 1Hz and 2MHz using the 16-bit *Timer1*. The *PWM* library by Sam Knight is contained within a *.zip* file available at https://code.google.com/archive/p/arduino-pwm-frequency-library/downloads. Download the *Arduino PWM Frequency Library .zip* file and store on the computer or laptop.

Extract the *PWM* folder from the *.zip* file and install the *PWM* library using installation method 2, as described in Chapter 3.

The sketch (see Listing 22-8) produces a square wave with frequency 10kHz on pin 10 with the duty cycle defined by the output of a potentiometer on analog pin A0. The potentiometer output value is divided by 4, as maximum values of the potentiometer output and the pwmWrite() function are 1023 and 255, respectively.

The InitTimersSafe() and SetPinFrequencySafe(pin, freq) instructions do not impact *Timer0*, which controls the delay(), millis() and micros() functions. Either of the two *Timer1* pins—Arduino pins 9 or 10—can output the square wave.

Listing 22-8. Square Wave with PWM

```
#include <PWM.h>                    // include PWM library
unsigned long freq = 10000;         // required frequency (Hz)
int potPin = A0;                    // potentiometer pin
int PWMpin = 10;                    // use pin 9 or 10 (Timer1)
int setFreq;

void setup()
{
  pinMode(PWMpin, OUTPUT);          // define PWMpin as OUTPUT
  InitTimersSafe();                 // does not impact Timer0
  setFreq = SetPinFrequencySafe(PWMpin, freq); // does not impact Timer0
}

void loop()
{                                   // output square wave with duty cycle
  pwmWrite(PWMpin, analogRead(potPin)/4); // determined by potentiometer
}
```

Square waves can be generated with timer register manipulation, in a similar procedure to triggering interrupts, as outlined in Chapter 20. In Fast PWM 8-bit mode, *Timer1* counts to 255 (2^8–1), resets to zero and starts counting again. When *Timer1* matches the value in the *OCR1B* register, the square wave has value *LOW* and when *Timer1* overflows or resets to zero, the square wave has value *HIGH* (see Figure 22-8). If the value in the *OCR1B* register is based on the output of a potentiometer, then the duty cycle of the square wave can be changed by altering the potentiometer output. The maximum values of the analog-to-digital converter (ADC) and the *OCR1B* register are 1023 and 255, respectively, so the value from the potentiometer output is either divided by 4 or mapped with the `map(analogRead(potPin),0,1023,0,255)` instruction, where *potPin* is the Arduino pin connected to the potentiometer.

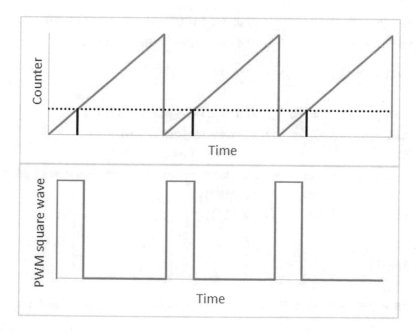

Figure 22-8. *PWM square wave*

The *COM1A1* and *COM1B1* registers enable outputs from *OCR1A* and *OCR1B* on pins *OC1A* and *OC1B*, which correspond to Arduino pins 9 and 10, respectively (see Figure 18-1). In Listings 22-9 and 22-10, the *OCR1B* register is used to generate a square wave, which is output on Arduino pin 10.

In Fast PWM 8-bit mode, *Timer1* overflows in $\dfrac{pre-scalar \times 256}{16 \times 10^{6}}$ seconds, which is equal to 16µs with prescalar of one, which corresponds to a square wave with frequency 62.5kHz. If the prescalar is increased to 256, the time for *Timer1* to overflow is 4.1ms, resulting in a square wave with frequency 244Hz.

Listing 22-9 generates a square wave with a frequency of 62.5kHz and the output from a potentiometer controls the duty cycle of the square wave.

Listing 22-9. Square Wave with Timer1 Fast PWM 8-bit Mode

```
int PWMpin = 10;            // define PWM pin on Arduino pin 10
int potPin = A0;            // define potentiometer on pin A0

void setup()
{
  pinMode(PWMpin, OUTPUT);   // define PWMpin as OUTPUT
  TCCR1A = 0;                // initialise register TCCR1A
  TCCR1B = 0;                // initialise register TCCR1B
    // set compare output mode and set pre-scalar to 1 with Fast PWM 8-bit mode
  TCCR1A |= (1<<WGM10) | (1<<COM1B1);
  TCCR1B |= (1<<CS10)  | (1<<WGM12);
}

void loop()
{
  OCR1B = analogRead(potPin)/4;     // change OCR1B register and duty cycle
}
```

The square wave frequencies generated using the Fast PWM 8-bit mode are constrained by *Timer1* counting to 255 and the values of the prescalar: 1, 8, 64, 256, and 1024, which result in frequencies of 62500, 7812.5, 976.56, 244, and 61Hz, respectively. However, with the Fast PWM mode, the overflow value of *Timer1* can be varied to generate square waves with frequencies between 1Hz and 4MHz. In Fast PWM mode, the value that *Timer1* counts up to is set by $\dfrac{16 \times 10^6}{pre-scalar \times frequency}$, such that *Timer1* overflows faster with higher values of the prescalar and the required square wave frequency, so that a square wave with the required frequency is generated. The *OCR1A* register is set to $\dfrac{16 \times 10^6}{pre-scalar \times frequency}$, but reduced by one as the counter starts from zero. While the *OCR1A* register controls the square wave frequency, the *OCR1B* register controls the duty cycle of the square wave through mapping the potentiometer output.

The required frequency determines the value of the prescalar, as the value of the *Timer1* overflow must be an integer; otherwise, the resulting frequency will not equal the required frequency. For example, prescalars of 1 and 256 are necessary to generate square waves with frequencies of 200kHz and 2Hz, with the *Timer1* overflow values equal to 80 and 31250, respectively.

Listing 22-10 generates a square wave with frequency 50kHz with a prescalar of one, although a prescalar of 8 or 64 could also be used. The term F_CPU is the microcontroller clock speed, which is a system constant, equal to 16MHz. Instructions for setting the *TCCR1B* register to different values of the prescalar are given in Table 22-4.

Table 22-4. *TCCR1B Register and Prescalar Values*

Prescalar	Instruction
1	TCCR1B |= (1<<CS10) | (1<<WGM12) | (1<<WGM13);
8	TCCR1B |= (1<<CS11) | (1<<WGM12) | (1<<WGM13);
64	TCCR1B |= (1<<CS10) | (1<<CS11) | (1<<WGM12) | (1<<WGM13);
256	TCCR1B |= (1<<CS12) | (1<<WGM12) | (1<<WGM13);
1024	TCCR1B |= (1<<CS10) | (1<<CS12) | (1<<WGM12) | (1<<WGM13);

Listing 22-10. Square Wave with Timer1 Fast PWM Mode

```
int PWMpin = 10;          // define PWM pin on Arduino pin 10
int potPin = A0;          // define potentiometer on pin A0
unsigned long freq = 50000; // required square wave frequency
int prescalar = 1;        // define pre-scalar
int overflow;

void setup()
{
  Serial.begin(9600);     // define Serial output baud rate
  pinMode(PWMpin, OUTPUT);   // define PWMpin as OUTPUT
  TCCR1A = 0;              // initialise register TCCR1A
  TCCR1B = 0;             // initialise register TCCR1B
        // set compare output mode and set pre-scalar to 1 with Fast PWM mode
  TCCR1A |= (1<<WGM10) | (1<<WGM11) | (1<<COM1B1);
  TCCR1B |= (1<<CS10)  | (1<<WGM12) | (1<<WGM13);
  overflow = F_CPU / (freq*prescalar);   // Timer1 overflow value
  Serial.println(overflow); // print Timer1 overflow value
  OCR1A = overflow-1;       // counter starts at zero
}
```

```
void loop()
{                                    // change OCR1B register and duty cycle
  OCR1B = map(analogRead(potPin),0,1023,0,overflow);
}
```

Square Wave and Servo Motor

A square wave with frequency 50Hz and duty cycle between 2.5% and 12.5% generates a signal with pulse width between 0.5ms and 2.5ms, which rotates a servo motor from 0° to 180°, as outlined in Chapter 8. With the servo motor connected to Arduino pin 10 and Listing 22-10 modified to generate the required square wave, the servo motor rotation can be controlled with the potentiometer. A prescalar of 64 is required to generate integer values for the *Timer1* overflow of 5000 and with a required frequency of 50Hz, the duty cycles of 2.5% and 12.5% are generated with *OCR1B* values of 125 and 625, respectively. Changes to Listing 22-10 include defining variables,

```
unsigned long freq = 50;      // square wave frequency
int prescalar = 64;           // define pre-scalar
```

setting the prescalar to 64 in the void setup() function,

```
TCCR1B |= (1<<CS10) |(1<<CS11) | (1<<WGM12) | (1<<WGM13)
```

and changing the void loop() function to

```
                              // duty cycle between 2.5% and 12.5%
OCR1B = map(analogRead(potPin),0,1023,.025*overflow,.125*overflow);
delay(10)                                 // time for servo to move
```

The PWM library could be used to generate the square wave for driving the servo motor, rather than setting the *Timer1* register. A square wave of frequency 50Hz and a duty cycle up to 12.5% can be generated with the *PWM* library, which only requires changing the frequency in Listing 22-8.

```
unsigned long freq = 50;                  // required frequency (Hz)
```

And changing the `void loop()` function to

```
pwmWrite(PWMpin, analogRead(potPin)/32);  // duty cycle up to 12.5%
delay(10)                                 // time for servo to move
```

Summary

Sounds of specific frequencies were generated with a Piezo transducer and with frequencies inversely related to the incident light on a light dependent resistor to imitate an electro-Theremin. Square waves were produced with pulse width modulation (PWM) and from timer register manipulation to control the movement of a servo motor.

Components List

- Arduino Uno and breadboard

- Piezo transducer

- Switch: 4× tactile

- Resistor: 220Ω and 2×4.7kΩ

- Capacitor: 0.1µF and 22µF

- LED

- Light dependent resistor (or photoresistor): 2×

- Potentiometer: 2×10kΩ

- Servo motor: SG90

- Voltage regulator: L4940V5

- Battery: 9V

CHAPTER 23

DC Motors

The DC (direct current) motor has many applications in robotics, portable power tools, and electric vehicles. DC motors are driven by the force generated in a magnetic field. Passing a current through an electromagnet, which is a coil of wire wrapped around a metallic rod, generates a magnetic field and reversing the current changes the polarity of the electromagnet. Given that same-pole magnets repel and dissimilar-pole magnets attract, then mounting two electromagnets on a rotor enclosed within a permanent magnet and alternating the current through the electromagnets turns the rotor as the magnets sequentially attract and repel.

The direction of rotation is controlled with an H-bridge, which is essentially formed by two pairs of transistor switches, on opposite sides of the motor, and the direction of current, through the motor, changes as each "diagonally opposite" pair of switches opens (see Figure 23-1). The L298N motor driver board can control two 6V DC motors and if the supply voltage is less than 12V, the voltage regulator provides a 5V output pin for powering an Arduino (see Figure 23-2). If the supply voltage is greater than 12V, then the jumper behind power connections must be disconnected.

© Neil Cameron 2019
N. Cameron, *Arduino Applied*, https://doi.org/10.1007/978-1-4842-3960-5_23

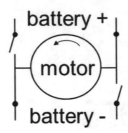

Figure 23-1. *H-bridge*

The L298N motor driver board controls the direction of rotation and speed of the motors by incorporating an H-bridge for each motor with PWM. The order of the control pins, on the L298N motor driver board, is *ENA, IN1,* and *IN2* for the left motor and *IN3, IN4,* and *ENB* for the right motor (see Table 23-1). For the left motor, setting pin *IN1* or *IN2* to *HIGH* and the other pin to *LOW* turns the motor forward or backward, respectively. Motor speed is controlled using Pulse Width Modulation (PWM), outlined in Chapter 1, on the *ENA (Enable motor A)* and *ENB* pins. The instruction to set the speed of the left motor is analogWrite(ENA, speed), where *speed* is a value between 0 and 255. If the *ENA* and *ENB* pins are not required for controlling the motor speed, then jumpers can be placed across the pins to connect them to 5V, resulting in full motor speed. If the two motors turn in the opposite direction from each other, then the connecting wires of one motor should be reversed.

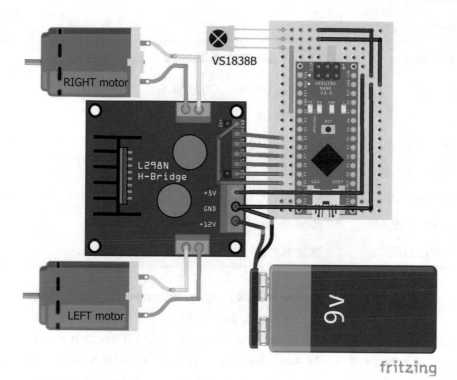

Figure 23-2. *L298N and DC motors*

Table 23-1. *L298N and DC Motors*

Component	Connect to Arduino		and to
	Nano	**Uno**	
L298 12V	Battery 9V	Battery 9V	
L298 GND	Battery GND	Battery GND	Nano or Uno GND
L298 5V	Nano VIN	Uno VIN	
L298 ENA	Nano pin D9	Uno pin 9	
L298 IN1	Nano pin D8	Uno pin 8	
L298 IN2	Nano pin D7	Uno pin 7	

(continued)

Table 23-1. (*continued*)

Component	Connect to Arduino	and to
L298 IN3	Nano pin D6	Uno pin 6
L298 IN4	Nano pin D5	Uno pin 5
L298 ENB	Nano pin D10	Uno pin 10
L298 motor connect	DC motors	DC motors
IR sensor OUT	Nano pin D2	Uno pin 2
IR sensor GND	Nano GND	Uno GND
IR sensor VCC	Nano VIN	Uno VIN

An Arduino Nano is used in this chapter because it is smaller than the Arduino Uno (see Figure 23-3). The Arduino Nano has two more analog inputs than the Arduino Uno and has a mini USB connection. The pin layouts of the Arduino Nano and Uno are similar, as indicated in Table 23-1, so the schematics and sketches are applicable to both the Arduino Nano and Arduino Uno. Note that from January 2018, Arduino released a new bootloader for the Arduino Nano and the relevant processor must be selected.

Within the Arduino IDE, in the *Tools* ➤ *Board* menu, select *Arduino Nano*. In the *Tools* ➤ *Processor* menu, select either *ATmega328P (Old Bootloader)* or *ATmega328P* (if the Arduino Nano was sold by Arduino before or after January 2018).

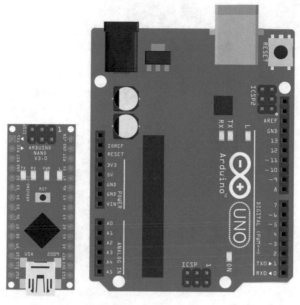

Figure 23-3. *Arduino Nano and Arduino Uno*

On the L298N motor driver board, the *ENA* and *ENB* pins for
controlling the motor speed are connected to PWM pins 9 and 10 on the
Arduino Nano. Digital (D) pins 3, 5, 6, 9, 10 and 11 on the Arduino Nano
can be used for variable output voltage with PWM (see Figure 23-4). The
restrictions on PWM pins outlined in Chapter 18 apply to the Arduino
Nano, which means that analogWrite() on Nano PWM pins D9 and D10
is disabled by the *Servo* library, on Nano PWM pins D10 and D11 by SPI
and on Nano PWM pins D3 and D11 by the tone() function. The *IRRemote*
library for infrared remote control also uses *Timer2*, which disables Nano
PWM pins D3 and D11 for analogWrite().

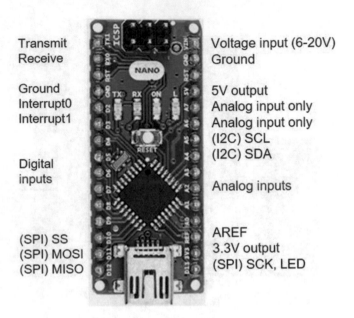

Transmit	Voltage input (6-20V)
Receive	Ground
Ground	5V output
Interrupt0	Analog input only
Interrupt1	Analog input only
	(I2C) SCL
	(I2C) SDA
Digital	
inputs	Analog inputs
(SPI) SS	AREF
(SPI) MOSI	3.3V output
(SPI) MISO	(SPI) SCK, LED

Figure 23-4. *Arduino Nano*

If the voltage supply to the motors is too low, either by setting the motor speed too low or the battery power is low, then the motors produce a buzzing sound and stop turning. A sketch should ensure that the minimum speed value in an `analogWrite()` instruction is at least 50. Likewise, a fully charged 9V battery is required as the voltage drop across the L298N motor driver board is 2V.

Motor Control Set in the Sketch

The sketch (see Listing 23-1) uses functions for moving forward or backward and for turning right or left, for a given period of time, with the `motor()` function controlling the speed and direction of rotation of each motor. The motor speed is set higher when moving forward or backward than when turning right or left. The route taken by the robot car is defined in the `void loop()` function. The motors move forward for 1500ms, then turn right for 500ms, move forward and turn left, move forward and turn left again, move forward and turn right, move forward and then move backward to the starting position.

Listing 23-1. Route Defined in Sketch

```
int IN1 = 8;                    // left motor forward and backward pins
int IN2 = 7;
int IN3 = 6;                    // right motor forward and backward pins
int IN4 = 5;
int ENA = 9;                    // control pin left motor
int ENB = 10;                   // control pin right motor

void setup()
{
  pinMode(IN1, OUTPUT);         // define motor pins as OUTPUT
  pinMode(IN2, OUTPUT);
  pinMode(IN3, OUTPUT);
  pinMode(IN4, OUTPUT);
  pinMode(ENA, OUTPUT);         // define motor enable pins as OUTPUT
  pinMode(ENB, OUTPUT);
}

void loop()
{
  direction("forward",1500);    // move forward for 1500ms
  direction("right",500);       // turn right for 500ms
  direction("forward",1000);
  direction("left",500);        // turn left for 500ms
  direction("forward",1500);
  direction("left",500);
  direction("forward",1000);
  direction("right",500);
  direction("forward",1500);
  direction("backward",4500);   // move backward for 4500ms
}
```

```
void direction(String direct, int runTime) // function to set motor direction
{
  if(direct == "forward") motor(1, 0, 1, 0, "fast"); // both motors forward
  else
  if(direct == "backward") motor(0, 1, 0, 1, "fast"); // both motors backward
  else                                                // left forward,
  if(direct == "right") motor(1, 0, 0, 1, "slow"); // right backward
  else                                                // left backward,
  if(direct == "left") motor(0, 1, 1, 0, "slow");   // right forward
  else
  if(direct == "stop") motor(0, 0, 0, 0, " ");  // both motors stop
  delay(runTime);                      // run time (ms) for motors
}

void motor(int leftF, int leftB, int rightF ,int rightB, String speed)
{                                 // motor function
  float bias = 1.0;              // bias on motor speed
  digitalWrite(IN1, leftF);   // control pin IN1 left motor forward
  digitalWrite(IN2, leftB);   // control pin IN2 left motor backward
  digitalWrite(IN3, rightF);  // control pin IN3 right motor forward
  digitalWrite(IN4, rightB);  // control pin IN4 right motor backward
  if(speed == "fast")
  {
    analogWrite(ENA, 100);        // higher speed when moving
    analogWrite(ENB, 100*bias);   // forward or backward
  }
  else
  {
    analogWrite(ENA, 80);         // lower speed when turning
    analogWrite(ENB, 80*bias);    // compensation on right motor
  }
}
```

If the right motor turns slower than the left motor, the PWM value is increased to compensate, by increasing the value of the variable bias.

Motor Speed

The relationship between motor speed and the `analogWrite()` instruction can be derived with a potentiometer, to change the motor speed (see Figure 23-5), and a Hall effect switch (see Chapter 3) to determine the time taken for a revolution with a small magnet attached to the wheel. Motor speed increases non-linearly with potentiometer value, with a greater change in motor speed at lower potentiometer values and a maximum motor speed of 230rpm (see Figure 23-6). Measurement of motor speed with photoelectric encoders is outlined later in the chapter. Listing 23-2 is based on the Hall effect sketch (see Listing 3-8) in Chapter 3 and applies to the motor on the right-hand side of the L298N motor driver board.

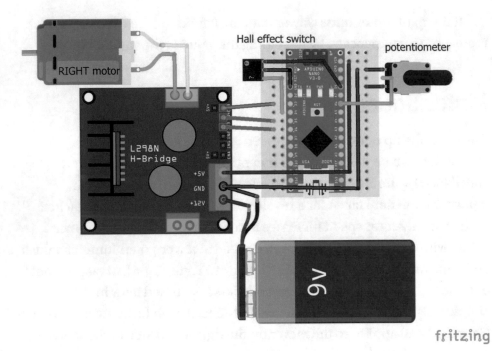

Figure 23-5. *Potentiometer control of DC motor speed*

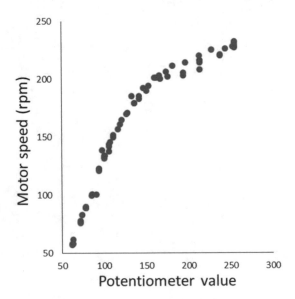

Figure 23-6. *Potentiometer and DC motor speed*

Listing 23-2. Hall Effect Sensor and DC Motor Speed

```
int hallPin = 4;                   // Hall effect switch pin
int hallState = LOW;               // set state to LOW
int IN3 = 6;                       // motor forward and backward pins
int IN4 = 5;
int ENB = 3;                       // motor enable pin
int potPin = A6;                   // potentiometer pin
unsigned long time = 0;            // time (ms) per revolution
float hallrpm;
int reading, speed;

void setup()
{
  Serial.begin(9600);             // set baud rate for Serial Monitor
  pinMode(hallPin, INPUT_PULLUP); // pull-up resistor on Hall effect switch pin
  pinMode(IN3, OUTPUT);           // define motor pins as OUTPUT
  pinMode(IN4, OUTPUT);
  digitalWrite(IN3,1);            // set motor to forward rotation
  digitalWrite(IN4,0);
}

void loop()
{
  reading = analogRead(potPin);        // read potentiometer
  speed = map(reading, 0, 1023, 0, 255); // map potentiometer value
  analogWrite(ENB,speed);              // set motor speed
  reading = digitalRead(hallPin);      // read Hall switch
  if(reading != hallState)             // Hall switch state changed
  {
    if (reading == HIGH && hallState == LOW) // start of new revolution
    {
      time = millis() - time;       // time (ms) since last revolution
      hallrpm = 60000.0/time;       // revolutions per minute
      Serial.print(speed);Serial.print("\t"); // potentiometer value
```

```
    Serial.println(hallrpm,0);   // display motor speed (rpm) with 0DP
    time = millis();             // update revolution time
  }
  hallState = reading;           // update Hall switch state
 }
}
```

Motor Control with Infrared Remote Control

In Chapter 10, an infrared (IR) remote control was used to turn on or off LEDs depending on which button was pressed on the remote control. Similarly, the rotation of the two DC motors can be associated with buttons on the remote control. To receive the infrared signal, an infrared sensor, VS1838B, is connected to pin 2 of the Arduino Nano (see Figure 23-2) and Listing 23-1 is updated to include the following instructions at the start of the sketch, with the `irrecv.enableIRIn()`instruction to initialize the IR receiver included in the `void setup()` function.

```
#include <IRremote.h>         // include IRemote library
int IRpin = 2;                // IR sensor pin
IRrecv irrecv(IRpin);         // associate irrecv with IRremote library
decode_results reading;       // IRremote reading
```

The `void loop()` function of Listing 23-3 is replaced to read the infrared signal and the remote control signal is also mapped with a `switch case` sequence to the corresponding function for controlling the motors to move for 500ms. Note that the hexadecimal signal codes are only an example.

Listing 23-3. DC Motor Control with Infrared Remote Control

```
void loop()
{
  if(irrecv.decode(&reading))       // read the IR signal
  {
    switch(reading.value)           // switch ... case for button signals
    {
      case 0xC0E014D: direction("forward",500); break;  // forward
      case 0x9FFCDC4D: direction("backward",500); break;  // backward
      case 0x348ADD0F: direction("right",500); break;  // turn right
      case 0x7E57898D: direction("left",500); break;  // turn left
      case 0x4B0AA72C: direction("stop",500); break;  // stop
    }
    irrecv.resume();                // receive the next infrared signal
  }
}
```

As noted, the *IRRemote* library for infrared remote control uses *Timer2*, which disables Nano PWM pins D3 and D11 for analogWrite() on the L298N motor driver board *ENA* and ENB pins.

Motor Control with Wireless Communication

In Chapter 17, nRF24L01 wireless transceiver modules enabled communication between two devices. The nRF24L01 transceiver modules can be used, in conjunction with a joystick, such as a KY-023 module, to control the DC motors remotely. One nRF24L01 module transmits PWM values derived from the joystick readings to the receiving nRF24L01 module, which controls the motor speeds with the PWM values. The transmitting nRF24L01 module and joystick are connected to an Arduino Uno or Nano (see Figure 23-7 and Table 23-2) and the receiving nRF24L01 module, two DC motors, and the L298N motor driver board are attached to an Arduino Nano (see Figure 23-8 and Table 23-3).

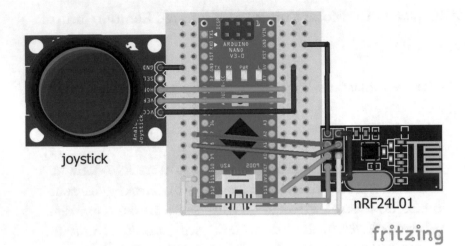

Figure 23-7. *Joystick and transmitting nRF24L01 module*

Table 23-2. *Joystick and Transmitting nRF24L01 Module*

Component	Connect to	
Joystick VCC	Nano 5V	Uno 5V
Joystick VER (Y)	Nano pin A5	Uno pin A3
Joystick HOR (X)	Nano pin A6	Uno pin A4
Joystick GND	Nano GND	Uno GND
nRF24L01 GND	Nano GND	Uno GND
nRF24L01 CE	Nano pin D7	Uno pin 7
nRF24L01 SCK	Nano pin D13	Uno pin 13
nRF24L01 MISO	Nano pin D12	Uno pin 12
nRF24L01 VCC	Nano 3V3	Uno 3.3V
nRF24L01 CSN	Nano pin D8	Uno pin 8
nRF24L01 MOSI	Nano pin D11	Uno pin 11

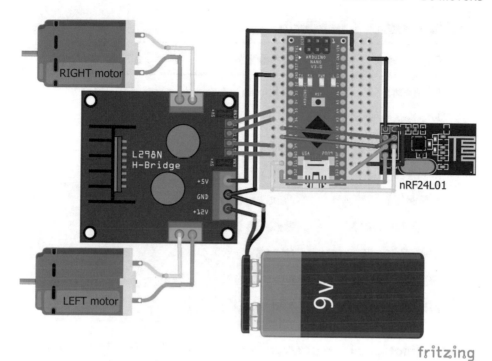

Figure 23-8. *DC motors and receiving nRF24L01 module*

Table 23-3. *DC Motors and Receiving nRF24L01 Module*

Component	Connect to	and to
L298 12V	Battery 9V	
L298 GND	Battery GND	Nano GND
L298 5V	Nano VIN	
L298 ENA	5V jumper	
L298 IN1	Nano PWM pin D10	
L298 IN2	Nano PWM pin D9	
L298 IN3	Nano PWM pin D6	
L298 IN4	Nano PWM pin D5	

(*continued*)

447

Table 23-3. (*continued*)

Component	Connect to	and to
L298 ENB	5V jumper	
L298 motor connect	DC motors	
nRF24L01 GND	Nano GND	
nRF24L01 CE	Nano pin D7	
nRF24L01 SCK	Nano pin D13	
nRF24L01 MISO	Nano pin D12	
nRF24L01 VCC	Nano 3V3	
nRF24L01 CSN	Nano pin D8	
nRF24L01 MOSI	Nano pin D11	

The motor speed and direction of rotation can be directly controlled with PWM inputs to the L298N motor driver board *IN1, IN2, IN3,* and *IN4* pins, as the Arduino Nano has several PWM pins. For example, to move forward at half speed, the instruction is

```
analogWrite(IN1, 128);
analogWrite(IN2, 0);
analogWrite(IN3, 128);
analogWrite(IN4, 0);
```

Jumpers are placed across the ENA and ENB pins to 5V, as the ENA and ENB pins are not required to control motor speed, when using PWM (see Figure 23-8).

The control pins of the L298N motor driver board are connected to Arduino Nano PWM pins 5, 6, 9, and 10 to use analogWrite() instructions in the motor() function. The analogWrite(pin, value) instruction automatically sets the pinMode status of a pin to *OUTPUT*, so when only using the analogWrite(), the pinMode(pin, OUTPUT) instruction is not required. Although, inclusion of the `pinMode(pin, OUTPUT)` instruction may be helpful to identify which pins are used in the sketch.

The motor speed and direction of rotation can be controlled with a joystick (see Listing 23-4), which consists of two potentiometers for controlling the left-right direction (X-axis) and the forward-backward direction (Y-axis). The joystick values range from 0 to 1023, with 0 corresponding to right and forward, 1023 mapping to left and backward and 512 equivalent to the "rest" position of the joystick. The left-right, *LR*, and forward-backward, *FB*, joystick readings are converted to PWM values for the left and right motors as the sum (*FB* + *LR*) and difference (*FB* – *LR*) of the *FB* and *LR* readings. The sum retains the magnitude of the forward-backward reading and the difference increases the speed of one motor and reduces the speed of the other motor to make a turn. Different scalars for the *FB* and *LR* readings are used to alter the sensitivity of the joystick to movements in the two axes.

Listing 23-4. Joystick and Transmitting nRF24L01

```
#include <SPI.h>            // include SPI library
#include <RF24.h>           // include RF24 library
RF24 radio(7, 8);           // associate radio with RF24 library
byte addresses[ ][6] = {"12"};
typedef struct              // define a structure to contain
{                           // PWM values for the
   int right, left;         // left and right motors
} dataStruct;
dataStruct data;            // name the structure
int LRpin = A5;  // Nano A5 Uno A4 (horizontal) left-right (X-axis)
int FBpin = A6;  // Nano A6 Uno A3 (vertical) forward-backward (Y-axis)
int LR, FB;
int minPWM = 50;            // minimum PWM value
int LRscalar = 2;           // scalars for joystick sensitivity
int FBscalar = 2;
```

```
void setup()
{
 radio.begin();                              // initialise radio
 radio.openWritingPipe(addresses[0]);   // open transmitting pipe
}

void loop()
{
  LR = map(analogRead(LRpin), 0, 1023, -255, 255); // joystick left = 0
  FB = map(analogRead(FBpin), 0, 1023, 255, -255); // joystick forward = 0
  data.left = FB/FBscalar + LR/LRscalar;   // sum of scaled readings
  data.right = FB/FBscalar - LR/LRscalar; // difference scaled readings
  data.left = constrain(data.left, -255, 255); // constrain PWM values
  data.right = constrain(data.right, -255, 255);
  if(abs(data.left) < minPWM) data.left = 0; // zero if < minimum value
  if(abs(data.right) < minPWM) data.right = 0;
  radio.write(&data, sizeof(data));           // transmit PWM values
  delay(50);                                  // delay 50ms
}
```

The sketch for the receiving nRF24L01 module is given in Listing 23-5.

Listing 23-5. DC Motors and Receiving nRF24L01

```
#include <SPI.h>              // include SPI library
#include <RF24.h>             // include RF24 library
RF24 radio(7, 8);             // associate radio with RF24 library
byte addresses[ ][6] = {"12"};
typedef struct                // define a structure to contain
{                             // PWM values for the
  int right, left;            // left and right motors
} dataStruct;
dataStruct data;        // name the structure
int IN1 = 10;           // left motor forward and backward on PWM pins
int IN2 = 9;
```

```
int IN3 = 6;            // right motor forward and backward
int IN4 = 5;

void setup()
{
  radio.begin();                  // initialise radio
  radio.openReadingPipe(0, addresses[0]); // open receiving pipe
  radio.startListening();   // initialise receive
}

void loop()
{
  if(radio.available())     // signal received
  {
    radio.read(&data,sizeof(data));     // read data values
                                        // forward
    if(data.left>0 && data.right>0) motor(data.left, 0, data.right, 0);
    else                              // backward
    if(data.left<0 && data.right<0) motor(0, -data.left, 0, -data.right);
    else                              // turn left
    if(data.left<0 && data.right>0) motor(0, -data.left, data.right, 0);
    else                              // turn right
    if(data.left>0 && data.right<0) motor(data.left, 0, 0, -data.right);
    else motor(0, 0, 0, 0);            // stop
  }
}

void motor(int leftF, int leftB, int rightF ,int rightB)
{
  analogWrite(IN1, leftF);    // control pin IN1 left motor forward
  analogWrite(IN2, leftB);    // control pin IN2 left motor backward
  analogWrite(IN3, rightF);   // control pin IN3 right motor forward
  analogWrite(IN4, rightB);   // control pin IN4 right motor backward
}
```

Motor Control with Accelerometer

The direction and degree of tilt of the GY-521 module, incorporating an accelerometer, can be used to control the direction and speed of rotation of the motors. The schematic for the GY-521 module with the transmitting nRF24L01 module (see Figure 23-9) is similar to schematic with the joystick (see Figure 23-7). Note that jumpers are placed across the *ENA* and *ENB* pins of the L298N motor driver board and 5V, as the *ENA* and *ENB* pins are not required to control motor speed (see Table 23-4). The sketch (see Listing 23-6) for the GY-521 and transmitting nRF24L01 modules is based on the accelerometer and gyroscope sketch (see Listing 3-13) in Chapter 3 with the *RF24* library for transmitting the transformed roll and pitch MPU-6050 values to the Arduino Nano or Uno to drive the motors. The sketch for the receiving nRF24L01 module is unchanged (see Listing 23-5).

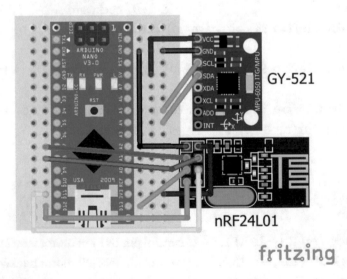

Figure 23-9. *GY-521 and transmitting nRF24L01*

The GY-521 module is orientated as in Figure 23-9, with the top-bottom and left-right axes corresponding to pitch and roll, respectively.

Table 23-4. *GY-521 and Transmitting nRF24L01*

Component	Connect to	
GY-521 VCC	Nano 5V	Uno 5V
GY-521 GND	Nano GND	Uno GND
GY-521 SCL	Nano pin A5	Uno pin A5
GY-521 SDA	Nano pin A4	Uno pin A4
nRF24L01 GND	Nano GND	Uno GND
nRF24L01 CE	Nano pin D7	Uno pin 7
nRF24L01 SCK	Nano pin D13	Uno pin 13
nRF24L01 MISO	Nano pin D12	Uno pin 12
nRF24L01 VCC	Nano 3V3	Uno 3.3V
nRF24L01 CSN	Nano pin D8	Uno pin 8
nRF24L01 MOSI	Nano pin D11	Uno pin 11

Listing 23-6. GY-521 and Transmitting nRF24L01

```
#include<Wire.h>                     // include Wire library
int I2Caddress = 0x68;               // I2C address of MPU-6050
float accelX, accelY, accelZ;        // values from MPU-6050
float roll, pitch, sumsquare;
#include <SPI.h>                     // include SPI library
#include <RF24.h>                    // include RF24 library
RF24 radio(7, 8);                    // associate radio with RF24 library
byte addresses[ ][6] = {"12"};
```

```
typedef struct                          // define a structure
{
  int right, left;                      // PWM values for the DC motors
} dataStruct;
dataStruct data;
int minPWM = 50;                        // minimum PWM value
int FB, LR;
int LRscalar = 1;                       // scalar for accelerometer sensitivity

void setup()
{
  Serial.begin(9600);
  Wire.begin();                             // initiate I2C bus
  Wire.beginTransmission(I2Caddress);       // transmit to device at I2Caddress
  Wire.write(0x6B);                         // PWR_MGMT_1 register
  Wire.write(0);                            // set to zero to wake up MPU-6050
  Wire.endTransmission(1);                  // end of transmission
  radio.begin();                            // initialise radio
  radio.openWritingPipe(addresses[0]);  // open transmitting pipe
}

void loop()
{
  Wire.beginTransmission(I2Caddress); // transmit to device at I2Caddress
  Wire.write(0x3B);                       // start reading from register 0x3B
  Wire.endTransmission(0);                // transmission not finished
  Wire.requestFrom(I2Caddress,6,true);    // request data from 6 registers
  accelX=Wire.read()<<8|Wire.read();  // combine AxHigh and AxLow values
  accelY=Wire.read()<<8|Wire.read();  // combine AyHigh and AyLow values
  accelZ=Wire.read()<<8|Wire.read();  // combine AzHigh and AzLow values
```

```
accelX = accelX/pow(2,14);
accelY = accelY/pow(2,14);          // scale X, Y and Z measurements
accelZ = accelZ/pow(2,14);
sumsquare = sqrt(accelX*accelX+accelY*accelY+accelZ*accelZ);
accelX = accelX/sumsquare;
accelY = accelY/sumsquare;  // adjusted accelerometer measurements
accelZ = accelZ/sumsquare;
roll = atan2(accelY, accelZ)*180/PI; // roll angle
pitch = -asin(accelX)*180/PI;          // pitch angle
LR = map(pitch, -90, 90, -255, 255); // tilt module left or right
FB = map(roll, -90, 90, -255, 255);   // tilt module forward or backward
data.left = FB + LR/LRscalar;         // sum of scaled readings
data.right = FB - LR/LRscalar;       // difference of scaled readings
data.left = constrain(data.left, -255, 255); // constrain PWM values
data.right = constrain(data.right, -255, 255);
if(abs(data.left) < minPWM) data.left = 0; // zero PWM values if
if(abs(data.right) < minPWM) data.right = 0; // less than minimum value
radio.write(&data, sizeof(data));     // transmit PWM values
delay(50);                            // delay 50ms
}
```

An OLED display, outlined in Chapter 13, can display the motor speed values, derived from the MCU-6050 accelerometer with the transmitting nRF24L01 module. The following instructions are included at the start of Listing 23-6 to define the OLED display.

```
#include <Adafruit_GFX.h>           // include Adafruit GFX library
#include <Adafruit_SSD1306.h>        // include Adafruit SSD1306 library
Adafruit_SSD1306 oled(-1)   // associate display with Adafruit_SSD1306 library
int FBspeed, LRspeed;                // define speed variables for OLED
```

with instructions to initialize the OLED Display in the void setup() function (see Listing 23-7) and instructions to display the motor speeds in the void loop() function (see Listing 23-8).

Listing 23-7. Initialize OLED Display with an I2C Address

```
oled.begin(SSD1306_SWITCHCAPVCC, 0x3C);
oled.clearDisplay();              // clear OLED display
oled.setTextColor(WHITE);         // set font colour
oled.setTextSize(2);              // set font size
oled.display();                   // start display instructions
```

Listing 23-8. Display Motor Speeds on OLED

```
FBspeed = data.left;
LRspeed = data.right;
oled.clearDisplay();              // clear OLED display
oled.setCursor(0,0);              // position cursor at (0, 0)
oled.print("left: ");            // display text and motor speed
oled.println(FBspeed);            // followed by a carriage return
oled.print("right: ");           // display text and motor speed
oled.print(LRspeed);
oled.display();                   // start display instructions
```

The OLED display display.print(data.left) instruction displays a character rather than an integer, which is resolved by including the FBspeed = data.left and display.print(FBspeed) instructions and similarly for *LRspeed* and *data.right,* in the void loop() function.

Motor Control with Photoelectric Encoder

 The HC-020K (left) and FC-03 (right) photoelectric encoders contain an infrared LED and phototransistor sensor, which passes current when light is detected, and an LM393 comparator that converts the change in current to a digital value. An encoder wheel, containing a number of slots, is attached to the DC motor and the photoelectric encoder is positioned around the encoder wheel. When the DC motor rotates, the photoelectric encoder counts the number of encoder wheel slots passing between the infrared LED and phototransistor sensor. With s slots in the encoder wheel and N slots counted in t seconds, the speed of the DC motor is $60 \times N/s \times t$ rpm. For example, with 20 slots in the encoder wheel, then 10 slots counted in 500ms equates to 60rpm.

A 100nF capacitor is required between the signal (OUT) and GND pins of the HC-202K photoelectric encoder and between the D0 and GND pins of the FC-03 photoelectric encoder, otherwise the number of counts is increased by a factor of approximately four. The A0 output of the FC-03 photoelectric encoder does not require a capacitor to be fitted. The photoelectric encoder signal pins are connected to the interrupt pins of the Arduino Uno (2 and 3) or Nano (D2 and D3), with the VCC pins connected to 5V (see Figure 23-10 and Table 23-5).

Table 23-5. *DC Motors with Photoelectric Encoders*

Component	Connect to	and to
L298 12V	Battery 9V	
L298 GND	Battery GND	Nano GND
L298 5V	Nano VIN	
L298 ENA	5V jumper	
L298 IN1	Nano PWM pin D10	
L298 IN2	Nano PWM pin D9	
L298 IN3	Nano PWM pin D6	
L298 IN4	Nano PWM pin D5	
L298 ENB	5V jumper	
L298 motor connect	DC motors	
FC-03 encoder A0 pins	Nano pins D2 and D3	
FC-03 encoder VCC	Nano 5V	
FC-03 encoder GND	Nano GND	

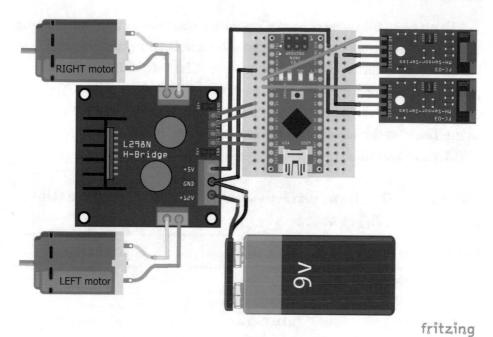

Figure 23-10. *DC motors and photoelectric encoders*

To measure the speed of a DC motor, the two sketches in Table 23-6 use interrupts (as outlined in Chapter 20) with the *TimerOne* library and the millis() function to count the number of encoder wheel slots in the fixed time period of 0.5 seconds. The motor turns at a fixed speed and is powered on Arduino PWM pins 5 and 6. With the *TimerOne* library, the *timerISR* and *counter* interrupts occur after the fixed time period and after the photoelectric encoder detects a slot, respectively. With the millis() function, *counter* is the only interrupt and the *count* variable is declared as volatile, as it is referenced in both the sketch and the ISR (outlined in Chapter 20). Note that the *TimerOne* library measures time in microseconds, while millis() measures time in milliseconds.

To measure the speed of two DC motors, rather than only one DC motor, the Arduino interrupt pins, 2 and 3, are connected to the photoelectric encoder output corresponding to each motor. The two DC motors are powered by Arduino PWM pins 5 and 6 and by PWM pins 9 and 10. The encoder slot *counter* interrupts must be controlled by the `millis()` function, as the *TimerOne* library disables the `analogWrite()`instruction on Arduino PWM pins 9 and 10.

Table 23-6. *DC Motors and Photoelectric Encoders with TimerOne Library or millis() Function*

TimerOne library	Use millis( )	Comments
#include <TimerOne.h>		
	unsigned long Atime = 0;	
float fixTime = 0.5;	int fixTime = 500;	rpm every 0.5s
	float chkTime;	
float rpm;	float rpm;	
int count=0;	volatile int count = 0;	
int IN1 = 6;	int IN1 = 6;	motor pins
int IN2 = 5;	int IN2 = 5;	
int slot = 20;	int slot = 20;	number of wheel slots
void setup()	void setup()	
{	{	
Serial.begin(9600);	Serial.begin(9600);	Serial baud rate
Timer1.initialize(50000);		TimerOne for 0.5s
attachInterrupt (0, counter, RISING);	attachInterrupt (0, counter, RISING);	counter interrupts
Timer1.attachInterrupt (timerISR);		timerISR interrupt
analogWrite(IN1, 60);	analogWrite(IN1, 60);	motor set ~60 rpm
analogWrite(IN2, 0);	analogWrite(IN2, 0);	
}	}	

(continued)

Table 23-6. (*continued*)

TimerOne library	Use millis( )	Comments
void loop()	void loop()	
{}	{	
	if (millis() - Atime >= fixTime)	rpm after fixTime
void timerISR()		rpm after 0.5s
{	{	
noInterrupts();	noInterrupts();	stop interrupts
	chkTime = (millis() - Atime)/1000.0;	
rpm = 60*count/(slot*fixTime);	rpm = 60*count/(slot*chkTime);	calculate rpm
Serial.print("rpm = ");	Serial.print("rpm = ");	
Serial.println(rpm, 0);	Serial.println(rpm, 0);	
count = 0;	count = 0;	reset counter
	Atime = millis();	reset elapsed time
interrupts();	interrupts();	restart interrupts
	}	
}	}	
void counter()	void counter()	interrupt ISR
{	{	
count++;	count++;	increment count
}	}	

The distance travelled by the robot car can be monitored with the photoelectric encoder. The number of encoder wheel slots that must pass the photoelectric encoder for the robot car to move a distance, D, is $D \times s/\pi \times d$, where s is the number of encoder wheel slots and d is the diameter of the robot car wheel. For the robot car to turn right or left, the number of encoder wheel slots that must pass the photoelectric encoder is $s \times W/4 \times d$, where W is the distance between the midpoint of the two wheels. The value of $s \times W/4 \times d$ should be rounded up to an integer with the turnSlot = round(s * W /(4 * d)) instruction.

The photoelectric encoders can be used to move the robot car through an exact route by determining the number of slots required to pass the photoelectric encoder to move a given distance. The same route taken in Listing 23-1, which moved the robot car for a given time in each direction of the route, is taken in Listing 23-9, but the robot car is moved a set distance in each direction of the route, with substantially more "accuracy."

Listing 23-9 includes two interrupts to count the number of encoder wheel slots passing the photoelectric encoder of each DC motor. The direction() function specifies the direction and distance to move, sets the direction of rotation of each DC motor and then a while() instruction monitors the values of the counters, which correspond to the number of encoder wheel slots passing the photoelectric encoder. The DC motors are not synchronized and the DC motors stop after both photoelectric encoders count the required number of slots. The DC motor speed is defined in the motor() function, with the sketch using values of 100 and 80 for forward or backward and for turn right or left, respectively.

Listing 23-9. Distance Travelled by the Robot Car

```
int IN1 = 10;              // left wheel forward and backward
int IN2 = 9;
int IN3 = 6;               // right wheel forward and backward
int IN4 = 5;
float W = 13.0;            // distance (cm) between mid-point of wheels
float d = 6.7;             // diameter (cm) of wheel
int slot = 20;             // number of encoder wheel slots
float turnSlot = slot * W /(4 * d);   // number of slots to turn right/left
float cmSlot = slot/(PI*d);      // number of slots to move one cm
volatile int countR = 0;         // counter for encoder wheel slots
volatile int countL = 0;
int FBspeed = 100;               // forward/backward speed
int LRspeed = 80;                // left/right turn speed
```

```
void setup()
{
  attachInterrupt(0, counterR, RISING); // interrupts to count encoder wheel
  attachInterrupt(1, counterL, RISING); // slots passing photoelectric encoder
}

void loop()
{
  direction("forward", 40);              // function to define direction
  direction("right", 0);                 // and distance (cm)
  direction("forward", 30);
  direction("left", 0);
  direction("forward", 20);
  direction("left", 0);
  direction("forward", 30);
  direction("right", 0);
  direction("forward", 50);
  direction("backward", 110);
  direction("stop", 0);
  delay(5000);                           // delay 5s on completing route
}

void direction(String direct, int dist) // function controlling DC motors
{
  int Nslots;                                 // number of slots to count
  if(direct == "forward" || direct == "backward")Nslots = dist*cmSlot;
  else if(direct == "right" || direct == "left") Nslots = turnSlot;
  else if(direct == "stop")
  {
    Nslots = 0;
    countL = 1;                          // to stop, set counters above slot limit
    countR = 1;
  }
```

```
  Serial.println(Nslots);        // set motor then count slots
       if(direct == "forward")  motor(1, 0, 1, 0, FBspeed);
  else if(direct == "backward") motor(0, 1, 0, 1, FBspeed);
  else if(direct == "right")    motor(1, 0, 0, 1, LRspeed);
  else if(direct == "left")     motor(0, 1, 1, 0, LRspeed);
                         // wait until slot limit reached by both motors
  while (countR <= Nslots || countL <= Nslots) { }
  if(countR > Nslots && countL > Nslots)
  {                          // both wheels have moved the required distance
    motor(0, 0, 0, 0, 0);               // reset all variables
    delay(500);
    countR = 0;
    countL = 0;
  }
}

void motor(int leftF, int leftB, int rightF ,int rightB, int cspeed)
{
  analogWrite(IN1, leftF * cspeed);   // forward speed of left motor
  analogWrite(IN2, leftB * cspeed);   // backward speed of left motor
  analogWrite(IN3, rightF * cspeed);  // forward speed of right motor
  analogWrite(IN4, rightB * cspeed);  // backward speed right motor
}

void counterR()
{                       // interrupt to count number of encoder wheel
  countR++;             // slots passing right wheel encoder
}

void counterL()
{                       // interrupt to count number of encoder wheel
  countL++;             // slots passing left wheel encoder
}
```

Summary

DC motors powered a robot car controlled by an Arduino Nano or Arduino Uno with the route taken either defined in the sketch or controlled by infrared remote control or wirelessly using transceivers with a joystick or by tilting an accelerometer module. DC motor speed was determined using a Hall effect sensor and by photoelectric encoders. The distance travelled was controlled by photoelectric encoders.

Components List

- Arduino Nano or Uno and breadboard: 2×

- DC motors: 2×

- Motor driver board: L298N

- Battery: 9V

- Infrared sensor: VS1838B

- Infrared remote control

- Hall effect sensor

- Magnet

- Potentiometer: 10kΩ

- Joystick

- Wireless transceiver module: 2× nRF24L01

- Accelerometer and gyroscope module: GY-521

- OLED display: 128×32 pixel

- Photoelectric encoder: 2× HC-020K or 2× FC-03

- Capacitor: 2× 100nF

- Encoder wheel: 2×

CHAPTER 24

Robot Car

Building a robot car combines devices outlined in several chapters, with DC motors in Chapter 23, a servo motor in Chapter 8, an ultrasonic distance sensor in Chapter 3, an OLED display in Chapter 13, and an RGB LED in Chapter 14. The obstacle-avoiding robot car detects the distance to surrounding objects in front of the robot car, and if the distance is below a threshold, the robot car stops and scans left and right to determine the direction away from the nearest obstacle. An RGB LED indicates the direction of the turn. The distances from the robot car are shown on the OLED display (see Figure 24-1).

With several devices requiring connection to the Arduino Nano, there are some constraints on pin availability. Arduino Nano PWM pins D9 and D10 are used by the *Servo* library for controlling the SG90 servo motor, which excludes those pins from being used to enable motors on the L298N motor driver board with PWM. Arduino Nano pins A4 and A5 are the SDA and SCK pins for I2C communication with the OLED display. Arduino Nano pins A6 and A7 are for analog input only and not for digital input. The same constraints apply to the Arduino Uno, apart from the A6 and A7 pins.

N. Cameron, *Arduino Applied*, https://doi.org/10.1007/978-1-4842-3960-5_24

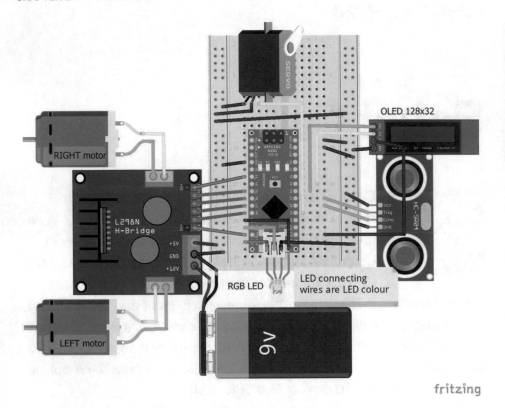

Figure 24-1. *Robot car with servo, scanner, RGB, LED, and OLED*

The motor enable pins, *ENA* and *ENB* of the L298N motor driver board, and the I2C SCK and SDA pins, of the OLED display, are connected to Arduino Nano PWM and analog pins, respectively, but all other connections are to Arduino Nano digital pins or analog pins treated as digital pins (see Figure 24-1). The OLED display VCC pin is connected to 3.3V, while the Arduino Nano VIN, SG90 servo motor and HC-SR04 ultrasonic distance sensor VCC pins are connected to the 5V rail. Pin connections are given in Table 24-1, which is also applicable to the Arduino Uno with the exception of analog pins A6 and A7.

The SG90 servo motor and HC-SR04 ultrasonic scanner are powered from the 5V rail. The GND pins of the Arduino Nano, L298N motor driver board, servo motor, ultrasonic scanner and OLED display are all connected together.

Table 24-1. *Robot Car with Servo, Scanner, RGB LED, and OLED*

Connect to	Arduino Nano pins		Connect to
	TX1	VIN	5V rail
	RX0	GND	OLED GND
			HC-SR04 GND
	RST	RST	
L298N GND	GND	5V	HC-SR04 VCC
Servo motor GND			Servo motor VCC
	D2	A7	
ENB right motor	D3 PWM	A6	
	D4	A5	OLED SCK
IN4 right motor	D5	A4	OLED SDA
IN3 right motor	D6	A3	HC-SR04 Trig pin
IN2 left motor	D7	A2	HC-SR04 Echo pin
IN1 left motor	D8	A1	Servo motor pin
RGB LED red	D9	A0	
RGB LED green	D10	REF	
ENA left motor	D11 PWM	3V3	OLED VCC
RGB LED blue	D12	D13	

The sketch (see Listing 24-1) includes the libraries *Servo* for the SG90 servo motor, *NewPing* for the HC-SR04 ultrasonic distance sensor, with *Adafruit GFX* and *Adafruit SSD1306* for the OLED display. After defining the libraries and the device pins connected to the Arduino Nano, the sketch clears the OLED display and defines the *OUTPUT* pins of the L298N motor driver board and the RGB LED. In the void loop() function, the distance in front of the robot car is measured and if greater that 20cm, the robot car moves forward. Otherwise, the robot car stops, measures the distances to the left and right of the robot car, then the robot car turns in the direction with the greater distance, provided it is longer than 15cm. If all distances are short, then the robot car moves backward and distances are measured again. An RGB LED indicates when the robot car meets an obstacle (blue), turns left (green), turns right (red) or moves backward (yellow). To best visualize the colors, place a ping-pong ball on top of the RGB LED.

The sketch includes the functions: turn(), direction(), motor(), scan(), and distance(). The turn() function turns on and off the red, green, or blue LED to indicate a right or left turn or scanning and calls the direction() function. The direction() function controls the direction of rotation of the DC motors based on the keywords *forward, backward, left,* or *right*, which are determined from the distance to the nearest obstacle as measured by the ultrasonic scanner. The motor() function controls the speed of rotation of the DC motors with the analogWrite() instruction to the motor control pins *ENA* and *ENB* on the L298N motor driver board and the digitalWrite() instruction to the DC motor control pins *IN1, IN2, IN3* and *IN4*. The scan() function moves the servo motor to the scanning angle, scans the distance and calls the distance() function, which displays, on the OLED display, the distance in front of the obstacle-avoiding robot car.

The sketch is long, but when broken down into the component parts as functions, the sketch only contains instructions that have been outlined in previous projects.

Listing 24-1. Robot Car with Servo, Scanner, RGB LED, and OLED

```
#include <Servo.h>              // include Servo library
Servo servo;                    // associate servo with Servo library
int servoPin = A1;              // servo motor pin
#include <NewPing.h>            // include NewPing library
int trigPin = A2;               // ultrasound trigger pin
int echoPin = A3;               // ultrasound echo pin
int maxdist = 70;               // set maximum scan distance (cm)
NewPing sonar(trigPin, echoPin, maxdist);   // associate sonar with
                                            // NewPing library
#include <Adafruit_GFX.h>       // include Adafruit GFX library
#include <Adafruit_SSD1306.h>   // include Adafruit SSD1306 library
Adafruit_SSD1306 oled(-1);      // associate oled with Adafruit_SSD1306 library
int redLED = 10;
int greenLED = 12;              // RGB LED pins
int blueLED = 13;
int IN1 = 8;                    // left motor forward and backward pins
int IN2 = 7;
int IN3 = 6;                    // right motor forward and backward pins
int IN4 = 5;
int ENA = 11;                   // left motor enable pin
int ENB = 3;                    // right motor enable pin
int scanTime = 250;             // set time between scans (ms)
int turnTime = 500;             // time to make turn or move backward
int motorSpeed;
float bias = 0.95;              // bias speed of right motor
float leftDist, rightDist, frontDist, frontDistR, frontDistL;
```

```
void setup()
{
  servo.attach(servoPin);        // attach servo motor pin
  oled.begin(SSD1306_SWITCHCAPVCC, 0x3C); // OLED display and I2C address
  oled.setTextColor(WHITE);      // set font colour
  oled.setTextSize(2);           // set font size
  oled.clearDisplay();           // clear OLED display
  oled.display();                // start display instructions
  pinMode(redLED, OUTPUT);
  pinMode(greenLED, OUTPUT);     // define RGB LED pins as OUTPUT
  pinMode(blueLED, OUTPUT);
  pinMode(trigPin, OUTPUT);      // define trigger pin as OUTPUT
  pinMode(IN1, OUTPUT);
  pinMode(IN2, OUTPUT);          // define motor pins as OUTPUT
  pinMode(IN3, OUTPUT);
  pinMode(IN4, OUTPUT);
}

void loop()
{
  servo.write(100);             // scan front left (100°), return distance
  frontDistL = (sonar.ping_median(5)/2.0)*0.0343;
  delay(50);
  servo.write(80);              // scan front right (80°), return distance
  frontDistR = (sonar.ping_median(5)/2.0)*0.0343;
  frontDist = min(frontDistL,frontDistR); // minimum of front distances
  distance("front", frontDist);
```

```
if(frontDist >20) direction("forward",100); // move forward if clear
else
{
    direction("stop", 100);              // stop to start scanning
    digitalWrite(blueLED, HIGH);         // turn on blue LED to indicate
                                         // scanning
    leftDist = scan(170, "left");    // scan 170° and return distance
    rightDist = scan(10, "right");   // scan 10° and return distance
    digitalWrite(blueLED, LOW);          // turn off blue LED
    if(rightDist <15 && leftDist <15)   // move back if clear
    {                                    // distance <15cm
      digitalWrite(greenLED, HIGH); // turn on red and green LEDs
      turn(redLED, "backward");          // to create yellow colour
      digitalWrite(greenLED, LOW);
    }
    else if(leftDist > rightDist) turn(greenLED, "left"); // turn left
    else if(rightDist > leftDist) turn(redLED, "right"); // turn right
  }
}

void turn (int LED, String direct) // function to turn right or left
{
    digitalWrite(LED, HIGH);             // turn on LED
    direction(direct, turnTime);         // call function to control motors
    digitalWrite(LED, LOW);              // turn off LED
}

void direction(String direct, int runTime) // function to set motor direction
{
  if(direct == "forward") motor(1, 0, 1, 0, 1); // both motors forward fast
```

```
  else
  if(direct == "backward") motor(0, 1, 0, 1, 1); // both motors
                                                 // backward fast
  else if(direct == "right") motor(1, 0, 0, 1, 0); // left forward,
                                                 // right backward
  else if(direct == "left") motor(0, 1, 1, 0, 0); // left backward,
                                                 // right forward
  else if(direct == "stop") motor(0, 0, 0, 0, 0); // both motors stop
  delay(runTime);                           // run time (ms) for motors
}

void motor(int leftF, int leftB, int rightF ,int rightB, int speed)
{
  digitalWrite(IN1, leftF);      // control pin IN1 left motor forward
  digitalWrite(IN2, leftB);      // control pin IN2 left motor backward
  digitalWrite(IN3, rightF);     // control pin IN3 right motor forward
  digitalWrite(IN4, rightB);     // control pin IN4 right motor back
  if(speed == 1) motorSpeed = 90;  // higher speed when moving forward
  else motorSpeed = 80;            // or backward than when turning
  analogWrite(ENA, motorSpeed);    // left motor speed
  motorSpeed = motorSpeed*bias;
  analogWrite(ENB, motorSpeed);    // right motor speed
}

float scan(int angle, String direct) // function to scan distance at angle
{
  servo.write(angle);                  // rotate servo motor
  delay(scanTime);                     // delay between scans
  float dist = (sonar.ping_median(5)/2.0)*0.0343; // check distance (cm)
  distance(direct, dist);              // display to distance on OLED
  servo.write(90);                     // rotate servo motor
  delay(scanTime);                     // delay between scans
  return dist;
}
```

```
void distance (String direct, float dist)  // function to display on OLED
{
  direct = direct +": ";
  oled.clearDisplay();              // clear OLED display
  oled.setCursor(0,0);              // position cursor at (0, 0)
  oled.print(direct);              // print text
  oled.print(dist, 0);             // print number with 0DP
  oled.display();                  // start display instructions
}
```

PID Controller

The balancing robot, outlined in the next section, requires a PID controller to manage the process of reacting to changes in the vertical angle of the robot by altering the direction and speed of rotation of the DC motors. A brief description and an example of a PID controller are given.

PID controllers are used in many systems to manage process inputs and control process outputs, with cruise control in a car being an example. The PID controller monitors the difference between the required input (called the *setpoint*) and the observed *input,* and uses a feedback mechanism to change the process *output.* In the example of a car, the *setpoint* is the required speed, the *input* is the actual speed, and the *output* is the amount of petrol or diesel injected into the fuel injection system, which alters the engine speed and the speed of the car.

The difference between the PID *setpoint* and observed PID *input* is the error. There are three components in a PID *output*—proportional, integral, and derivative, which are derived from the current error, the cumulative error, and the rate of change in the error. The PID *output* is $K_p e + K_i t \sum e + K_d b_e$, where K_p, K_i and K_d are the coefficients of the proportional, integral and derivative terms for the error, e, the cumulative error, $\sum e$, and the rate of change in the error, b_e, respectively, with t the time interval between successive PID evaluations. The rate of change in the error, b_e, is calculated as *(error – previous error)/t*. If the PID *setpoint* is constant, then the rate of change in the error is the negative rate of change in the PID *input* or *(previous input - input)/t*, as error is equal to *setpoint – input*.

Changing the proportional coefficient, K_p, directly changes the PID *output*, but results in oscillation of the PID *input* about the PID *setpoint*. If the PID *output* only consists of the proportional component, then the mean *input* is always below the *setpoint*, as the *output* is proportional to the error, which is fixed for a given *input*. Increasing the integral coefficient, K_i, increases the rate at which the PID *input* reaches the PID *setpoint*, but there is a time lag while the integral component accumulates. A combination of the proportional and integral components results in the PID *input* reaching the PID *setpoint* quickly, with little oscillation about the PID *setpoint*. The derivative component prevents the PID *output* from changing too quickly.

An example of a PID control system is to maintain constant ambient light on a light dependent resistor (LDR) by controlling the brightness of an LED facing the LDR (see Figure 24-2 and Table 24-2). If the reading of the incident light on the LDR (*input*) differs from the required amount (*setpoint*), then the LED brightness (*output*) is updated.

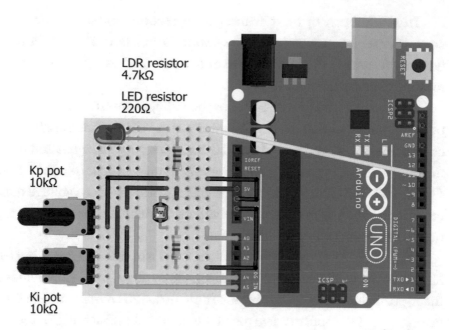

Figure 24-2. *PID controller with LDR and LED*

Table 24-2. *PID Controller with LDR and LED*

Component	Connect to	and to
potentiometers GND	Arduino GND	
Kp, Ki potentiometer signals	Arduino pin A4, A5	
potentiometers VCC	Arduino 5V	
LDR top	Arduino 5V	
LDR bottom	4.7kΩ resistor	Arduino GND
LDR bottom	Arduino pin A0	
LED long leg	Arduino PWM pin 11	
LED short leg	220Ω resistor	Arduino GND

477

The *PID* library by Brett Beauregard is recommended for PID controller sketches, when the PID *setpoint* is constant. The *PID* library is available within the Arduino IDE and is installed using installation method 3, as outlined in Chapter 3.

The sketch (see Listing 24-2) uses the voltage output from potentiometers to alter the coefficients K_p and K_i. Note that the PID coefficients K_p, K_i and K_d and the PID variables *setpoint, input* and *output* must be defined, in a sketch using the *PID* library, as double rather than float. The LDR is combined with a 4.7kΩ resistor to form a voltage divider (see Figure 24-2), with the voltage divider's output voltage converted to a digital value, as outlined in Chapter 3.

Increasing the K_p coefficient results in increasing the PID *input*, but when K_p exceeds a threshold, the PID *input* starts to oscillate. Increasing values of the K_i coefficient reduces the response time of the PID *output* and the time taken for the PID *input* to reach the PID *setpoint*. Note that the PID *setpoint* in Listing 24-2 is constant and that the derivative component, K_d, is set to zero.

Listing 24-2. PID Controller with LDR and LED

```
#include <PID_v1.h>              // include PID library
double Kp=0;
double Ki=0;                     // PID coefficients
double Kd=0;
double input, output, setpoint;  // PID variables
                                 // associate pid with PID_v1 library
PID pid(&input, &output, &setpoint, Kp, Ki, Kd, DIRECT);
int PIDtime = 20;                // time (ms) between PID evaluations
int LDRpin = A0;                 // LDR pin
int KpPin = A4;                  // Kp potentiometer pin
int KiPin = A5;                  // Ki potentiometer pin
int LEDpin = 11;                 // LED on a PWM pin
unsigned long chkTime;
```

```
void setup()
{
  pid.SetMode(AUTOMATIC);      // start PID control
  pid.SetSampleTime(PIDtime);  // constant PID evaluation time interval
  setpoint = 500;              // constant PID setpoint
  chkTime = millis();
}

void loop()
{
  if(millis()-chkTime > PIDtime)             // new PID evaluation
  {
    Kp = analogRead(KpPin) *3.0/1023;    // Kp (0 to 3) from potentiometer
    Ki = analogRead(KiPin) *15.0/1023;   // Ki (0 to 15) from potentiometer
    input = analogRead(LDRpin);   // read LDR value as PID input
    pid.SetTunings(Kp, Ki, Kd);   // update PID coefficients
    pid.Compute();                // evaluate PID
    analogWrite(LEDpin, output);  // LED brightness is PID output
    chkTime - millis();           // reset time to next PID evaluation
  }
}
```

PID control with an adjustable *setpoint* variable and K_i coefficient values requires calculation of the three PID components, given that the *PID* library assumes a constant PID setpoint. In Listing 24-3, the voltage output from potentiometers varies the *setpoint* and the K_i coefficient. To prevent the integral component from accumulating beyond limits, known as *windup*, the integral component is constrained when the new error term is added to the previous integral and when included in the PID *output* calculation, with values of 0 and 255 used in the sketch. The PID *output* variable is also constrained between 0 and 255. Given that the K_i coefficient is a variable, the calculation of the integral component error term incorporates the current K_i coefficient rather than multiplying the sum of the error terms by a constant K_i coefficient.

Note that in Listing 24-3, the error and derivative coefficients, K_p and K_d, are defined at the start of the sketch, but can be determined from a potentiometer output as with the integral coefficient, K_i. When using PID to control the LED brightness, zero values for K_p and K_d are sufficient.

Listing 24-3. PID Control with Variable Setpoint

```
float Kp=0;
float Ki=0;                          // PID coefficients
float Kd=0;
float input, output, setpoint;       // PID variables
int PIDtime = 20;         // time (ms) between PID evaluations
int LDRpin = A0;          // LDR pin
int setPin = A4;          // setpoint potentiometer pin
int KiPin = A5;           // Ki potentiometer pin
int LEDpin = 11;          // LED on a PWM pin
unsigned long chkTime;
float pTime, error, lastError, integral, derivative;

void setup()
{
  pTime = PIDtime/1000.0; // PID evaluation time (s)
  chkTime = millis();
}

void loop()
{
  if(millis()-chkTime > PIDtime)
  {
    setpoint = analogRead(setPin);   // setpoint from potentiometer
    Ki = analogRead(KiPin) *15.0/1023;   // Ki (0 to 15) from potentiometer
    input = analogRead(LDRpin); // read LDR value as PID input
    error = setpoint-input;       // PID error
                                  // constrained PID integral and error
    integral = constrain(integral,0,255) + error*Ki*pTime;
```

```
derivative = (error - lastError)/pTime;    // PID derivative
lastError = error;                         // retain last error
                                           // evaluate PID output
output = Kp*error + constrain(integral,0,255) + Kd*derivative;
output = constrain(output, 0, 255); // constrain PID output
analogWrite(LEDpin, output); // LED brightness is PID output
chkTime = millis();                // reset time to next PID evaluation
  }
}
```

Balancing Robot

The balancing robot (see Figure 24-3 and Table 24-3) uses the Arduino Nano, DC motors, the L298N motor driver board and the GY-521 module, which includes an MPU-6050 accelerometer and gyroscope sensor, as outlined in Chapter 3. Wireless communication of the PID coefficients transmitted with the nRF24L01 module, was outlined in Chapter 17. The GY-521 module is positioned low in the balancing robot and on the same axis as the DC motors; while the Arduino Nano, L298N motor driver board, and battery are positioned high in the robot to generate an inverted pendulum. The pitch angle of the robot, detected by the GY-521 module, is the PID *input*, the PID *setpoint* is the angle of the robot when the robot is balanced and the PID *output* is the direction and speed of rotation of the DC motors.

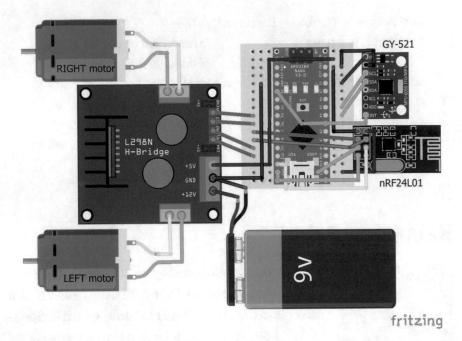

Figure 24-3. *Balancing robot with nRF24L01 and accelerometer*

Table 24-3. *Balancing Robot with nRF24L01 and Accelerometer*

Connect to	Arduino Nano pins		Connect to
	TX1	VIN	5V rail
	RX0	GND	GY-521 GND
			nRF24L01 GND
	RST	RST	
L298N GND	GND	5V	GY-521 VCC
GY-521 INT	D2	A7	
	D3	A6	
	D4	A5	GY-521 SCK

(continued)

Table 24-3. (*continued*)

Connect to	Arduino Nano pins		Connect to
IN4 right motor	D5 PWM	A4	GY-521 SDA
IN3 right motor	D6 PWM	A3	
nRF24L01 CE	D7	A2	
nRF24L01 CSN	D8	A1	
IN2 left motor	D9 PWM	A0	
IN1 left motor	D10 PWM	REF	
nRF24L01 MOSI	D11	3V3	nRF24L01 VCC
nRF24L01 MISO	D12	D13	nRF24L01 SCK

Determining PID Coefficients

The three PID components are the error or difference between the PID *setpoint* and *input* for the proportional component, the cumulative sum of errors for the integral component and the difference between the current error and previous error for the derivative component. The three PID components are multiplied by the K_p, K_i, and K_d PID coefficients to determine the PID *output*.

There are several methods for determining optimal values of the PID coefficients. The Ziegler-Nichols method sets the integral and derivative coefficients, K_i and K_d, to zero. The proportional coefficient is increased from zero, reaching a value, K, when the PID *input* starts to oscillate. The period of the input oscillation, T, is measured with an oscilloscope. The PID coefficients—K_p, K_i, and K_d— are then set to $0.6K$, $1.2K/T$ and $0.075KT$, respectively.

Without an oscilloscope, PID coefficients can be determined empirically using potentiometers to vary values of the K_p, K_i, and K_d coefficients (see Figure 24-4). The integral and derivative coefficients, K_i and K_d, are set to zero and the value of the proportional coefficient, K_p, is increased from zero until the robot starts to balance. The integral coefficient, K_i, and then the derivative coefficient K_d are increased to improve the stability of the robot. Empirical values of K_p, K_i and K_d are wirelessly transmitted with an nRF24L01 module to a receiving nRF24L01 module connected to the Arduino Nano attached to the balancing robot. An OLED display connected to the transmitting Arduino Nano displays values of the PID coefficients K_p, K_i and K_d.

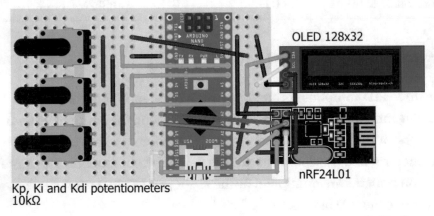

Figure 24-4. nRF24L01 transmit K_p, K_i, and K_d values

Table 24-4. *nRF24L01 Transmit K_p, K_i, and K_d Values*

Connect to	Arduino Nano pins		Connect to
	TX1	VIN	5V rail
	RX0	GND	OLED GND
			nRF24L01 GND
	RST	RST	
potentiometers GND	GND	5V	potentiometers VCC
	D2	A7	K_d potentiometer signal
	D3	A6	K_i potentiometer signal
	D4	A5	OLED SCK
	D5	A4	OLED SDA
	D6	A3	K_p potentiometer signal
nRF24L01 CE	D7	A2	
nRF24L01 CSN	D8	A1	
	D9	A0	
	D10	REF	
nRF24L01 MOSI	D11	3V3	OLED VCC
			nRF24L01 VCC
nRF24L01 MISO	D12	D13	nRF24L01 SCK

Circular Buffer

Noise from a potentiometer results in variation in the transmitted PID coefficients, which can be reduced by ignoring values that differ from the current mean value by set amount. The circular buffer holds several potentiometer values from which the mean value is calculated, with the size of the circular buffer fixed. The circular buffer replaces the "oldest" value with the current value, if the current value differs sufficiently from the mean value. In the sketch (see Listing 24-4), the circular buffer holds 10 (*nVal*) values and ignores values that differ from the mean by less than 5 (*minVal*). For example, if the buffer size is three and the sequence of potentiometer values is 5, 5, 5, 4, 11, 14, then the mean value is 5 for the first four values, as the value of 4 is ignored since it differs by only one from the mean. With value 11, the new mean value is 7 and the buffer consists of (5, 5, 11), and with the value 14, the new mean is 10 and the buffer consists of (5, 11, 14).

In Listing 24-4, circular buffers reduce the noise variation on three potentiometers used to define the K_p, K_i and K_d coefficients, with each buffer containing 10 (*nVal*) values and a minimum deviation of at least 5 (*minVal*) before a new value is included in the circular buffer. The getKvalues() function updates the circular buffer for each potentiometer with the K_p, K_i, and K_d coefficients constrained to values less than 40, 10, and 1, respectively. The coefficient values are displayed on the OLED display and then transmitted to the nRF24L01 receiver module. In practice, the robot was balanced with PID K_p, K_i, and K_d, coefficients of 32, 2.5, and 0.2 respectively, but the coefficient values are dependent on the specific robot, and a wide range of values should be examined.

Listing 24-4. Determining PID Coefficients with a Circular Buffer

```
#include <SPI.h>                      // include SPI library
#include <RF24.h>                     // include RF24 library
RF24 radio(7, 8);                     // associate radio with RF24 library
byte addresses[][6] = {"12"};
typedef struct                        // define a structure
{
   float Kp, Ki, Kd;                  // PID coefficients
} dataStruct;
dataStruct data;
#include <Adafruit_GFX.h>    // include Adafruit GFX library
```

```
#include <Adafruit_SSD1306.h>   // include Adafruit SSD1306 library
Adafruit_SSD1306 oled(-1);   // associate oled with Adafruit_SSD1306 library
int Kpins[3] = {A3, A6, A7};   // Kp, Ki and Kd potentiometer pins
const int nVal = 10;           // number of values in circular buffer
int val[3][nVal];              // circular buffer for three variables
int value;
int sum[] = {0, 0, 0};         // sum of circular buffer values
int n[] = {0, 0, 0};           // index of current values in buffer
int minVal = 5;                // minimum deviation from mean
int K[3];                      // mean values of circular buffer

void setup()
{
  radio.begin();                               // initialise radio
  radio.openWritingPipe(addresses[0]);   // open transmitting pipe
  oled.begin(SSD1306_SWITCHCAPVCC, 0x3C);  // OLED display and I2C address
  oled.clearDisplay();             // clear OLED display
  oled.setTextColor(WHITE);        // set font colour
  oled.setTextSize(1);             // set font size
  oled.display();                  // start display instructions
  for (int i=0; i<3; i++)
  {
    for (int j=0; j<nVal; j++) val[i][j] = 0; // set circular buffer
  }                                          // values to zero
}

void loop()
{
    getKvalues();                // function to update circular buffer
    data.Kp = K[0] *40.0/1023; // Kp (0 to 40) from potentiometer
    data.Ki = K[1] *10.0/1023; // Ki (0 to 10) from potentiometer
    data.Kd = K[2] *1.0/1023;  // Kd (0 to 1) from potentiometer
```

```
    oled.clearDisplay();          // clear OLED display
    oled.setCursor(0,0);          // position cursor at (0, 0)
    oled.print("Kp: ");           // display text and Kp value
    oled.println(data.Kp);        // followed by a carriage return
    oled.print("Ki: ");           // display text and Ki value
    oled.println(data.Ki);
    oled.print("Kd: ");                     // display text and Kd value
    oled.print(data.Kd);
    oled.display();                         // start display instructions
    radio.write(&data, sizeof(data)); // transmit Kp and Kd values
    delay(50);
}

void getKvalues()                 // function to update circular buffer
{
  for (int i=0; i<3; i++)         // repeat for each PID coefficient
  {
    value = analogRead(Kpins[i]);     // read current potentiometer value
    if(value>0)
    {
      if(abs(value-K[i]) > minVal)    // potentiometer value differs
      {                               // sufficiently from mean value
        sum[i] = sum[i] - val[i][n[i]]; // subtract "oldest" value from buffer
        val[i][n[i]] = value;   // replace "oldest" with current value
        sum[i] = sum[i] + value; // update circular buffer total
        n[i]++;                        // increment index of current value
        if(n[i] > nVal-1) n[i] = 0;   // when at end of circular buffer
      }
    }
    else                      // reset circular buffer to zero
```

```
{                              // when potentiometer value is zero
  for (int j=0; j<nVal; j++) val[i][j] = 0;
  sum[i]=0;
}
K[i] = sum[i]/nVal;      // mean values of circular buffer
}
}
```

Quaternion Measurements

Accelerometer measurements provide an estimate of the pitch angle, as outlined in Chapter 3. The estimated pitch angle can be improved by combining the accelerometer and gyroscope measurements into quaternions, which is performed by the Invensense DMP (Digital Motion Processor) of the MPU-6050 sensor on the GY-521 module. Quaternions consist of four components, a magnitude and three directional components, which parameterize the angle of rotation. The quaternion components, accelerometer and gyroscope measurements are stored by the MPU-6050 sensor in a 10-byte FIFO (first-in, first-out) buffer, when the MPU-6050 sensor interrupt pin is set to *HIGH*, to indicate that updated positional measurements are available. Quaternions are outlined in the Appendix.

Estimates of the pitch angle using quaternion components or only accelerometer measurements were broadly similar, but the latter are more variable. For example, when the GY-521 module was tilted forward and backward, the change in estimated pitch angle was smoother using quaternion components than when using accelerometer measurements (see Figure 24-5). The accelerometer pitch angles differed from the quaternion pitch angles between –5° and 9° (see Figure 24-5, secondary axis). For the balancing robot, noise in the estimated pitch angle must be minimized, so calculation of the pitch angle from quaternion measurements is recommended; however, there is an initial lag before the quaternion components stabilize.

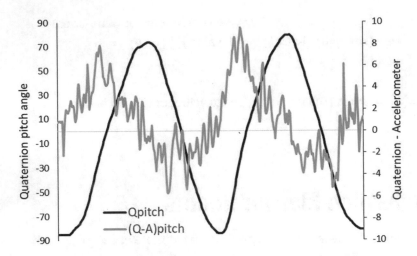

Figure 24-5. *Estimated pitch angle*

The *MPU6050* and *I2Cdev* libraries by Jeff Rowberg enable access to the MPU-6050 sensor's FIFO buffer, which holds the quaternion measurements. A *.zip* file containing the *MPU6050* and *I2Cdev* libraries can be downloaded from https://github.com/jrowberg/i2cdevlib/.

Extract the *MPU6050* and *I2Cdev* folders from the *.zip* file and install the libraries using installation method 2, as described in Chapter 3.

The balancing robot sketch (see Listing 24-5) includes instructions from the *Examples* ➤ *MPU6050* ➤ *MPU6050_DMP6* sketch in the *MPU6050* library to access the quaternion measurements. Prior to use, the MPU6050 sensor should be calibrated with the *Examples* ➤ *MPU6050* ➤ *IMU_Zero* sketch to determine offset values for the gyroscope X, Y, and Z axes and the accelerometer Z axis. PID K_p, K_i, and K_d coefficients, defined with potentiometers using circular buffers to reduce noise, are transmitted with a nRF24L01 module using Listing 24-4 to the receiving nRF24L01 module attached to the balancing robot.

Table 24-5 shows the structure of the FIFO buffer as outlined in the *Arduino* ➤ *Libraries* ➤ *MPU6050* ➤ *MPU6050_6Axis_MotionApps20.h* file.

Table 24-5. *FIFO Buffer Structure*

	Quarternion				Gyroscope			Accelerometer		
Value	w	x	y	z	x	y	z	x	y	z
Register	0, 1	4, 5	8, 9	12, 13	16, 17	20, 21	24, 25	28, 26	32, 33	36, 37

Quaternion values are combined with the following instructions.

```
qw = ((fifoBuffer[0] << 8)  | fifoBuffer[1]);
qx = ((fifoBuffer[4] << 8)  | fifoBuffer[5]);
qy = ((fifoBuffer[8] << 8)  | fifoBuffer[9]);
qz = ((fifoBuffer[12] << 8) | fifoBuffer[13]);
```

The symbols <<8 and | indicate that the left-hand value is moved by 8 positions and added to the right-hand value, as outlined in the "Accelerometer and Gyroscope" section of Chapter 3.

In the balancing robot sketch (see Listing 24-5), the pitch angle corresponding to a balanced robot is defined as the PID *setpoint* and the pitch angle of the moving robot is defined as the PID *input*, which is constrained to have absolute values of less than 25°. Motor speed, which is the PID *output*, is constrained to a value of at least 60, otherwise the motors do not turn sufficiently. The interval between PID evaluations of 20ms is sufficient to achieve a balancing robot. In practice, PID coefficients of 32, 2.5, and 0.2 for K_p, K_i, and K_d, respectively, balanced a robot, with higher K_p values required on carpet surface compared to wooden flooring.

Listing 24-5 is long, but consists of groups of instructions that have been used in projects in other Chapters. As usual, the start of the sketch includes libraries, defines variables and pins associated with the MPU-6050 accelerometer and gyroscope sensor, the nRF24L01 receiver module, and the L298N motor driver board. The void setup() function consists primarily of instructions to access the FIFO buffer of the MPU-6050 sensor, which were derived from the *Examples* ➤ *MPU6050* ➤ *MPU6050_DMP6* sketch. The void loop() function consists of two halves, with the first half receiving the transmitted PID coefficients: K_p, K_i, and K_d, calculating the pitch angle from the quaternion values and then the PID output, calculated from the PID error, integral, and derivative components, to adjust the DC motor speed.

The second half of the void loop() function combines the eight FIFO buffer values to form the four scaled quaternion values. The motor() function sets the DC motor speed on the Arduino Nano PWM pins and the DMPdataReady() function is an interrupt indicating that data is available from the MPU-6050 sensor.

Listing 24-5. Balancing Robot

```
#include <I2Cdev.h>                 // include I2Cdev library
#include <MPU6050_6Axis_MotionApps20.h> // include MPU6050 library
#if I2CDEV_IMPLEMENTATION == I2CDEV_ARDUINO_WIRE
  #include <Wire.h>                  // include Wire library
#endif
MPU6050 mpu;                         // associate mpu with MPU6050 library
uint8_t mpuIntStatus;                // MPU-6050 interrupt status
volatile bool mpuInterrupt = false;  // if MPU-6050 interrupt is HIGH
bool DMPinit = false;                // DMP initialisation status
uint8_t DMPstatus;                   // device status (0 = success, !0 = error)
uint16_t fifoPacket;                 // DMP packet size (default 42 bytes)
uint16_t fifoCount;                  // number of bytes in FIFO
uint8_t fifoBuffer[64];              // FIFO storage buffer
int I2Caddress = 0x68;               // I2C address of MPU-6050
#include <SPI.h>                     // include SPI library
#include <RF24.h>                    // include RF24 library
RF24 radio(7, 8);                    // associate radio with RF24 library
byte addresses[ ][6] = {"12"};
```

```
typedef struct                    // define a structure
{
  float K1, K2, K3;               // transmitted PID coefficients
} dataStruct;
dataStruct data;
float Kp = 0, Ki = 0, Kd = 0; // PID coefficients
int pidTime = 20;                 // interval between PID evaluations (ms)
unsigned long chkTime = 0;
int IN1 = 10;                     // left wheel forward and backward pins
int IN2 = 9;
int IN3 = 6;                      // right wheel forward and backward pins
int IN4 = 5;
int inputLimit = 25;              // limit on pitch angle (-25, 25)
int outMin = 60;                  // minimum output to turn on motors
int LEDpin = 3;
float qw = 0, qx = 0, qy = 0, qz = 0, pitch; // quaternion values
                                             // from MPU-6050
float integral = 0;
float input, output, setpoint, error, lastError, derivative, pTime,
      sumsquare;
int mSpeed;

void setup()
{
  Serial.begin(115200);                  // set baud rate to 115200
  #if I2CDEV_IMPLEMENTATION == I2CDEV_ARDUINO_WIRE
    Wire.begin();                        // initialise I2C
    Wire.setClock(400000);               // set I2C clock speed to 400kHz
  #elif I2CDEV_IMPLEMENTATION == I2CDEV_BUILTIN_FASTWIRE
    Fastwire::setup(400, true);          // library for fast I2C access
  #endif
  mpu.initialize();                      // initialise mpu
  DMPstatus = mpu.dmpInitialize();   // set DMPstatus variable
```

```
  mpu.setXGyroOffset(10);
  mpu.setYGyroOffset(-20);        // gyro X, Y and Z and accelZ offsets
  mpu.setZGyroOffset(100);          // from IMU_Zero in MPU6050 library
  mpu.setZAccelOffset(1730);
  if (DMPstatus == 0)      // DMP (Digital Motion Processor)initialised
  {
    mpu.setDMPEnabled(true);                        // start DMP
    attachInterrupt(0, DMPdataReady, RISING); // interrupt on GY-521 module
    mpuIntStatus = mpu.getIntStatus();
    DMPinit = true;                              // DMP initialised
    fifoPacket = mpu.dmpGetFIFOPacketSize();   // DMP packet size
  }
  else Serial.print("DMP initialization failed");
  radio.begin();                                  // initialise radio
  radio.openReadingPipe(0, addresses[0]);       // open reading pipe
  radio.startListening();
  motor(0, 0, 0, 0);           // initialise motor to zero
  pinMode(LEDpin, OUTPUT);     // define LED pin as OUTPUT
  setpoint = 2;                // setpoint angle with robot balanced
  integral = 0;
  pTime = pidTime/1000.0;      // PID evaluation time (s)
  delay(1000);
}

void loop()
{                                  // MPU6050 data available
  while (!mpuInterrupt && fifoCount < fifoPacket)
  {
    if(millis()-chkTime > pidTime)    // PID evaluation
    {
      if(radio.available())                // transmitted data available
        {
          radio.read(&data,sizeof(data));
```

```
      Kp = data.K1;                    // update PID coefficients
      Ki = data.K2;
      Kd = data.K3;               // flash LED received transmission
      digitalWrite(LEDpin, !digitalRead(LEDpin));
    }
  pitch = -asin(2.0*(qx*qz-qw*qy))*180/PI; // constrain pitch angle
  input = constrain(-pitch, -inputLimit, inputLimit);
  error = setpoint - input;  // PID error and integral components
  integral = constrain(integral,-255,255) + error*Ki*pTime;
  derivative = (error - lastError)/pTime; // PID derivative component
  lastError = error;                     // update last error
                                         // evaluate PID output
  output=Kp*error + constrain(integral,-255,255) + Kd*derivative;
  mSpeed = constrain(output, -255,255);    // limit motor speed
  if(mSpeed > outMin) motor(mSpeed, 0, mSpeed, 0);
  else if(mSpeed < -outMin) motor(0, -mSpeed, 0, -mSpeed);
  else motor(0, 0, 0, 0);          // output low, zero motor speed
  chkTime=millis();
  }
}
fifoCount = mpu.getFIFOCount();      // get current FIFO count
mpuInterrupt = false;                // reset interrupt flag
mpuIntStatus = mpu.getIntStatus();   // check for overflow
                                     // when getIntStatus fifth bit = 1
if (bitRead(mpuIntStatus,4) == 1 || fifoCount == 1024)
{
  mpu.resetFIFO();                   // reset FIFO
  Serial.println("FIFO overflow");
}
else if(bitRead(mpuIntStatus,1) == 1) // check if DMP data ready
{                                    // getIntStatus second bit = 1
  while (fifoCount < fifoPacket) fifoCount = mpu.getFIFOCount();
  mpu.getFIFOBytes(fifoBuffer, fifoPacket); // read data packet from FIFO
```

```
        fifoCount -= fifoPacket;        // update FIFO byte number
        qw = ((fifoBuffer[0] << 8) | fifoBuffer[1]);
        qx = ((fifoBuffer[4] << 8) | fifoBuffer[5]);   // quaternion values
        qy = ((fifoBuffer[8] << 8) | fifoBuffer[9]);
        qz = ((fifoBuffer[12] << 8) | fifoBuffer[13]);
        qw = qw/16384.0;                // divide quaternion by 2¹⁴
        qx = qx/16384.0;
        qy = qy/16384.0;
        qz = qz/16384.0;
    }
}

void motor(int leftF, int leftB, int rightF ,int rightB)
{                                       // control motors
    float bias = 1.0;
    analogWrite(IN1, leftF*bias);   // bias left or right motor speed
    analogWrite(IN2, leftB*bias);   // as required
    analogWrite(IN3, rightF);
    analogWrite(IN4, rightB);
}

void DMPdataReady()                     // interrupt from MPU-6050
{
    mpuInterrupt = true;
}
```

Summary

An obstacle-avoiding robot car used an ultrasonic distance sensor
mounted on a servo motor to detect obstacles, with the distance-
to-obstacle information provided on an OLED display. Use of a PID
controller was illustrated by maintaining constant ambient light on a
light dependent resistor through controlling the brightness of an adjacent
LED. A circular buffer was described to reduce noise from potentiometer

output. Quaternion measurement system provided more stable readings of the pitch angle from the accelerometer and gyroscope module than the accelerometer readings alone. A balancing robot was built with the accelerometer and gyroscope module controlling the DC motors through a PID controller with a circular buffer to reduce noise on potentiometer values used to derive the PID coefficients.

Components List

- Arduino Uno and breadboard

- Arduino Nano and breadboard

- DC motors: 2×

- Motor driver board: L298N

- Battery: 9V

- Ultrasonic distance sensor: HC-SR04

- Servo motor: SG90

- OLED display: 128×32 pixels

- RGB LED or module

- Potentiometers: 3× 10kΩ

- LED

- Light dependent resistor (or photoresistor)

- Resistor: 220Ω and 4.7kΩ

- Wireless transceiver module: 2× nRF24L01

- Accelerometer and gyroscope module: GY-521

CHAPTER 25

Wi-Fi Communication

Wi-Fi technology allows communication between a device and a wireless local area network (WLAN). Devices such as personal computers and printers, digital cameras and mobile phones can connect to a Wi-Fi access point over a distance of 20m indoors with greater distances outdoors. Like Bluetooth (see Chapter 16) and wireless (see Chapter 17) communication, Wi-Fi operates at 2.4GHz.

Some Arduino Wi-Fi shields that connect to the Arduino Uno are based on the ESP8266 Wi-Fi microchip. The NodeMCU ESP8266 based microcontroller is more powerful than the Arduino Uno and can be programmed using the Arduino IDE. The NodeMCU ESP8266 is used for Wi-Fi communication in this chapter. The WeMos D1 mini is based on the ESP8266 microcontroller. It has Wi-Fi communication, and it can be used instead of the NodeMCU ESP8266.

NodeMCU ESP8266

The NodeMCU ESP8266 operates at 3.3V and is powered through a micro USB connection, which is also used to upload instructions and communicate with a computer or laptop. The micro USB cable can be connected to 5V, given the 3.3V voltage regulator, and there are three

© Neil Cameron 2019
N. Cameron, *Arduino Applied*, https://doi.org/10.1007/978-1-4842-3960-5_25

3.3V output pins, a voltage input (5V) pin and four ground pins for connecting to other devices (see Figure 25-1). The general-purpose input/output (GPIO) pins are used for transmitting and receiving serial data (GPIO 1 and 3, respectively) with I2C (GPIO 4 and 5) and SPI (GPIO 12 to 15) communication. There are four PWM pins (GPIO 4, 12, 14, and 15) and one analog-to-digital converter pin (A0). There are two LEDs: one beside pin D0 and the other beside the micro-USB connection on pins GPIO 2 and 16, respectively, with the latter equal to LED_BUILTIN and active *LOW*. The Reset button is used to restart the microcontroller. The GPIO pins are not 5V tolerant and the maximum current supply of a pin is 12mA.

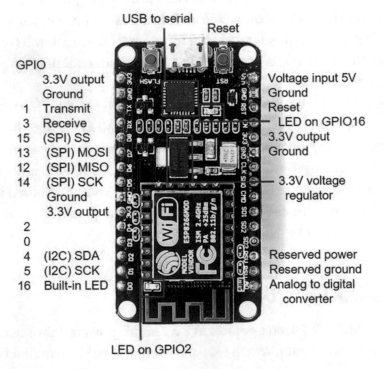

Figure 25-1. *NodeMCU ESP8266*

Several steps are required prior to running sketches on the NodeMCU ESP8266. First, the CP2012 Virtual COM Port (VCP) USB to UART driver is installed on the computer.

1. Download the *VCP.zip* file from www.silabs.com/ products/development-tools/software/usb-to- uart-bridge-vcp-drivers.

2. Extract the *CP210x Universal Windows Driver* folder.

3. Double-click the *CP210x VCP Installer* using either the x64 or x86 version for 64-bit or 32-bit operating systems, respectively.

4. To determine if a computer has a 32-bit or a 64-bit operating system, select *Control Panel* ➤ *System and Security* ➤ *System.* The system type is displayed.

5. Go to github.com/esp8266/Arduino.

6. In the *Installing with Boards Manager* section, copy the http://arduino.esp8266.com/stable/ package_esp8266com_index.json link.

7. Open the Arduino IDE with a new sketch.

8. Select *File* ➤ *Preferences.*

9. Paste the link into the *Additional Boards Manager URLs* box and click *OK.*

The *ESP8266* libraries are installed in the Arduino IDE.

1. Select *Tools* ➤ *Board* ➤ *Boards Manager.*

2. Enter **8266** in *Filter* to display *esp8266 by ESP8266 Community.*

3. Click *Install.*

4. Connect the *NodeMCU ESP8266* to the computer or laptop, but do not use a USB charging cable.

5. In *Tools* ➤ *Board*, select *NodeMCU 1.0 (ESP-12E Module)*.

6. In *Tools* ➤ *CPU Frequency*, select *160 MHz*.

7. In *Tools* ➤ *Port*, choose the appropriate COM channel.

8. The NodeMCU ESP8266 setup is verified by running the blink sketch, available in the Arduino IDE under *File* ➤ *Examples* ➤ *ESP8266*.

In the Arduino IDE, a pin can be referred to by the GPIO pin number or by D#, such as int LEDpin = 2 or int LEDpin = D4.

WeMos D1 Mini

WeMos D1 mini development board is based on the ESP-8266EX microcontroller, and has Wi-Fi functionality (see Figure 25-2). The WeMos D1 mini operates at 3.3V and is powered through the micro USB connection. The micro USB cable can be connected to 5V, given the 3.3V voltage regulator, and there is a 3.3V output pin, a 5V output pin and a ground pin for connecting to other devices. There is one analog-to-digital converter pin (A0), SPI (GPIO 12 to 15) and I2C (GPIO 4 and 5) communication, and nine digital input pins, which are all PWM except GPIO 16. The built-in LED is on pin D4 or GPIO 2 and is active *LOW*. The Reset button is used to restart the microcontroller. The GPIO pins are not 5V tolerant and the maximum current supply of a pin is 12mA.

Reset	1 Transmit
A0 ADC	3 Receive
16	5 (I2C) SCL
14 (SPI) SCK	4 (I2C) SDA
12 (SPI) MISO	0
13 (SPI) MOSI	2 Built-in LED
15 (SPI) SS	Ground
3.3V output	5V output

Figure 25-2. *WeMos D1 mini*

The CH340G USB to UART driver for the WeMos Di mini development board has to be installed.

1. Go to wiki.wemos.cc/downloads.

2. Select *CH340G Driver* ➤ *Windows*.

3. Save the *ch341ser_win.zip* file on the desktop.

4. Open the *.zip* file and move the *CH341SER* application to the desktop.

5. Right-click the *CH341SER* application.

6. Select *Run as administrator* and install the driver.

7. Restart the computer to install the driver.

The *ESP8266* libraries have to be installed, as outlined in the NodeMCU ESP8266 section.

1. In the Arduino IDE, from *Tools* ➤ *Board*, select *LOLIN (WEMOS) D1 R2 & mini*.

2. In *Tools* ➤ *CPU Frequency*, select 160 MHz.

3. In *Tools* ➤ *Port*, select the relevant port.

Wi-Fi and Web Server

A series of sketches illustrates communicating with a Wi-Fi network, establishing a web server and managing HTTP (Hypertext Transfer Protocol) requests. The first sketch (see Listing 25-1) connects to a Wi-Fi network and updates a webpage. The Wi-Fi network SSID (Service Set Identifier) and password are required to access the Wi-Fi network. The SSID is the name of the local wireless network and both the SSID and password are generally located on the base of the router. The default HTTP COM port is 80 and the `ESP8266WebServer server` instruction is sufficient, rather than `ESP8266WebServer server(80)`. While waiting for the Wi-Fi connection, the sketch uses a delay of 500ms. When the Wi-Fi connection is established, the IP (Internet Protocol) address of the Wi-Fi network is displayed on the serial monitor.

When the IP address is entered to a web browser, such as Mozilla Firefox, the `server.on("/", message)` instruction initiates the `message()` function, which sends an HTTP status code, the content type and the content to the web browser. Note that in the `server.on()` instruction, the `message()` function does not have brackets, as the `message()` function does not return a variable. In the sketch, the status code *200* indicates a successful HTTP request by the server, which is that a valid URL (Uniform Resource Locator, or web address) exists and the content of the plain text string *msg* is displayed on the webpage. The status code *404* indicates that server could not find the requested URL.

Listing 25-1. Connect to Wi-Fi Network and Update Webpage

```
#include <ESP8266WiFi.h>        // library to connect to Wi-Fi network
#include <ESP8266WebServer.h>   // library for webserver functionality
ESP8266WebServer server;        // declare webserver
char* ssid = "xxxx";            // change xxxx to your Wi-Fi ssid
char* password = "xxxx";        // change xxxx to your Wi-Fi password
```

```
void setup()
{
  Serial.begin(115200);              // define Serial output at 115200 baud
  WiFi.begin(ssid, password);        // initialise Wi-Fi
  while (WiFi.status() != WL_CONNECTED) delay(500); // wait for Wi-Fi connection
  Serial.print("IP address: ");
  Serial.println(WiFi.localIP());    // display IP address of Wi-Fi network
  server.on("/",message);            // message function when webpage loaded
  server.begin();                    // initialise server
}

void message()                       // function for main webpage
{
  String msg = "webserver connected";   // define msg as string
  server.send (200, "text/plain",msg);  // send response with plain text
}

void loop()
{
  server.handleClient();             // manage incoming HTTP requests
}
```

The second sketch builds on Listing 25-1, by turning on or off the built-in LED and a second LED when the webpage is reloaded and displays the status of the LEDs on the webpage (see Figure 25-3).

Three changes are required to Listing 25-1. At the start of the sketch, define the LED pins by including the following instructions.

```
int LEDpin = 16;                     // built-in LED on GPIO 16
int LED2pin = D8;                    // second LED on pin D8 or GPIO 15
```

Within the void setup() function, add the following instructions.

```
server.on("/LED", LED);              // turn LED on or off when website loads
pinMode(LEDpin, OUTPUT);             // built-in LED pin as output
pinMode(LED2pin, OUTPUT);            // second LED pin as output
```

Include the instructions (see Listing 25-2) for the void LED() function, noting that GPIO pin 16 is active *LOW*.

Listing 25-2. void LED() Function

```
void LED()
{
  digitalWrite(LEDpin, !digitalRead(LEDpin)); // turn built-in LED on or off
  digitalWrite(LED2pin, !digitalRead(LEDpin)); // turn LED2 on or off
  String msg;                              // define msg as string
  if (digitalRead(LEDpin) == HIGH) msg = "LEDs off"; // GPIO16 active LOW
  else msg = "LEDs on";
  server.send(200,"text/plain", msg); // send response in plain text
}
```

Inclusion of the two LEDs requires the two LED pin definition instructions at the start of the updated sketch, the two pinMode() instructions in the void setup() function and the void LED() function. The purpose of the new server.on("/LED", LED) instruction added in the void setup() function is to call the void LED() function when the webpage *IP address/LED* is loaded.

For example, if the IP address of the Wi-Fi network is *192.168.1.3*, then reloading the webpage with IP address *192.168.1.3/LED* results in both the built-in LED and the second LED being turned on or off and the corresponding *LEDs on* or *LEDs off* message is displayed on the webpage. Note that IP addresses are case sensitive. The GPIO pin 16 is active *LOW*, while pin D8 or GPIO pin 15 is active *HIGH*, so the state of the pin for the second LED is the opposite state for the built-in LED. If the instruction for LED2 is digitalWrite(LED2pin, !digitalRead(LED2pin)), then the two LEDs are not on at the same time.

The third sketch (see Listing 25-3) illustrates entering information by a URL request string to instruct the server to display particular sensor readings on the webpage. The BMP280 sensor can measure temperature, pressure or predict altitude. One of the three measurements is made and displayed on the webpage through a URL request. If the IP address of the Wi-Fi network is *192.168.1.3*, then loading the webpage with address *192.168.1.3/BMP?sensor=T* or *192.168.1.3/BMP?sensor=P* or *192.168.1.3/BMP?sensor=A* results in temperature, pressure, or predicted altitude displayed on the webpage. In the sketch, the `String sensor = server.arg("sensor")` instruction searches for the *sensor* string in the IP address and the subsequent string is parsed, which is either `"T"` or `"P"` or `"A"`, corresponding to the temperature, pressure, or predicted altitude. Note the ? character in the address, which separates the URL (*192.168.1.3/BMP*) from the search parameter (*sensor*) and its value (`"T"` or `"P"` or `"A"`).

The BMP280 sensor was outlined in Chapter 4 and as the NodeMCU ESP8266 operates on 3.3V, then the logic level converter used in Chapter 4 is not required (see Figure 25-3 and Table 25-1). The NodeMCU ESP8266 and other components in the schematic can require more power than supplied through the USB computer or laptop output. A DC-DC step-down (buck) converter set to 3.8V and 1A output can be used as an external power source. The default I2C address of the BMP280 module is *0x77*, but as the SD0 pin is pulled to GND, the I2C address is *0x76*.

LDR resistor
4.7kΩ
LED resistors
220Ω

LDR   BMP280

power source

fritzing

Figure 25-3. *ESP8266 with LED, LDR and BMP820 sensor*

Table 25-1. *ESP8266 with LED, LDR, and BMP820 Sensor*

Component	Connect to	and to
BMP280 VCC	ESP8266 3V3	
BMP280 GND	ESP8266 GND	GND rail
BMP280 SDI	ESP8266 pin D2	
BMP280 SCK	ESP8266 pin D1	
BMP280 SD0	GND rail	
LDR left	ESP8266 pin A0	
LDR left	4.7kΩ resistor	GND rail
LDR right	ESP8266 3V3	
LED long legs	ESP8266 pin D7, D8	
LED short legs	220Ω resistor	GND rail

Listing 25-3. ESP8266 with LED, LDR, and BMP820 Sensor

```
#include <ESP8266WiFi.h>          // library to connect to Wi-Fi network
#include <ESP8266WebServer.h>   // library for webserver functionality
ESP8266WebServer server;    // associate server with ESP8266WebServer library
char* ssid = "xxxx";          // change xxxx to your Wi-Fi ssid
char* password = "xxxx";    // change xxxx to your Wi-Fi password
#include <Wire.h>              // include Wire library
#include <Adafruit_Sensor.h>          // include Unified Sensor library
#include <Adafruit_BMP280.h>          // include BMP280 library
Adafruit_BMP280 bmp;      // associate bmp with Adafruit_BMP280 library
int BMPaddress = 0x76; // I2C address of BMP280
float reading;
String letter, msg;

void setup()
{
  Serial.begin(115200);             // define Serial output at 115200 baud
  WiFi.begin(ssid, password);   // initialise Wi-Fi
  while (WiFi.status() != WL_CONNECTED) delay(500); // wait for Wi-Fi
                                                    // connection
  Serial.print("IP address: ");
  Serial.println(WiFi.localIP());   // display IP address of Wi-Fi network
  server.on("/BMP", BMP); // display temperature, pressure or altitude
  server.begin();               // initialise server
  bmp.begin(DMPaddress);   // initialise BMP280 sensor
}

void BMP()            // function for /BMP webpage
{                     // look for string "sensor" in URL and value T, P or A
  letter = server.arg("sensor");   // T entered on browser, read temperature
```

```
 if(letter == "T") reading = bmp.readTemperature();
                               // P entered on browser, read pressure
 else if(letter == "P") reading = bmp.readPressure()/100.0;
 else if(letter == "A")      // A entered on browser, read altitude
 {
    reading = 10.0 + bmp.readPressure()/100.0; // assumed sea level pressure
    reading = bmp.readAltitude(reading);   // predicted altitude
 }
 msg = letter +": "+ String(reading); // string "T" or "P" or "A" and reading
 server.send(200,"text/plain", msg);    // activated by sensor=T, P or A
}

void loop()
{
  server.handleClient();
}
```

Note that in each of the sketches (see Listing 25-1 and 25-3), the void loop() function contains only the server.handleClient() instruction and instructions for each webpage are included in the separate message(), LED(), and BMP() functions. In earlier chapters, variables were declared at the start of the sketch, but to emphasize that all instructions for a webpage are included in a function, the required variables are declared within the each function.

Wi-Fi and HTML

Listings 25-1, 25-2, and 25-3 display plain text on the webpage, as defined by the server.send(200, "text/plain", msg) instruction, where *msg* is a string containing the text to display. The server.send() instruction can also provide HTML (Hyper Text Markup Language) for building webpages. HTML is outside the scope of the text, but www.w3schools.com is recommended for information on HTML and CSS (Cascading Style Sheets), which are used to build and define the style of webpages.

Briefly, an HTML page consists of a head section, where the webpage title and styles are defined, and a body section, which contains the webpage content. The sections are bracketed with <head> </head> and <body> </body>. Style defines font types and sizes, headers, spacing, and so forth, and is bracketed by <style> </style>. A specific item within a webpage can be separately formatted and bracketed by <span> </span>.

HTML code for the webpage can be included in the main sketch, but it can also be included as an additional file; for example, *htmlCode.h,* which makes both the main sketch and HTML code for the webpage easier to interpret. The additional file is created in the Arduino IDE by selecting the triangle below the serial monitor button, on the right-hand side of the IDE, and choosing *New Tab* from the drop-down menu. *New Tab* should be titled *htmlCode.h.*

The *htmlCode.h* file is accessed by the main sketch, with the following instructions.

```
char* pageCode =          // three lines to include character pointer
#include "htmlCode.h"      // html code for webpage
;                         // line only includes a semi-colon
```

pageCode is a pointer to the memory address of the HTML code, which is implemented with the server.send (200, "text/html", pageCode) instruction.

For example, Listing 25-4 includes the HTML code for a webpage as a *string literal,* which consists of the HTML code bracketed by R"(and)", noting the double apostrophes before and after the single brackets. The string literal must only contain the HTML code without comments. The webpage consists of two buttons to control an LED, with the buttons both named *LED,* but with values of *ON* and *OFF.*

Listing 25-4. HTML Code for Webpage As String Literal

```
R"(
<!DOCTYPE html>
<html>
<head>
<title>Arduino Applied</title>
<style> body {font-family: Arial}
.button {padding: 15px 15px; font-size: 20px}
.button:focus {background-color: lime}
</style>
</head>
<body>
<h1>Arduino Applied</h1>
<span style='font-size: 20px'>LED</span>
<form action='/' method='post'>
<input type='submit' class='button' name='LED' value='ON'>
<span class='checkmark'></span> 
<input type='submit' class='button' name='LED' value='OFF'}>
<span class='checkmark'></span>
</form>
</body>
</html>
)"
```

When a button is selected on the webpage, as detected by the server.
hasArg() instruction, the value of the selected button is obtained as a URL
request by the server.arg() instruction, as used in Listing 25-3, and the
LED is turned on or off (see Listing 25-5). Note that the instruction server.
send(200, "text/html", pageCode) is sending HTML code and not plain
text, as in Listings 25-1, 25-2, and 25-3.

Listing 25-5. Control an LED with a Webpage Button

```
#include <ESP8266WiFi.h>        // library to connect to Wi-Fi network
#include <ESP8266WebServer.h>   // library for webserver functionality
ESP8266WebServer server;        // associate server with ESP8266WebServer library
char* ssid = "xxxx";            // change xxxx to your Wi-Fi ssid
char* password = "xxxx";        // change xxxx to your Wi-Fi password
int LEDpin = D8;                // LED pin D8 or GPIO 15
String LEDvalue = "OFF";        // default value
char* pageCode =                // three lines to include
#include "htmlCode.h"   // html code for webpage without comments
;                               // line only includes a semi-colon

void setup()
{
  Serial.begin(115200);         // define Serial output at 115200 baud
  WiFi.begin(ssid, password);   // initialise Wi-Fi
  while (WiFi.status() != WL_CONNECTED) delay(500); // wait for Wi-Fi
                                                    // connection
  Serial.print("IP address: ");
  Serial.println(WiFi.localIP());   // display IP address of Wi-Fi network
  pinMode(LEDpin, OUTPUT);          // LED pin as output
  server.on("/", webpage); // run webpage function as webpage loaded
  server.begin();                   // initialise server
}

void webpage()                  // function to collect data for webpage
{
  button();                     // obtain LED button status
  server.send (200, "text/html", pageCode);   // publish webpage
}
```

```
void button()                   // function to obtain LED button status
{                               // read LED button state
  if (server.hasArg("LED")) LEDvalue = server.arg("LED");
  if (LEDvalue == "ON") digitalWrite(LEDpin, HIGH); // turn LED on or off
  else digitalWrite(LEDpin, LOW);
  delay(1000);          // delay for 1s to retain button colour
}

void loop()
{
  server.handleClient();
}
```

If the HTML code for the webpage does not include any variables, then the HTML code can be incorporated as a string literal, as shown in Listings 25-4 and 25-5. However, if a variable is included in the HTML code, then the HTML code must be included in the main sketch.

In Listing 25-6, the webpage consists of a list of time information, a list of BMP280 sensor data and buttons to control an LED. Date and time information is obtained from the Network Time Protocol (NTP) service with information provided by a local server pool. Details of server pools are available at www.pool.ntp.org and the IP address of the local server pool is required in the sketch. The NTP data is accessed using the *NTPtimeESP* library by Andreas Spiess. A *.zip* file containing the library is available at github.com/SensorsIot/NTPtimeESP. The *NTPtimeESP* library is installed using library installation method 1 or 2, as described in Chapter 3.

The two parameters of the NTP.getNTPtime() instruction are time zone and *0* or *1* for European Summer Time. In the two string arrays, *months* and *weekdays*, the first element, *[0]*, is blank so that the months[] and weekday[] variables directly refer to elements in the corresponding array, such as "May" is equal to months[5], which is the sixth element of the array. Date and time information are converted into strings in the format *dd mmm yy* and *hh:mm:ss*, respectively, for inclusion in the HTML code.

The HTML code for the webpage is contained in the string *page* using the `String buildPage()` function. Note that the `buildPage()` function returns a string, so the function is defined as `String buildPage()`, in contrast to `void webpage()` that does not return a variable. In the `String buildPage()` function, the string *page* is incremented, line by line, to include the HTML code for the webpage and to incorporate the date and time strings with the BMP280 sensor measurements. Each increment of HTML code is bracketed by double apostrophes and followed by a semicolon. For example, `page += "<style> body {font-family: Arial}";`. The date and time information strings and the strings for BMP280 sensor measurements are not bracketed by double apostrophes, because otherwise the webpage would display the name of the string or the name of the measurement, rather than the value of the string or measurement.

The webpage includes time and sensor information grouped into two lists and in the HTML code the lists are bracketed with `<ul> </ul>` and items within a list are bracketed by `<li> </li>`.

The sketch (see Listing 25-6) is structured to include libraries and define variables in the first section, the `void setup()` function connects to the local Wi-Fi network and calls the `webpage()` function, when the webpage of the local Wi-Fi network is loaded. The `webpage()` function calls the `button()` function to update the LED state, updates the BMP280 measurements, calls the `getTime()` function to obtain date and time information from the NTP service, and then the webpage is updated by the `String buildPage()` function.

If the IP address of the Wi-Fi network is *192.168.1.3*, then the webpage loaded is titled *Arduino Applied*. The date, time, and BMP280 measurements are displayed, and updated every two seconds. Clicking the *ON* or *OFF* LED button turns on or off the LED, connected to the NodeMCU ESP8266 on GPIO pin D8. The NodeMCU ESP8266 does not need to be connected to a computer or laptop, as the information for the webpage is forwarded to the web browser on the computer or laptop displaying the webpage by using the local Wi-Fi network.

Listing 25-6. HTML Webpage

```
#include <ESP8266WiFi.h>          // library to connect to Wi-Fi network
#include <ESP8266WebServer.h>   // library for webserver functionality
ESP8266WebServer server;     // associate server with ESP8266WebServer library
char* ssid = "xxxx";             // change xxxx to your Wi-Fi ssid
char* password = "xxxx";         // change xxxx to your Wi-Fi password
#include <Wire.h>                // Wire library
#include <Adafruit_Sensor.h>     // Unified Sensor library
#include <Adafruit_BMP280.h>     // BMP280 library
Adafruit_BMP280 bmp;  // associate bmp with Adafruit_BMP280 library
int BMPaddress = 0x76;           // I2C address of BMP280
int LEDpin = D8;                 // LED pin GPIO 15 defined as D8
String LEDvalue = "OFF";
#include <NTPtimeESP.h>          // include NTPtime library
                                 // associate NTP with NTPtime library
NTPtime NTP("uk.pool.ntp.org");       // UK server pool for NTPtime
String stringTime, stringDate, stringDay;
String days[ ] = {" ","Sunday","Monday","Tuesday","Wednesday",
                    "Thursday","Friday","Saturday"};
String months[ ] = {" ","Jan","Feb","Mar","Apr","May","Jun","Jul",
                        "Aug","Sep","Oct","Nov","Dec"};
strDateTime dateTime;
float temperature, pressure, altitude, BasePressure;
byte hh, mm, ss, month, day, dayofweek;
int yr;

void setup()
{
  Serial.begin(115200);          // define Serial output at 115200 baud
  WiFi.begin(ssid, password); // initialise Wi-Fi and wait for
  while (WiFi.status() != WL_CONNECTED) delay(500); // wait for Wi-Fi
                                                    // connection
```

```
  Serial.print("IP address: ");
  Serial.println(WiFi.localIP());  // display IP address of Wi-Fi network
  pinMode(LEDpin, OUTPUT);         // LED pin as output
  server.on("/", webpage);  // run webpage function as webpage loaded
  server.begin();               // initialise server
  bmp.begin(BMPaddress);    // initialise BMP280 sensor
}

void webpage()               // function to collect data for webpage
{
  button();                  // obtain LED button status
  temperature = bmp.readTemperature();   // BMP280 measurements
  pressure = bmp.readPressure()/100.0; // temperature and pressure
  BasePressure = pressure + 10.0;    // assumed sea level pressure
  altitude = bmp.readAltitude(BasePressure);  // predicted altitude
  getTime();                            // obtain date and time
  server.send (200, "text/html", buildPage()); // publish webpage
  delay(1000);                          // delay 1000ms
}

void getTime()                           // function to get NTP time
{
  dateTime = NTP.getNTPtime(0, 1);       // get date and time
  if(dateTime.valid)
    {
    hh = dateTime.hour;                // extract hour (0 to 24)
    mm = dateTime.minute;              // extract minutes
    ss = dateTime.second;              // extract seconds
    yr = dateTime.year;                // extract year
    month = dateTime.month;            // extract month
    day = dateTime.day;                // extract day (1 to 31)
    dayofweek = dateTime.dayofWeek;    // extract day of week (1 to 7)
    if(ss<10) stringTime = ":0"+String(ss); // leading zero for seconds <10
    else stringTime = ":"+String(ss);
```

```
   if(mm<10) stringTime = String(hh)+":0"+String(mm) + stringTime;
   else stringTime = String(hh)+":"+String(mm) + stringTime;
   stringDate = String(day)+" "+String(months[month])+"
              "+String(yr);
   stringDay = days[dayofweek];      // convert data to strings
   }
}

void button()                        // function of LED button status
{                                    // read LED button state
  if (server.hasArg("LED")) LEDvalue = server.arg("LED");
  if (LEDvalue == "ON") digitalWrite(LEDpin, HIGH); // turn LED on or off
  else digitalWrite(LEDpin, LOW);
}

String buildPage()                   // function to build webpage
{
  String page = "<!DOCTYPE html><html><head>"; // head section and
  page += "<meta http-equiv='refresh' content='1'>"; // webpage refresh rate (s)
  page += "<title>Arduino Applied</title>";
  page += "<style> body {font-family: Arial}";   // define styles
  page += ".button {padding: 15px 15px; font-size: 20px}
</style></head>";
  page += "<body><h1> Arduino Applied </h1>";    // body section
  page += "<span style='font-size: 20px'>Time of day</span>";
                                                 // date and time
  page += "<ul><li>Time: <span style='font-size:30px'>"
           +stringTime+"</span></li>";
  page += "<li>Date: "+stringDate+"</li>";
  page += "<li>Day of week: "+stringDay+"</li></ul>";
  page += "<p><span    style='font-size:   20px'>Sensor</span></p>";
                                                 //sensor readings
  page += "<ul><li>Temperature: ";
```

```
page += "<span style='font-size:30px'>"+String(temperature)
        +"&deg;C</span></li>";
page += "<li>Pressure: "+String(pressure)+" hPa</li>";
page += "<li>Altitude: "+String(altitude)+" m</li></ul>";
page += "<span style='font-size: 20px'>LED</span>";
page += "<form action='/' method='post'>";   // LED buttons
page += "<input type='submit' class='button' name='LED' value='ON'>";
page += "<span class='checkmark'></span> ";
page += "<input type='submit' class='button' name='LED' value='OFF'>";
page += "<span class='checkmark'></span></form>";
page += "</body></html>";
return page;                              // return HTML code
}

void loop()
{
  server.handleClient();
}
```

Wi-Fi and Internet Access

Communication between devices on different Wi-Fi networks requires a different solution than communication between devices within a Wi-Fi network. The MQTT (Message Queuing Telemetry Transport) protocol enables communication between devices and an MQTT broker to allow information to be passed between one device and the MQTT broker and between the MQTT broker and a second device, with the two devices on different Wi-Fi networks. The MQTT broker enables information to be passed between devices without breaching firewall safeguards. When a device on a Wi-Fi network requests information from the Internet, the information is allowed through the network's firewall as the request came from the Wi-Fi network. Provision of information to the MQTT broker is termed *publish* and *subscribe* is the term to access information from the MQTT broker. Adafruit.io and Cayenne are two MQTT brokers and the Cayenne MQTT broker is used in the chapter.

Cayenne (see `mydevices.com/cayenne/features`) provides a dashboard to display information from devices connected to a NodeMCU ESP8266 (see Figure 25-4). The Cayenne dashboard is visible locally or remotely on `cayenne.mydevices.com/cayenne/dashboard/start` or with the Cayenne app, available from Google Play. Information from devices can be displayed numerically, as a dial and graphically, with binary variables displayed as *ON/OFF*. A device can be switched on or off from the Cayenne dashboard, providing both local and remote access to a device.

An *IFTTT* (If This, Then That) function enables triggering of events based on the output from devices connected to a NodeMCU ESP8266 and visible on the Cayenne dashboard. For example, if the incident light increases above a threshold on a light dependent resistor, connected to a NodeMCU ESP8266, due to a door opening or time of day, then an *IFTTT* instruction is sent to the MQTT broker to forward an email or text message to an email address or mobile phone number stored on the Cayenne dashboard.

Figure 25-4. *Cayenne dashboard and app*

All MQTT brokers require a username and password. For Cayenne, information is available at `mydevices.com/cayenne`. Accessing Cayenne with the NodeMCU ESP8266 requires the Cayenne-*MQTT-ESP* library, with a *.zip* file containing the library available at `github.com/myDevicesIoT/`

Cayenne-MQTT-ESP. The Cayenne-*MQTT-ESP* library is installed using library installation method 1 or 2, as described in Chapter 3.

Communication between the NodeMCU ESP8266 and Cayenne MQTT is through virtual channels, which can be arbitrarily numbered *V0*, *V1*, *V2*, and so forth. The instruction to send data to the Cayenne dashboard is Cayenne.virtualWrite(virtual channel, variable, type code, unit code), where the *type* and *unit* codes define attributes of the variable. Several variables are given in Table 25-2, with the corresponding *type* and *unit* codes. For example, if the variable *light* is a measure of luminosity in lux, then the instruction to send, on virtual channel *V3*, the value of *light* to the Cayenne dashboard is Cayenne.virtualWrite(V3, light, "lum", "lux").

Including *type* and *unit* code in the Cayenne.virtualWrite() instruction automatically configures the Cayenne dashboard with the variable description and unit of measurement. Note that Cayenne.virtualWrite() instructions are limited to 60 per minute, so Listings 25-7 and 25-8 have a two-second interval between the MQTT messages.

Table 25-2. *Variable Type Names and Codes*

Description	Type Name	Type Code
Barometric pressure	TYPE_BAROMETRIC_PRESSURE	"bp"
Luminosity	TYPE_LUMINOSITY	"lum"
Relative humidity	TYPE_RELATIVE_HUMIDITY	"rel_hum"
Temperature	TYPE_TEMPERATURE	"temp"
Description	**Unit Name**	**Unit Code**
Hectopascal	UNIT_HECTOPASCAL	"hpa"
Lux	UNIT_LUX	"lux"
Fahrenheit	UNIT_FAHRENHEIT	"f"
Celsius	UNIT_CELSIUS	"c"

The instructions to read an integer variable on virtual channel 3 in the Cayenne dashboard is

```
CAYENNE_IN(3)                              // define virtual channel number 3
{
  int variable = getValue.asInt();  // read value of integer variable
}
```

`getValue.asDouble()` and `getValue.asString()` read a real number and a string, respectively, with the channel number not including a "V", as included in the `Cayenne.virtualWrite()` instruction.

Information on declaring devices or variables, such as LED status or an LDR reading, on the Cayenne dashboard is available at `mydevices. com/cayenne/docs/features/#features-dashboard`. Cayenne dashboard devices are defined by following these steps.

1. Select *Add new* at the top left-hand side of the dashboard.

2. Select *Device/Widget* ➤ *Custom Widgets* ➤ *Button*.

3. Enter the chosen device name.

4. Select *Data* ➤ *Digital Actuator* ➤ *Unit* ➤ *Digital (0/1)*.

5. Select the virtual channel number to correspond with the sketch.

6. Choose an icon and select *Add Widget*.

To define a Cayenne dashboard variable, follow these steps.

1. Select *Add new* ➤ *Device/Widget* ➤ *Custom Widgets* ➤ *Value*.

2. Enter the chosen device name.

3. Enter **Analog Sensor**.

4.   Select the virtual channel number.

5.   Choose an icon and select *Add Widget*.

Figure 25-5 shows examples of a defined variable, *light*, and a device, *LED*, for the Cayenne dashboard.

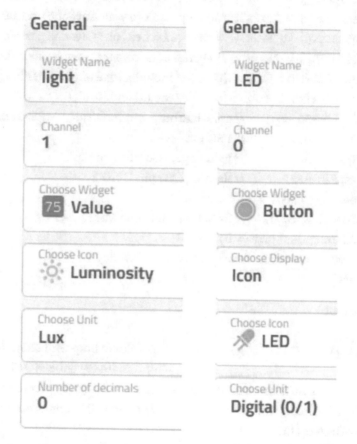

Figure 25-5. *Cayenne variables and devices*

Listing 25-7 displays on a Cayenne webpage or app (see Figure 25-4) temperature and pressure measurements from a BMP280 sensor, ambient light using a light dependent resistor, a time counter and a button to turn on or off an LED. The sensor readings are displayed on the Cayenne dashboard.

Listing 25-7. Cayenne, *ESP8266 with LED, LDR, and BMP820 Sensor*

```
#include <CayenneMQTTESP8266.h> // Cayenne MQTT library
char ssid[] = "xxxx";       // change xxxx to your Wi-Fi ssid
char wifipass[] = "xxxx"; // change xxxx to your Wi-Fi password
char username[] = "xxxx"; // change xxxx to your Cayenne username
char mqttpass[] = "xxxx"; // change xxxx to your Cayenne password
char clientID[] = "xxxx"; // change xxxx to your Cayenne client identity
#include <Adafruit_Sensor.h>     // include Adafruit_Sensor library
#include <Adafruit_BMP280.h>     // include Adafruit_BMP280 library
Adafruit_BMP280 bmp;   // associate bmp with Adafruit_BMP280 library
int LEDpin = D8;        // LED pin
int LDRpin = A0;        // light dependent resistor pin
int flashPin = 2;       // flashing LED pin GPIO 2
unsigned long count = 0;
int interval = 2000;    // 2s interval between MQTT messages
unsigned long lastTime = 0;
float temp, pressure, BasePressure, altitude;
int light;

void setup()
{
  bmp.begin(0x76);                    // initiate bmp with I2C address
                                      // initiate Cayenne MQTT
  Cayenne.begin(username, mqttpass, clientID, ssid, wifipass);
  pinMode(LEDpin, OUTPUT);            // define LED pins as output
  digitalWrite(LEDpin, LOW);
  pinMode(flashPin, OUTPUT);
}

void loop()
{
  Cayenne.loop();                     // Cayenne loop() function
```

```
if(millis()-lastTime > interval)
{
  temp = bmp.readTemperature(); // BMP280 temperature and pressure
  pressure = bmp.readPressure()/100.0;
  BasePressure = pressure + 10.0;        // assumed sea level pressure
  altitude = bmp.readAltitude(BasePressure); // predicted altitude (m)
  light = analogRead(LDRpin);            // ambient light intensity
  light = constrain(light, 0, 1023);   // constrain light reading
  count++;                               // increment counter
  if(count>99) count = 0;
  digitalWrite(flashPin, LOW);   // turn flashing LED on then off
  delay(10);
  digitalWrite(flashPin, HIGH);
                        // send readings to Cayenne on virtual channels
  Cayenne.virtualWrite(V1, temp, "temp", "c"); // define temperature reading
             // channel2 is flashPin so V2 is not used to avoid confusion
  Cayenne.virtualWrite(V3, pressure, "bp", "pa"); // define pressure reading
  Cayenne.virtualWrite(V4, altitude);
  Cayenne.virtualWrite(V5, light, "lum", "lux"); // define luminosity reading
  Cayenne.virtualWrite(V6, count);
  lastTime=millis();        // update time
  }
}

CAYENNE_IN(0)                 // Cayenne virtual channel 0
{
  digitalWrite(LEDpin, getValue.asInt());   // turn LED on or off
}
```

Listing 25-8 uses the Cayenne MQTT functionality to mimic an alarm system, which is triggered by the light intensity reading on a light dependent resistor, such as when a door is opened. If the light intensity increases above a threshold of 300 and the alarm setting on Cayenne MQTT is set to *ON* as indicated by the blue LED, then the red LED is turned on with an email and/or text notification that the event has occurred. If the alarm setting is off, then there is no response to changes in light intensity. The NodeMCU ESP8266 on-board LED is flashed every two seconds to indicate that the microcontroller is powered on.

If the alarm setting is on, then the light intensity reading is sent to Cayenne on virtual channel 1, but with a value of zero if the alarm is turned off. Virtual channels 0 and 3 of the Cayenne dashboard contain the LED and alarm states, which are used to turn on or off the corresponding LEDs or to indicate the alarm state (blue LED) and when the alarm has been triggered (red LED). The alarm, LED and email/ text notification triggers are defined in the Cayenne dashboard's IFTTT function.

Figure 25-6 shows the Cayenne dashboard with the alarm set to *ON* and a light intensity reading of 166, which is not high enough to trigger the LED to be turned on.

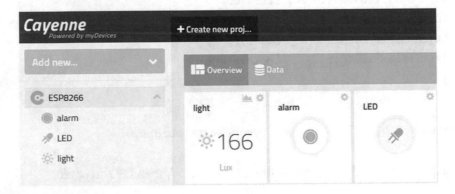

Figure 25-6. *Alarm, LED, and light intensity*

Listing 25-8. Alarm, LED, and Light Intensity

```
#include <CayenneMQTTESP8266.h>      // Cayenne MQTT library
char ssid[] = "xxxx";        // change xxxx to your Wi-Fi ssid
char wifipass[] = "xxxx";  // change xxxx to your Wi-Fi password
char username[] = "xxxx";  // change xxxx to your Cayenne username
char mqttpass[] = "xxxx";  // change xxxx to your Cayenne password
char clientID[] = "xxxx";  // change xxxx to your Cayenne client identity
int LEDpin = 15;             // LED pin GPIO 15 or D8
int alarmPin = 13;           // alarm pin GPIO 13 or D7
int LDRpin = A0;             // LDR on pin A0
int flashPin = 2;            // flashing LED pin GPIO 2
int reading, alarm;
int interval = 2000;         // 2s interval between LDR readings
unsigned long LDRtime = 0;

void setup()
{
  Serial.begin(9600);                  // initiate Cayenne MQTT
  Cayenne.begin(username, mqttpass, clientID, ssid, wifipass);
  pinMode(LEDpin, OUTPUT);             // define LED pins as output
  pinMode(alarmPin, OUTPUT);
  pinMode(flashPin, OUTPUT);
  alarm = 0;                           // set alarm as "OFF"
}

void loop()
{
  Cayenne.loop();                      // Cayenne loop() function
  if(millis()-LDRtime>interval)
  {
    LDRtime = millis();
    reading = analogRead(LDRpin);
// if alarm ON, then send LDR reading to Cayenne on channel V1, otherwise send zero
```

```
  if (alarm == 1) Cayenne.virtualWrite(V1, reading, "lum", "lux");
  else Cayenne.virtualWrite(V1, 0, "lum", "lux");
  delay(20);
 }
  digitalWrite(flashPin, LOW);    // LED GPIO 2 active LOW
  delay(10);                      // flash to indicate power on
  digitalWrite(flashPin, HIGH);
}

CAYENNE_IN(0)                     // Cayenne virtual channel 0
{
  digitalWrite(LEDpin, getValue.asInt());   // get LED status
}
CAYENNE_IN(3)                     // Cayenne virtual channel 3
{
  alarm = getValue.asInt();       // get alarm state
  digitalWrite(alarmPin, alarm);
}
```

The IFTTT (If This, Then That) function to trigger an event on the Cayenne dashboard is defined on the Cayenne dashboard and not in the sketch. Information on the IFTTT features of the Cayenne dashboard is available at mydevices.com/cayenne/docs/features/#features-triggers.

Four IFTTT triggers are required by the alarm system. When the light intensity increases above a threshold of 300, with the alarm setting on, the email and text notification of the event is triggered and a second trigger turns on the red LED on virtual channel 0, which triggers the alarm on virtual channel 3 to turn off, which then triggers the blue LED to turn off.

Cayenne IFTTT triggers are accessed by following these steps.

1. Select *User Menu* ➤ *Triggers and Alerts* at the top right-hand side of the Cayenne dashboard.

2. Select *New Trigger*.

3. Drag the *ESP8266* device into the *if* box.

4. Select the trigger, such as *light* in Figure 25-7.

5. Select the threshold.

6. Select either *Sensor above* or *Sensor below*.

7. Drag the *ESP8266* device into the *then* box.

8. Select the action, such as LED in Figure 25-7.

9. Select either *On(1)* or *Off (0)*.

10. Select *Save*.

When sending a notification as a text message, include the mobile phone number plus the *+country code* in the *Add custom recipient* box.

Figure 25-7. *Cayenne IFTTT trigger*

Figures 25-7 and 25-8 illustrate the IFTTT trigger to turn on the LED, on virtual channel 0, when the light intensity, on virtual channel 1, exceeds the threshold of 300 and the corresponding triggered email notification, respectively.

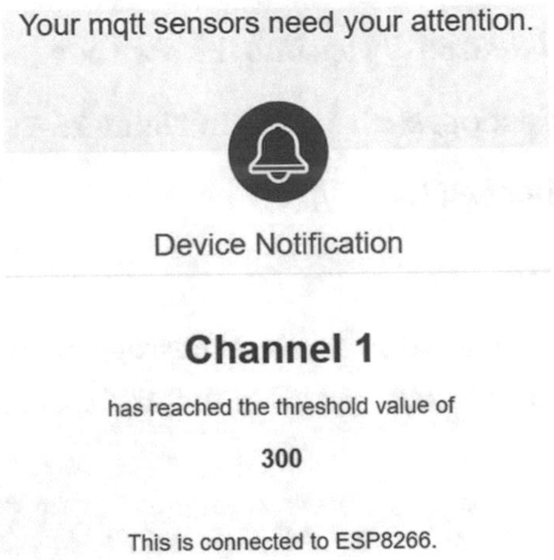

Your mqtt sensors need your attention.

Device Notification

Channel 1

has reached the threshold value of

300

This is connected to ESP8266.

Figure 25-8. *Cayenne IFTTT notification*

Summary

A NodeMCU ESP8266–based microcontroller is connected to a Wi-Fi network to establish a web server and manage HTTP requests to control a device and display requested sensor information on a webpage. HTML code for a webpage was included in a sketch to provide information from an external network, such as date and time. Access to an MQTT broker enabled sensor data to be uploaded to a webpage, with a sensor value above a threshold triggering an email or text message notification of the event.

Components List

- NodeMCU ESP8266

- LED: 2×

- Resistor: 2× 220Ω and 4.7kΩ

- Light dependent resistor (or photoresistor)

- Temperature sensor: BMP280

APPENDIX

Resistor Banding

Resistors are color coded for identification of their value, with the color bands read from left to right (see Figure A-1). With four bands, there can be a larger space between bands three and four. Gold and silver bands are always on the right-hand end of the resistor. Checking the resistance with a multimeter is recommended. The order of colors, from red to violet, is the same as in a rainbow. The diagram and a color band calculator is available www.digikey.co.uk.

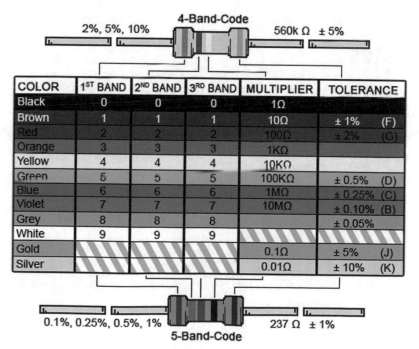

COLOR	1ST BAND	2ND BAND	3RD BAND	MULTIPLIER	TOLERANCE	
Black	0	0	0	1Ω		
Brown	1	1	1	10Ω	± 1%	(F)
Red	2	2	2	100Ω	± 2%	(G)
Orange	3	3	3	1KΩ		
Yellow	4	4	4	10KΩ		
Green	5	5	5	100KΩ	± 0.5%	(D)
Blue	6	6	6	1MΩ	± 0.25%	(C)
Violet	7	7	7	10MΩ	± 0.10%	(B)
Grey	8	8	8		± 0.05%	
White	9	9	9			
Gold				0.1Ω	± 5%	(J)
Silver				0.01Ω	± 10%	(K)

Figure A-1. *Resistor colour banding*

© Neil Cameron 2019
N. Cameron, *Arduino Applied*, https://doi.org/10.1007/978-1-4842-3960-5

The sequence of six resistor values between 100, 150, 220, 330, 470 and 680Ω is the E6 series, with resistor values having 20% tolerance. For example, the 220Ω resistor has an upper tolerance level of 264Ω, which equals the lower tolerance level of the next resistor in the series, the 330Ω resistor. The preferred resistor values between 10Ω and 100Ω, 100Ω, and 1kΩ, and so forth, are calculated as $L \times 10^{N/6}$, where L is the lower value of the range and N is the Nth resistor in the E6 series. If the resistor values are plotted on the logarithmic (base 10) scale, then the slope of the line is 1/6.

A similar procedure, $L \times 10^{N/12}$, is used to calculate the 12 preferred values of the E12 series, which has 10% tolerance. The E12 series between 100Ω and 1kΩ includes the E6 series plus the additional six values of 120, 180, 270, 390, 560, and 820Ω.

Resistors have different power ratings, with the ¼W and ½W resistors measuring 6.3mm and 9.2mm in length.

Libraries

The majority of the required libraries can be uploaded within the Arduino IDE, with the other libraries available through GitHub (`www.github.com`) or specific websites. Several libraries are already built-in to the Arduino IDE.

Table A-1. *Libraries with Information on the Author and Library Source*

Library	Author and source if not available through the Arduino IDE
AccelStepper	Mike McCauley
Adafruit BMP280	Adafruit
Adafruit GFX	Adafruit
Adafruit SSD1306	Adafruit
Adafruit ST7735	Adafruit
Adafruit Unified Sensor	Adafruit
AltSoftSerial	Paul Stoffregen
Cayenne_MQTT_ESP	myDevices
DHTlib (dht)	Rob Tillaart github.com/RobTillaart/Arduino
DS3231	Henning Karlsen
I2Cdev	Jeff Rowberg github.com/jrowberg/i2cdevlib
IRremote	Ken Shirriff
LiquidCrystal	Adafruit, built-in
LiquidCrystal_I2C	Frank de Brabander
LiveOV7670	Indrek Luuk github.com/indrekluuk/LiveOV7670
Low-Power	Rocket Scream Electronics
MD_KeySwitch	majicDesigns

(continued)

Table A-1. (*continued*)

Library	Author and source if not available through the Arduino IDE
MD_MAX72XX	majicDesigns
MD_Parola	majicDesigns
MFRC522	Miguel Balboa
MPU6050	Jeff Rowberg github.com/jrowberg/i2cdevlib
NeoGPS	SlashDevin
NewPing	Tim Eckel
NTPtimeESP	Andreas Spiess github.com/Sensorslot/NTPtimeESP
PID	Brett Beauregard
PinChangeInterrupt	NicoHood
PWM	Sam Knight code.google.com/archive/p/arduino-pwm-frequency-library/downloads
RF24	J Coliz
SD	SparkFun Electronics, built-in
Servo	Michael Margolis, built-in
SPI	Built-in
Stepper	Tom Igoe, built-in
TimerOne	Paul Stoffregen
toneAC	Tim Eckel playground.arduino.cc/Code/ToneAC
Wire	Built-in

Quaternion Measurements

Rotation in three dimensions can be described by rotation about the Z, Y, and X axes, corresponding to the yaw, pitch, and roll angles. An example of rotation about the three axes is an aircraft turning on the runway (yaw or heading), taking off (pitch or attitude), and turning in flight (roll or bank). Rotation about the axes can be written as R(yaw).

$$= \begin{bmatrix} \cos(yaw) & -\sin(yaw) & 0 \\ \sin(yaw) & \cos(yaw) & 0 \\ 0 & 0 & 1 \end{bmatrix},$$

$$R(pitch) = \begin{bmatrix} \cos(pitch) & 0 & \sin(pitch) \\ 0 & 1 & 0 \\ -\sin(pitch) & 0 & \cos(pitch) \end{bmatrix} \text{ and }$$

$$R(roll) = \begin{bmatrix} 1 & 0 & 0 \\ 0 & \cos(roll) & -\sin(roll) \\ 0 & \sin(roll) & \cos(roll) \end{bmatrix}.$$

If the order of the rotation sequence is about the Z axis, then about the Y axis and finally about the X axis, then the rotation matrix $R_{YPR} = R(yaw) R(pitch) R(roll)$ includes the following terms.

$$R_{YPR} = \begin{bmatrix} \cos(yaw)\cos(pitch) & \ldots & \ldots \\ \sin(yaw)\cos(pitch) & \ldots & \ldots \\ -\sin(pitch) & \sin(roll)\cos(pitch) & \cos(roll)\cos(pitch) \end{bmatrix}$$

If the rotation sequence is about the Z axis, then about the X axis and finally about the Y axis, then the rotation matrix $RYRP = R(yaw)$, $R(roll)$, $R(pitch)$ includes the following terms.

$$R_{YRP} = \begin{bmatrix} \dots & -\sin(yaw)\cos(roll) & \dots \\ \dots & \cos(yaw)\cos(roll) & \dots \\ -\sin(pitch)\cos(roll) & \sin(roll) & \cos(pitch)\cos(roll) \end{bmatrix}$$

The difference between the R_{YPR} and R_{YRP} matrices indicates the importance of defining the rotation sequence.

The rotation can also be parameterized by a quaternion, where w, x, y, and z are the quaternion magnitude, and three-directional components, such that the new position of a point, p, with coordinates (X, Y, Z) following the rotation is Rp.

The rotation matrix, R, is expressed in terms of the quaternion components as

$$R = \begin{bmatrix} 1-2(y^2+z^2) & 2(xy-wz) & 2(wy+xz) \\ 2(wz+xy) & 1-2(x^2+z^2) & 2(yz-wx) \\ 2(xz-wy) & 2(wx+yz) & 1-2(x^2+y^2) \end{bmatrix} = \begin{bmatrix} R_{11} & R_{12} & R_{13} \\ R_{21} & R_{22} & R_{23} \\ R_{31} & R_{32} & R_{33} \end{bmatrix}$$

The angle and axis of rotation is $\alpha = 2\,arccos\,(w)$ and $\begin{bmatrix} x \\ y \\ z \end{bmatrix} \alpha \,/\, sin\left(\dfrac{\alpha}{2}\right)$.

Interpretation of rotation matrix R depends on the rotation sequence. If R is equated to R_{YPR} or R_{YRP}, then given the quaternion, the rotation angles or Euler angles are as follows.

$$\text{YPR} \begin{bmatrix} roll \\ pitch \\ yaw \end{bmatrix} = \begin{bmatrix} arctan\left(\dfrac{2(wx+yz)}{1-2(x^2+y^2)} \right) \\ -arcsin(2(xz-wy)) \\ arctan\left(\dfrac{2(wz+xy)}{1-2(y^2+z^2)} \right) \end{bmatrix} = \begin{bmatrix} arctan(R_{32}/R_{33}) \\ -arcsin(R_{31}) \\ arctan(R_{21}/R_{11}) \end{bmatrix}$$

$$\text{YRP} \begin{bmatrix} roll \\ pitch \\ yaw \end{bmatrix} = \begin{bmatrix} arcsin(2(wx+yz)) \\ arctan\left(\dfrac{-2(xz-wy)}{1-2(x^2+y^2)} \right) \\ arctan\left(\dfrac{-2(xy-wz)}{1-2(x^2+z^2)} \right) \end{bmatrix} = \begin{bmatrix} arcsin(R_{32}) \\ arctan(-R_{31}/R_{33}) \\ arctan(-R_{12}/R_{22}) \end{bmatrix}$$

To complete the loop of quaternion to rotation matrix to Euler angles to quaternion, then given the Euler angles, the quaternion is

$$\begin{bmatrix} w \\ x \\ y \\ z \end{bmatrix} = \begin{bmatrix} cos(roll/2)cos(pitch/2)cos(yaw/2)+sin(roll/2)sin(pitch/2)sin(yaw/2) \\ sin(roll/2)cos(pitch/2)cos(yaw/2)-cos(roll/2)sin(pitch/2)sin(yaw/2) \\ cos(roll/2)sin(pitch/2)cos(yaw/2)+sin(roll/2)cos(pitch/2)sin(yaw/2) \\ cos(roll/2)cos(pitch/2)sin(yaw/2)-sin(roll/2)sin(pitch/2)cos(yaw/2) \end{bmatrix}$$

Quaternion components produced by the MPU-6050 DMP are multiplied by 2^{14}, while accelerometer measurements are multiplied by 2^{13}. The square root of the sum of squares of the quaternion components, each divided by 2^{14}, is essentially unity, but not for the accelerometer measurements.

Defining $|A| = \sqrt{a_X^2 + a_Y^2 + a_Z^2}$, where a_X, a_Y, and a_Z are the accelerometer measurements, each divided by 2^{13}, and $A_X = a_X/|A|$ and similarly for a_Y and a_Z, then roll and pitch angles are estimated only from accelerometer measurements as

$$
YPR \begin{bmatrix} roll \\ pitch \end{bmatrix} = \begin{bmatrix} arctan(A_Y / A_Z) \\ -arcsin(A_X) \end{bmatrix} = \begin{bmatrix} arctan(A_Y / A_Z) \\ arctan\left(-A_X / \sqrt{1-A_X^2}\right) \end{bmatrix}
$$

$$
YRP \begin{bmatrix} roll \\ pitch \end{bmatrix} = \begin{bmatrix} arcsin(A_Y) \\ arctan(-A_X / A_Z) \end{bmatrix} = \begin{bmatrix} arctan\left(A_Y / \sqrt{1-A_Y^2}\right) \\ arctan(-A_X / A_Z) \end{bmatrix}
$$

Note that the yaw angle cannot be estimated with only the accelerometer measurements.

To express an angle in degrees, rather than radians, multiply the angle by $180/\pi$.

As an example, with the GY-521 module tilted up along the Y axis, for a positive pitch, the quaternion measurements of 8312, 7278, 5139, and –10953 were divided by 2^{14}, with the resulting R matrix equal to
$\begin{bmatrix} -0.091 & 0.957 & -0.762 \\ -0.400 & -0.288 & -0.870 \\ -0.912 & 0.031 & 0.409 \end{bmatrix}$. The estimated roll, pitch and yaw angles are
4.39°, 65.81°, and –102.77°, with the YPR representation. Note that with the YRP representation, the estimated roll, pitch, and yaw angles are 1.80°, 65.87°, and –106.78°, respectively, emphasizing the importance of defining the rotation order.

The corresponding accelerometer measurements were -7281, 316, and 3074. After dividing the accelerometer measurements by 2^{13} and scaling, the estimated roll and pitch angles were 5.87° and 67.00°, which were of the same order of magnitude as the angles from the quaternion components.

Who's Who in Electronics

The names of variables used in electronics are listed in Table A-2 with details of those accredited with the discoveries. The corresponding dates indicate that the late 1700s and early 1800s must have been fascinating times in science. The list only includes variables outlined in the text, as otherwise the list would be substantially longer to include scientists such as James Clark Maxwell.

Table A-2. *Variables Used in Electronics, with Information on the Founders*

Variable	Name and Birth–Death	Country	Symbol
Baud rate	Jean-Maurice-Émile Baudot (1845–1903)	France	Bd baud
Bluetooth	King Harald Bluetooth (10th century), symbol combines the runic characters H and B	Scandinavia	ᛒ= ᚼ + ᛒ
Boolean	George Boole (1815–1864)	England	
Capacitance	Michael Faraday (1791–1867)	England	F farad
Charge	Charles–Augustin de Coulomb (1736–1806)	France	C coulomb

(*continued*)

Table A-2. (*continued*)

Variable	Name and Birth–Death	Country	Symbol
Current	André–Marie Ampère (1775–1836)	France	A amp
Energy	James Prescott Joule (1818–1889)	England	J joule
Frequency	Heinrich Hertz (1857–1894)	Germany	Hz hertz
Gray code	Frank Gray (1887–1969)	USA	
Hall effect	Edwin Hall (1855–1938)	USA	
Power	James Watt (1736–1819)	Scotland	W watt
Resistance	Georg Ohm (1789–1854)	Germany	Ω ohm
Voltage	Alessandro Volta (1745–1827)	Italy	V volt

Sources of Electronic Components

Components can be bought online from a variety of suppliers, such as those at the following websites.

- `store.arduino.cc`

- `www.rs-online.com`

- `www.aliexpress.com`

- `cpc.farnell.com`

- `www.banggood.com`

- `www.digikey.com`

- `www.gearbest.com`

- `www.jameco.com`

The longer delivery time from some sources may be offset by lower prices.

A starter kit (see Figure A-2) provides sufficient components for several chapters of the book.

Figure A-2. *Example of an Arduino starter kit*

Index

Printed in the United States
By Bookmasters